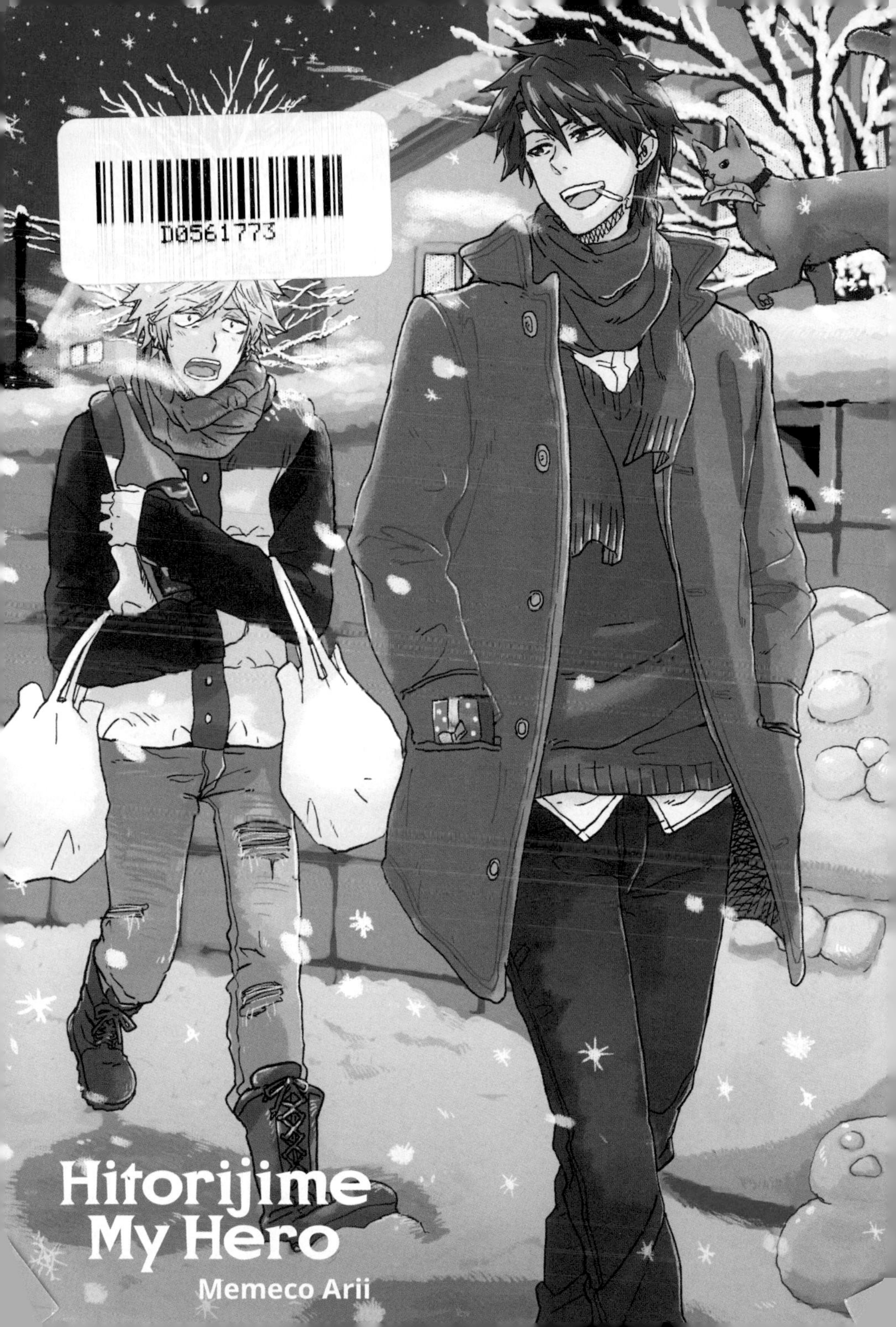
Hitorijime
My Hero
Memeco Arii

Hitorijime
My Hero
CONTENTS

Hitorijime My Hero volume 1 is a work of fiction. Names, characters, places, and incidents are the products of the author's imagination or are used fictitiously. Any resemblance to actual events, locales, or persons, living or dead, is entirely coincidental.

A Kodansha Comics Trade Paperback Original.

Hitorijime My Hero volume 1 copyright © 2012 Memeco Arii
English translation copyright © 2019 Memeco Arii

Published in the United States by Kodansha Comics,
an imprint of Kodansha USA Publishing, LLC, New York.

Publication rights for this English edition arranged through Kodansha Ltd., Tokyo.

First published in Japan in 2012 by Ichijinsha Inc., Tokyo.

ISBN 978-1-63236-771-6

Printed in the United States of America.

www.kodanshacomics.com

9 8 7 6 5 4

Translation: Anne Lee
Lettering: Michael Martin
Editing: Lauren Scanlan
Kodansha Comics Edition Cover Design: Phil Balsman

KC
KODANSHA COMICS

FIRESOLDIER
8
TOKYO
CO2

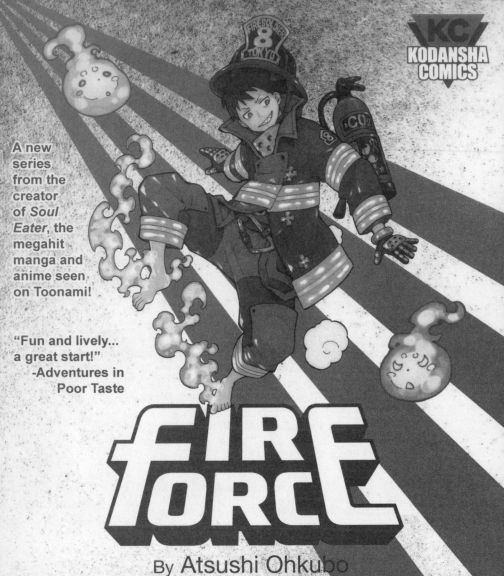

A new series from the creator of *Soul Eater*, the megahit manga and anime seen on Toonami!

"Fun and lively... a great start!"
-Adventures in Poor Taste

FIRE FORCE

By Atsushi Ohkubo

The city of Tokyo is plagued by a deadly phenomenon: spontaneous human combustion! Luckily, a special team is there to quench the inferno: The Fire Force! The fire soldiers at Special Fire Cathedral 8 are about to get a unique addition. Enter Shinra, a boy who possesses the power to run at the speed of a rocket, leaving behind the famous "devil's footprints" (and destroying his shoes in the process). Can Shinra and his colleagues discover the source of this strange epidemic before the city burns to ashes?

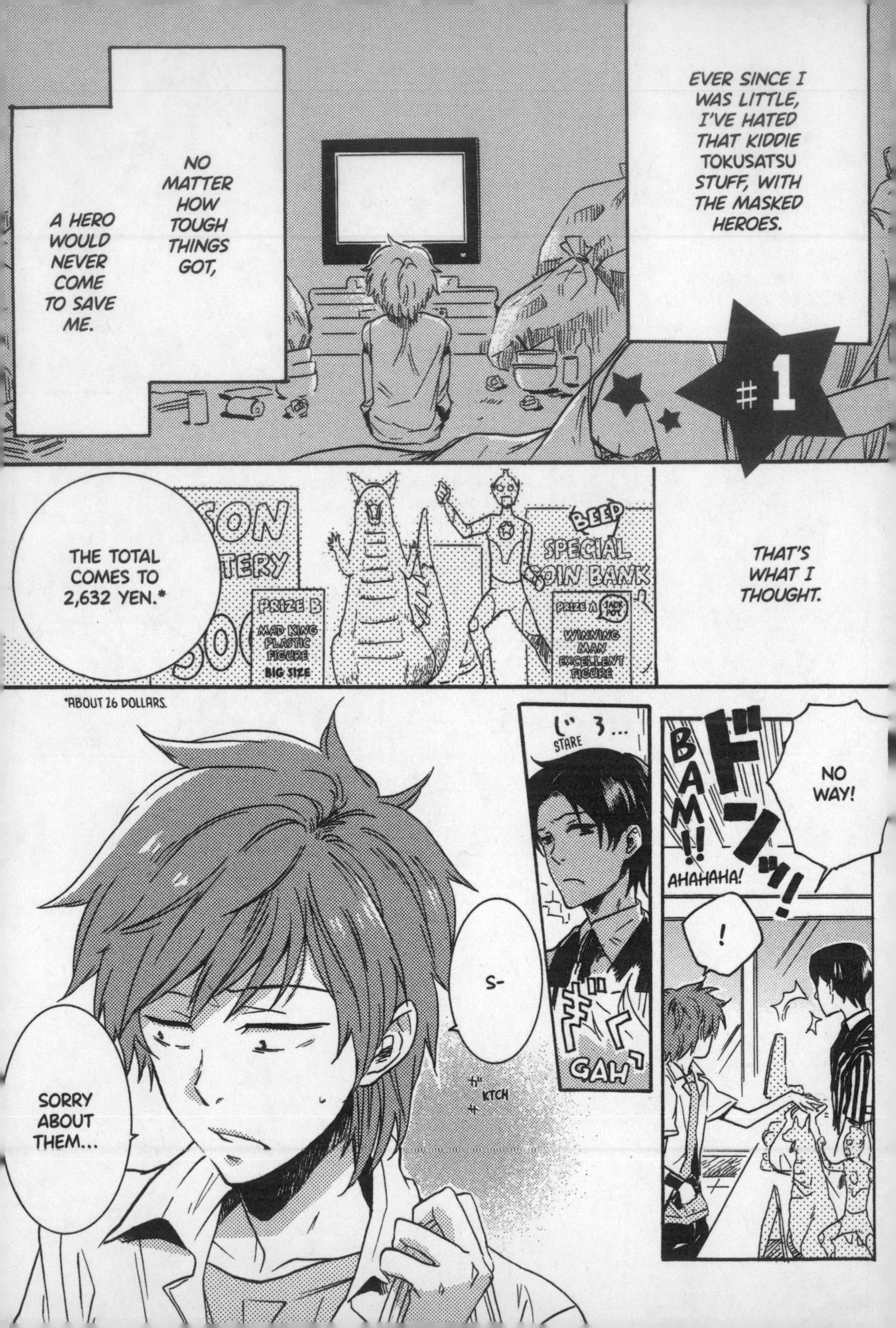
EVER SINCE I WAS LITTLE, I'VE HATED THAT KIDDIE TOKUSATSU STUFF, WITH THE MASKED HEROES.
#1
NO MATTER HOW TOUGH THINGS GOT,
A HERO WOULD NEVER COME TO SAVE ME.
THAT'S WHAT I THOUGHT.
BEEP
SPECIAL COIN BANK
PRIZE A JACKPOT WINNING MAN EXCELLENT FIGURE
PRIZE B MAD KING PLASTIC FIGURE BIG SIZE
THE TOTAL COMES TO 2,632 YEN.*
*ABOUT 26 DOLLARS.
NO WAY!
ドーンッ!! BAM!!
AHAHAHA!
!
じろ… STARE
ぎくっ GAH
S-
ガ KTCH
SORRY ABOUT THEM...

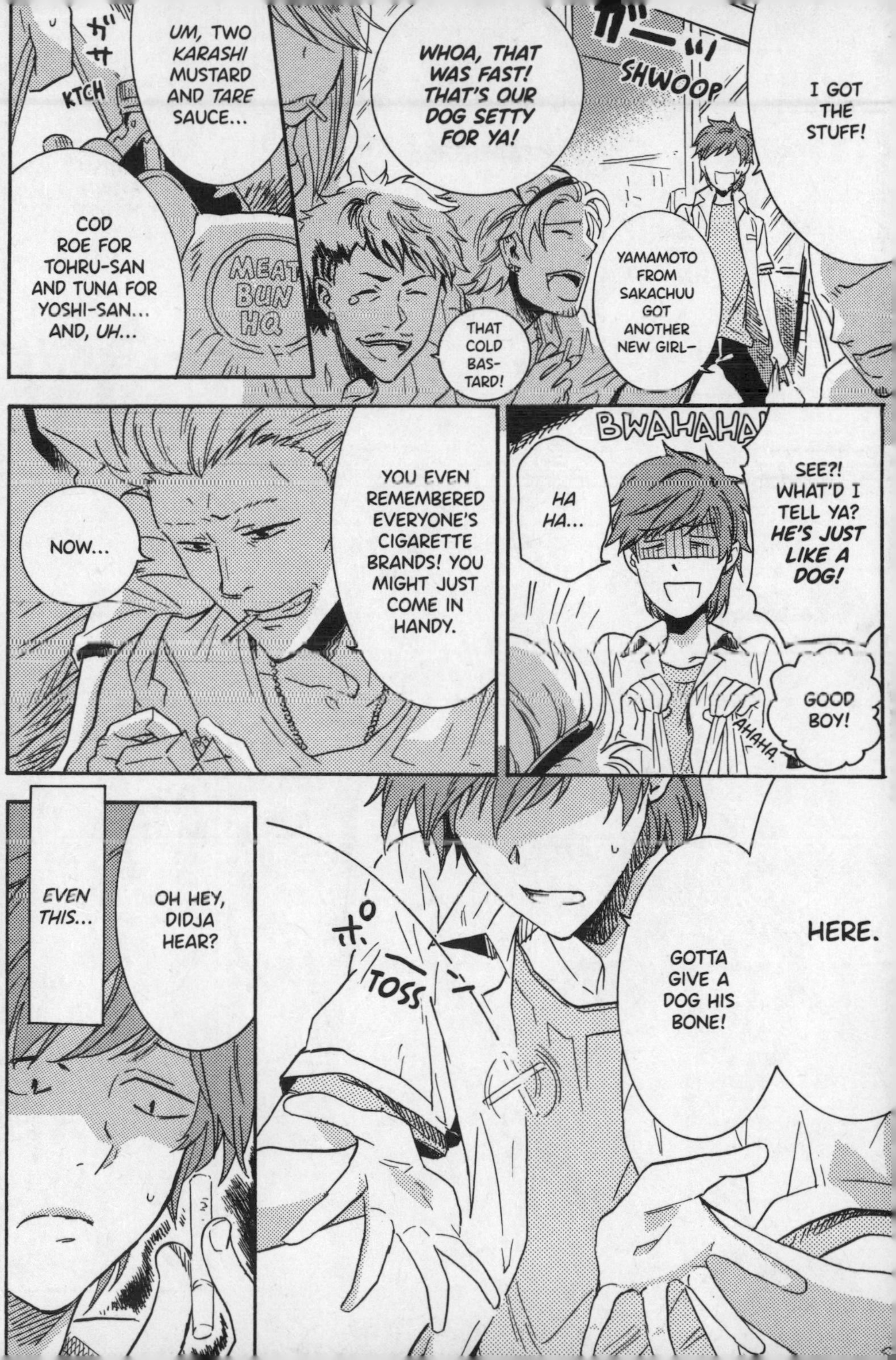
SHWOOP
I GOT THE STUFF!
WHOA, THAT WAS FAST! THAT'S OUR DOG SETTY FOR YA!
YAMAMOTO FROM SAKACHUU GOT ANOTHER NEW GIRL–
THAT COLD BAS-TARD!
UM, TWO KARASHI MUSTARD AND *TARE* SAUCE...
ガサ
KTCH
COD ROE FOR TOHRU-SAN AND TUNA FOR YOSHI-SAN... AND, *UH*...
MEAT BUN HQ
BWAHAHA
SEE?! WHAT'D I TELL YA? *HE'S JUST LIKE A DOG!*
HA HA...
GOOD BOY!
AHAHA
YOU EVEN REMEMBERED EVERYONE'S CIGARETTE BRANDS! YOU MIGHT JUST COME IN HANDY.
NOW...
HERE.
GOTTA GIVE A DOG HIS BONE!
TOSS
OH HEY, DIDJA HEAR?
EVEN THIS...

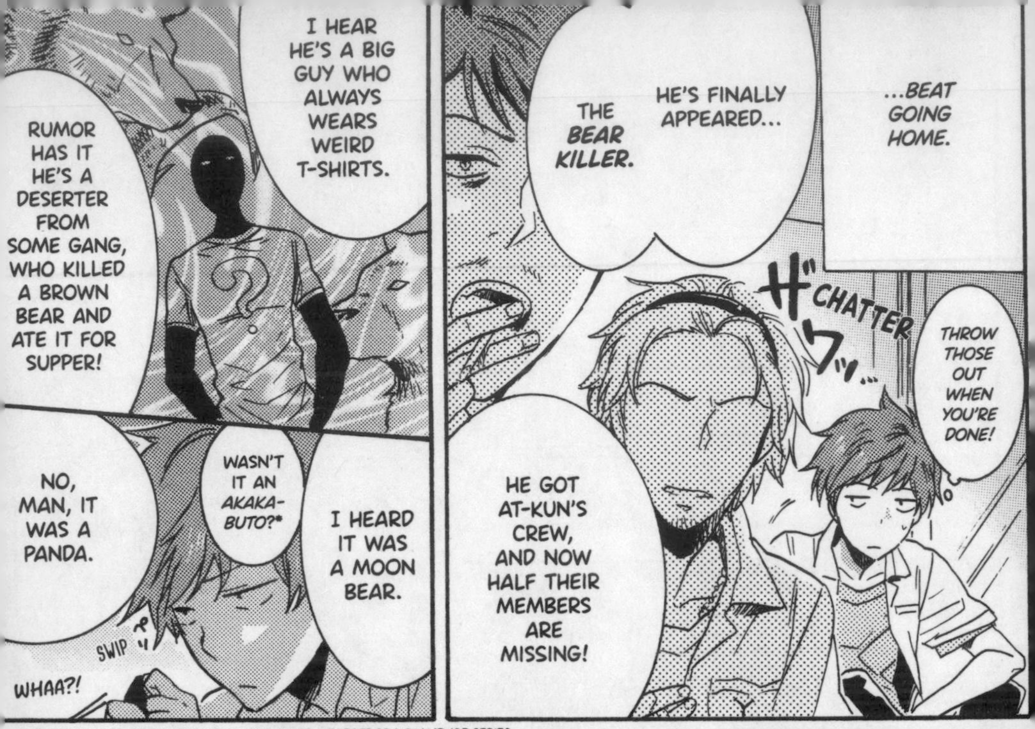
...BEAT GOING HOME.
HE'S FINALLY APPEARED...
THE *BEAR KILLER.*
CHATTER
THROW THOSE OUT WHEN YOU'RE DONE!
HE GOT AT-KUN'S CREW, AND NOW HALF THEIR MEMBERS ARE MISSING!
I HEAR HE'S A BIG GUY WHO ALWAYS WEARS WEIRD T-SHIRTS.
RUMOR HAS IT HE'S A DESERTER FROM SOME GANG, WHO KILLED A BROWN BEAR AND ATE IT FOR SUPPER!
I HEARD IT WAS A MOON BEAR.
WASN'T IT AN *AKAKABUTO?**
NO, MAN, IT WAS A PANDA.
SWIP
WHAA?!

*A FICTIONAL, MAN-EATING BEAR FROM THE *GINGA: NAGAREBOSHI GIN* MANGA SERIES..

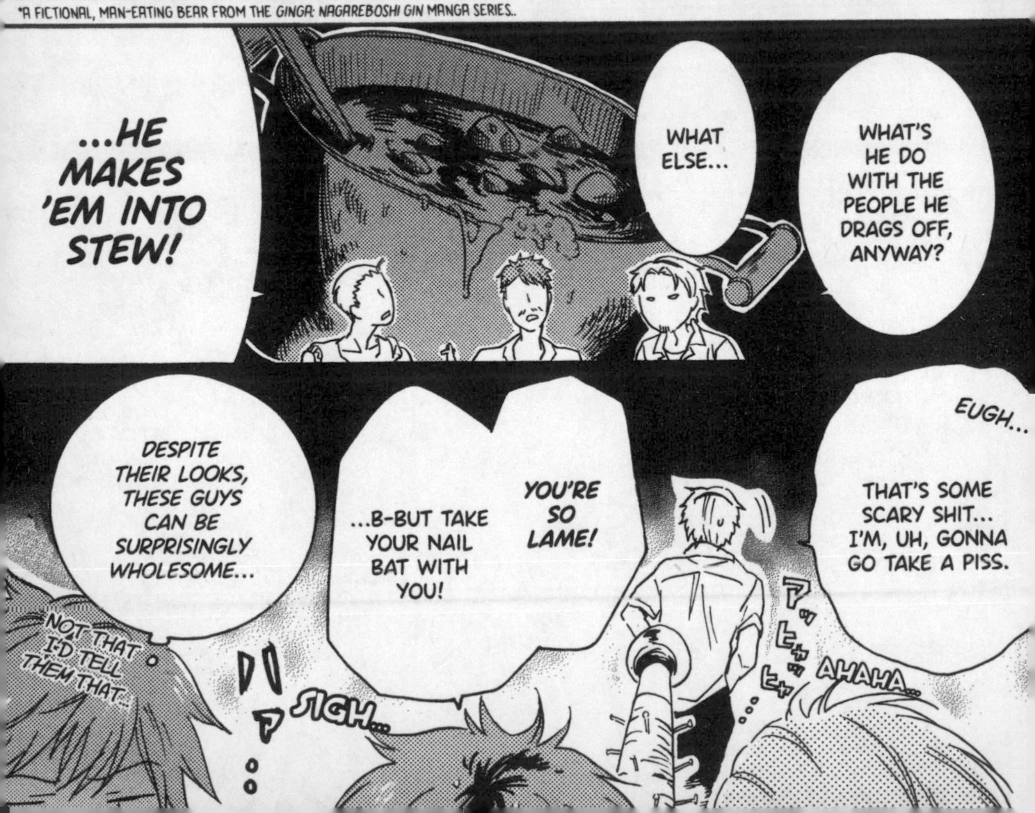
WHAT'S HE DO WITH THE PEOPLE HE DRAGS OFF, ANYWAY?
WHAT ELSE...
...HE MAKES 'EM INTO STEW!
EUGH...
THAT'S SOME SCARY SHIT... I'M, UH, GONNA GO TAKE A PISS.
AHAHA...
YOU'RE SO LAME!
...B-BUT TAKE YOUR NAIL BAT WITH YOU!
DESPITE THEIR LOOKS, THESE GUYS CAN BE SURPRISINGLY WHOLESOME...
NOT THAT I'D TELL THEM THAT...
SIGH...

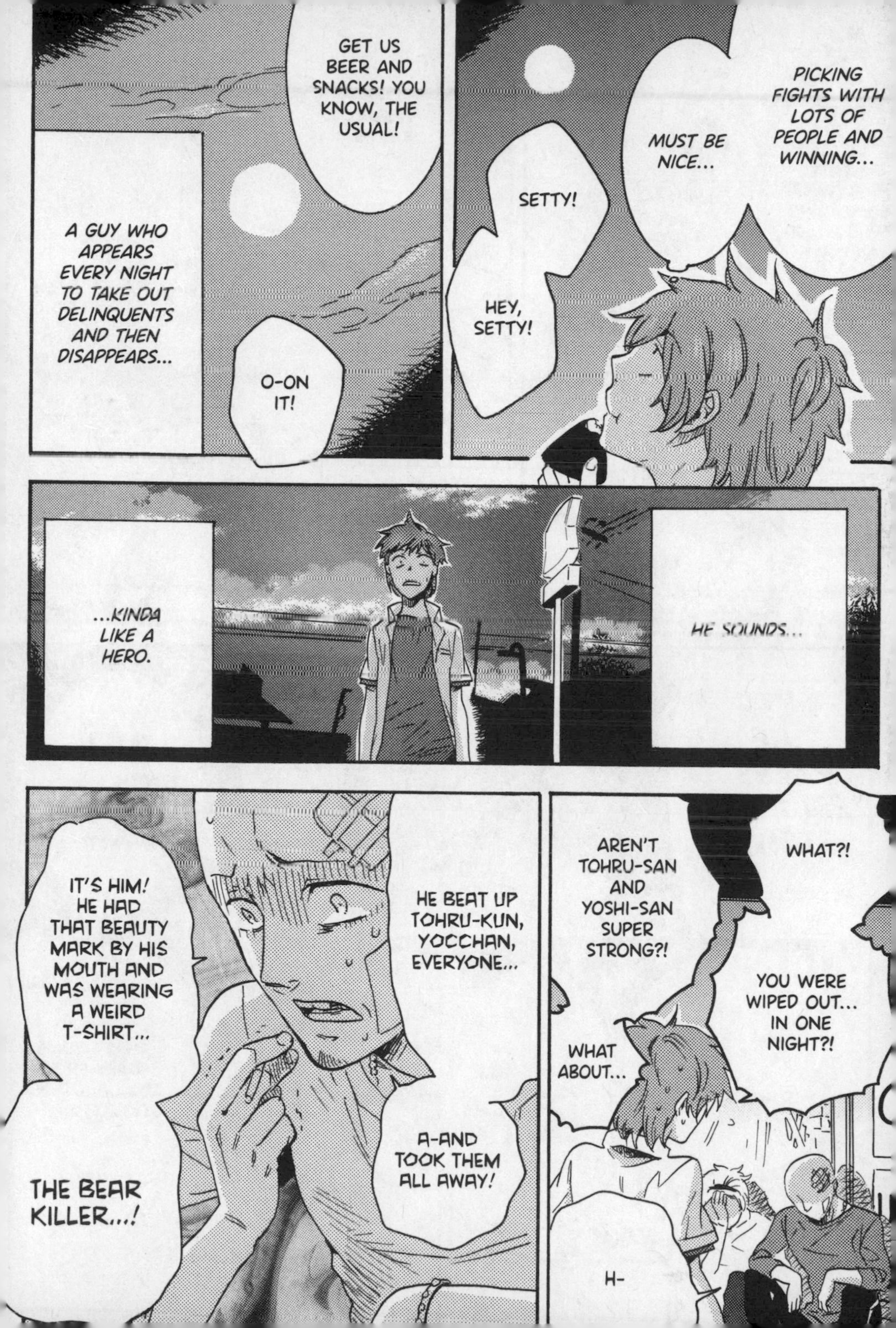
PICKING FIGHTS WITH LOTS OF PEOPLE AND WINNING...
MUST BE NICE...
SETTY!
HEY, SETTY!
GET US BEER AND SNACKS! YOU KNOW, THE USUAL!
A GUY WHO APPEARS EVERY NIGHT TO TAKE OUT DELINQUENTS AND THEN DISAPPEARS...
O-ON IT!
HE SOUNDS...
...KINDA LIKE A HERO.
WHAT?!
AREN'T TOHRU-SAN AND YOSHI-SAN SUPER STRONG?!
YOU WERE WIPED OUT... IN ONE NIGHT?!
WHAT ABOUT...
H-
HE BEAT UP TOHRU-KUN, YOCCHAN, EVERYONE...
IT'S HIM! HE HAD THAT BEAUTY MARK BY HIS MOUTH AND WAS WEARING A WEIRD T-SHIRT...
A-AND TOOK THEM ALL AWAY!
THE BEAR KILLER...!

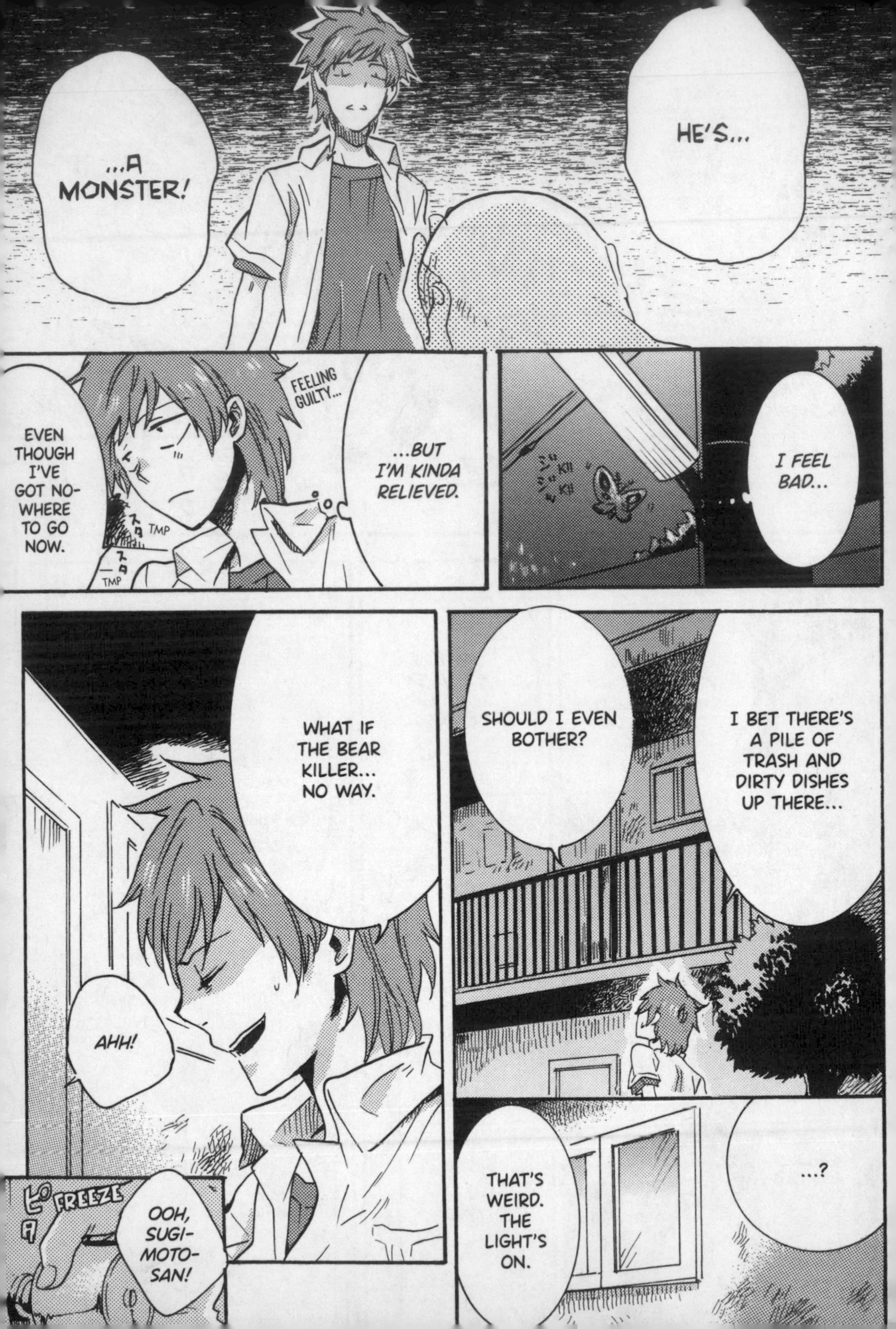
HE'S...
...A MONSTER!
I FEEL BAD...
KH
KH
...BUT I'M KINDA RELIEVED.
FEELING GUILTY...
EVEN THOUGH I'VE GOT NO-WHERE TO GO NOW.
TMP
TMP
I BET THERE'S A PILE OF TRASH AND DIRTY DISHES UP THERE...
SHOULD I EVEN BOTHER?
...?
THAT'S WEIRD. THE LIGHT'S ON.
WHAT IF THE BEAR KILLER... NO WAY.
AHH!
FREEZE
OOH, SUGI-MOTO-SAN!

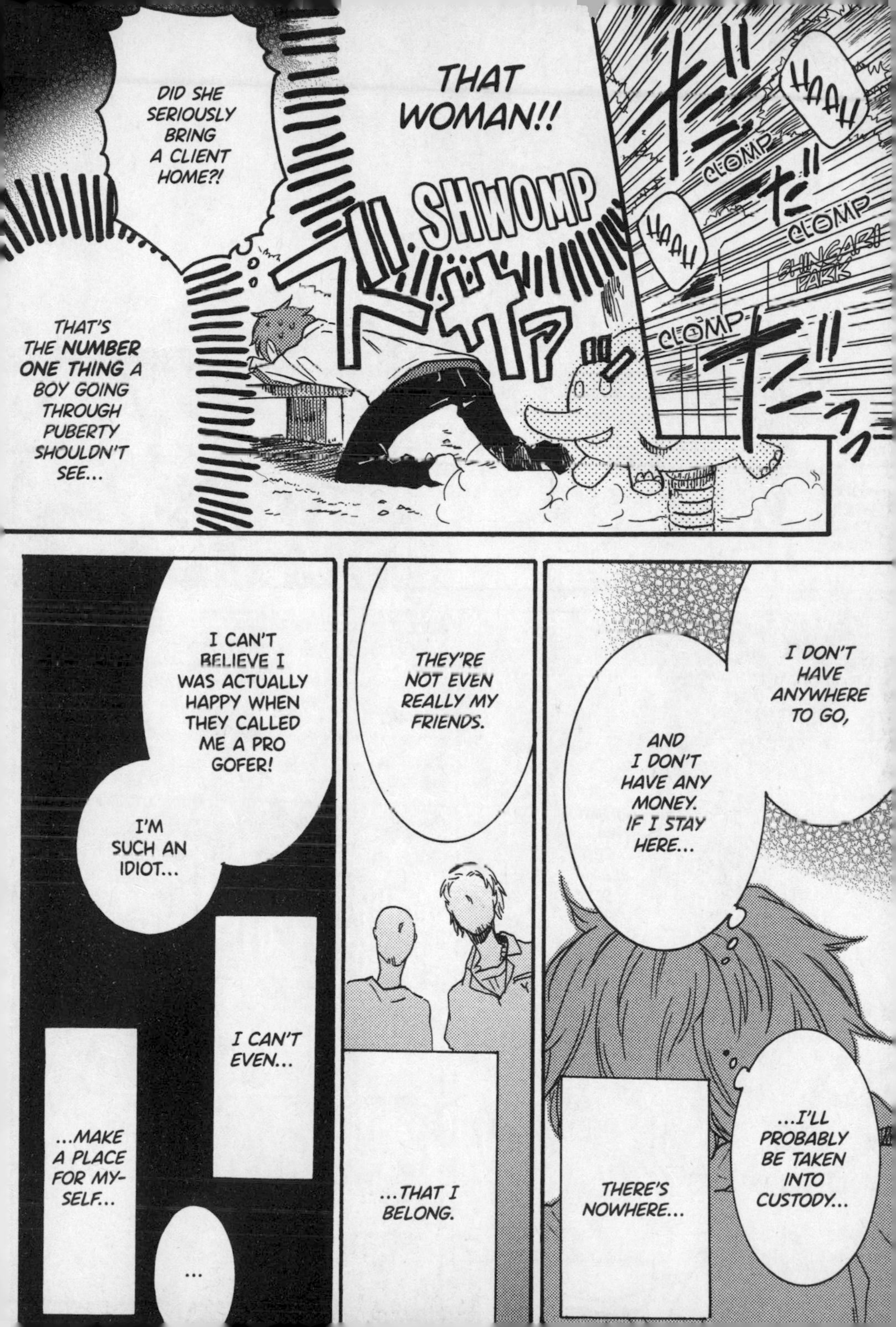
HAAH
CLOMP
CLOMP
SHINGARI PARK
HAAH
CLOMP
SHWOMP
THAT WOMAN!!
DID SHE SERIOUSLY BRING A CLIENT HOME?!
THAT'S THE NUMBER ONE THING A BOY GOING THROUGH PUBERTY SHOULDN'T SEE...
I DON'T HAVE ANYWHERE TO GO,
AND I DON'T HAVE ANY MONEY. IF I STAY HERE...
...I'LL PROBABLY BE TAKEN INTO CUSTODY...
THERE'S NOWHERE...
THEY'RE NOT EVEN REALLY MY FRIENDS.
...THAT I BELONG.
I CAN'T BELIEVE I WAS ACTUALLY HAPPY WHEN THEY CALLED ME A PRO GOFER!
I'M SUCH AN IDIOT...
I CAN'T EVEN...
...MAKE A PLACE FOR MY-SELF...
...

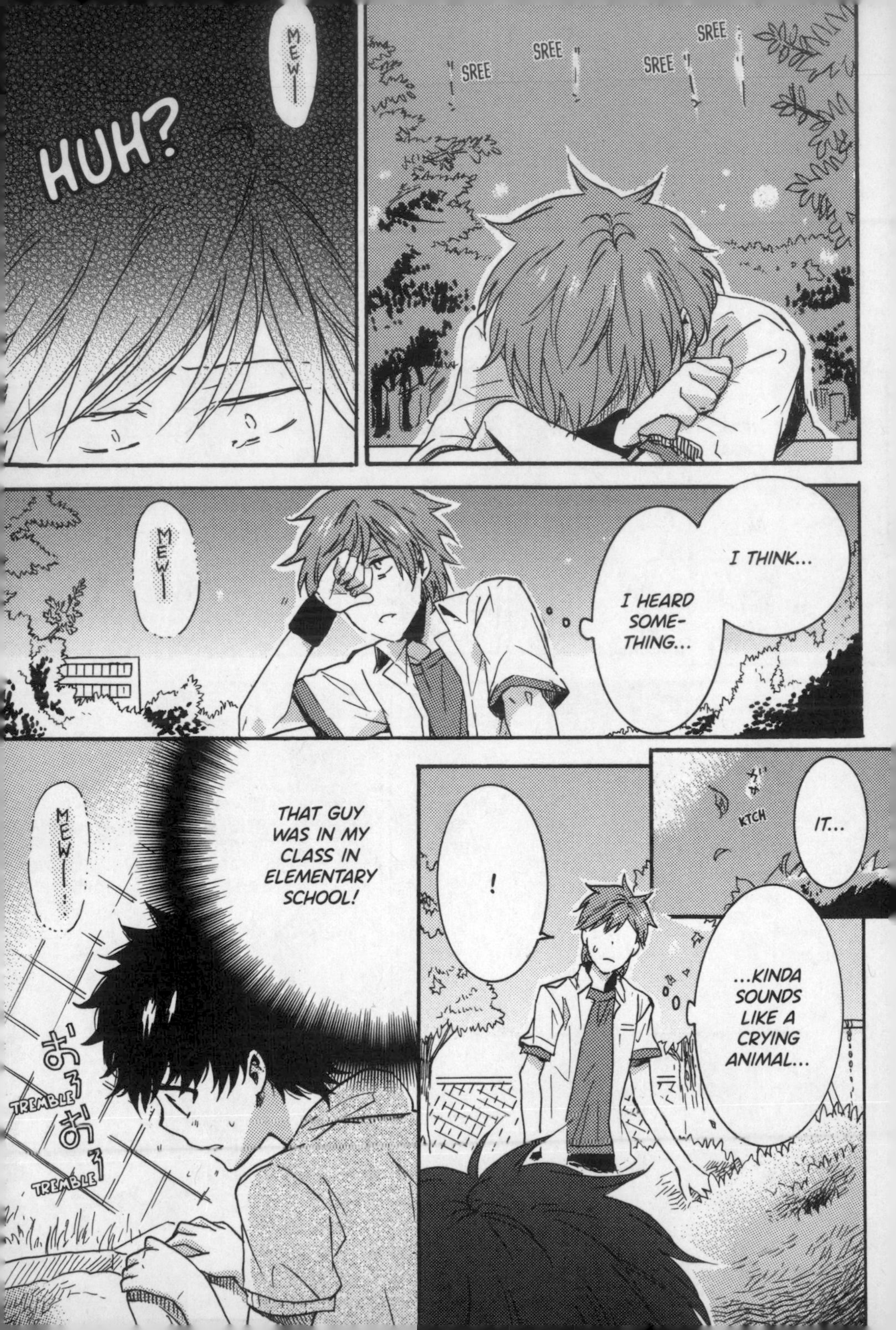

SREE
SREE
SREE
SREE
MEW!
HUH?
I THINK...
I HEARD SOME-THING...
MEW!
KTCH
IT...
...KINDA SOUNDS LIKE A CRYING ANIMAL...
!
THAT GUY WAS IN MY CLASS IN ELEMENTARY SCHOOL!
MEW!...
おろ TREMBLE
おろ TREMBLE

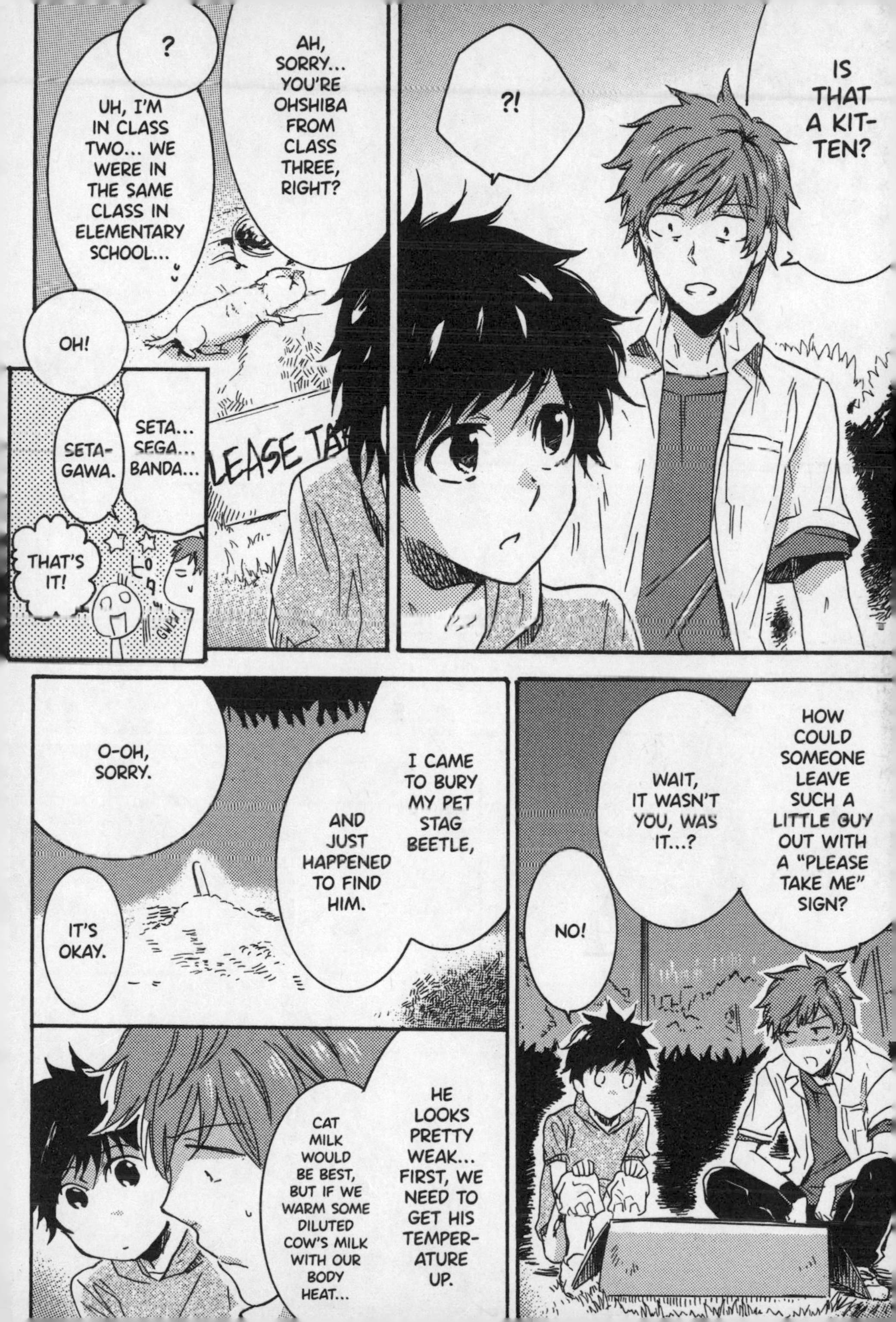
IS THAT A KIT-TEN?
?!
?
AH, SORRY... YOU'RE OHSHIBA FROM CLASS THREE, RIGHT?
UH, I'M IN CLASS TWO... WE WERE IN THE SAME CLASS IN ELEMENTARY SCHOOL...
OH!
SETA... SEGA... BANDA...
SETA-GAWA.
THAT'S IT!
HOW COULD SOMEONE LEAVE SUCH A LITTLE GUY OUT WITH A "PLEASE TAKE ME" SIGN?
WAIT, IT WASN'T YOU, WAS IT...?
NO!
I CAME TO BURY MY PET STAG BEETLE,
AND JUST HAPPENED TO FIND HIM.
O-OH, SORRY.
IT'S OKAY.
HE LOOKS PRETTY WEAK... FIRST, WE NEED TO GET HIS TEMPER-ATURE UP.
CAT MILK WOULD BE BEST, BUT IF WE WARM SOME DILUTED COW'S MILK WITH OUR BODY HEAT...

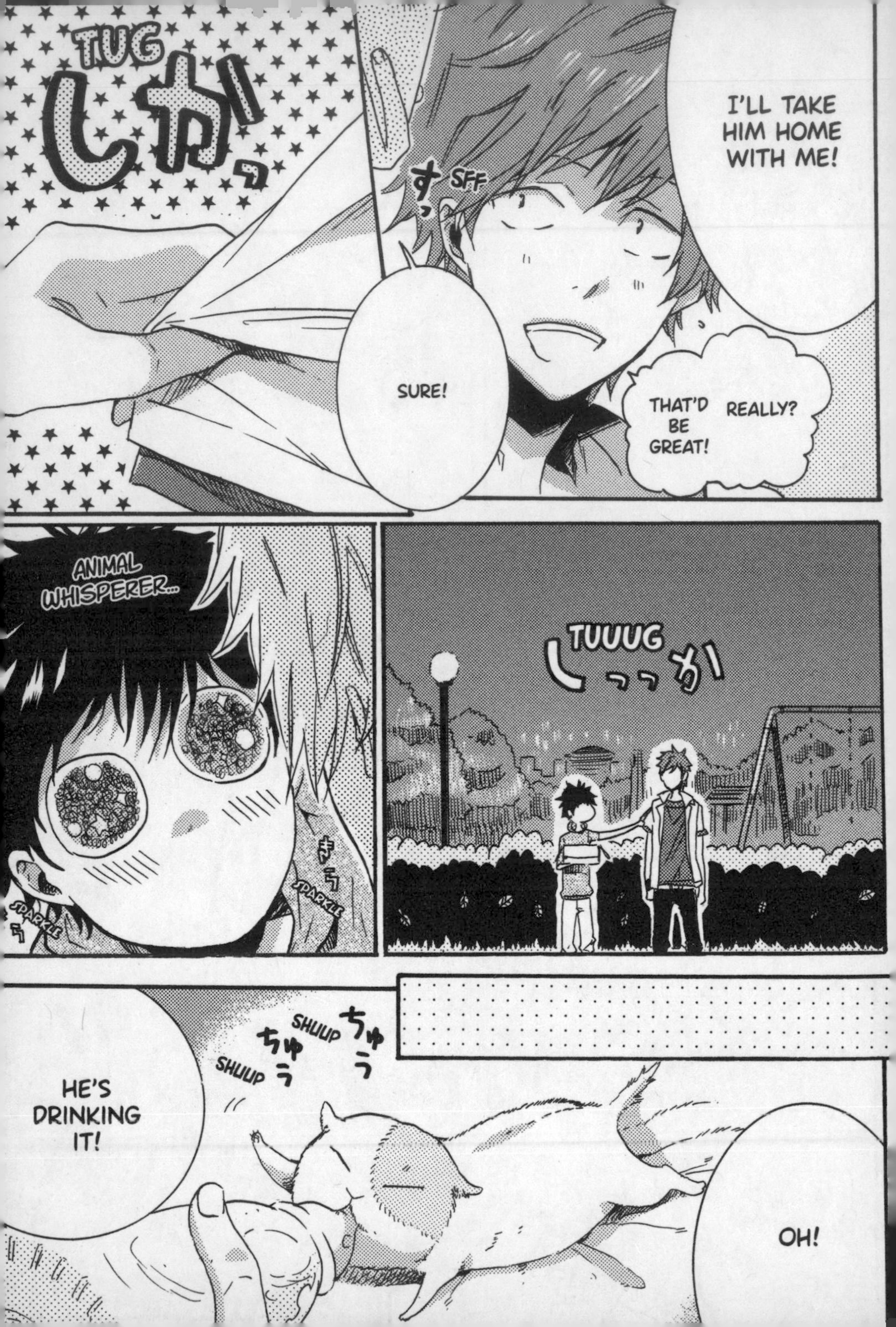
I'LL TAKE HIM HOME WITH ME!
REALLY? THAT'D BE GREAT!
SURE!
すっ SFF
TUG しかっ
TUUUG しっっっか
ANIMAL WHISPERER...
きら SPARKLE
きら SPARKLE
OH!
ちゅう SHUUP
ちゅう SHUUP
HE'S DRINKING IT!

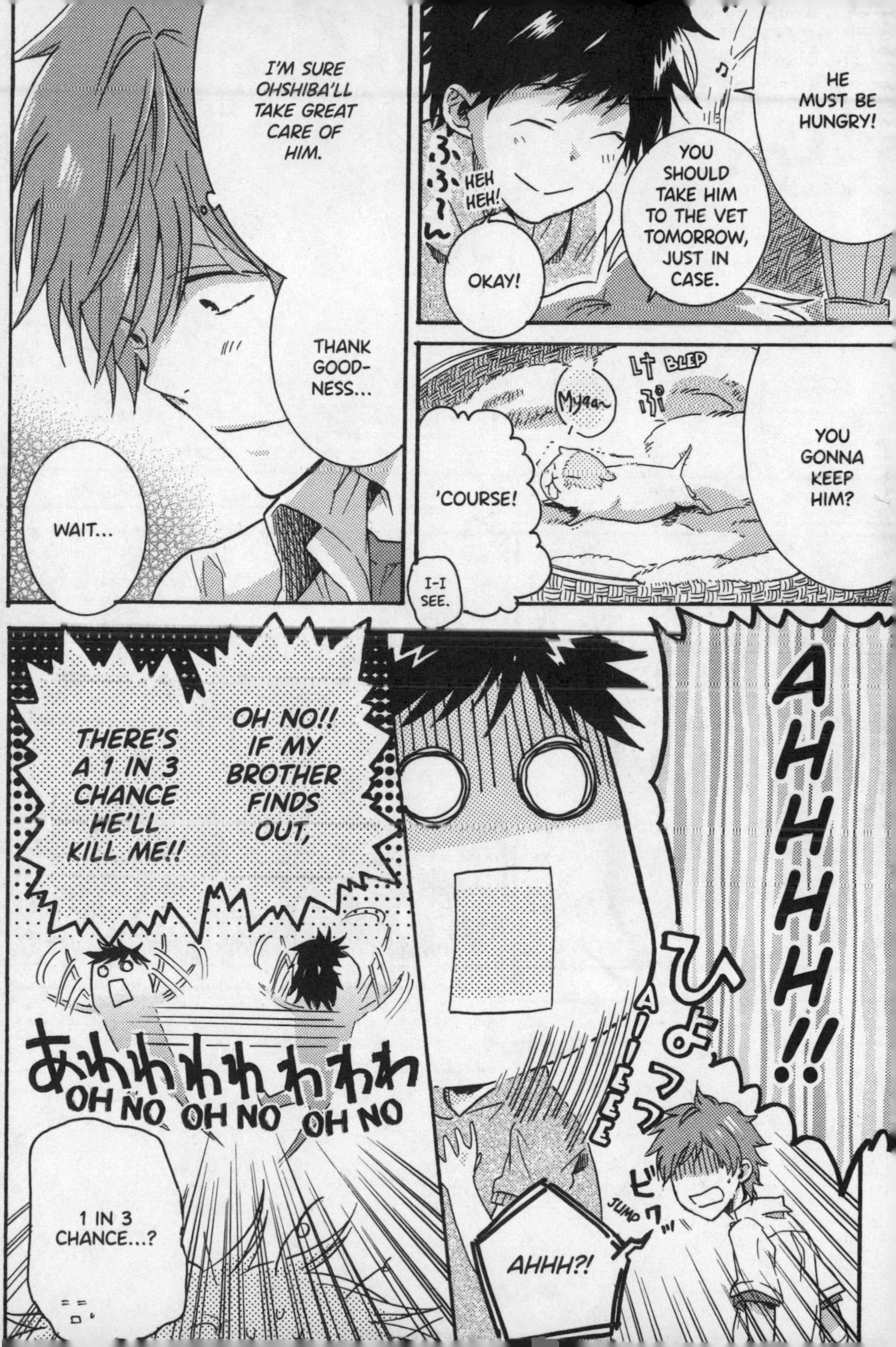
HE MUST BE HUNGRY!
YOU SHOULD TAKE HIM TO THE VET TOMORROW, JUST IN CASE.
ふふ～ん
HEH HEH!
OKAY!
YOU GONNA KEEP HIM?
けぷ BLEP
Myaa~
'COURSE!
I-I SEE.
I'M SURE OHSHIBA'LL TAKE GREAT CARE OF HIM.
THANK GOODNESS...
WAIT...
AHHHHH!!
ひょっ
AIIIEEE
ビクッ JUMP
AHHH?!
OH NO!! IF MY BROTHER FINDS OUT,
THERE'S A 1 IN 3 CHANCE HE'LL KILL ME!!
あわわわわわわ
OH NO OH NO OH NO
1 IN 3 CHANCE...?

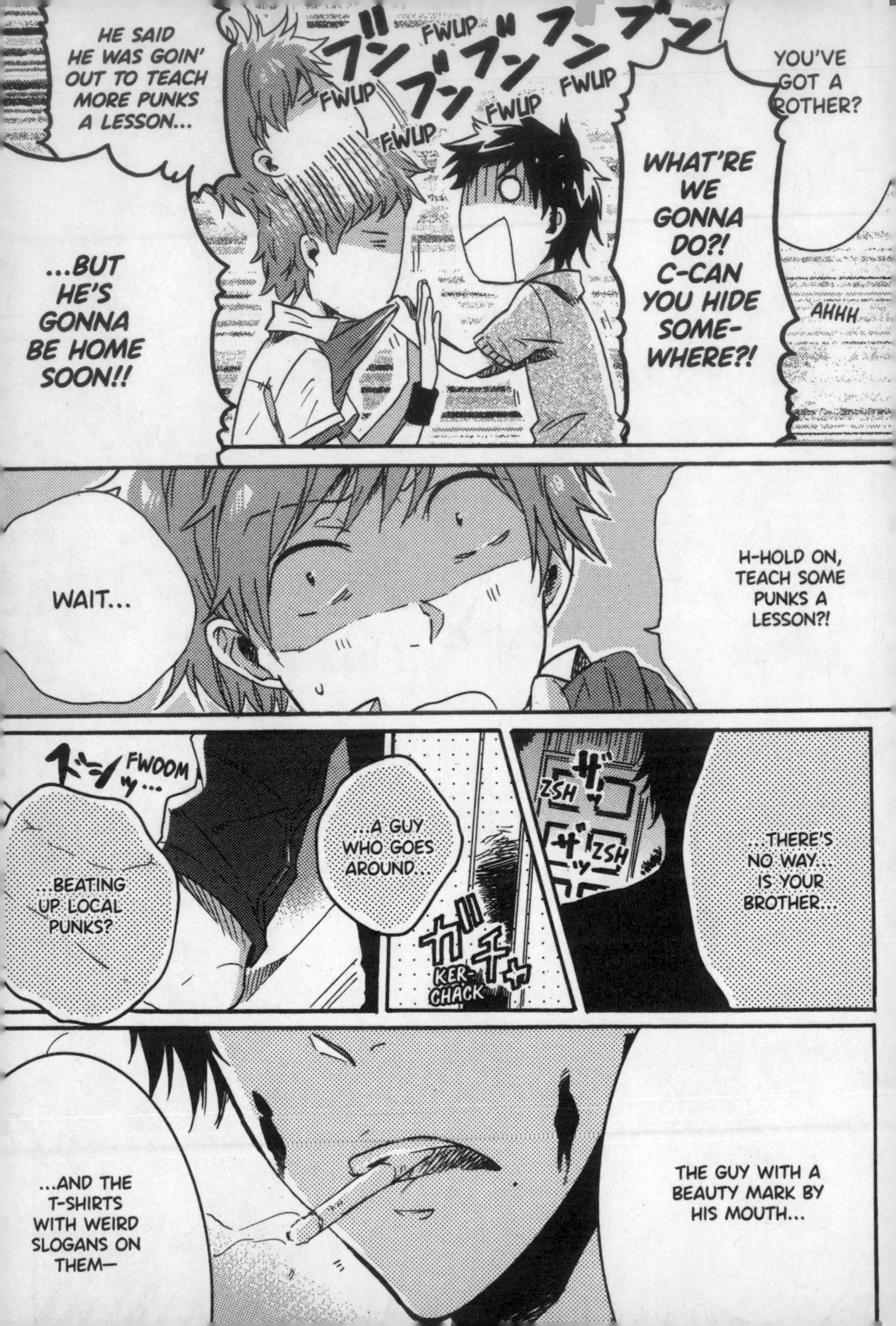
YOU'VE GOT A ROTHER?
AHHH
WHAT'RE WE GONNA DO?! C-CAN YOU HIDE SOME-WHERE?!
FWUP FWUP FWUP FWUP FWUP
HE SAID HE WAS GOIN' OUT TO TEACH MORE PUNKS A LESSON...
...BUT HE'S GONNA BE HOME SOON!!
H-HOLD ON, TEACH SOME PUNKS A LESSON?!
WAIT...
...THERE'S NO WAY... IS YOUR BROTHER...
ZSH ZSH
KER-CHACK
...A GUY WHO GOES AROUND...
FWOOM
...BEATING UP LOCAL PUNKS?
THE GUY WITH A BEAUTY MARK BY HIS MOUTH...
...AND THE T-SHIRTS WITH WEIRD SLOGANS ON THEM—

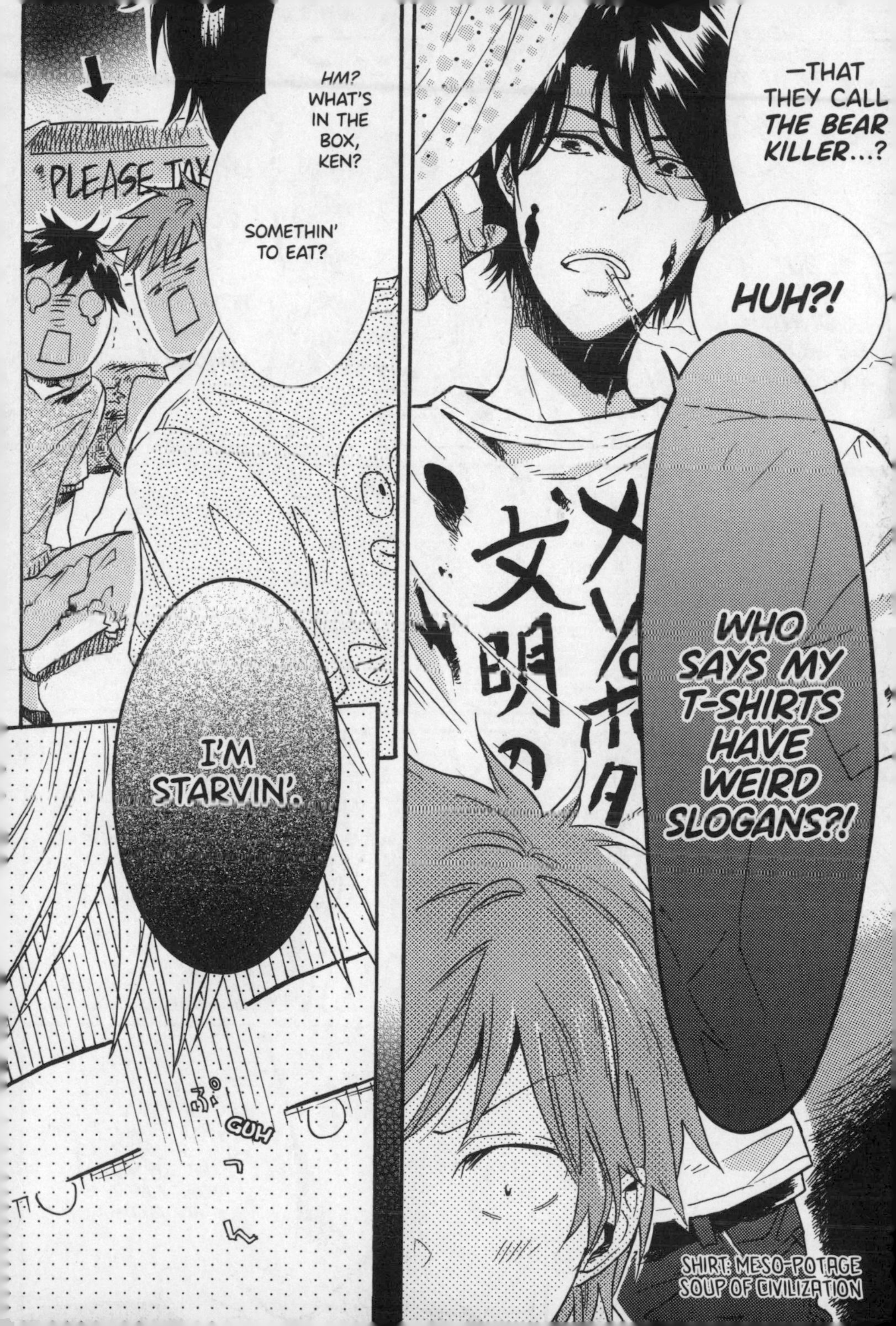
—THAT THEY CALL THE BEAR KILLER...?
HUH?!
WHO SAYS MY T-SHIRTS HAVE WEIRD SLOGANS?!
SHIRT: MESO-POTAGE SOUP OF CIVILIZATION
PLEASE TAK
HM? WHAT'S IN THE BOX, KEN?
SOMETHIN' TO EAT?
I'M STARVIN'.
GUH

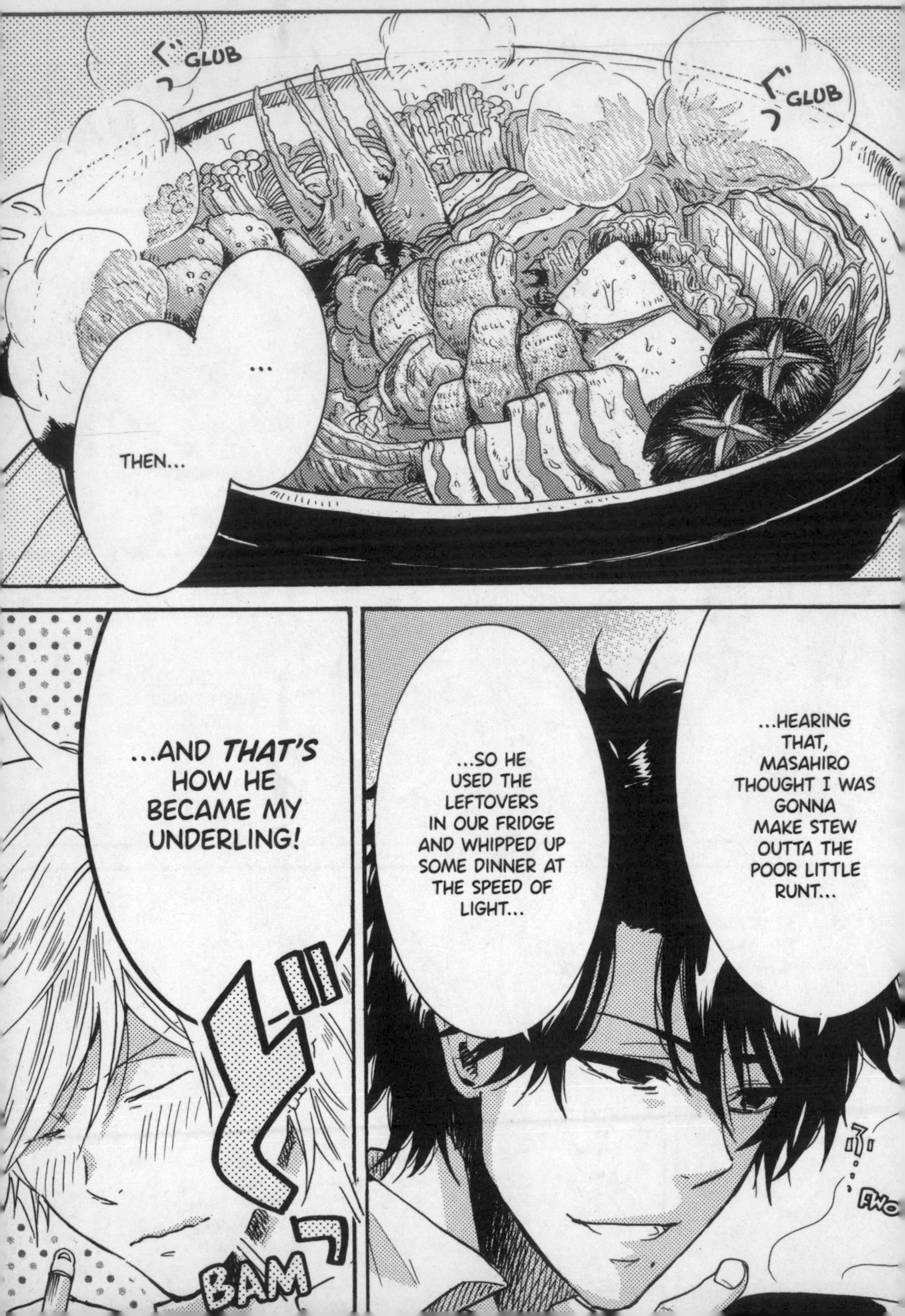
GLUB
GLUB
...
THEN...
...HEARING THAT, MASAHIRO THOUGHT I WAS GONNA MAKE STEW OUTTA THE POOR LITTLE RUNT...
...SO HE USED THE LEFTOVERS IN OUR FRIDGE AND WHIPPED UP SOME DINNER AT THE SPEED OF LIGHT...
FWO
...AND *THAT'S* HOW HE BECAME MY UNDERLING!
BAM

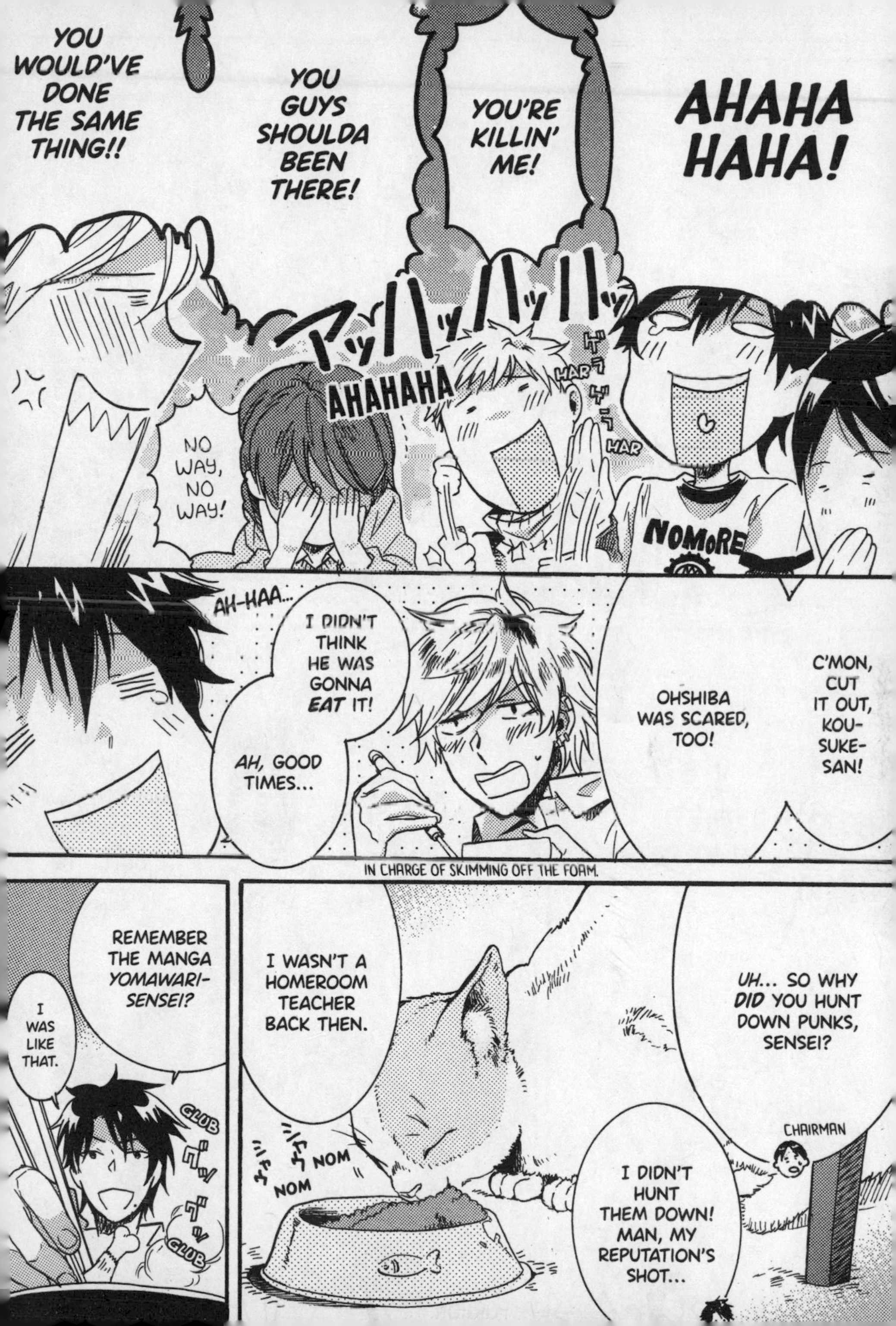
AHAHA HAHA!
YOU'RE KILLIN' ME!
YOU GUYS SHOULDA BEEN THERE!
YOU WOULD'VE DONE THE SAME THING!!
HAR
HAR
AHAHAHA
NO WAY, NO WAY!
C'MON, CUT IT OUT, KOU-SUKE-SAN!
OHSHIBA WAS SCARED, TOO!
I DIDN'T THINK HE WAS GONNA EAT IT!
AH, GOOD TIMES...
AH-HAA...
IN CHARGE OF SKIMMING OFF THE FOAM.
UH... SO WHY DID YOU HUNT DOWN PUNKS, SENSEI?
CHAIRMAN
I DIDN'T HUNT THEM DOWN! MAN, MY REPUTATION'S SHOT...
I WASN'T A HOMEROOM TEACHER BACK THEN.
NOM
NOM
REMEMBER THE MANGA YOMAWARI-SENSEI?
I WAS LIKE THAT.
GLUB
GLUB

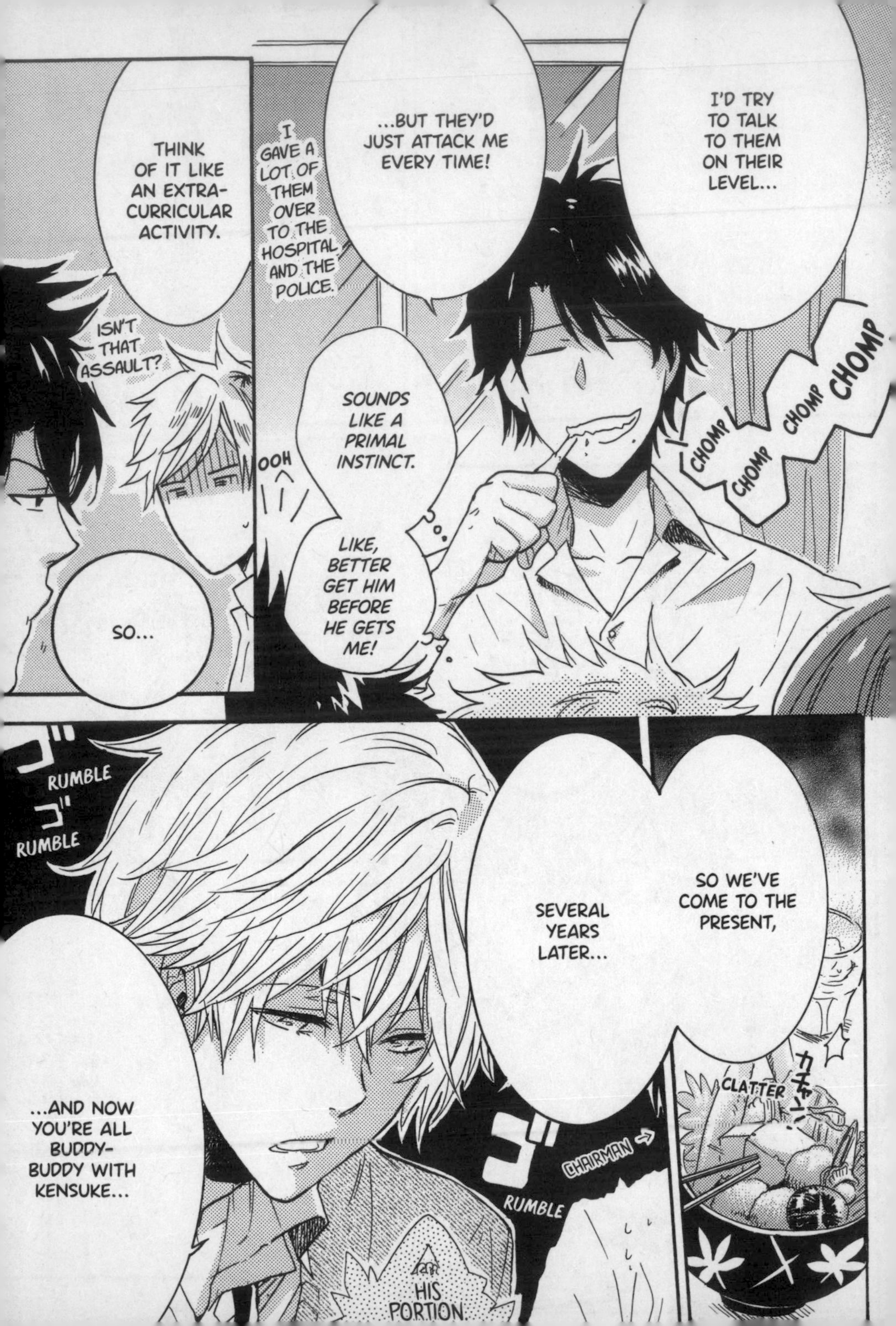
I'D TRY TO TALK TO THEM ON THEIR LEVEL...
...BUT THEY'D JUST ATTACK ME EVERY TIME!
I GAVE A LOT OF THEM OVER TO THE HOSPITAL AND THE POLICE.
CHOMP CHOMP CHOMP CHOMP
SOUNDS LIKE A PRIMAL INSTINCT.
OOH
LIKE, BETTER GET HIM BEFORE HE GETS ME!
THINK OF IT LIKE AN EXTRA-CURRICULAR ACTIVITY.
ISN'T THAT ASSAULT?
SO...
SO WE'VE COME TO THE PRESENT,
SEVERAL YEARS LATER...
CLATTER
CHAIRMAN
RUMBLE
RUMBLE
RUMBLE
...AND NOW YOU'RE ALL BUDDY-BUDDY WITH KENSUKE...
HIS PORTION

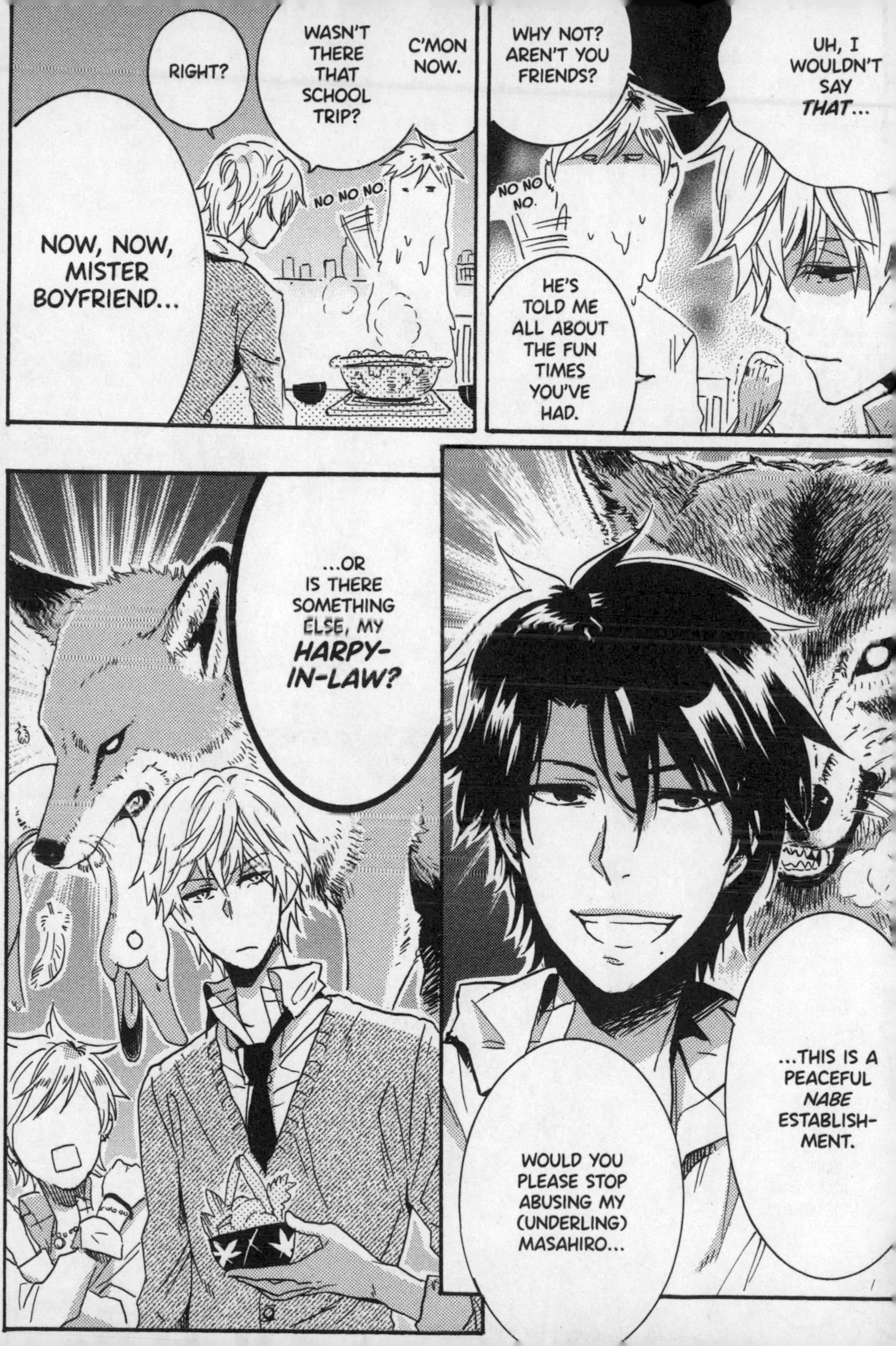
UH, I WOULDN'T SAY *THAT*...
WHY NOT? AREN'T YOU FRIENDS?
NO NO NO.
HE'S TOLD ME ALL ABOUT THE FUN TIMES YOU'VE HAD.
C'MON NOW.
WASN'T THERE THAT SCHOOL TRIP?
RIGHT?
NO NO NO.
NOW, NOW, MISTER BOYFRIEND...
...THIS IS A PEACEFUL *NABE* ESTABLISHMENT.
WOULD YOU PLEASE STOP ABUSING MY (UNDERLING) MASAHIRO...
...OR IS THERE SOMETHING ELSE, MY ***HARPY-IN-LAW?***

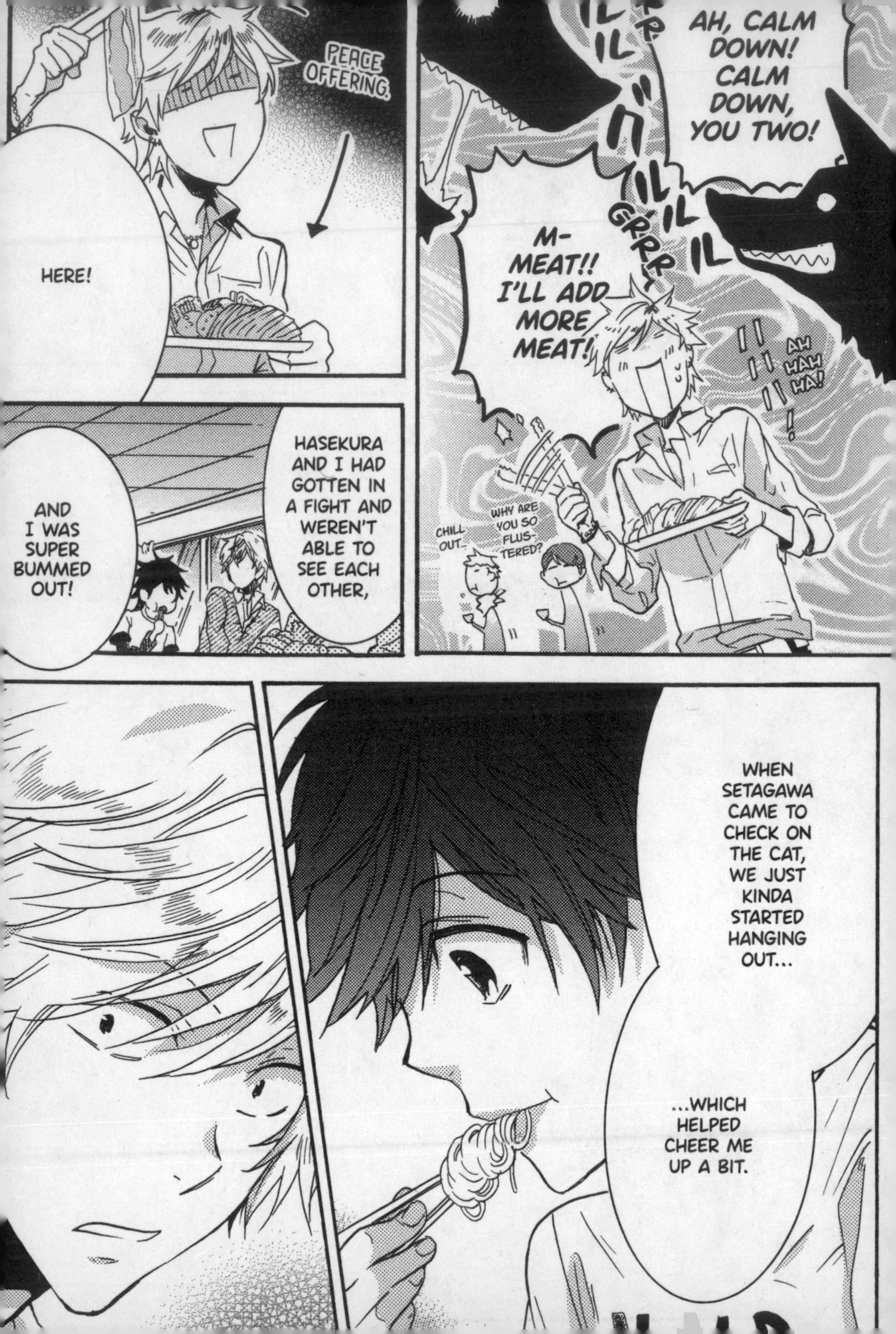
AH, CALM DOWN! CALM DOWN, YOU TWO!
GRRR
M-MEAT!! I'LL ADD MORE MEAT!
AH HAH HA!
WHY ARE YOU SO FLUS-TERED?
CHILL OUT..
PEACE OFFERING.
HERE!
HASEKURA AND I HAD GOTTEN IN A FIGHT AND WEREN'T ABLE TO SEE EACH OTHER,
AND I WAS SUPER BUMMED OUT!
WHEN SETAGAWA CAME TO CHECK ON THE CAT, WE JUST KINDA STARTED HANGING OUT...
...WHICH HELPED CHEER ME UP A BIT.

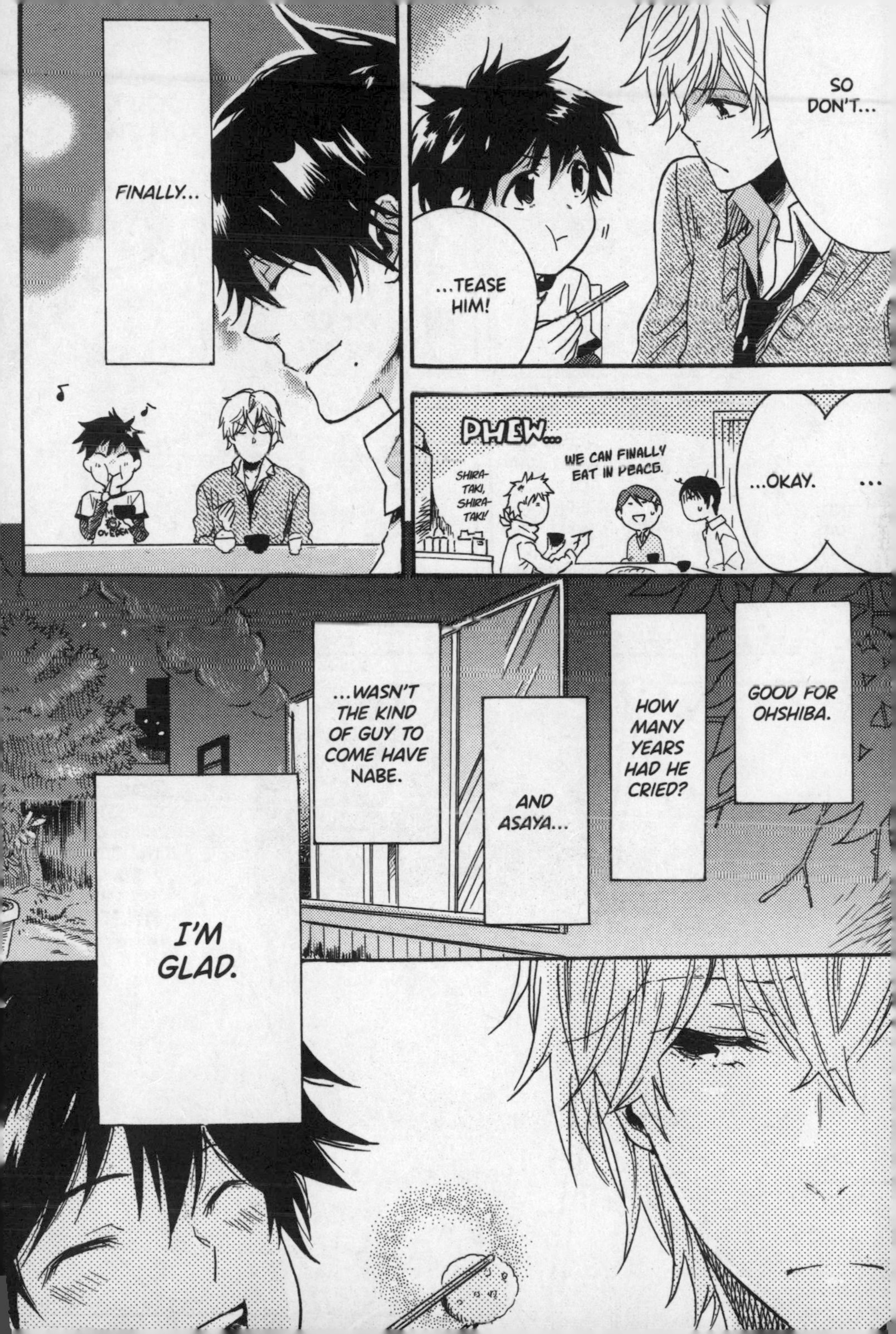
SO DON'T...
...TEASE HIM!
...
...OKAY.
PHEW...
WE CAN FINALLY EAT IN PEACE.
SHIRA-TAKI, SHIRA-TAKI!
FINALLY...
GOOD FOR OHSHIBA.
HOW MANY YEARS HAD HE CRIED?
AND ASAYA...
...WASN'T THE KIND OF GUY TO COME HAVE NABE.
I'M GLAD.

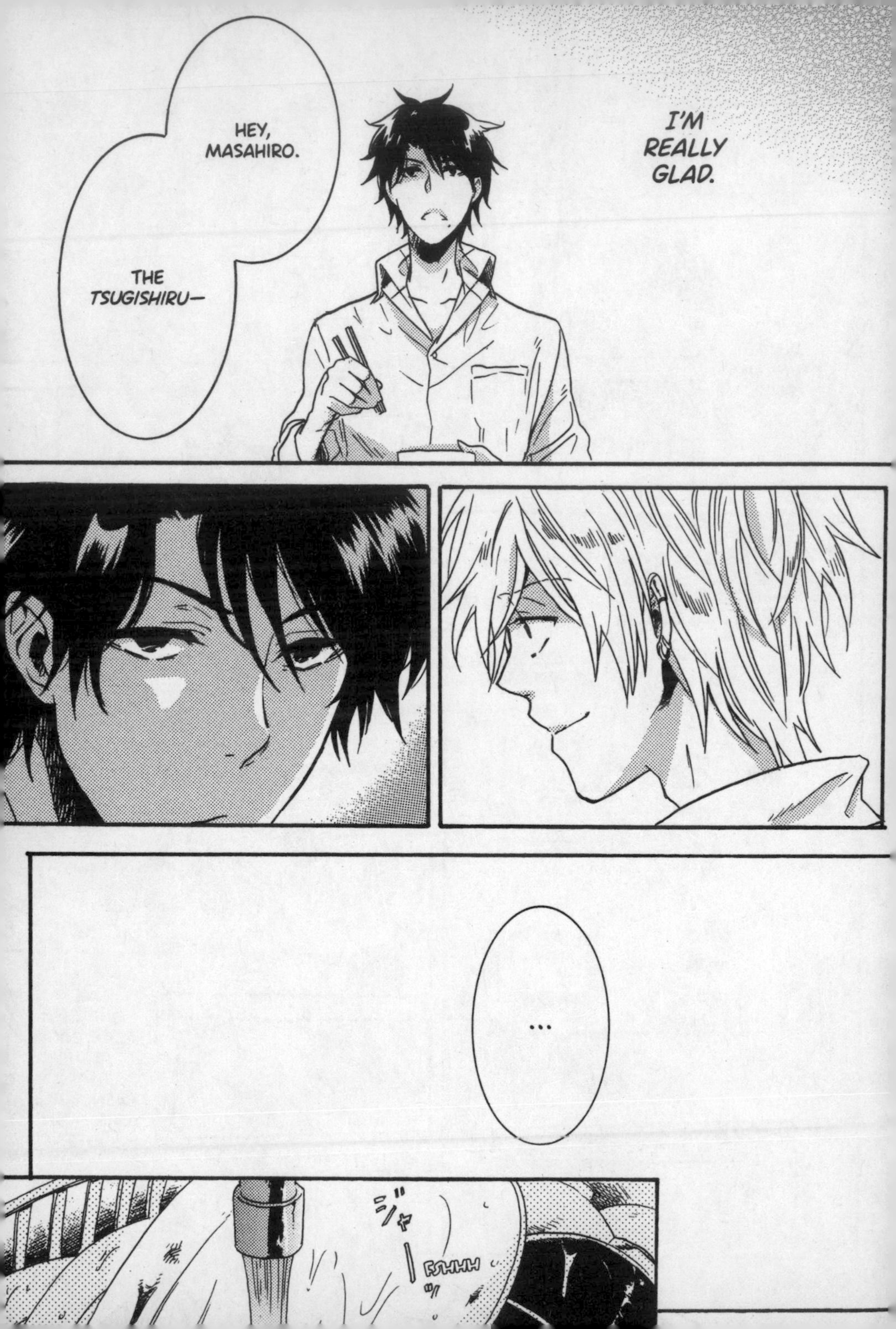
I'M REALLY GLAD.
HEY, MASAHIRO.
THE TSUGISHIRU—
...
FSHHH

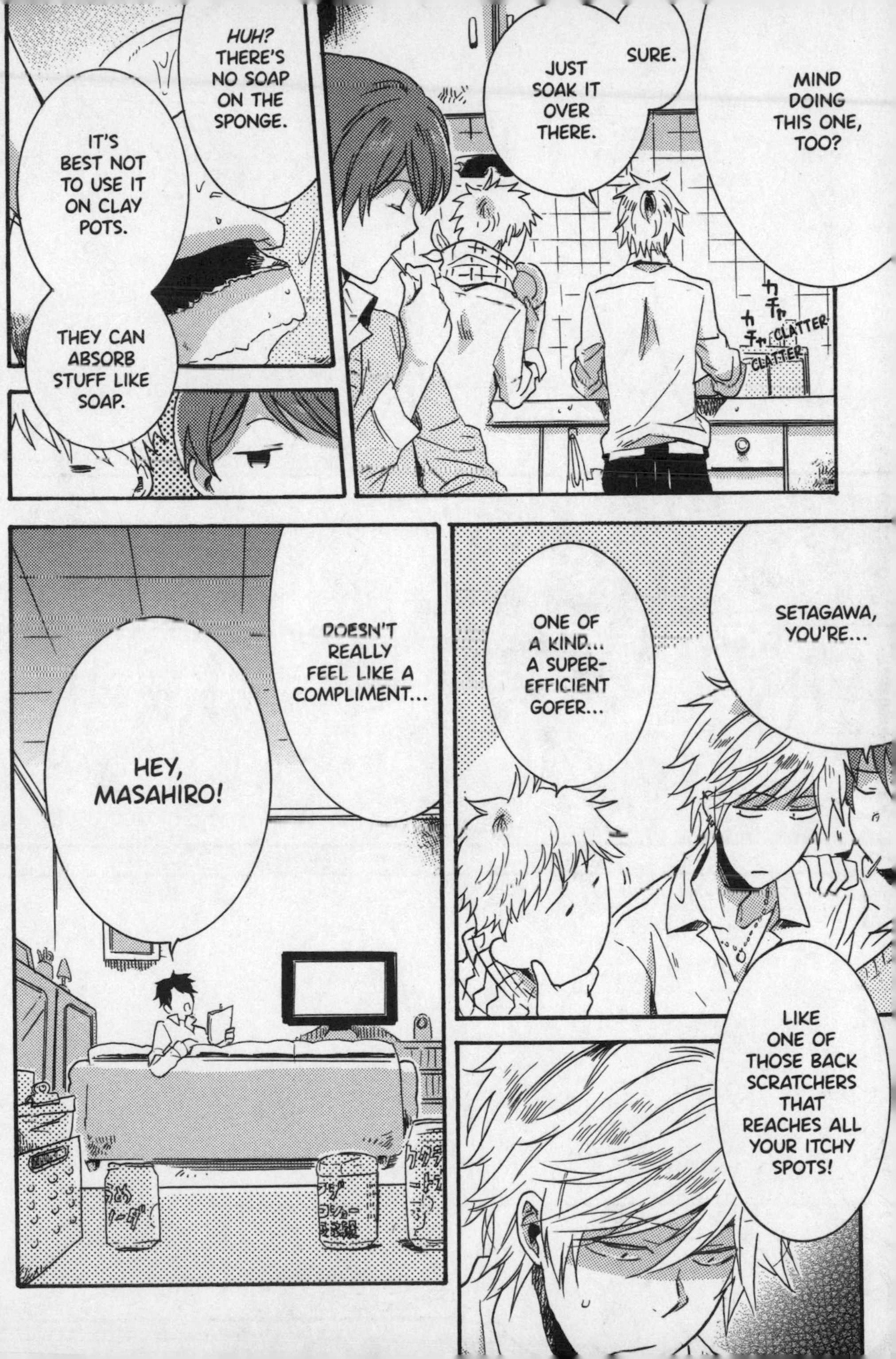
MIND DOING THIS ONE, TOO?
SURE.
JUST SOAK IT OVER THERE.
カチャカチャ
CLATTER CLATTER
HUH? THERE'S NO SOAP ON THE SPONGE.
IT'S BEST NOT TO USE IT ON CLAY POTS.
THEY CAN ABSORB STUFF LIKE SOAP.
SETAGAWA, YOU'RE...
ONE OF A KIND... A SUPER-EFFICIENT GOFER...
LIKE ONE OF THOSE BACK SCRATCHERS THAT REACHES ALL YOUR ITCHY SPOTS!
DOESN'T REALLY FEEL LIKE A COMPLIMENT...
HEY, MASAHIRO!

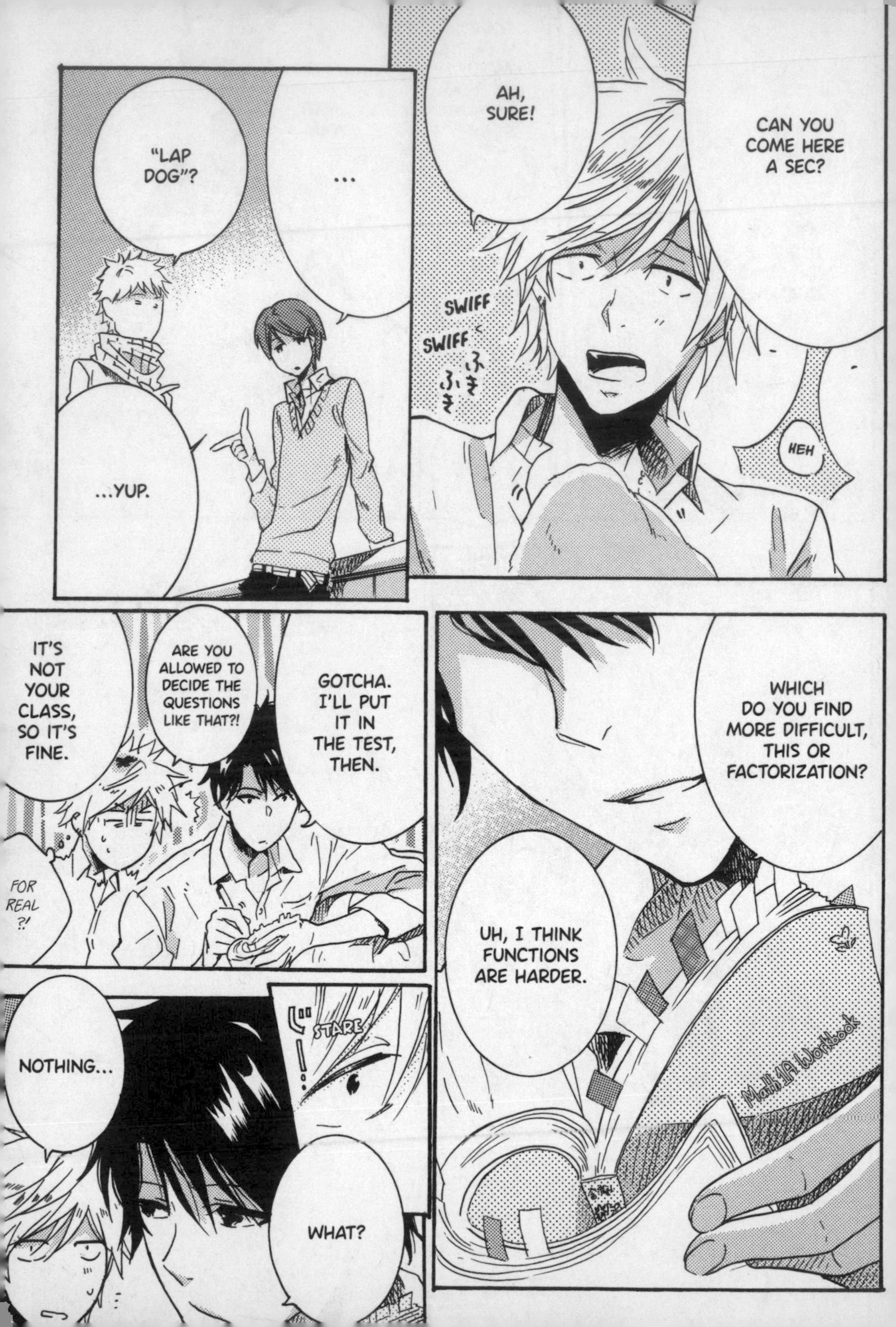
CAN YOU COME HERE A SEC?
AH, SURE!
HEH
SWIFF SWIFF
ふき ふき
...
"LAP DOG"?
...YUP.
WHICH DO YOU FIND MORE DIFFICULT, THIS OR FACTORIZATION?
UH, I THINK FUNCTIONS ARE HARDER.
Math 1A Workbook
GOTCHA. I'LL PUT IT IN THE TEST, THEN.
ARE YOU ALLOWED TO DECIDE THE QUESTIONS LIKE THAT?!
IT'S NOT YOUR CLASS, SO IT'S FINE.
FOR REAL ?!
じー
STARE
WHAT?
NOTHING...

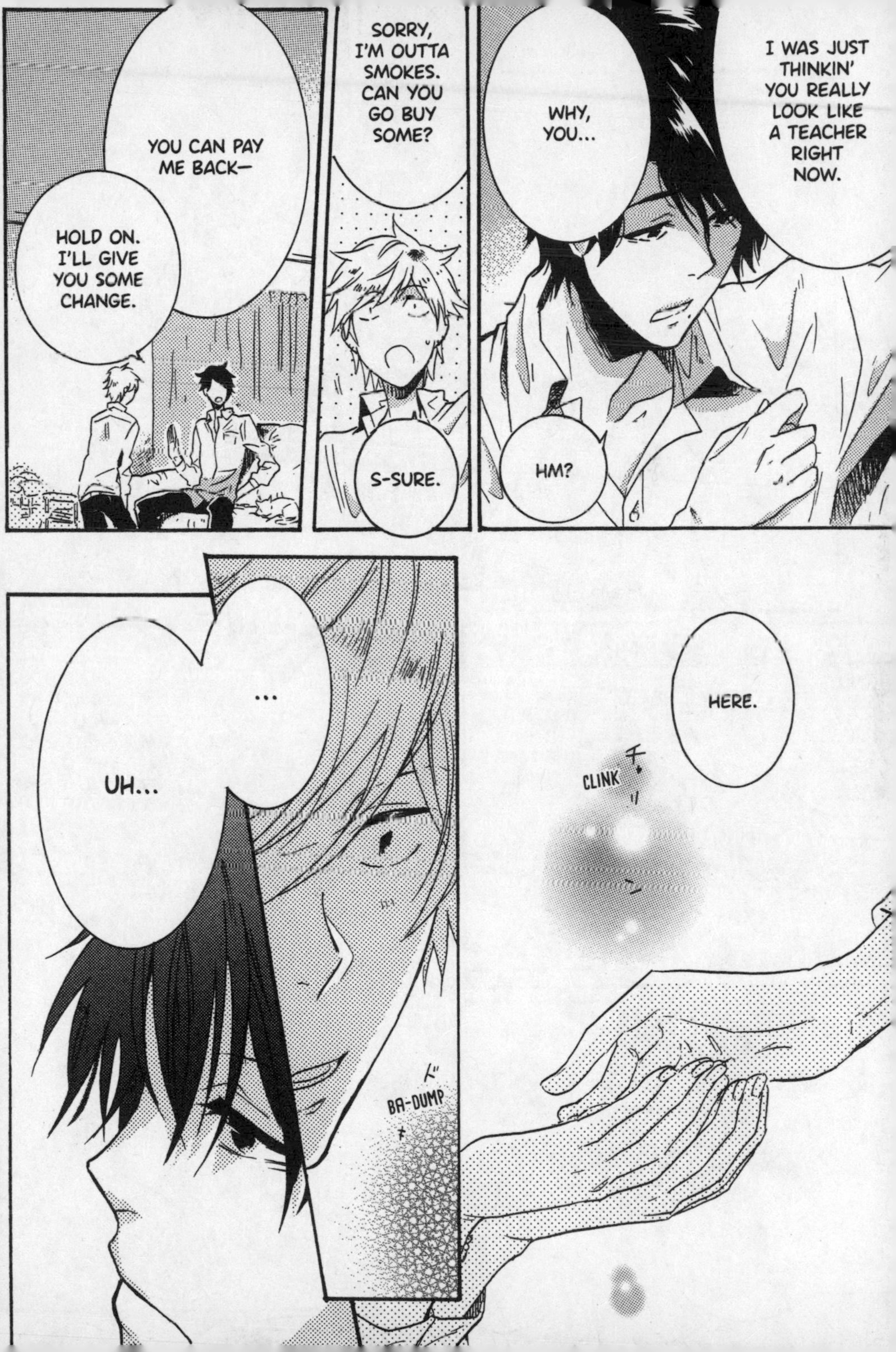
I WAS JUST THINKIN' YOU REALLY LOOK LIKE A TEACHER RIGHT NOW.
WHY, YOU...
HM?
SORRY, I'M OUTTA SMOKES. CAN YOU GO BUY SOME?
S-SURE.
YOU CAN PAY ME BACK—
HOLD ON. I'LL GIVE YOU SOME CHANGE.
HERE.
CLINK
...
UH...
BA-DUMP

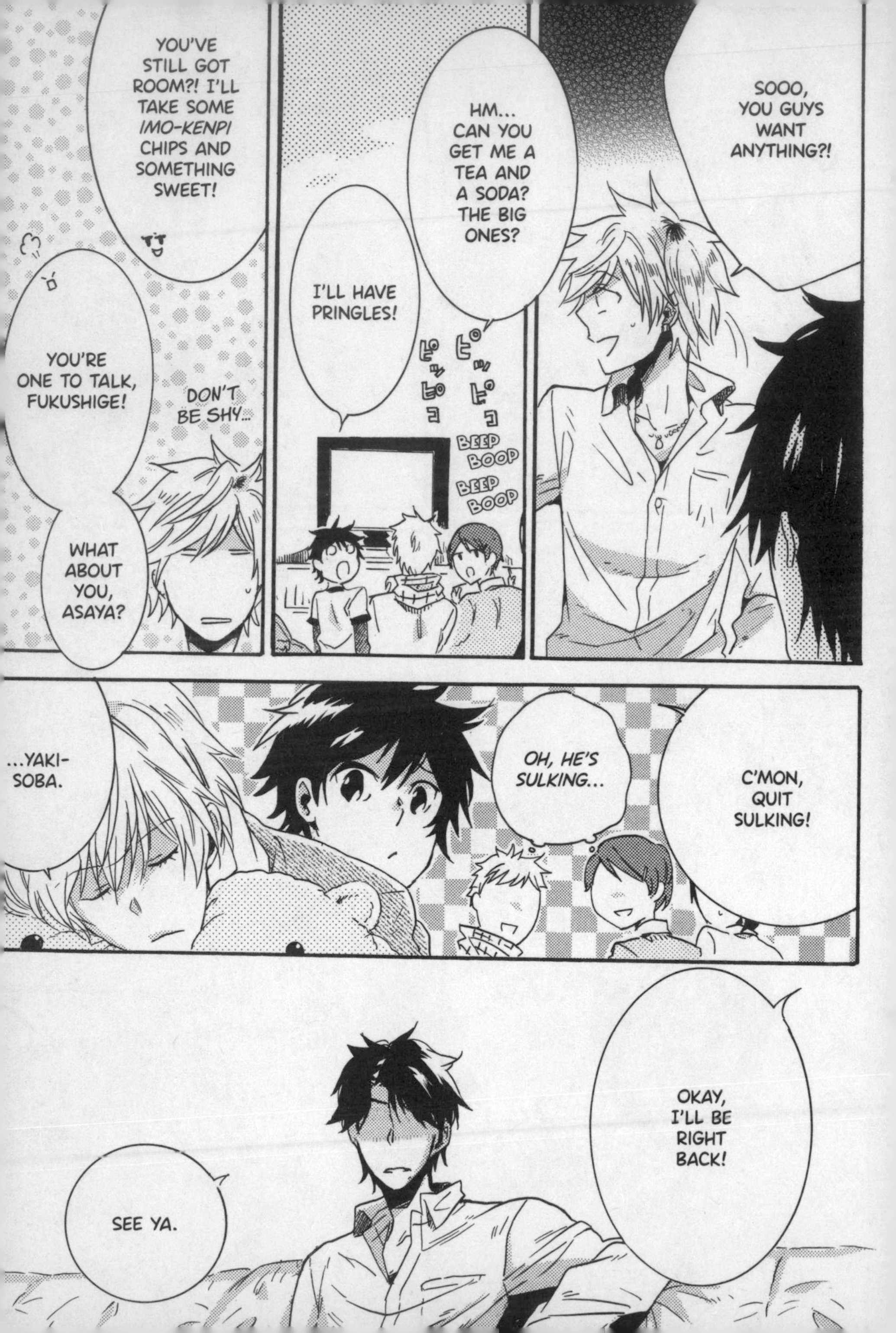
SOOO, YOU GUYS WANT ANYTHING?!
HM... CAN YOU GET ME A TEA AND A SODA? THE BIG ONES?
I'LL HAVE PRINGLES!
BEEP BOOP
BEEP BOOP
YOU'VE STILL GOT ROOM?! I'LL TAKE SOME *IMO-KENPI* CHIPS AND SOMETHING SWEET!
YOU'RE ONE TO TALK, FUKUSHIGE!
DON'T BE SHY...
WHAT ABOUT YOU, ASAYA?
C'MON, QUIT SULKING!
OH, HE'S SULKING...
...YAKI-SOBA.
OKAY, I'LL BE RIGHT BACK!
SEE YA.

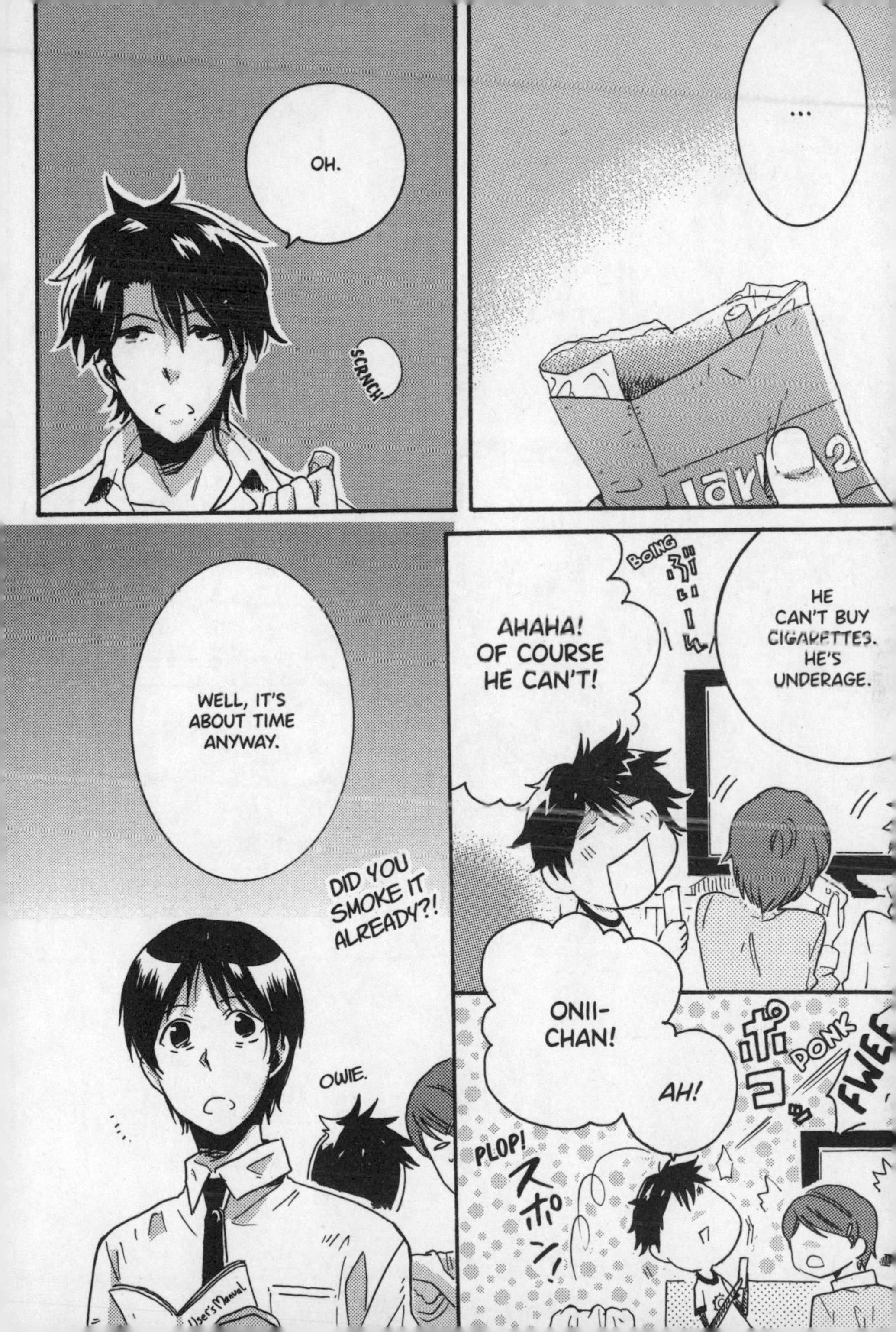
...
OH.
SCRNCH
HE CAN'T BUY CIGARETTES. HE'S UNDERAGE.
BOING
AHAHA! OF COURSE HE CAN'T!
ONII-CHAN!
PONK
ポコ
AH!
PLOP!
スポーン!
WELL, IT'S ABOUT TIME ANYWAY.
DID YOU SMOKE IT ALREADY?!
OWIE.
...
User's Manual

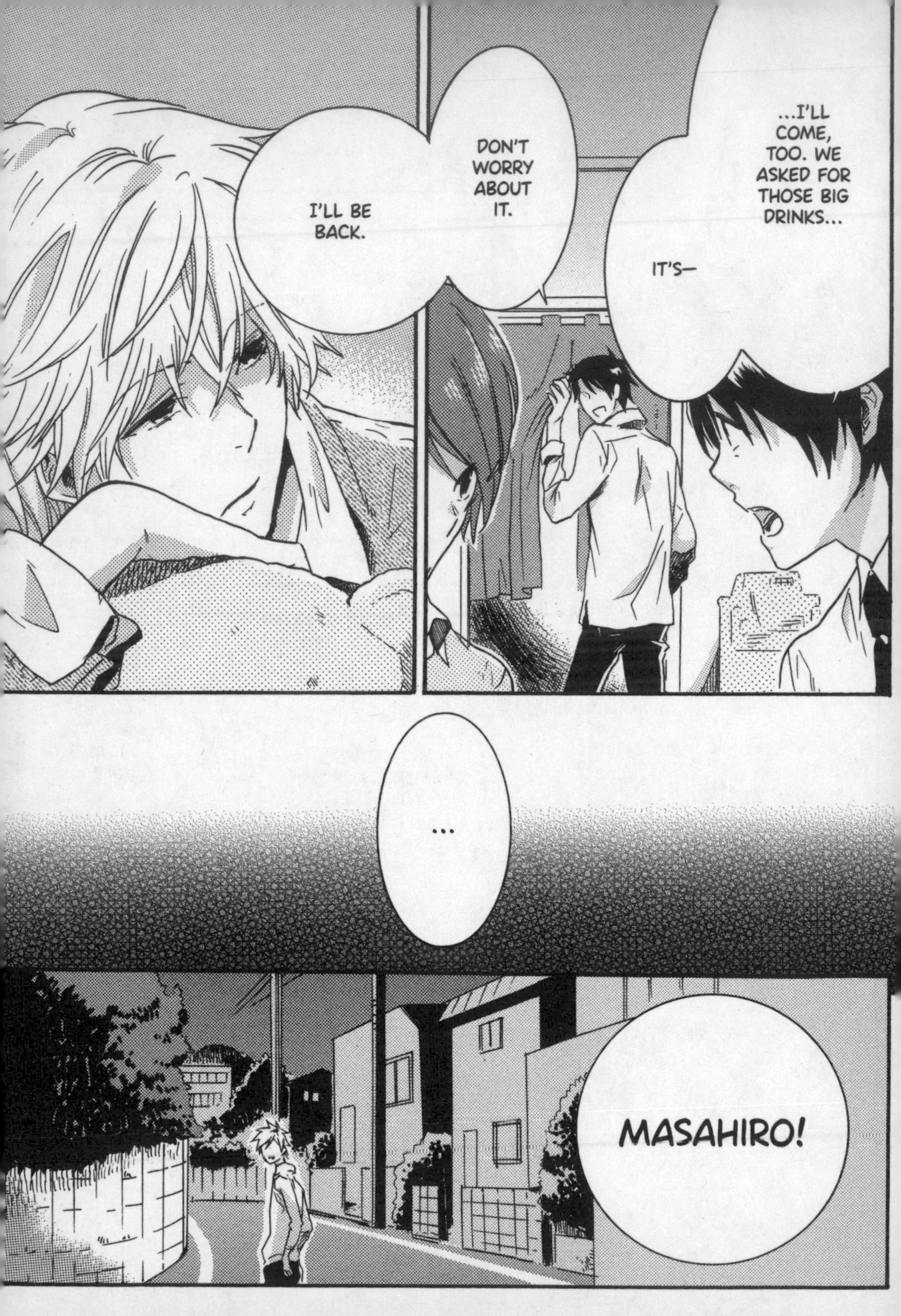

...I'LL COME, TOO. WE ASKED FOR THOSE BIG DRINKS...
IT'S—
DON'T WORRY ABOUT IT.
I'LL BE BACK.
...
MASAHIRO!

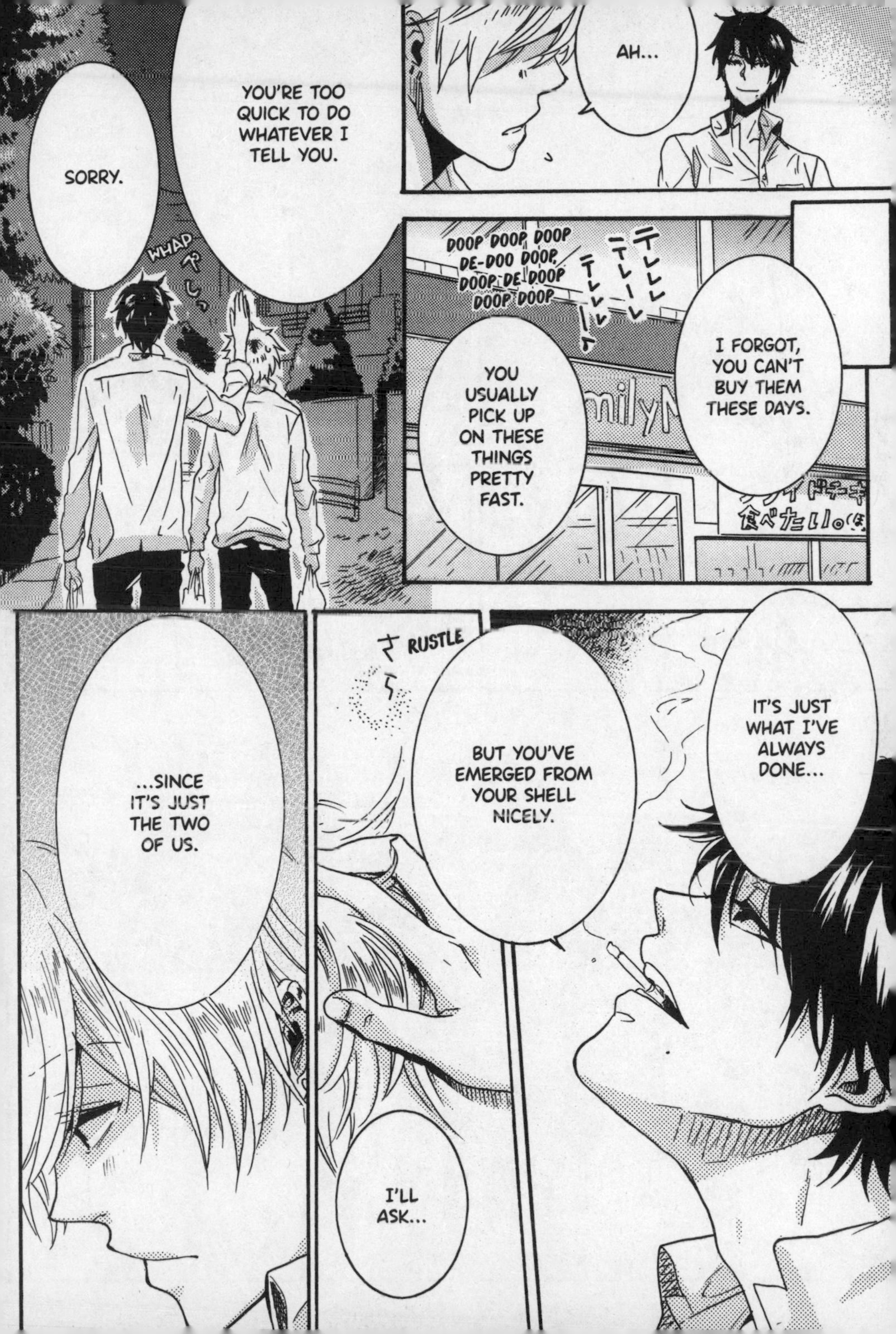
AH...
I FORGOT, YOU CAN'T BUY THEM THESE DAYS.
DOOP DOOP DOOP DE-DOO DOOP, DOOP DE DOOP DOOP DOOP
YOU USUALLY PICK UP ON THESE THINGS PRETTY FAST.
YOU'RE TOO QUICK TO DO WHATEVER I TELL YOU.
WHAP
SORRY.
IT'S JUST WHAT I'VE ALWAYS DONE...
BUT YOU'VE EMERGED FROM YOUR SHELL NICELY.
RUSTLE
I'LL ASK...
...SINCE IT'S JUST THE TWO OF US.

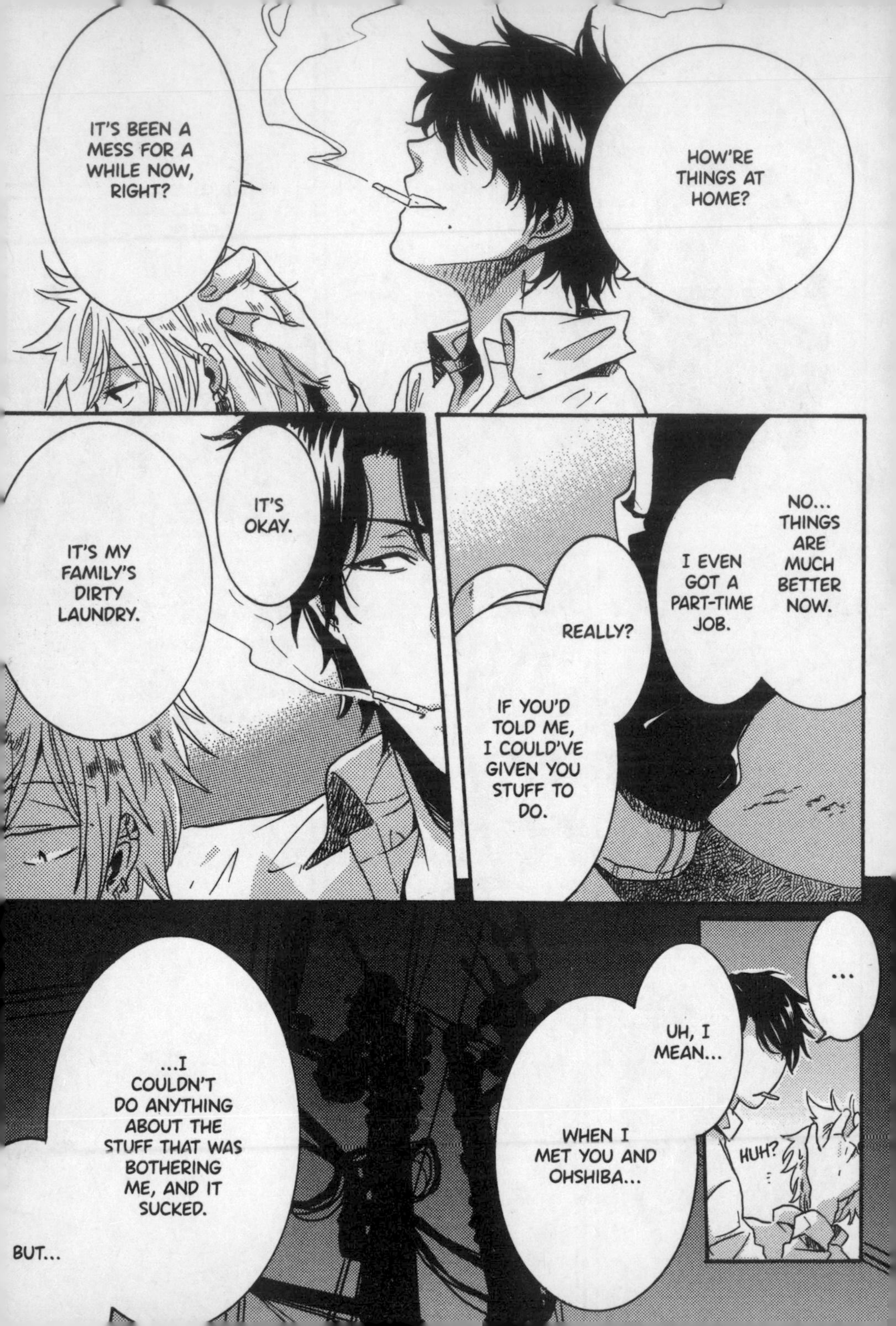
HOW'RE THINGS AT HOME?
IT'S BEEN A MESS FOR A WHILE NOW, RIGHT?
NO... THINGS ARE MUCH BETTER NOW.
I EVEN GOT A PART-TIME JOB.
REALLY?
IF YOU'D TOLD ME, I COULD'VE GIVEN YOU STUFF TO DO.
IT'S OKAY.
IT'S MY FAMILY'S DIRTY LAUNDRY.
...
HUH?
UH, I MEAN...
WHEN I MET YOU AND OHSHIBA...
...I COULDN'T DO ANYTHING ABOUT THE STUFF THAT WAS BOTHERING ME, AND IT SUCKED.
BUT...

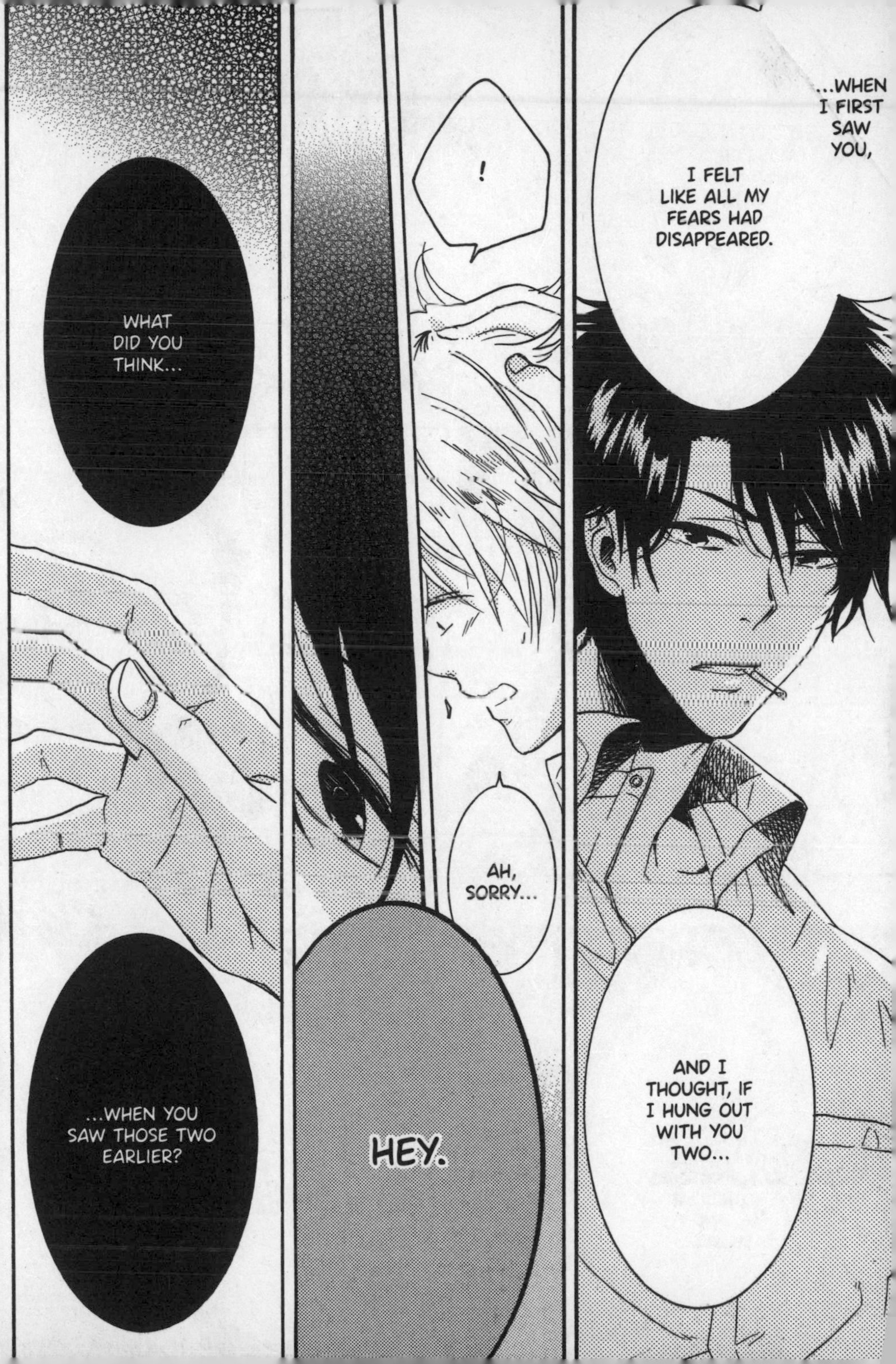
...WHEN I FIRST SAW YOU,
I FELT LIKE ALL MY FEARS HAD DISAPPEARED.
AND I THOUGHT, IF I HUNG OUT WITH YOU TWO...
!
AH, SORRY...
HEY.
WHAT DID YOU THINK...
...WHEN YOU SAW THOSE TWO EARLIER?

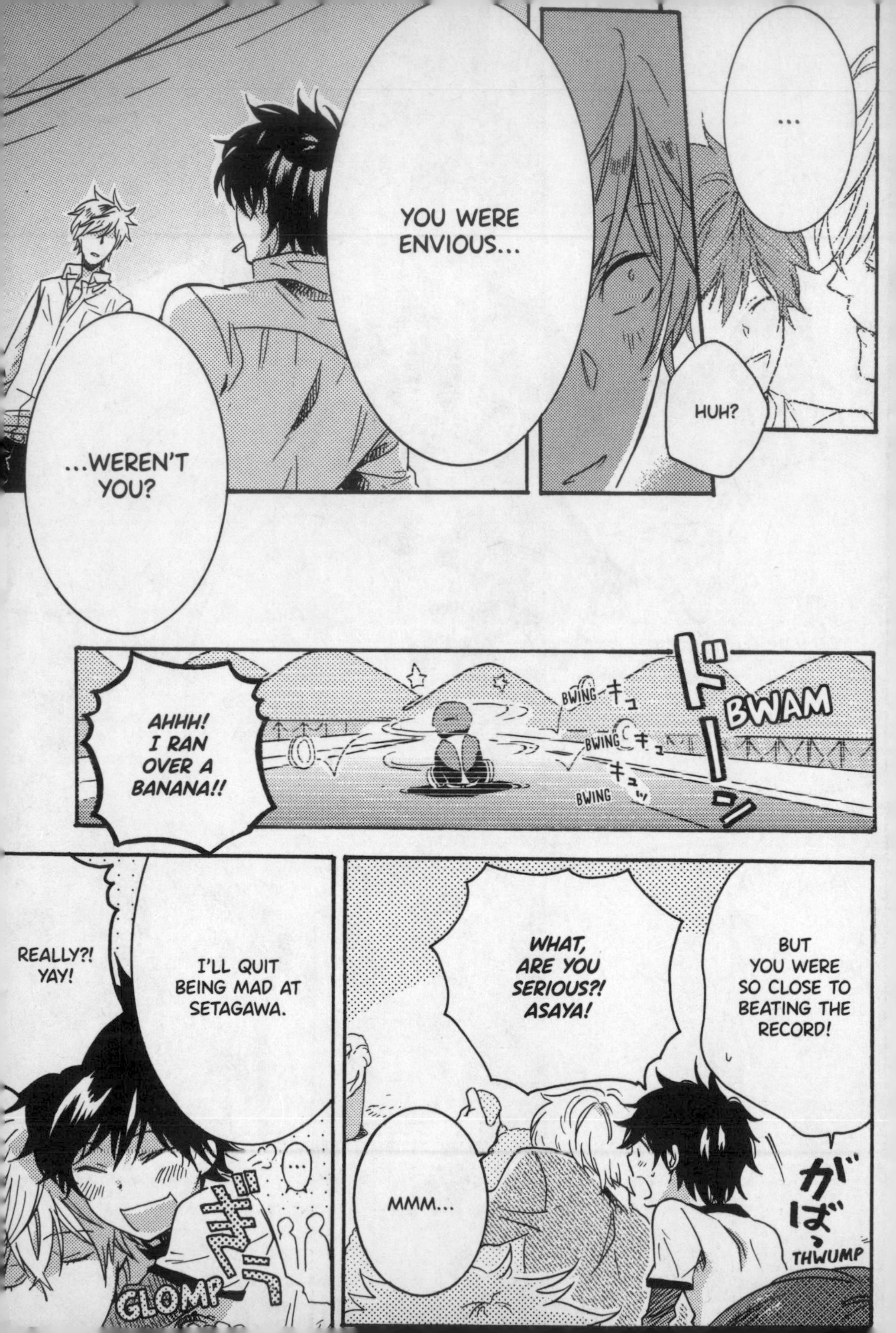
...
HUH?
YOU WERE ENVIOUS...
...WEREN'T YOU?
BWAM
ドーン
BWING
キュ
BWING
キュ
BWING
キュッ
AHHH! I RAN OVER A BANANA!!
BUT YOU WERE SO CLOSE TO BEATING THE RECORD!
WHAT, ARE YOU SERIOUS?! ASAYA!
MMM...
THWUMP
がばっ
I'LL QUIT BEING MAD AT SETAGAWA.
REALLY?! YAY!
...
GLOMP

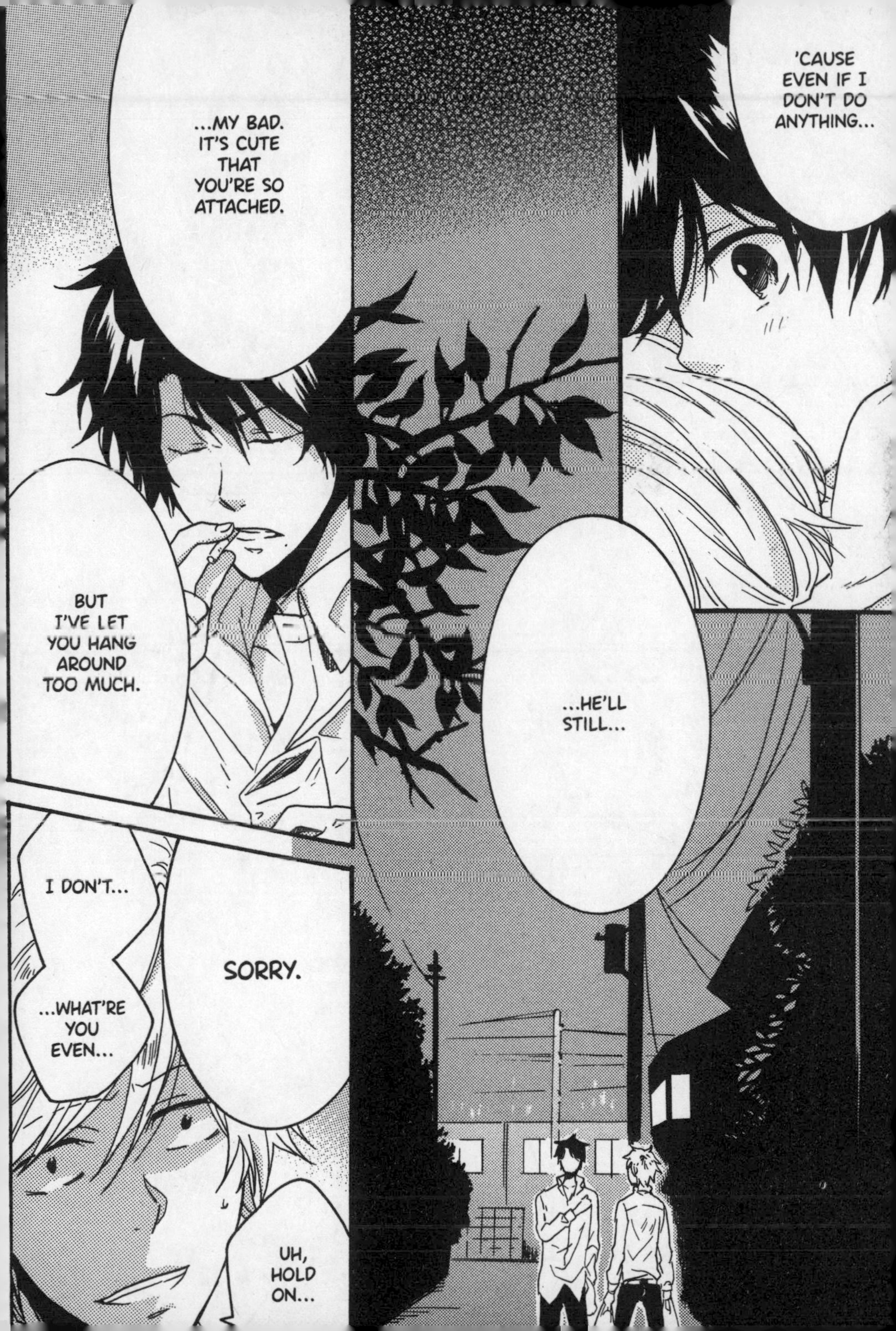
'CAUSE EVEN IF I DON'T DO ANYTHING...
...HE'LL STILL...
...MY BAD. IT'S CUTE THAT YOU'RE SO ATTACHED.
BUT I'VE LET YOU HANG AROUND TOO MUCH.
SORRY.
I DON'T...
...WHAT'RE YOU EVEN...
UH, HOLD ON...

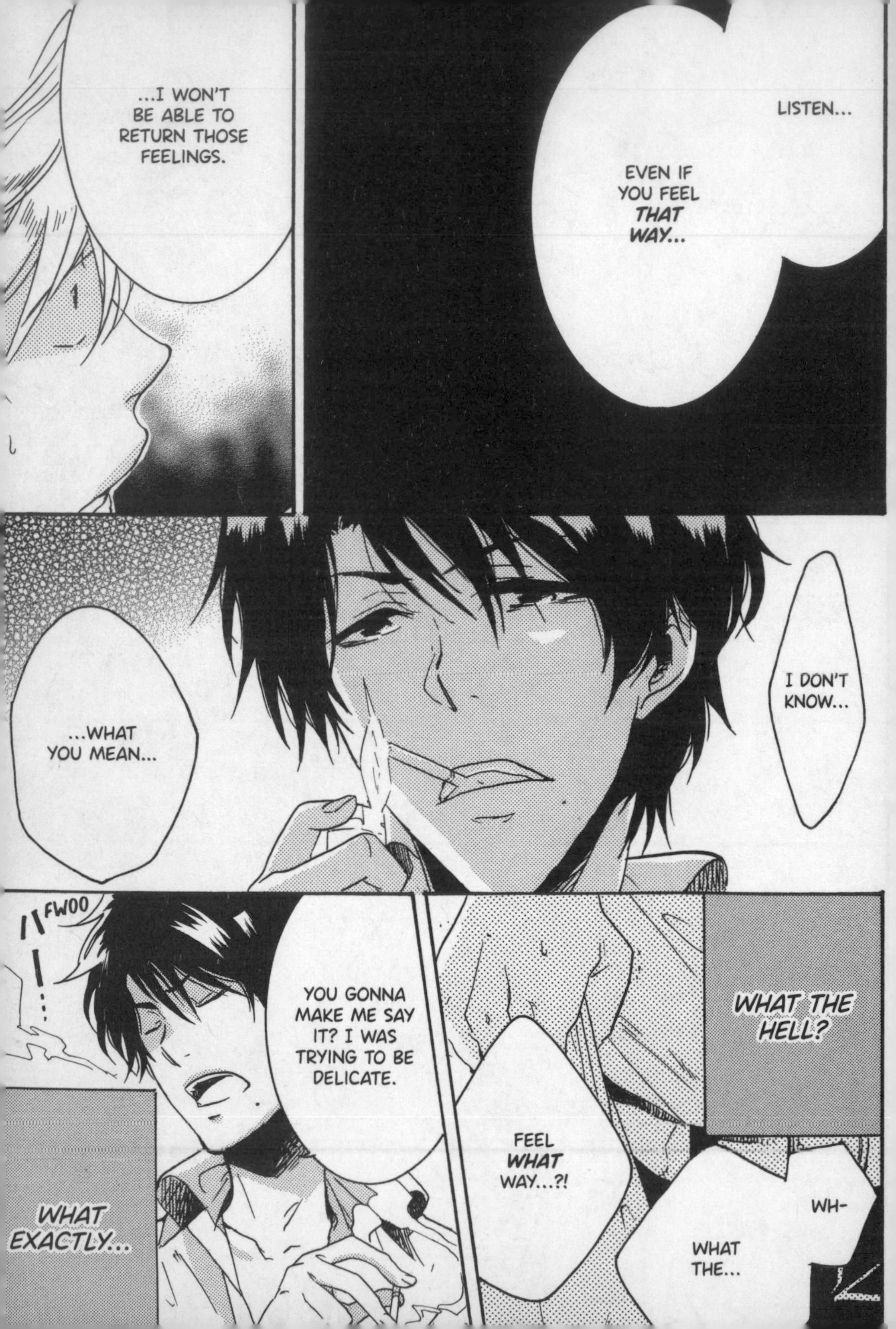
LISTEN...
EVEN IF YOU FEEL THAT WAY...
...I WON'T BE ABLE TO RETURN THOSE FEELINGS.
I DON'T KNOW...
...WHAT YOU MEAN...
WHAT THE HELL?
WH-
WHAT THE...
FEEL WHAT WAY...?!
FWOO
YOU GONNA MAKE ME SAY IT? I WAS TRYING TO BE DELICATE.
WHAT EXACTLY...

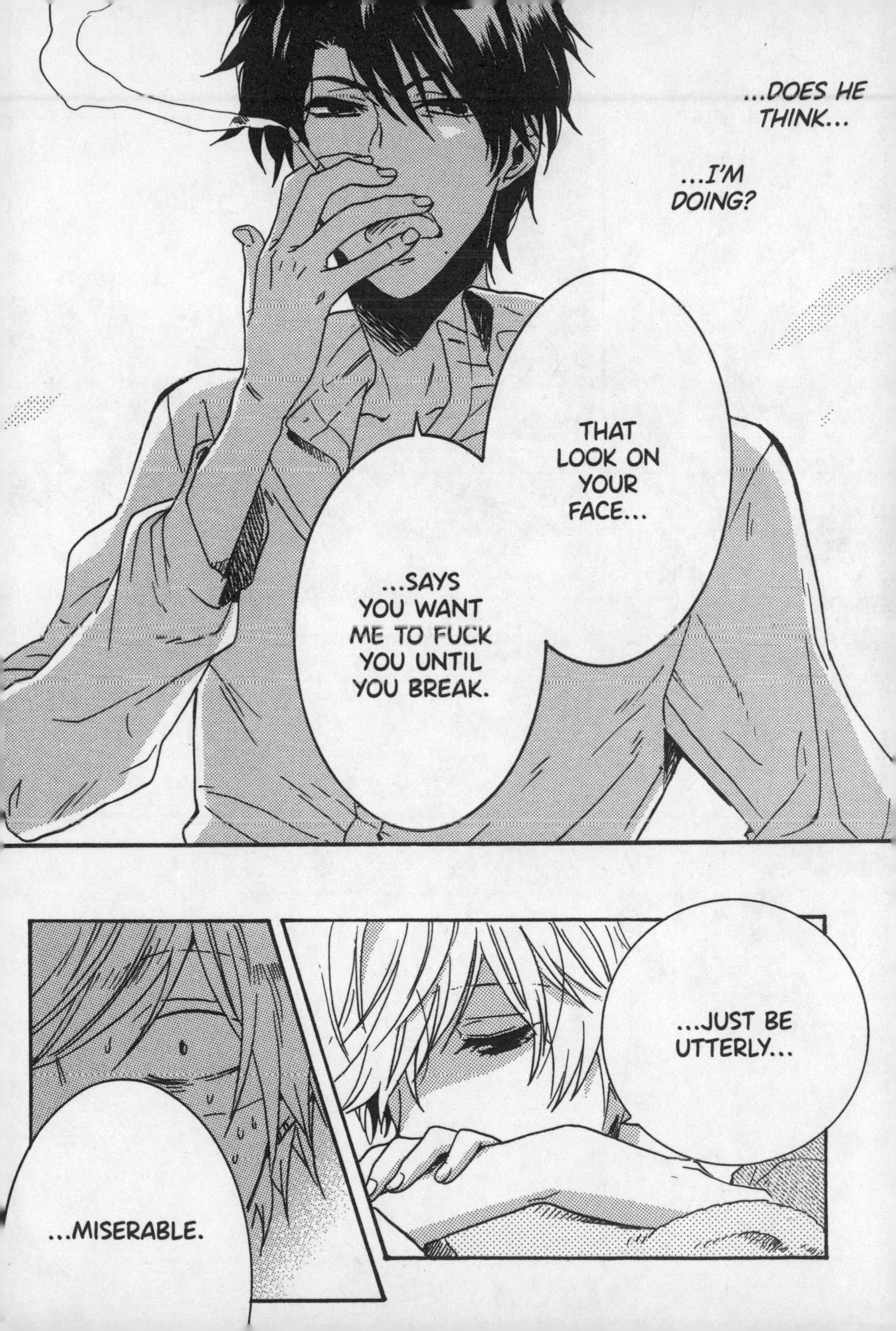
...DOES HE THINK...
...I'M DOING?
THAT LOOK ON YOUR FACE...
...SAYS YOU WANT ME TO FUCK YOU UNTIL YOU BREAK.
...JUST BE UTTERLY...
...MISERABLE.

Meet the Crew

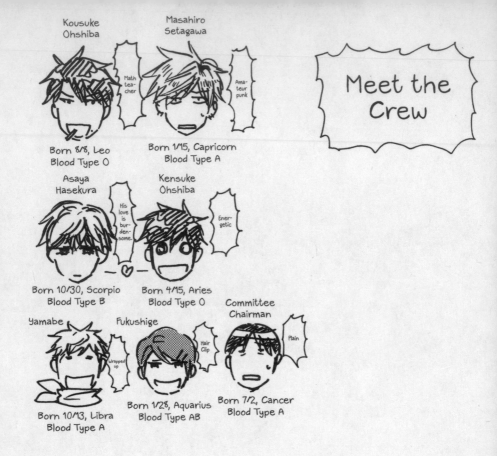

Kousuke Ohshiba
Math teacher
Born 8/8, Leo
Blood Type O
Masahiro Setagawa
Amateur punk
Born 1/15, Capricorn
Blood Type A
Asaya Hasekura
His love is burdensome.
Born 10/30, Scorpio
Blood Type B
Kensuke Ohshiba
Energetic
Born 4/15, Aries
Blood Type O
Yamabe
Wrapped up
Born 10/13, Libra
Blood Type A
Fukushige
Hair Clip
Born 1/28, Aquarius
Blood Type AB
Committee Chairman
Plain
Born 7/2, Cancer
Blood Type A

So, what's it called?
Food's good!
Wha?! Uh, it's sasanishiki!
LURCH
No, not the rice...
Oh, whatever.
PLEASE TAKE
Rice Bag

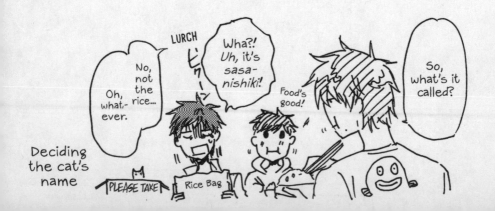

Deciding the cat's name

Hitorijime
My Hero

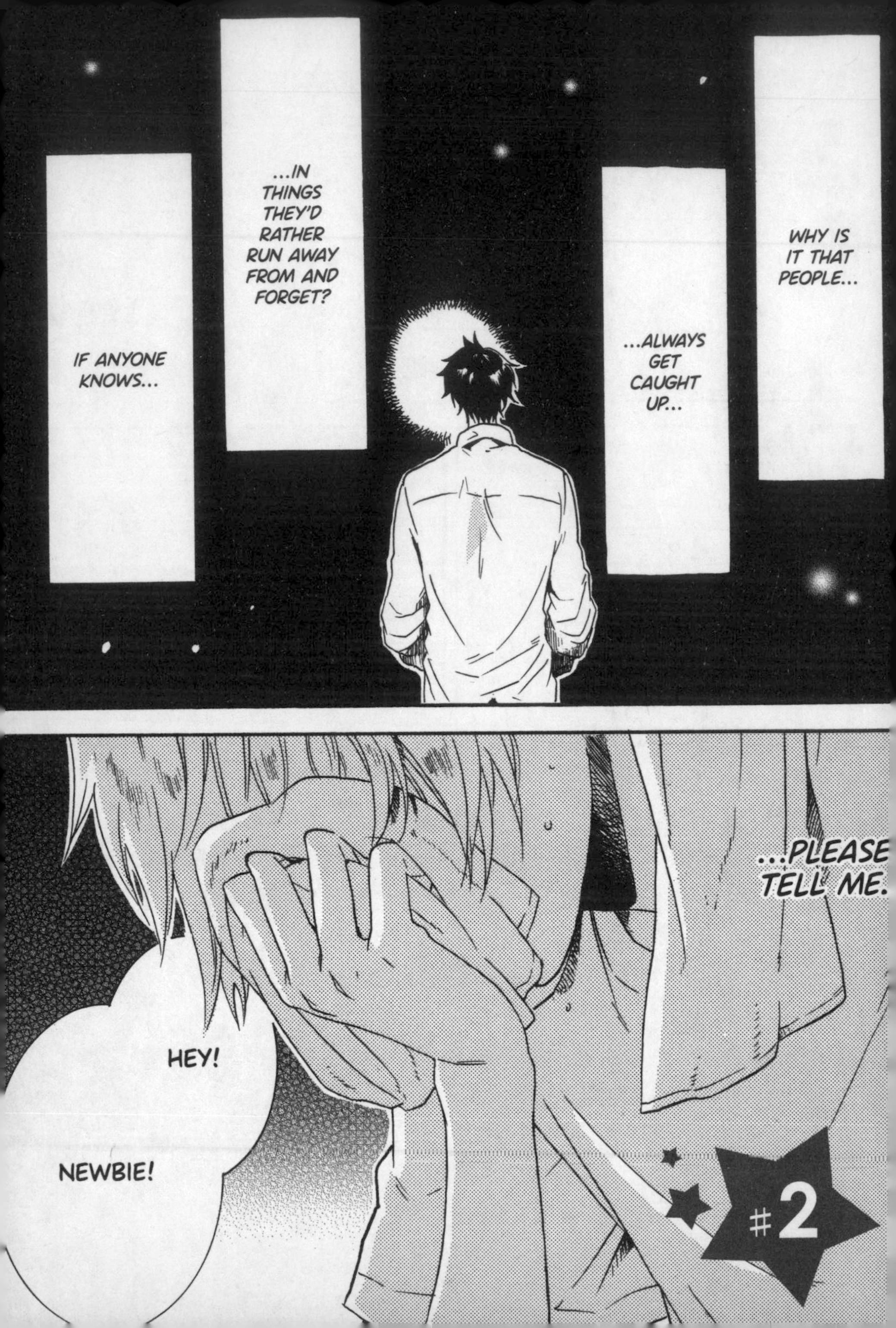
WHY IS IT THAT PEOPLE...
...ALWAYS GET CAUGHT UP...
...IN THINGS THEY'D RATHER RUN AWAY FROM AND FORGET?
IF ANYONE KNOWS...
...PLEASE TELL ME.
#2
HEY!
NEWBIE!

STORE CURTAIN: SHOUFUKU RAMEN

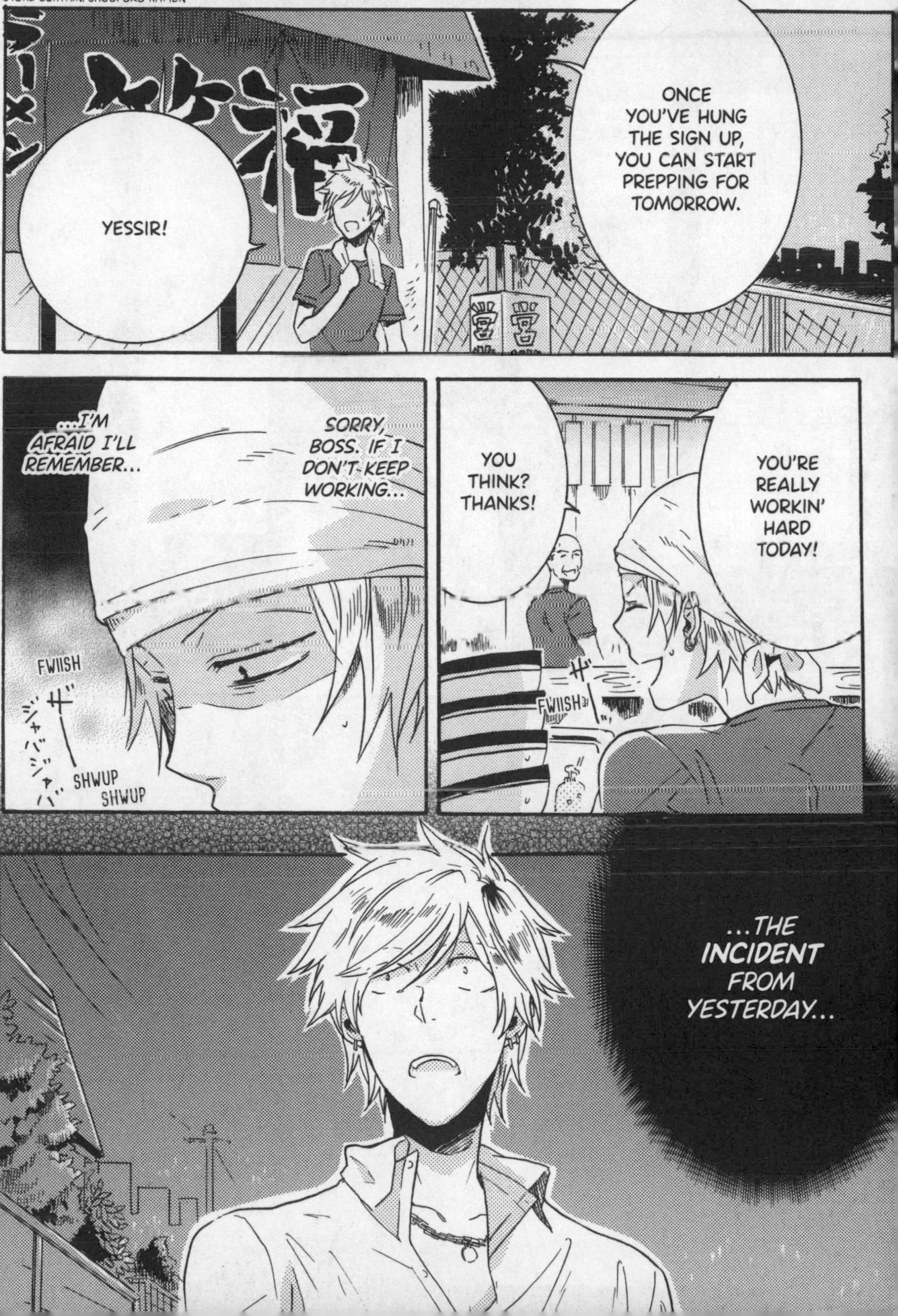
ONCE YOU'VE HUNG THE SIGN UP, YOU CAN START PREPPING FOR TOMORROW.
YESSIR!
YOU'RE REALLY WORKIN' HARD TODAY!
YOU THINK? THANKS!
FWIISH
SORRY, BOSS. IF I DON'T KEEP WORKING...
...I'M AFRAID I'LL REMEMBER...
FWIISH
SHWUP SHWUP
...THE INCIDENT FROM YESTERDAY...

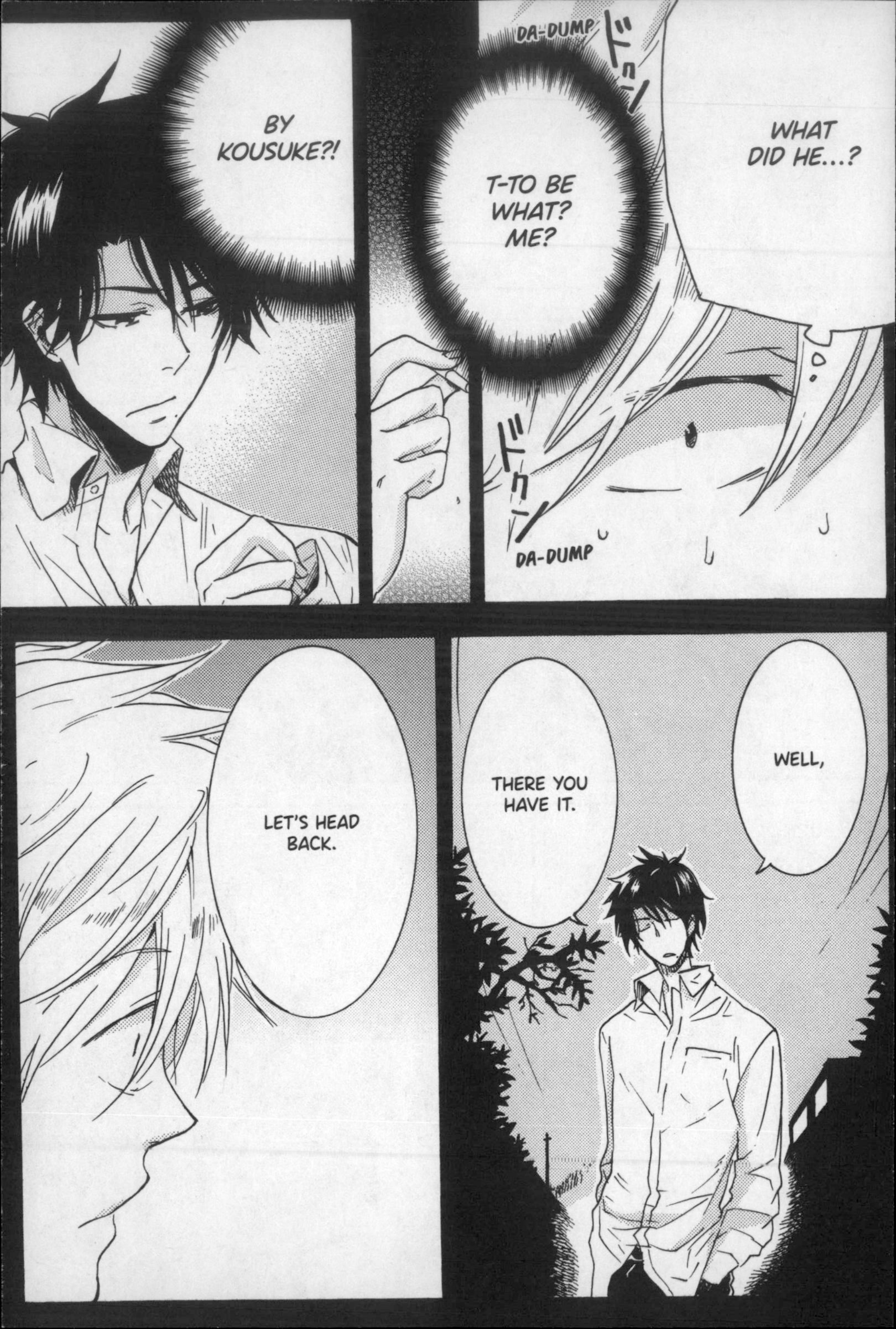
DA-DUMP
WHAT DID HE...?
T-TO BE WHAT? ME?
DA-DUMP
BY KOUSUKE?!
WELL,
THERE YOU HAVE IT.
LET'S HEAD BACK.

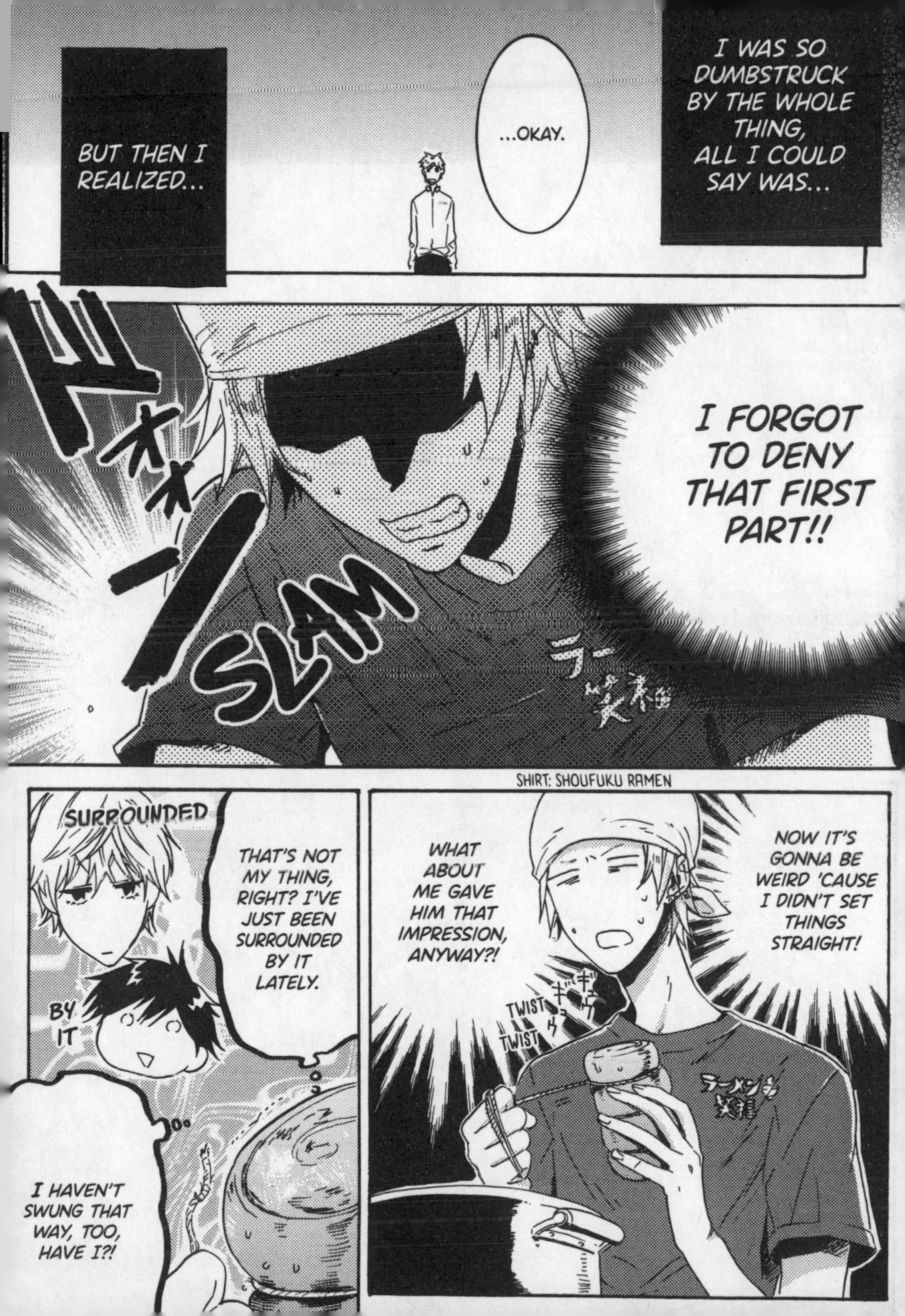
I WAS SO DUMBSTRUCK BY THE WHOLE THING, ALL I COULD SAY WAS...
...OKAY.
BUT THEN I REALIZED...
I FORGOT TO DENY THAT FIRST PART!!
SLAM
SHIRT: SHOUFUKU RAMEN
NOW IT'S GONNA BE WEIRD 'CAUSE I DIDN'T SET THINGS STRAIGHT!
WHAT ABOUT ME GAVE HIM THAT IMPRESSION, ANYWAY?!
TWIST TWIST
SURROUNDED
THAT'S NOT MY THING, RIGHT? I'VE JUST BEEN SURROUNDED BY IT LATELY.
BY IT
I HAVEN'T SWUNG THAT WAY, TOO, HAVE I?!

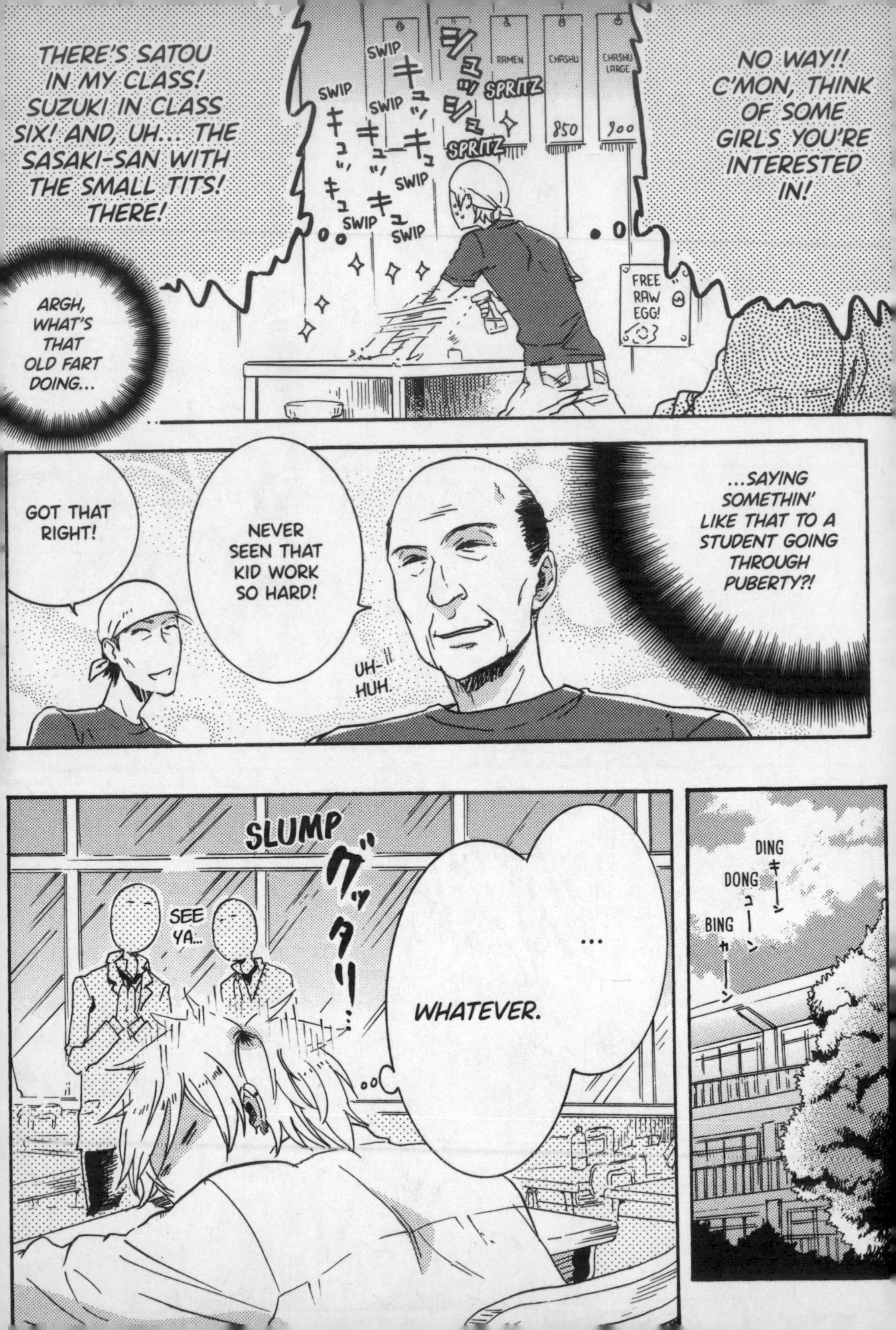
NO WAY!! C'MON, THINK OF SOME GIRLS YOU'RE INTERESTED IN!
CHASHU LARGE 900
CHASHU 850
RAMEN
SPRITZ
SPRITZ
SWIP
SWIP
SWIP
SWIP
SWIP
SWIP
FREE RAW EGG!
THERE'S SATOU IN MY CLASS! SUZUKI IN CLASS SIX! AND, UH... THE SASAKI-SAN WITH THE SMALL TITS! THERE!
ARGH, WHAT'S THAT OLD FART DOING...
...SAYING SOMETHIN' LIKE THAT TO A STUDENT GOING THROUGH PUBERTY?!
UH-HUH.
NEVER SEEN THAT KID WORK SO HARD!
GOT THAT RIGHT!
DING
DONG
BING
... WHATEVER.
SLUMP
グッタリ…
SEE YA...

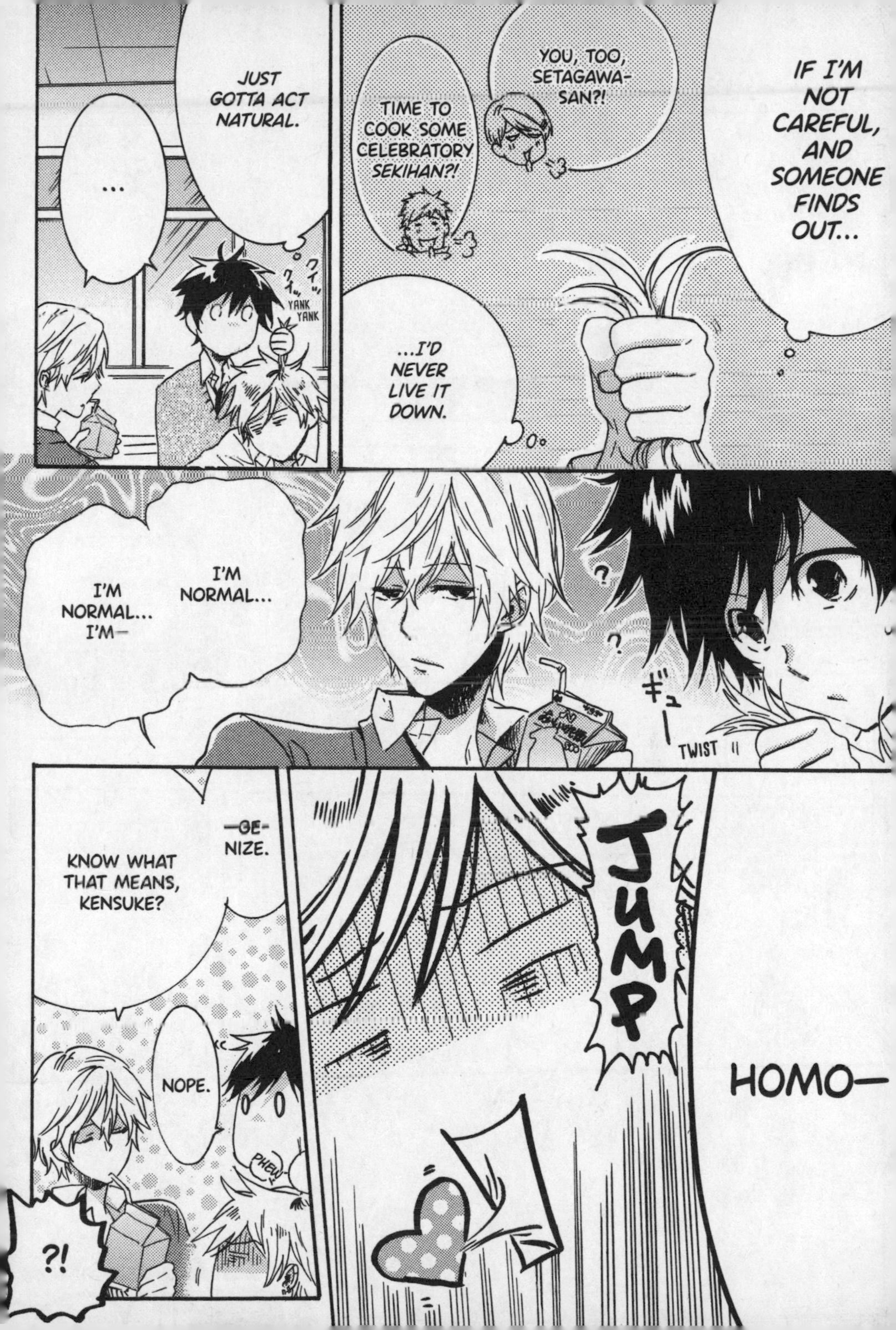
IF I'M NOT CAREFUL, AND SOMEONE FINDS OUT...
YOU, TOO, SETAGAWA-SAN?!
TIME TO COOK SOME CELEBRATORY SEKIHAN?!
...I'D NEVER LIVE IT DOWN.
JUST GOTTA ACT NATURAL.
...
YANK YANK
?
?
ギュー
TWIST
I'M NORMAL...
I'M NORMAL... I'M—
HOMO—
JUMP
—GE-NIZE.
KNOW WHAT THAT MEANS, KENSUKE?
NOPE.
PHEW
?!

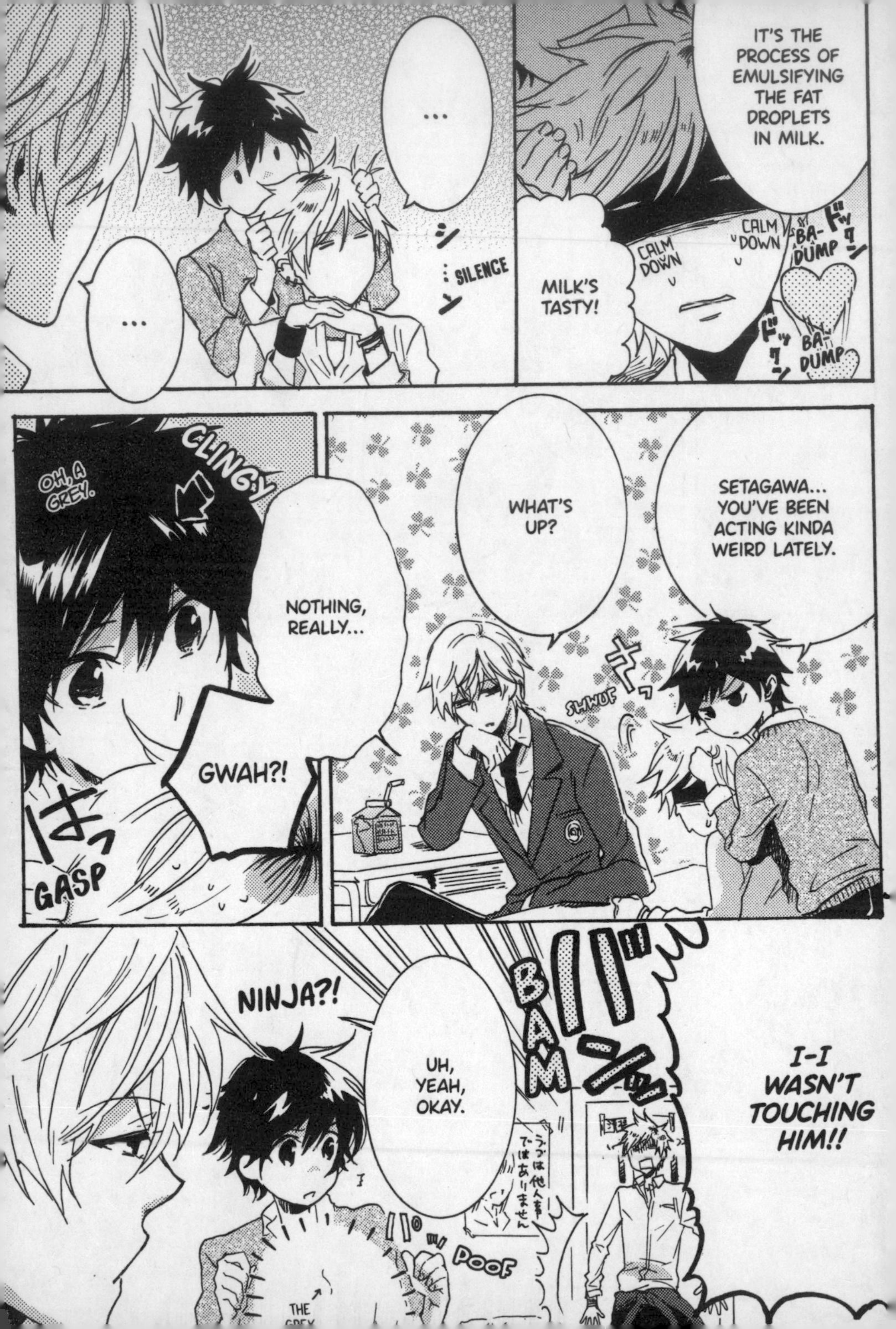
IT'S THE PROCESS OF EMULSIFYING THE FAT DROPLETS IN MILK.
BA-DUMP
CALM DOWN
CALM DOWN
MILK'S TASTY!
BA-DUMP
...
SILENCE
...
SETAGAWA... YOU'VE BEEN ACTING KINDA WEIRD LATELY.
WHAT'S UP?
SHWUF
NOTHING, REALLY...
CLINGY
OH, A GREY.
GWAH?!
GASP
I-I WASN'T TOUCHING HIM!!
BAM
ラブは他人事ではありません
UH, YEAH, OKAY.
NINJA?!
POOF
THE

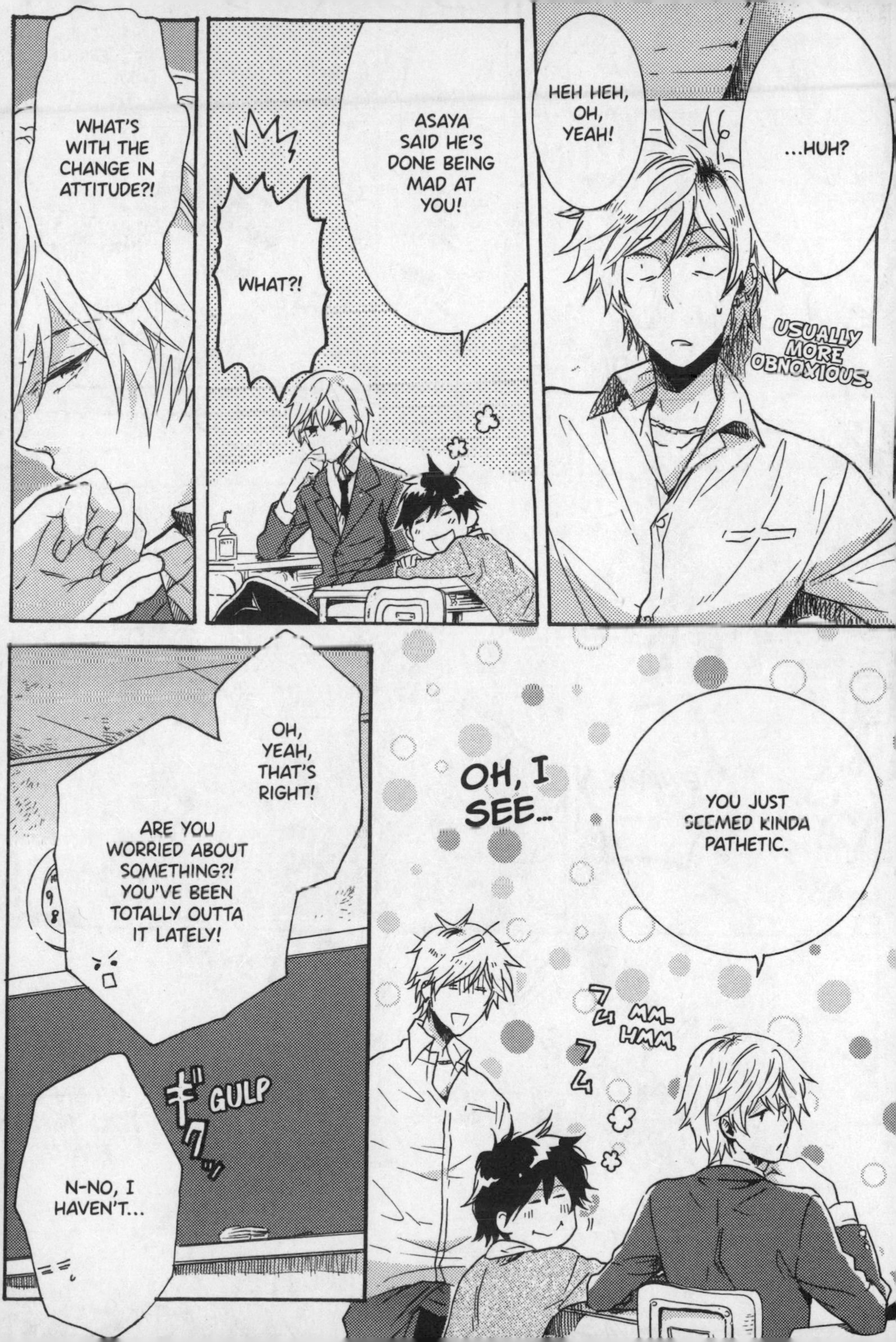
...HUH?
HEH HEH, OH, YEAH!
USUALLY MORE OBNOXIOUS.
ASAYA SAID HE'S DONE BEING MAD AT YOU!
WHAT?!
WHAT'S WITH THE CHANGE IN ATTITUDE?!
YOU JUST SEEMED KINDA PATHETIC.
OH, I SEE...
MM-HMM.
OH, YEAH, THAT'S RIGHT!
ARE YOU WORRIED ABOUT SOMETHING?! YOU'VE BEEN TOTALLY OUTTA IT LATELY!
GULP
N-NO, I HAVEN'T...

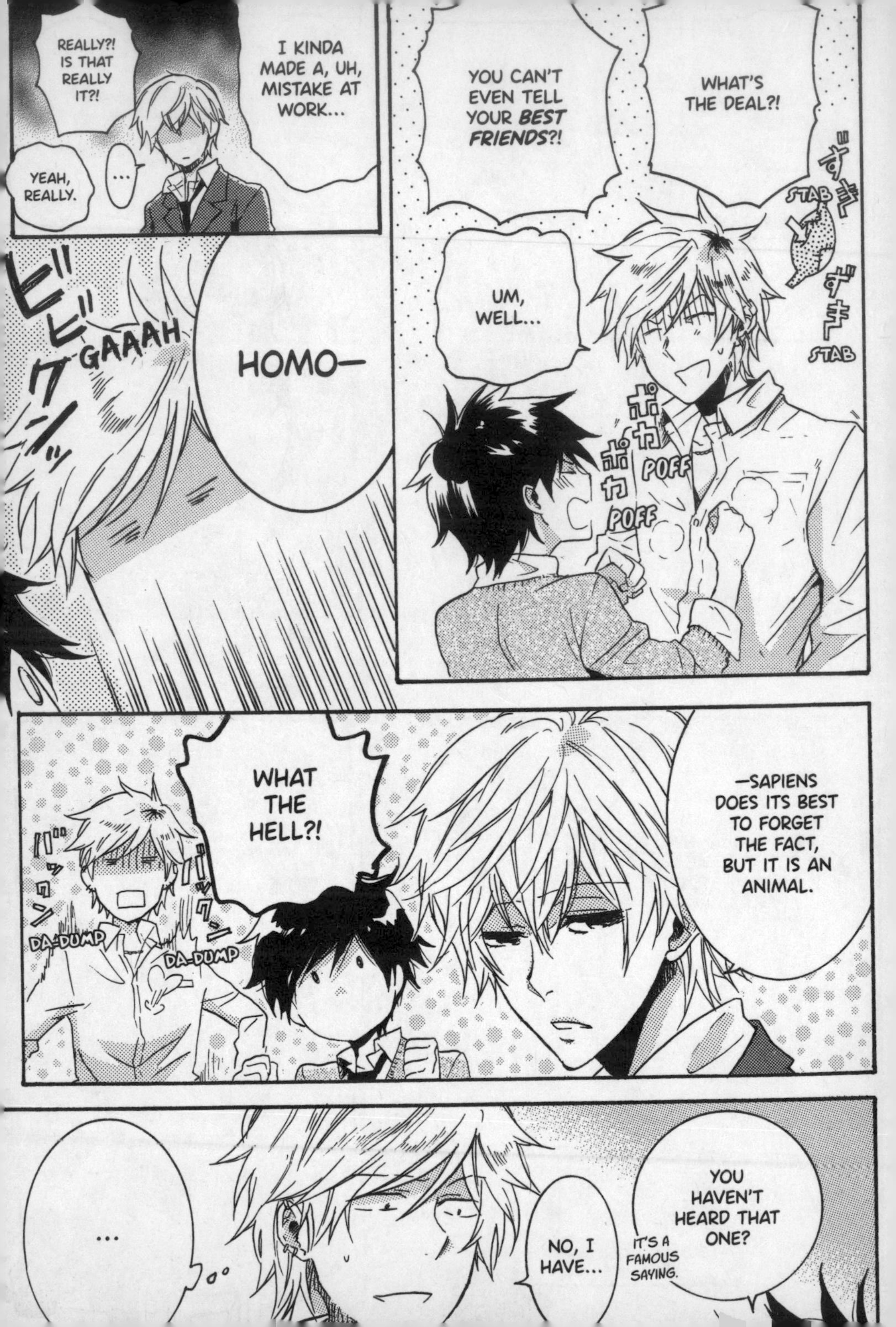

WHAT'S THE DEAL?!
YOU CAN'T EVEN TELL YOUR **BEST FRIENDS**?!
STAB
STAB
UM, WELL...
POFF
POFF
I KINDA MADE A, UH, MISTAKE AT WORK...
REALLY?! IS THAT REALLY IT?!
...
YEAH, REALLY.
HOMO—
GAAAH
—SAPIENS DOES ITS BEST TO FORGET THE FACT, BUT IT IS AN ANIMAL.
WHAT THE HELL?!
DA-DUMP
DA-DUMP
YOU HAVEN'T HEARD THAT ONE?
IT'S A FAMOUS SAYING.
NO, I HAVE...
...

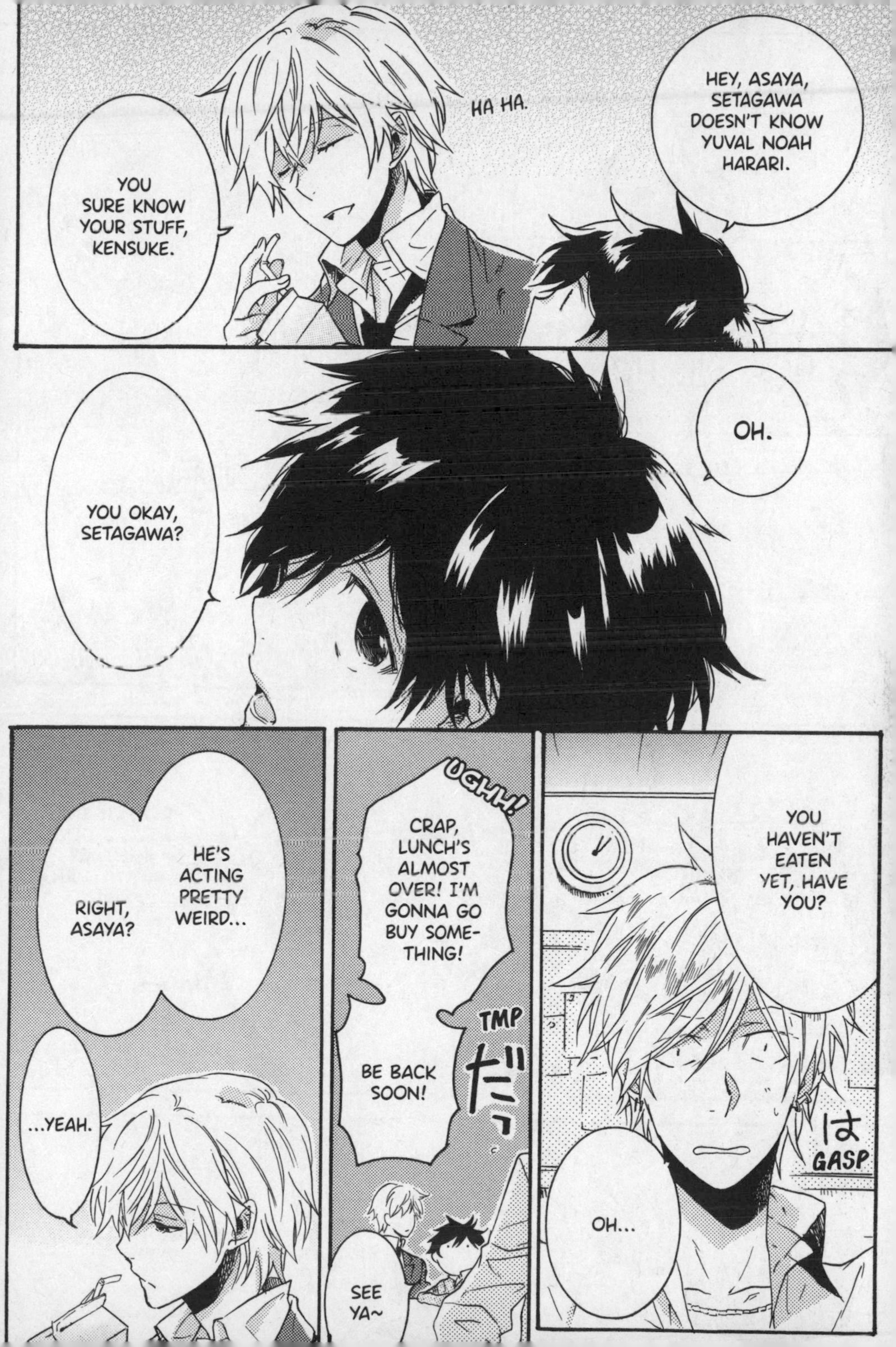
HEY, ASAYA, SETAGAWA DOESN'T KNOW YUVAL NOAH HARARI.
HA HA.
YOU SURE KNOW YOUR STUFF, KENSUKE.
OH.
YOU OKAY, SETAGAWA?
YOU HAVEN'T EATEN YET, HAVE YOU?
は
GASP
OH...
UGHH!
CRAP, LUNCH'S ALMOST OVER! I'M GONNA GO BUY SOME-THING!
TMP
だっ
BE BACK SOON!
SEE YA~
HE'S ACTING PRETTY WEIRD...
RIGHT, ASAYA?
...YEAH.

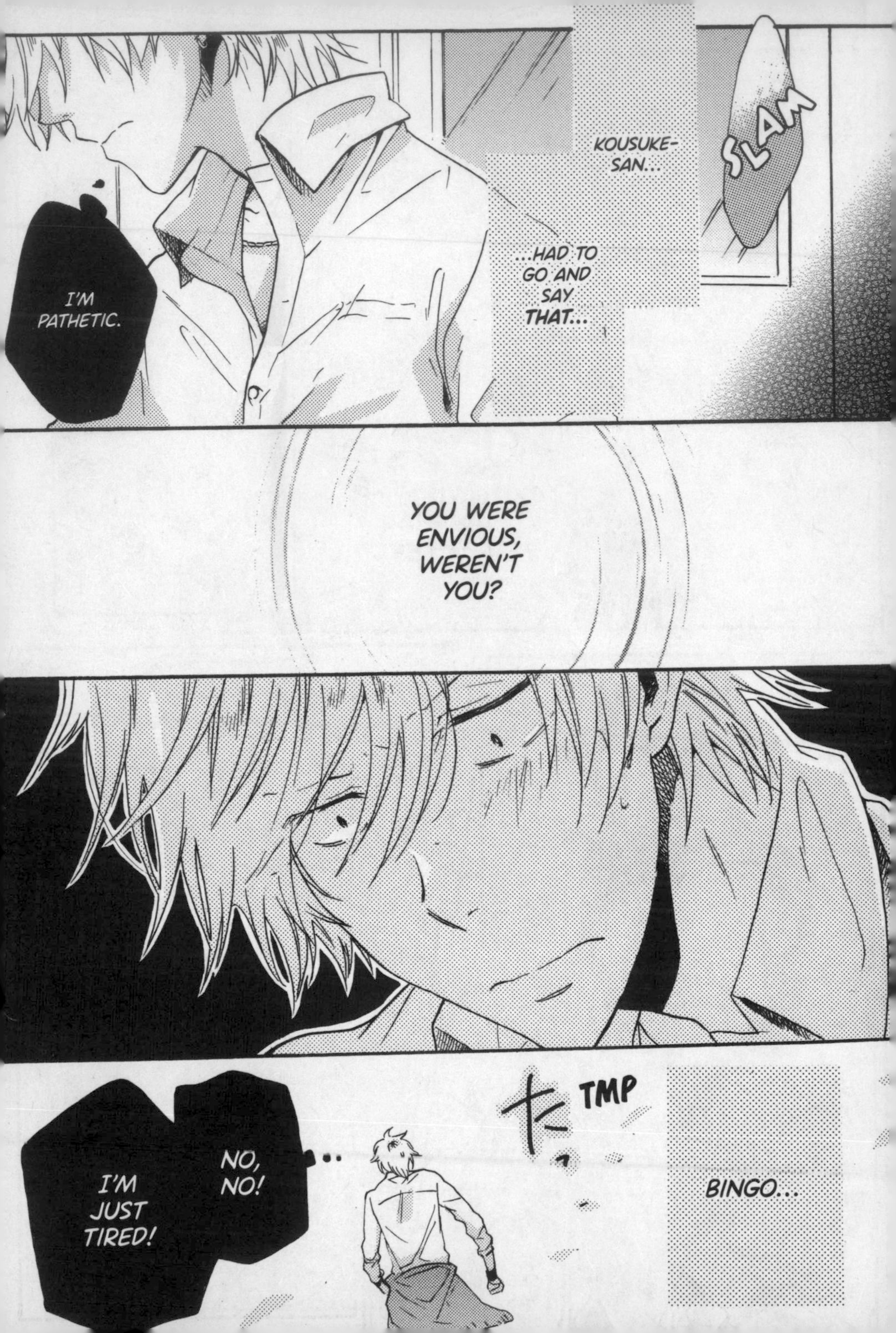
SLAM
KOUSUKE-SAN...
...HAD TO GO AND SAY THAT...
I'M PATHETIC.
YOU WERE ENVIOUS, WEREN'T YOU?
BINGO...
TMP
...
NO, NO!
I'M JUST TIRED!

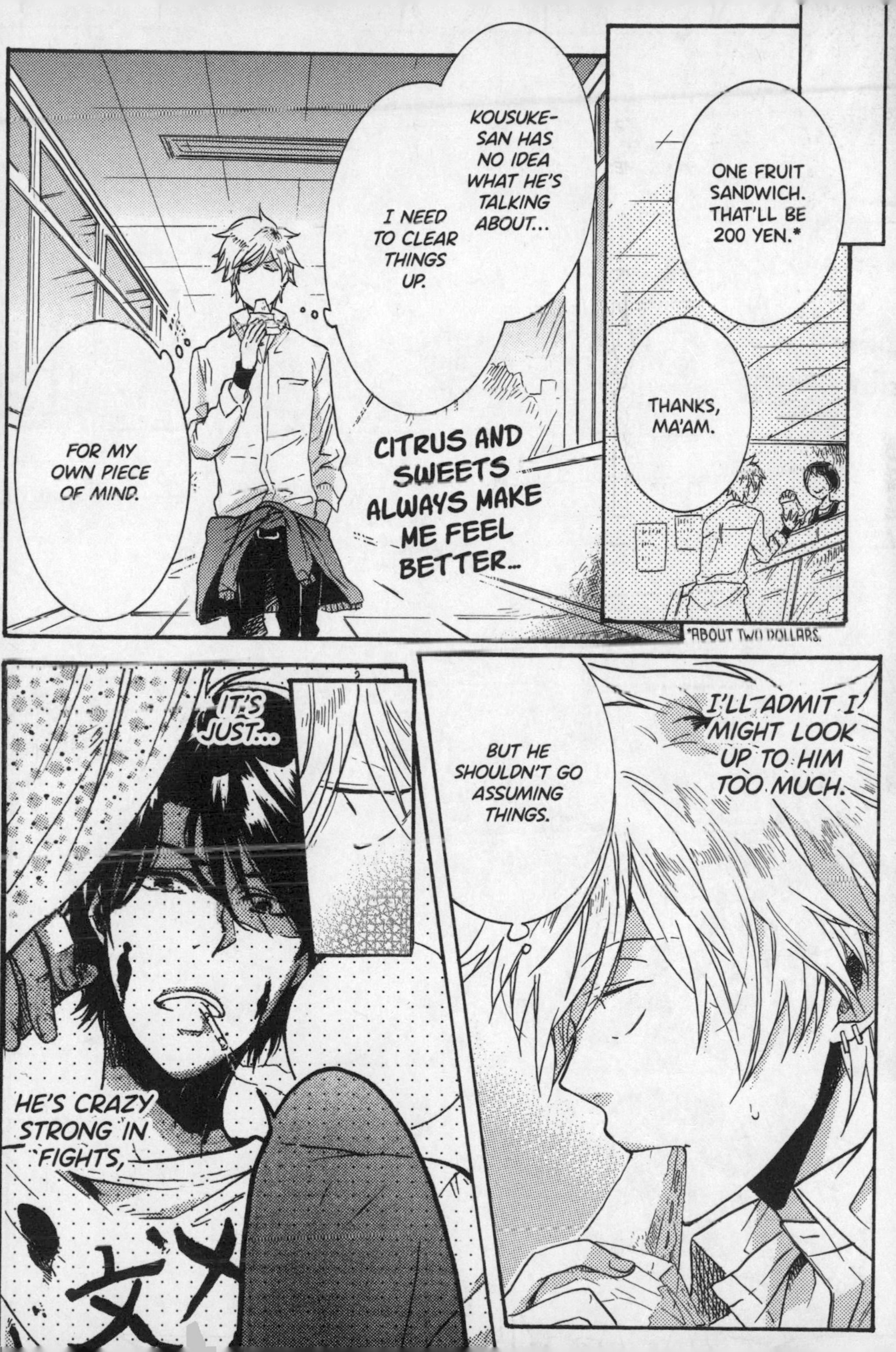
ONE FRUIT SANDWICH. THAT'LL BE 200 YEN.*
THANKS, MA'AM.
KOUSUKE-SAN HAS NO IDEA WHAT HE'S TALKING ABOUT...
I NEED TO CLEAR THINGS UP.
CITRUS AND SWEETS ALWAYS MAKE ME FEEL BETTER...
FOR MY OWN PIECE OF MIND.
I'LL ADMIT I MIGHT LOOK UP TO HIM TOO MUCH.
BUT HE SHOULDN'T GO ASSUMING THINGS.
IT'S JUST...
HE'S CRAZY STRONG IN FIGHTS,

*ABOUT TWO DOLLARS.

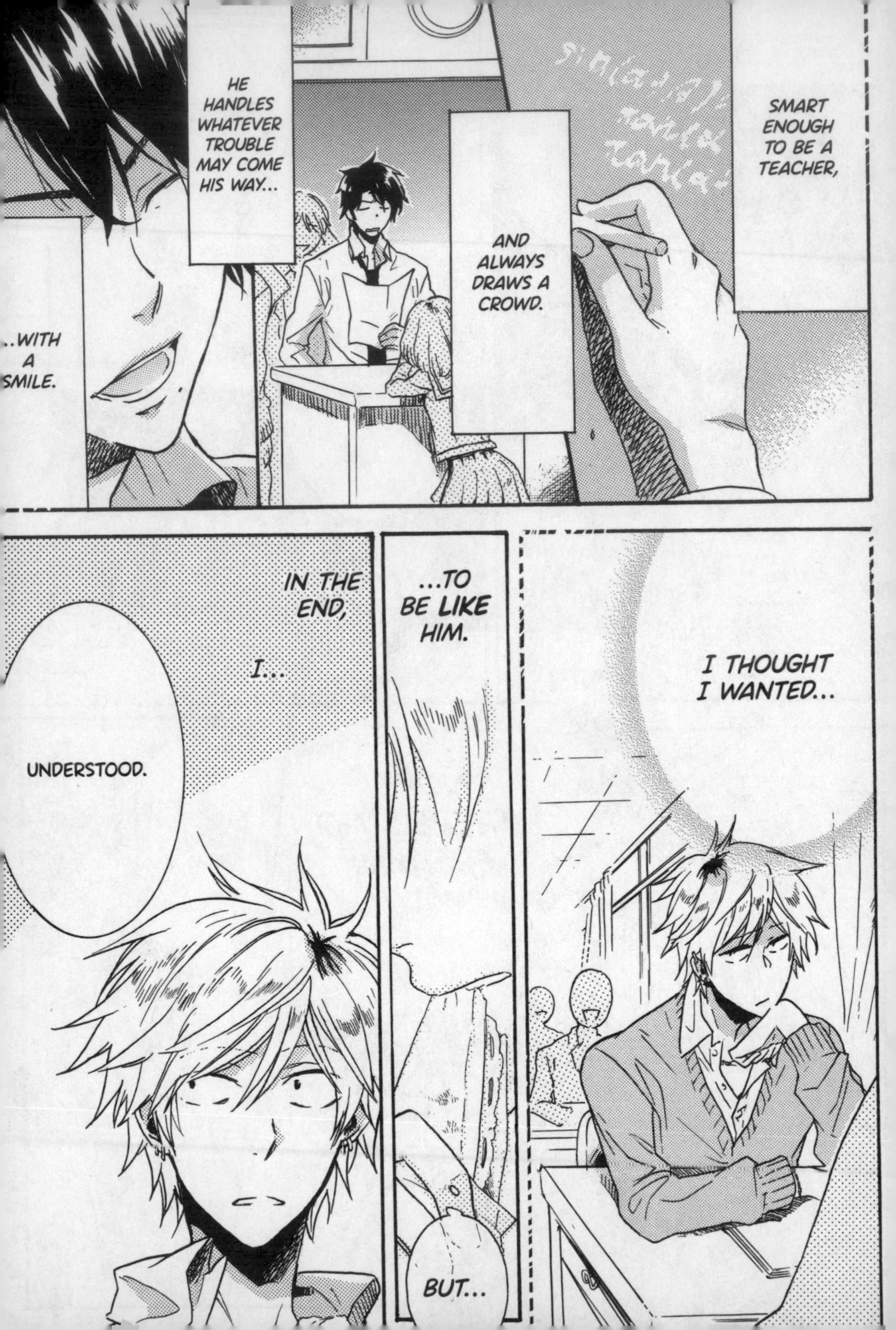
SMART ENOUGH TO BE A TEACHER,
AND ALWAYS DRAWS A CROWD.
HE HANDLES WHATEVER TROUBLE MAY COME HIS WAY...
...WITH A SMILE.
I THOUGHT I WANTED...
...TO BE LIKE HIM.
BUT...
IN THE END,
I...
UNDERSTOOD.

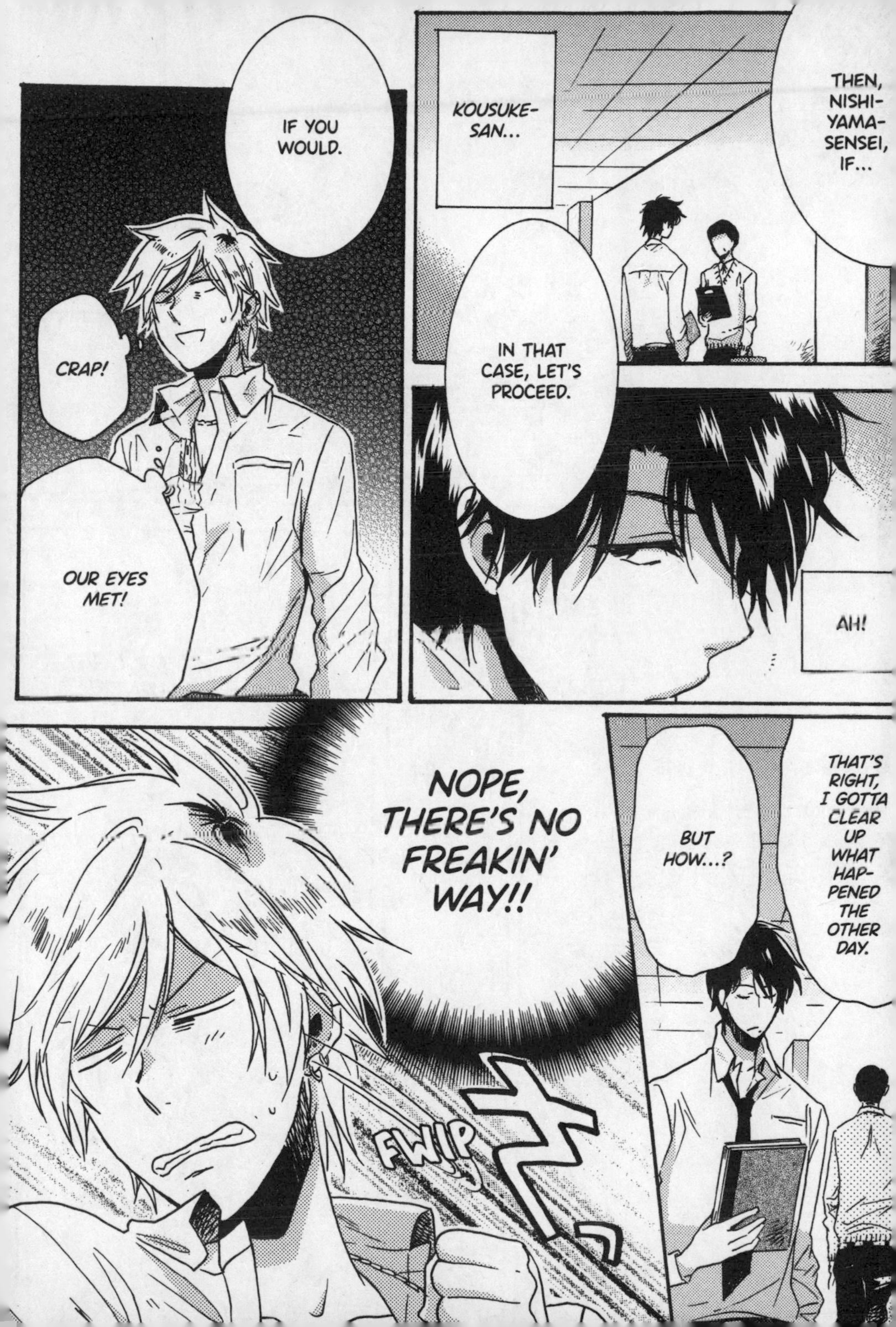
THEN, NISHIYAMA-SENSEI, IF...
KOUSUKE-SAN...
IN THAT CASE, LET'S PROCEED.
AH!
IF YOU WOULD.
CRAP!
OUR EYES MET!
THAT'S RIGHT, I GOTTA CLEAR UP WHAT HAPPENED THE OTHER DAY.
BUT HOW...?
NOPE, THERE'S NO FREAKIN' WAY!!
FWIP

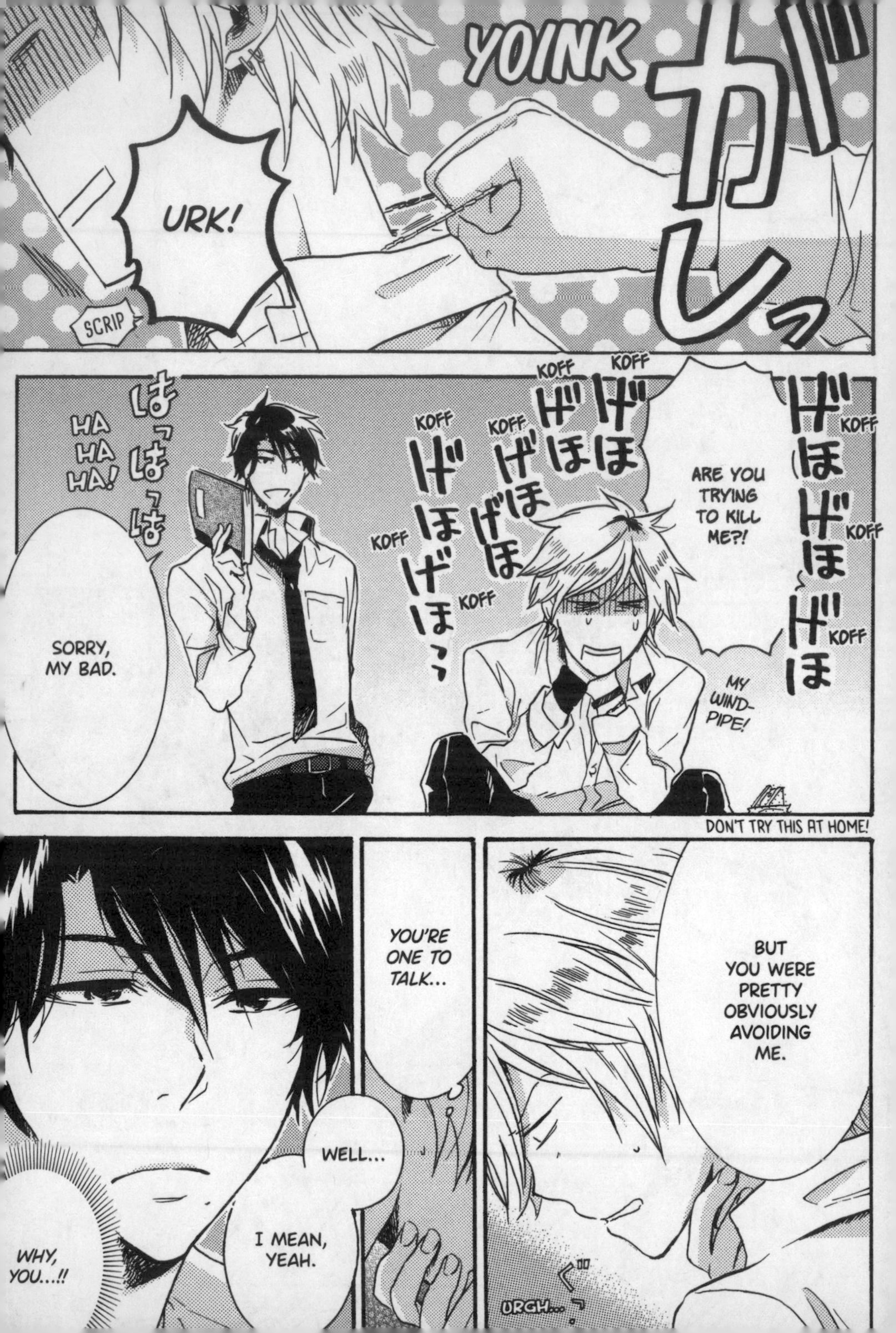
がしっ
YOINK
URK!
SCRIP
げほげほげほ
KOFF KOFF KOFF
ARE YOU TRYING TO KILL ME?!
MY WIND-PIPE!
げほげほ
げほげほ
げほげほっ
KOFF KOFF KOFF KOFF KOFF
はっはっは
HA HA HA!
SORRY, MY BAD.
DON'T TRY THIS AT HOME!
BUT YOU WERE PRETTY OBVIOUSLY AVOIDING ME.
URGH...
YOU'RE ONE TO TALK...
WELL...
I MEAN, YEAH.
WHY, YOU...!!

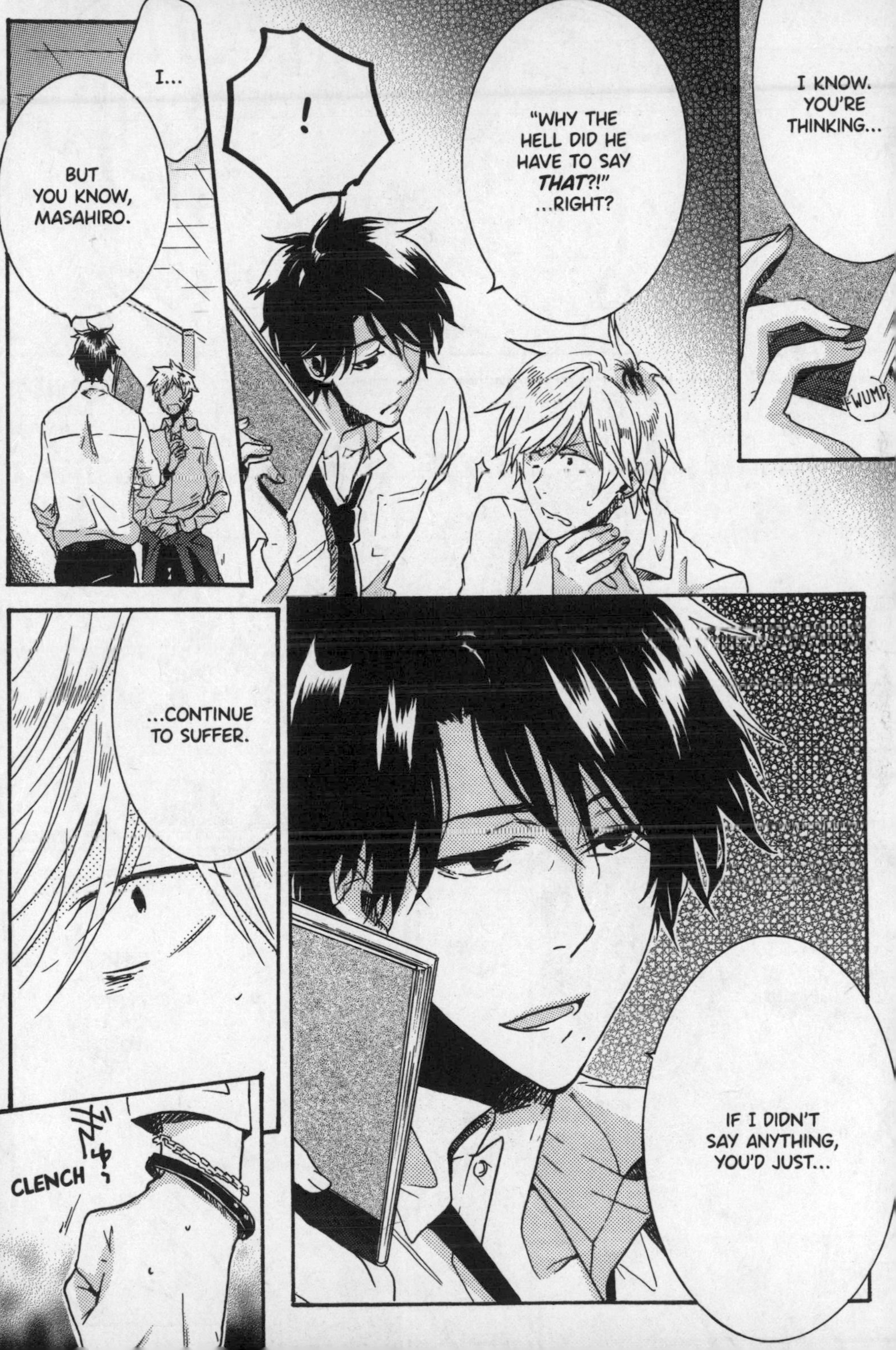
I KNOW. YOU'RE THINKING...
WUMP
"WHY THE HELL DID HE HAVE TO SAY *THAT*?!" ...RIGHT?
!
I...
BUT YOU KNOW, MASAHIRO.
IF I DIDN'T SAY ANYTHING, YOU'D JUST...
...CONTINUE TO SUFFER.
CLENCH

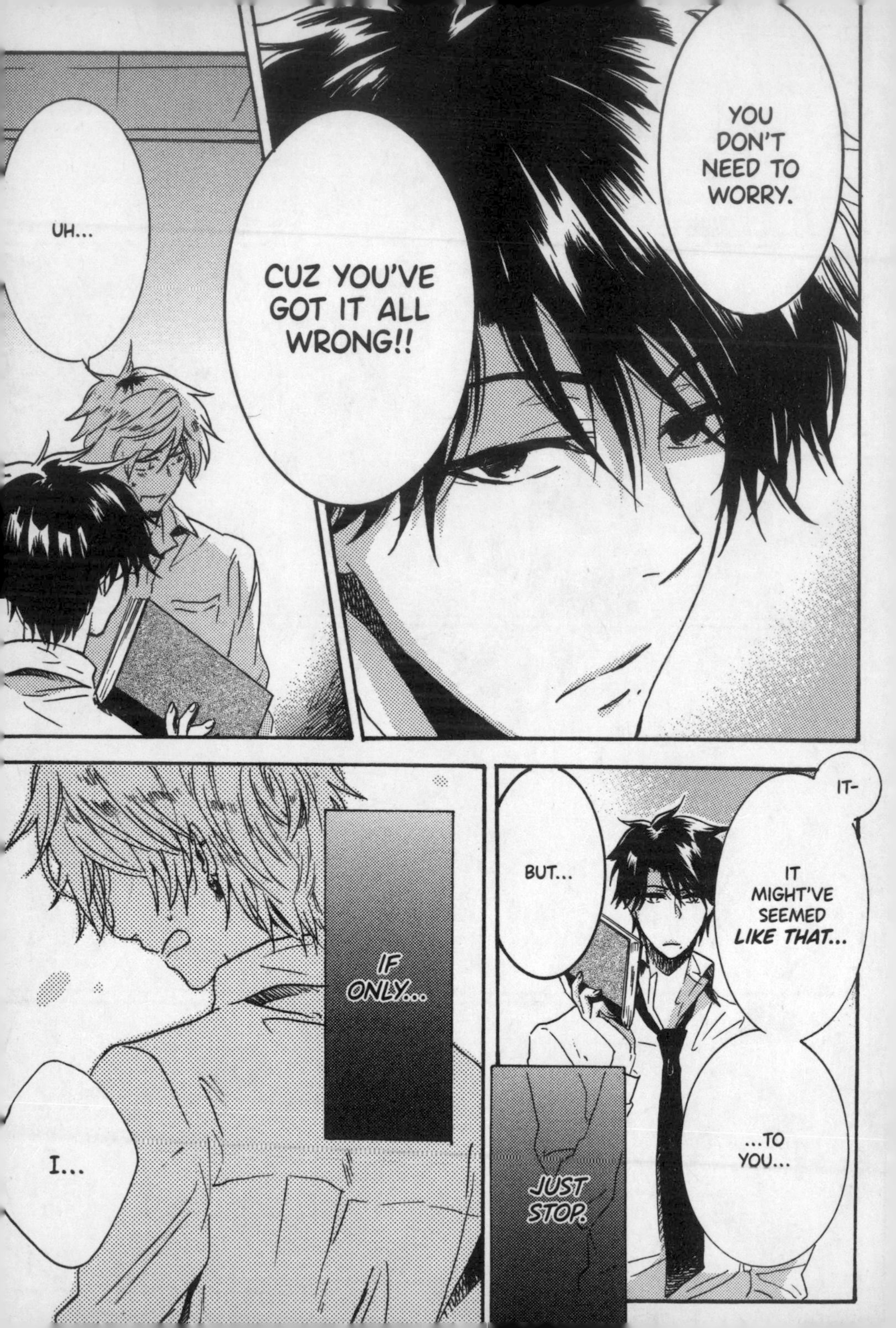
YOU DON'T NEED TO WORRY.
CUZ YOU'VE GOT IT ALL WRONG!!
UH...
IT-
IT MIGHT'VE SEEMED LIKE THAT...
...TO YOU...
BUT...
JUST STOP.
IF ONLY...
I...

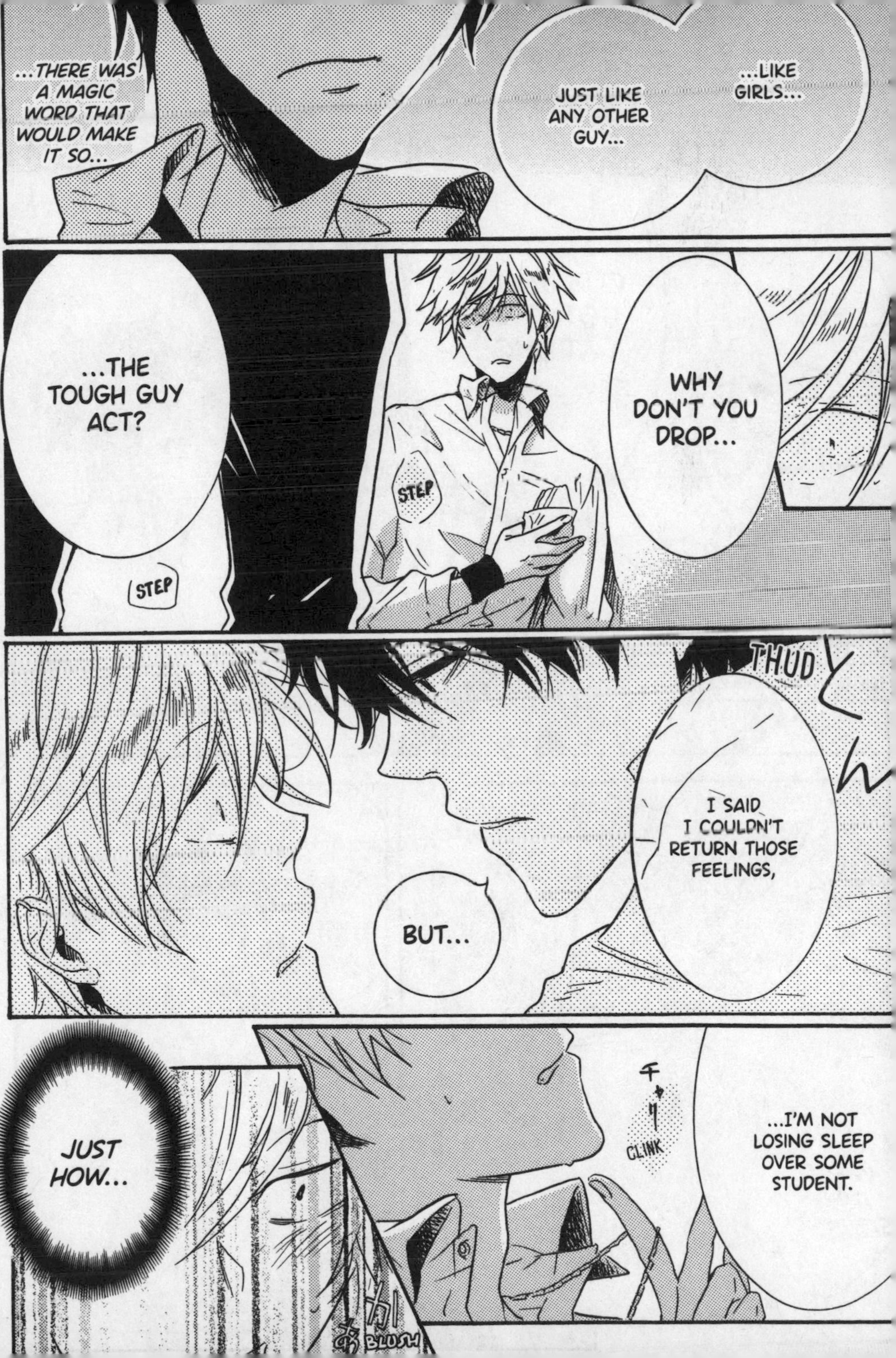
...LIKE GIRLS...
JUST LIKE ANY OTHER GUY...
...THERE WAS A MAGIC WORD THAT WOULD MAKE IT SO...
WHY DON'T YOU DROP...
STEP
STEP
...THE TOUGH GUY ACT?
THUD
I SAID I COULDN'T RETURN THOSE FEELINGS,
BUT...
...I'M NOT LOSING SLEEP OVER SOME STUDENT.
チャリ
CLINK
JUST HOW...
BLUSH

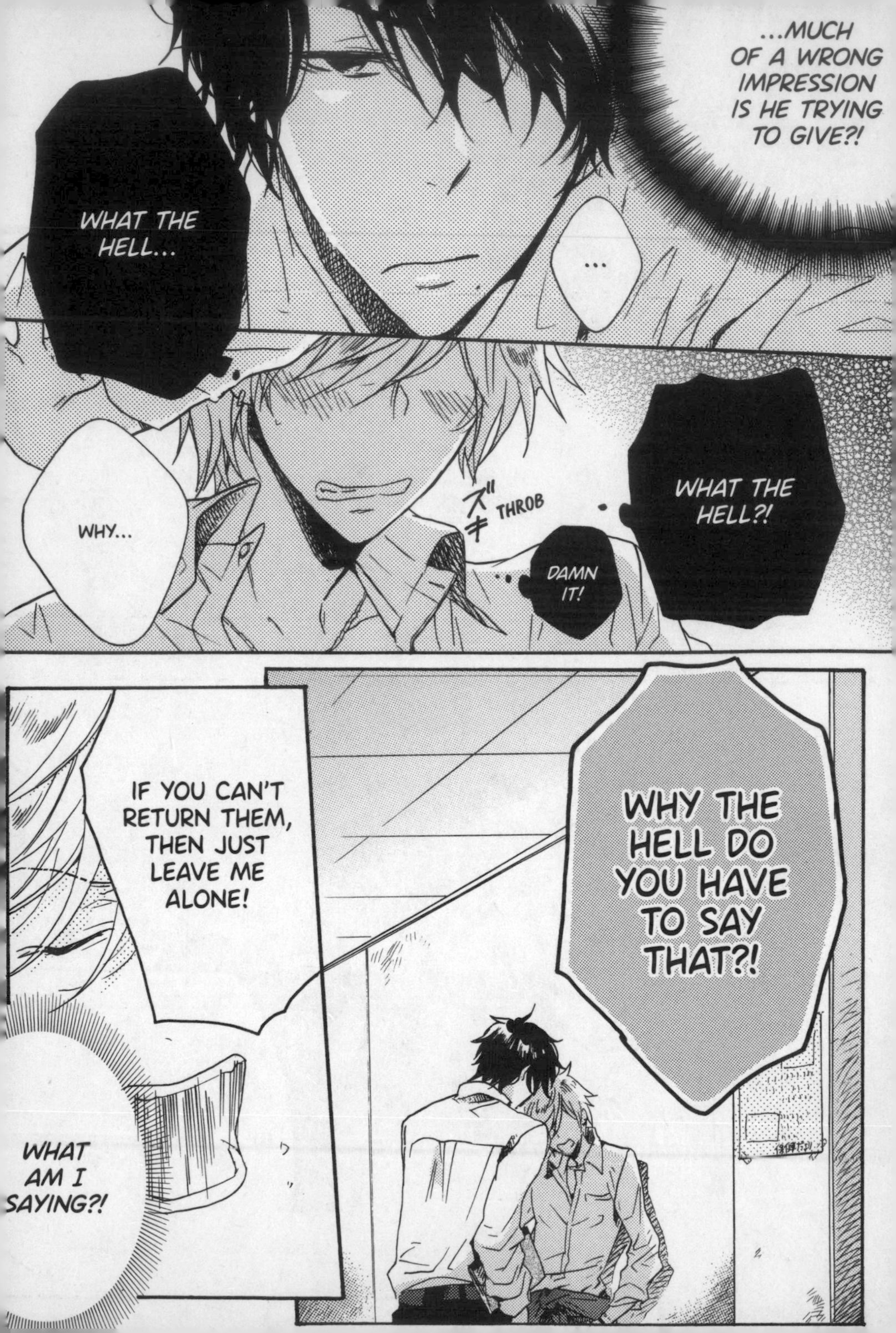
...MUCH OF A WRONG IMPRESSION IS HE TRYING TO GIVE?!
...
WHAT THE HELL...
WHAT THE HELL?!
DAMN IT!
ズキ THROB
WHY...
WHY THE HELL DO YOU HAVE TO SAY THAT?!
IF YOU CAN'T RETURN THEM, THEN JUST LEAVE ME ALONE!
WHAT AM I SAYING?!

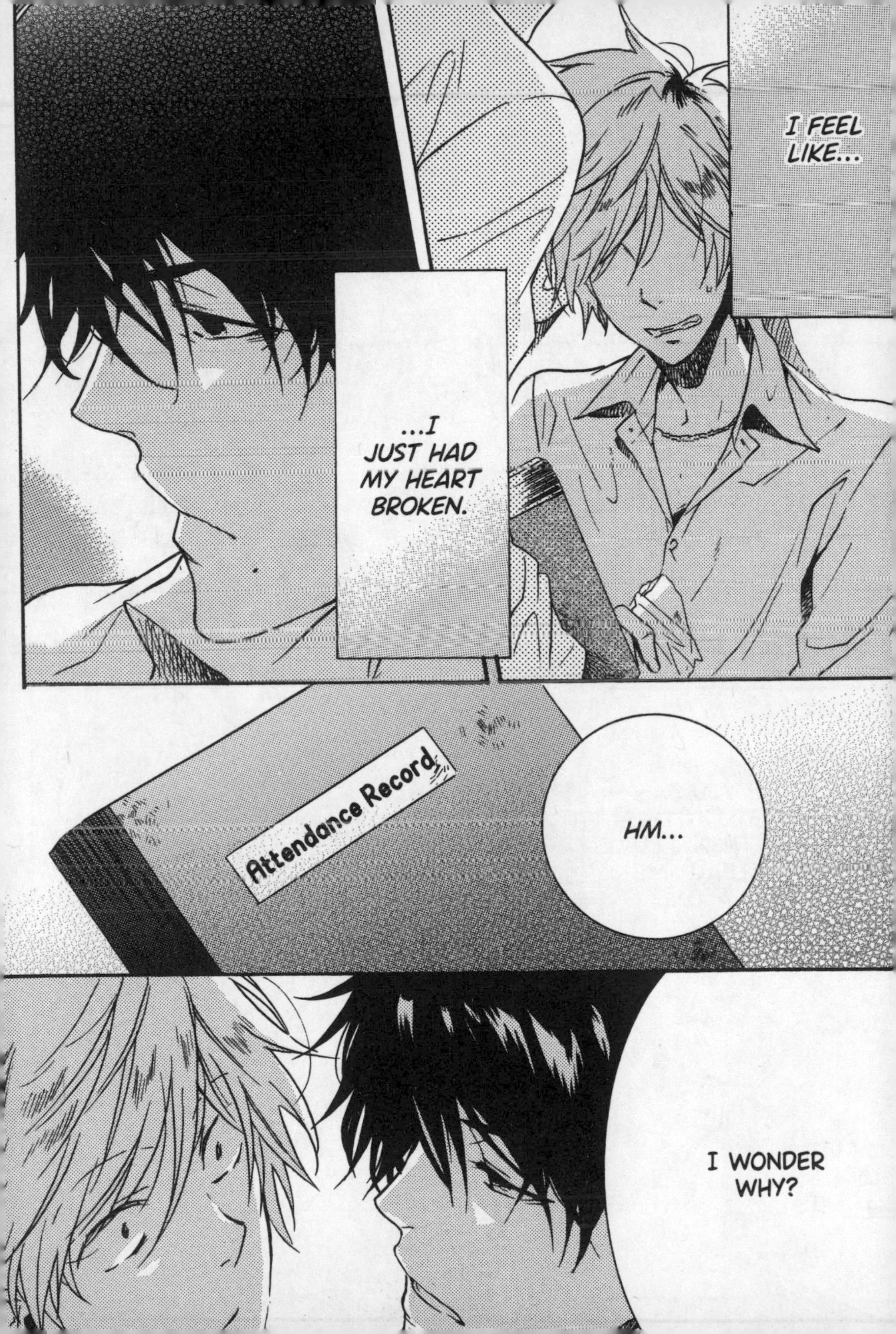
I FEEL LIKE...
...I JUST HAD MY HEART BROKEN.
HM...
Attendance Record
I WONDER WHY?

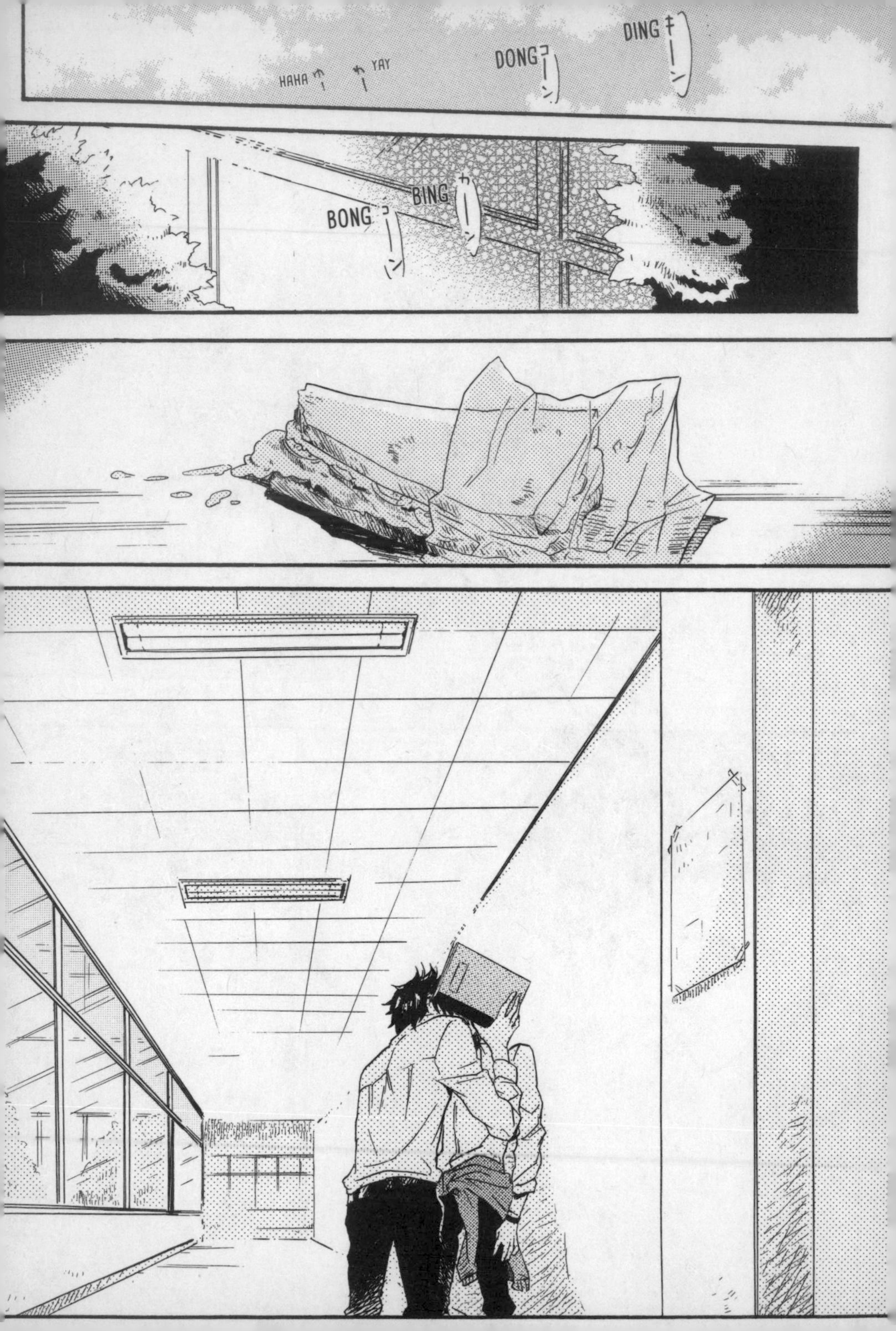
DING
DONG
YAY
HAHA
BING
BONG

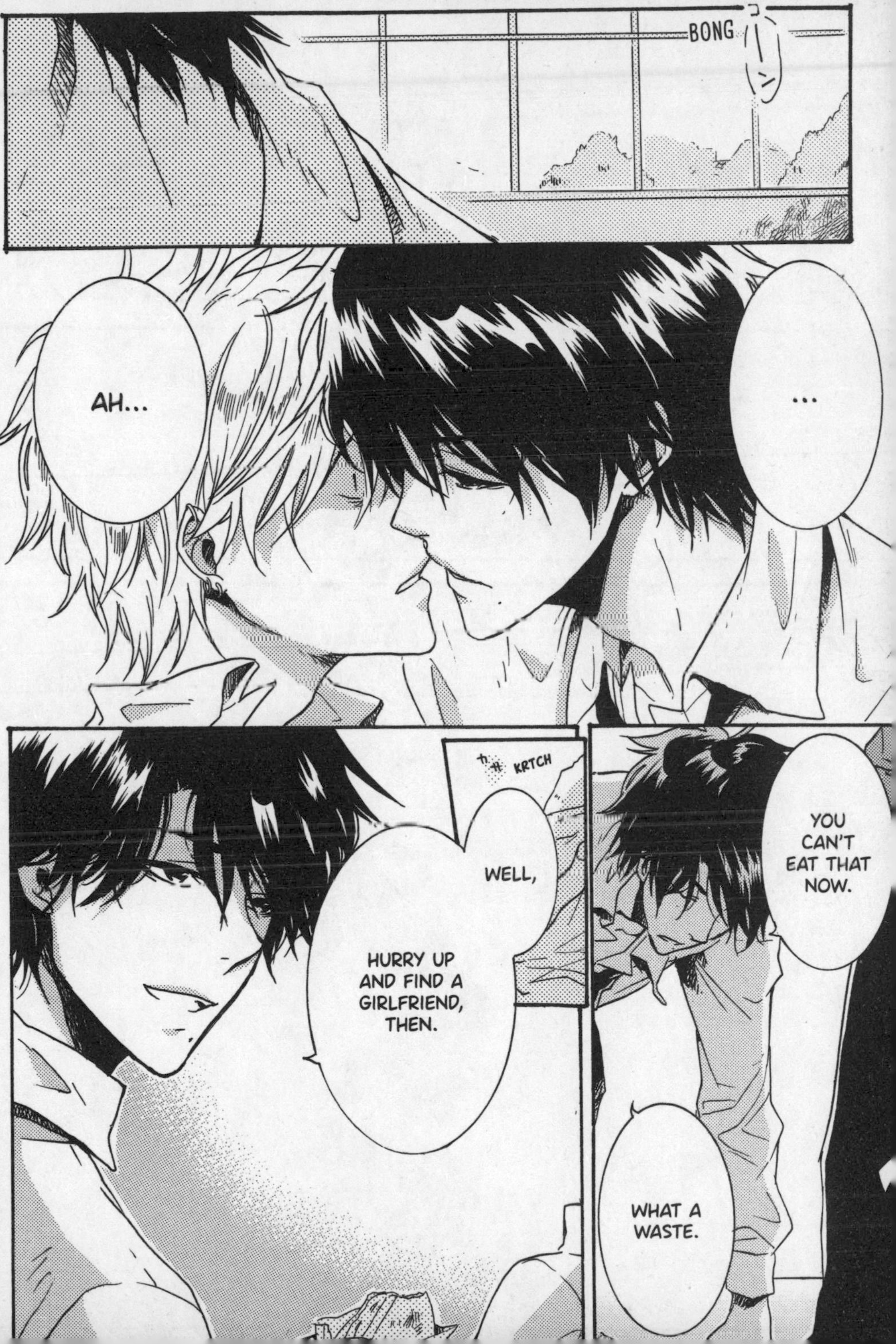
BONG
...
AH...
YOU CAN'T EAT THAT NOW.
WHAT A WASTE.
KRTCH
WELL,
HURRY UP AND FIND A GIRLFRIEND, THEN.

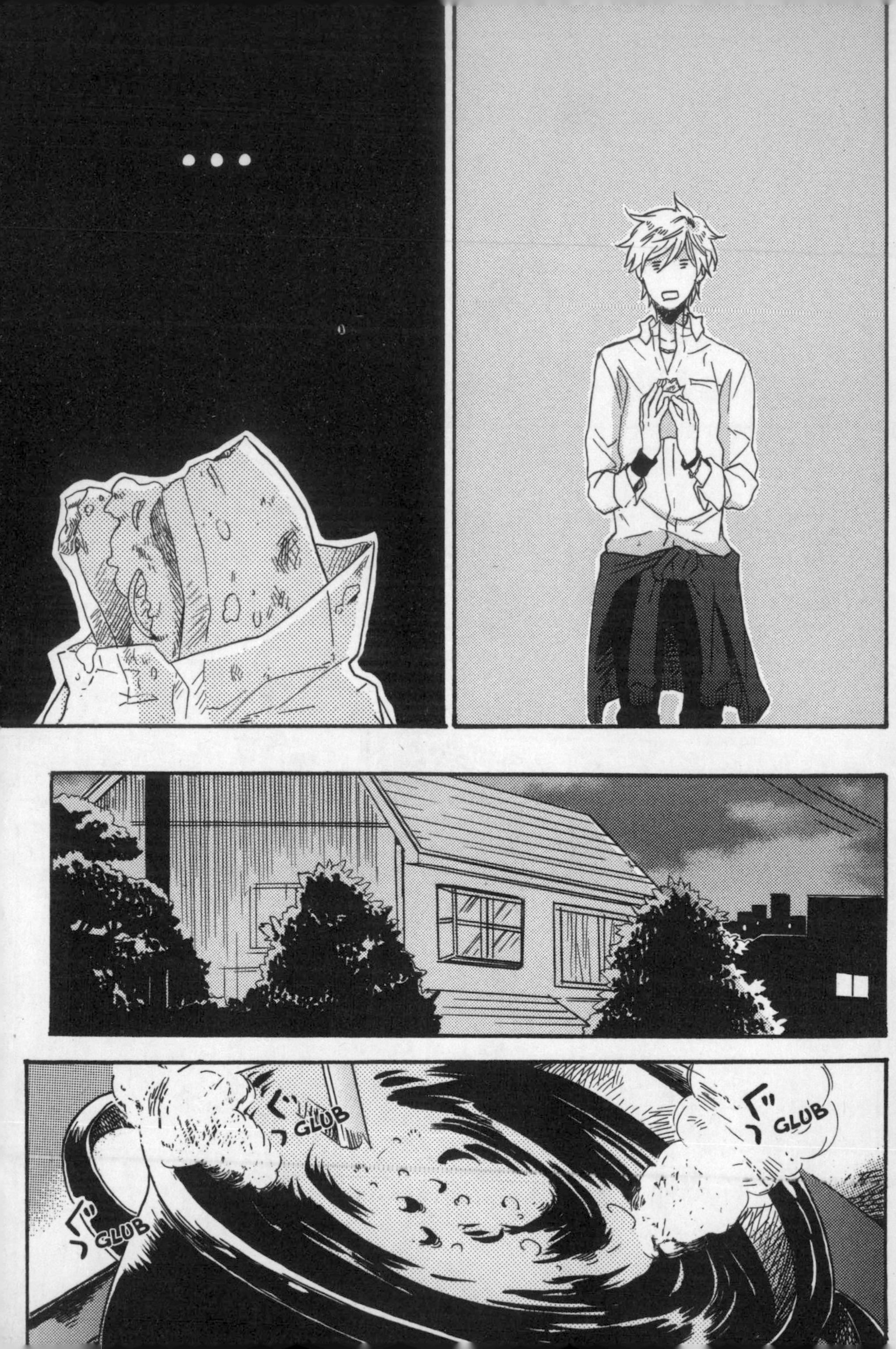
• • •
GLUB
GLUB
GLUB

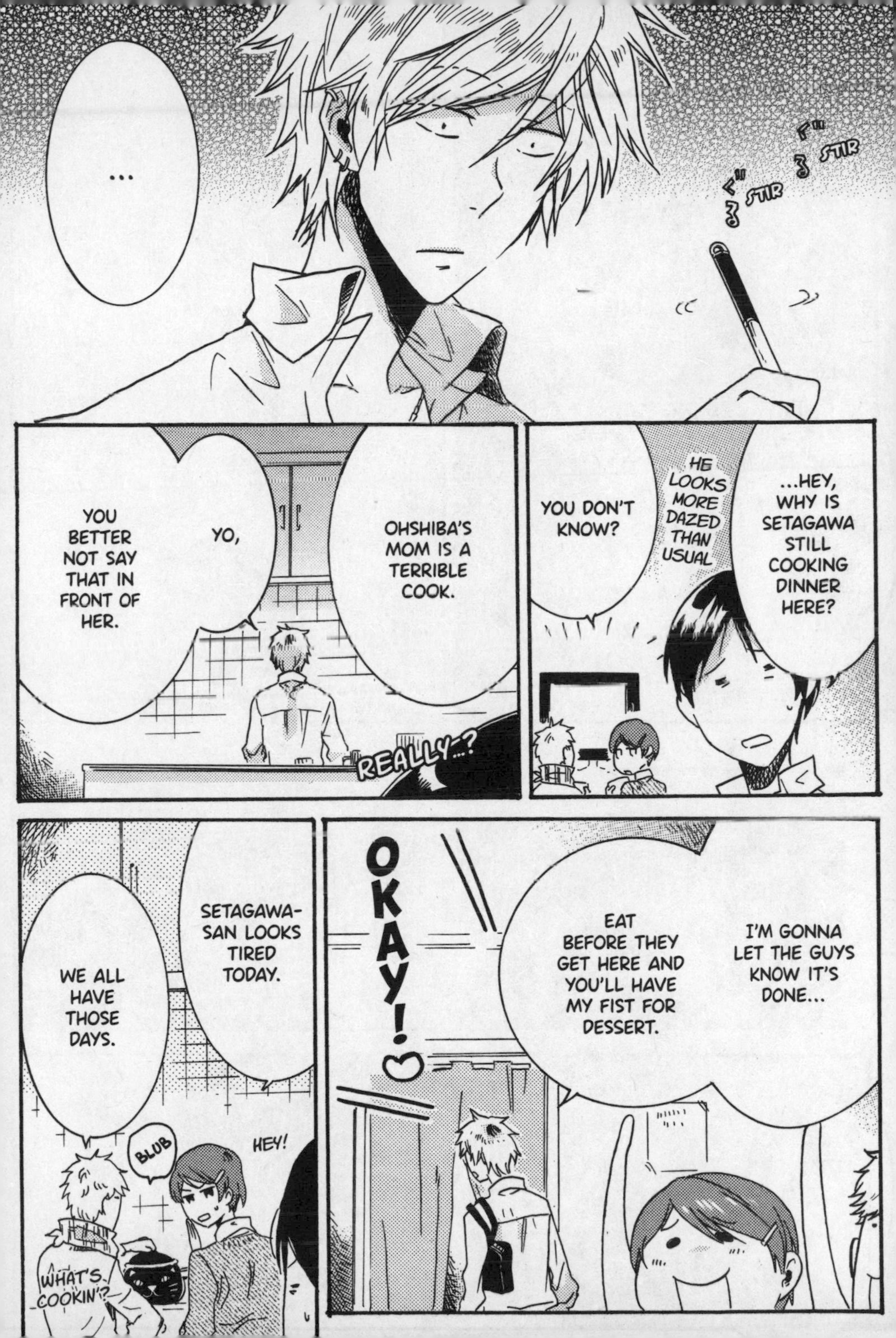
...
STIR STIR
...HEY, WHY IS SETAGAWA STILL COOKING DINNER HERE?
HE LOOKS MORE DAZED THAN USUAL
YOU DON'T KNOW?
OHSHIBA'S MOM IS A TERRIBLE COOK.
YO,
YOU BETTER NOT SAY THAT IN FRONT OF HER.
REALLY...?
I'M GONNA LET THE GUYS KNOW IT'S DONE...
EAT BEFORE THEY GET HERE AND YOU'LL HAVE MY FIST FOR DESSERT.
OKAY!
SETAGAWA-SAN LOOKS TIRED TODAY.
WE ALL HAVE THOSE DAYS.
HEY!
BLUB
WHAT'S COOKIN'?

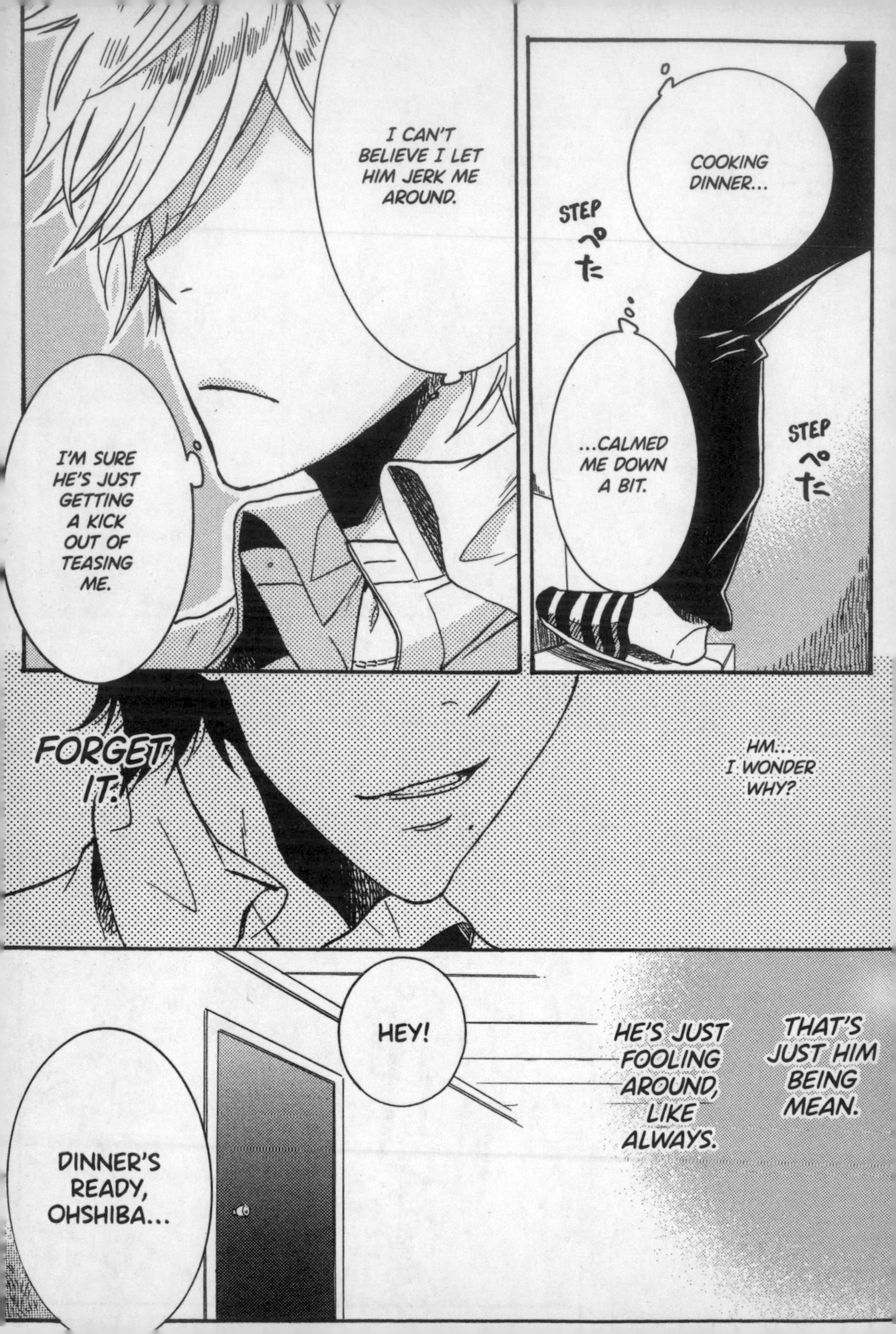
COOKING DINNER...
STEP ぺた
...CALMED ME DOWN A BIT.
STEP ぺた
I CAN'T BELIEVE I LET HIM JERK ME AROUND.
I'M SURE HE'S JUST GETTING A KICK OUT OF TEASING ME.
HM... I WONDER WHY?
FORGET IT.
THAT'S JUST HIM BEING MEAN.
HE'S JUST FOOLING AROUND, LIKE ALWAYS.
HEY!
DINNER'S READY, OHSHIBA...

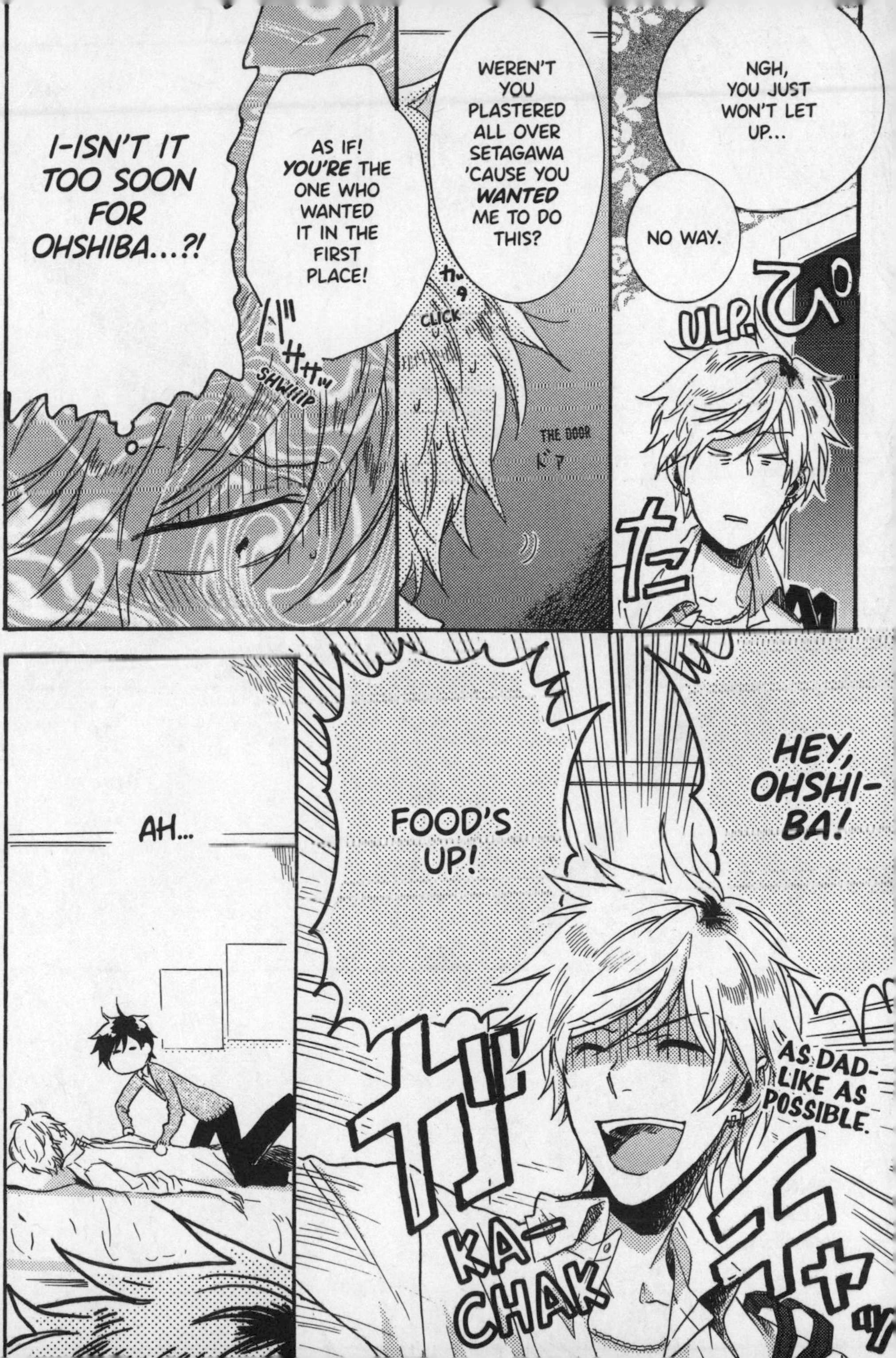
NGH, YOU JUST WON'T LET UP...
NO WAY.
ULP.
WEREN'T YOU PLASTERED ALL OVER SETAGAWA 'CAUSE YOU WANTED ME TO DO THIS?
CLICK
THE DOOR
AS IF! YOU'RE THE ONE WHO WANTED IT IN THE FIRST PLACE!
I-ISN'T IT TOO SOON FOR OHSHIBA...?!
SHWIIIP
HEY, OHSHI-BA!
FOOD'S UP!
AS DAD-LIKE AS POSSIBLE.
KA-CHAK
AH...

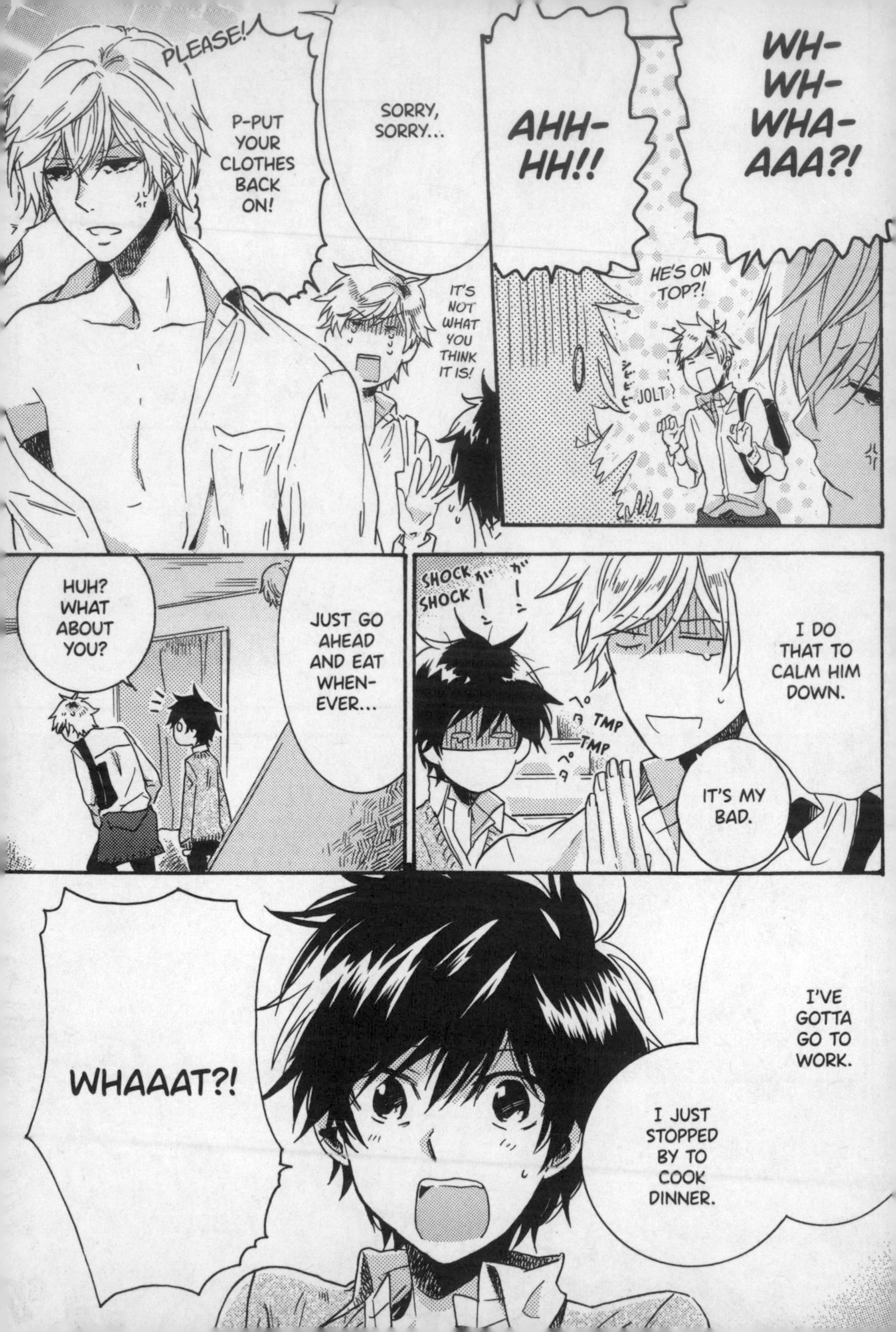
WH-WH-WHA-AAA?!
AHH-HH!!
HE'S ON TOP?!
JOLT
SORRY, SORRY...
IT'S NOT WHAT YOU THINK IT IS!
PLEASE!
P-PUT YOUR CLOTHES BACK ON!
SHOCK SHOCK
I DO THAT TO CALM HIM DOWN.
IT'S MY BAD.
TMP TMP
JUST GO AHEAD AND EAT WHEN-EVER...
HUH? WHAT ABOUT YOU?
I'VE GOTTA GO TO WORK.
I JUST STOPPED BY TO COOK DINNER.
WHAAAT?!

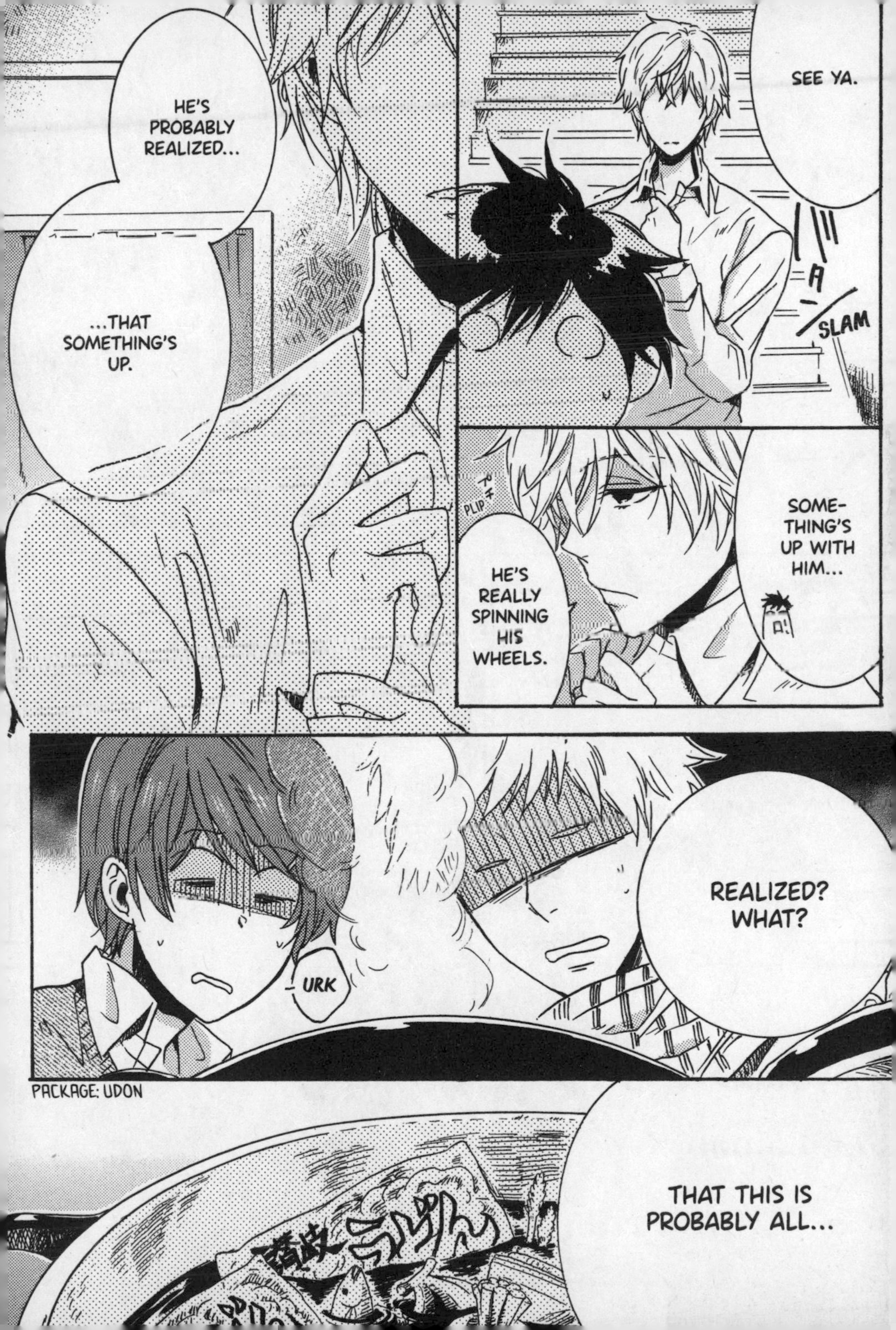
SEE YA.
SLAM
SOME-THING'S UP WITH HIM...
PLIP
HE'S REALLY SPINNING HIS WHEELS.
HE'S PROBABLY REALIZED...
...THAT SOMETHING'S UP.
REALIZED? WHAT?
URK
PACKAGE: UDON
THAT THIS IS PROBABLY ALL...

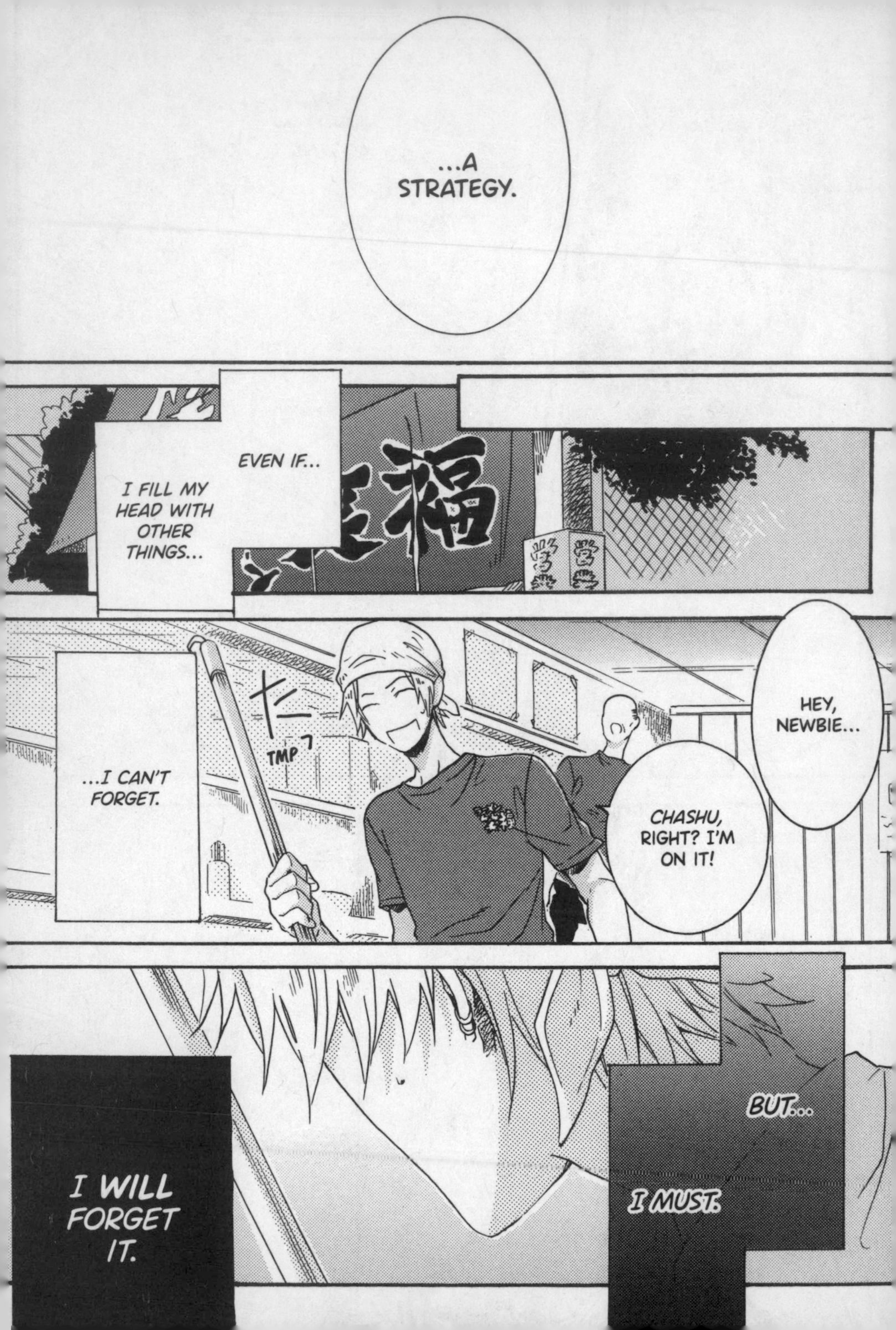
...A STRATEGY.
EVEN IF...
I FILL MY HEAD WITH OTHER THINGS...
HEY, NEWBIE...
CHASHU, RIGHT? I'M ON IT!
TMP
...I CAN'T FORGET.
BUT...
I MUST.
I WILL FORGET IT.

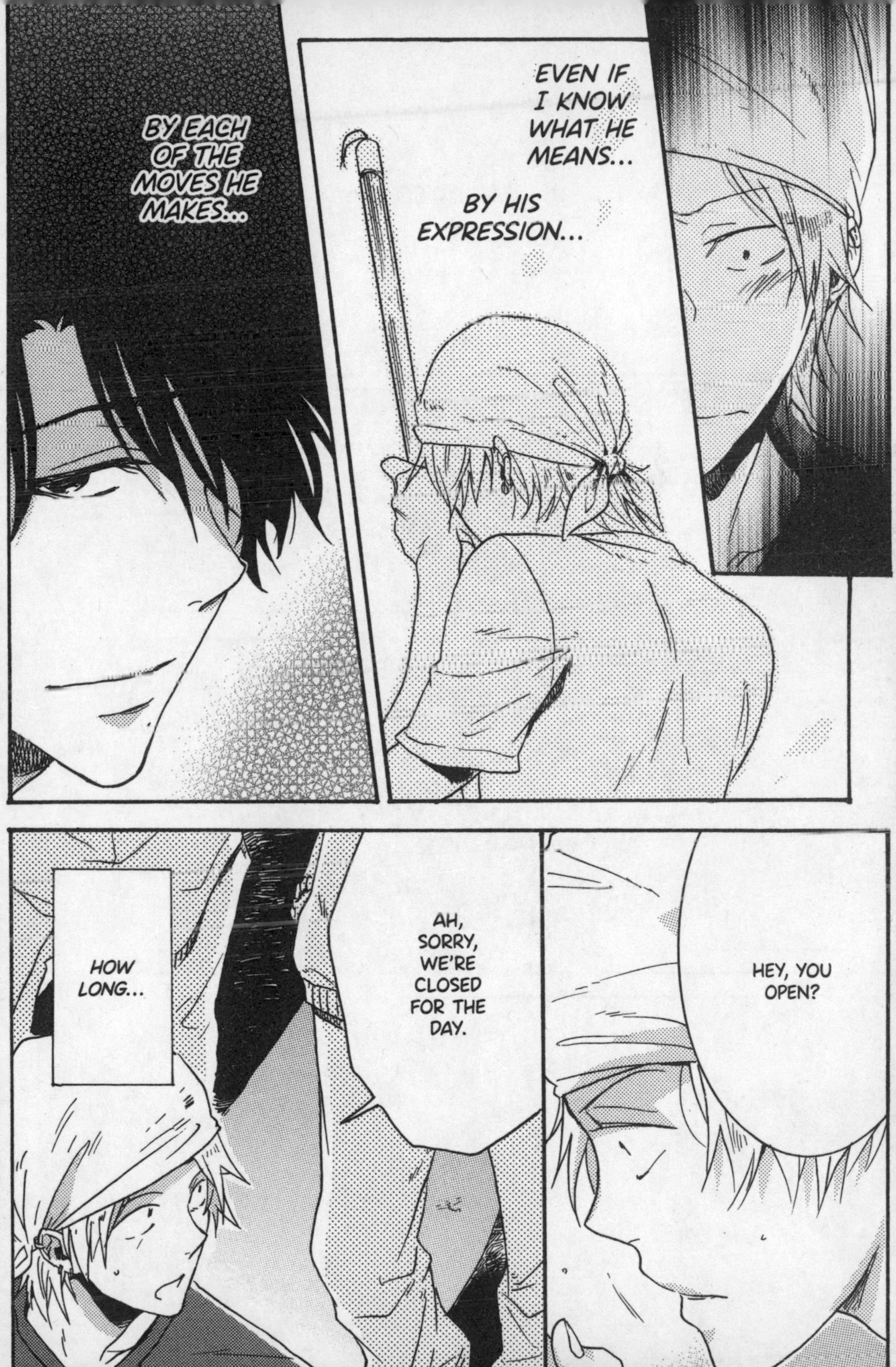
EVEN IF I KNOW WHAT HE MEANS...
BY HIS EXPRESSION...
BY EACH OF THE MOVES HE MAKES...
HEY, YOU OPEN?
AH, SORRY, WE'RE CLOSED FOR THE DAY.
HOW LONG...

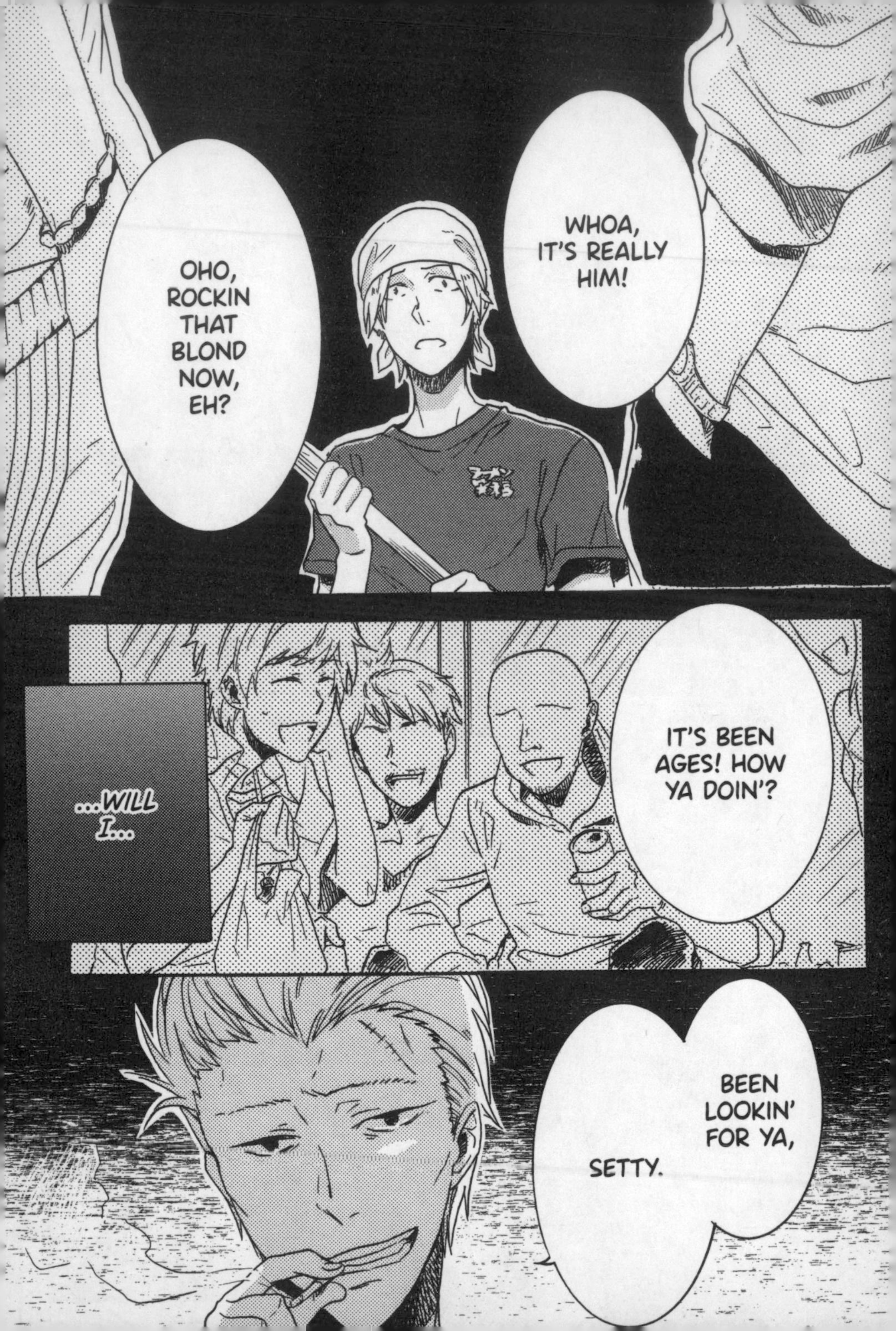
WHOA, IT'S REALLY HIM!
OHO, ROCKIN THAT BLOND NOW, EH?
IT'S BEEN AGES! HOW YA DOIN'?
...WILL I...
BEEN LOOKIN' FOR YA, SETTY.

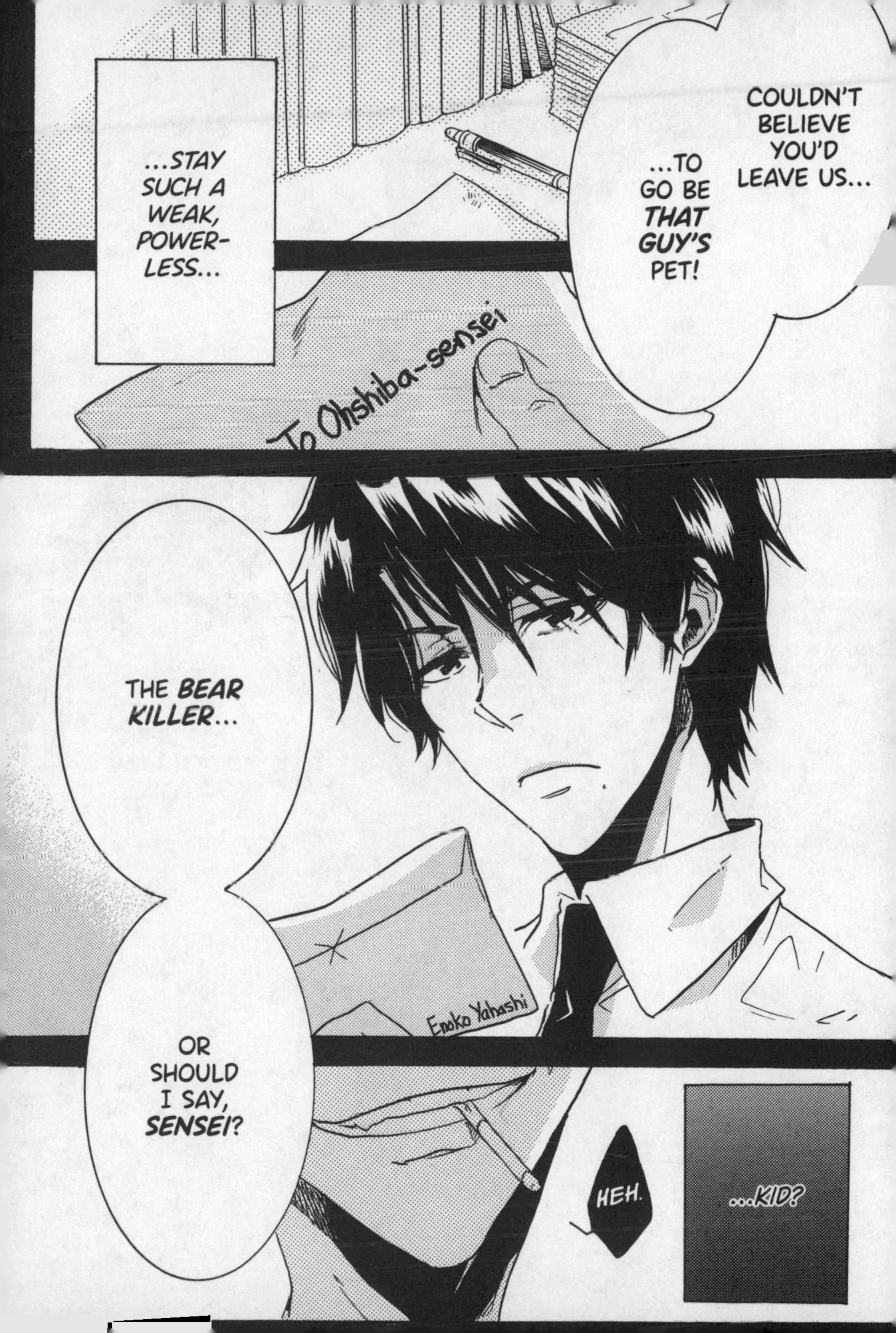
COULDN'T BELIEVE YOU'D LEAVE US...
...TO GO BE THAT GUY'S PET!
...STAY SUCH A WEAK, POWER-LESS...
To Ohshiba-sensei
THE BEAR KILLER...
Enoko Yahashi
OR SHOULD I SAY, SENSEI?
...KID?
HEH.

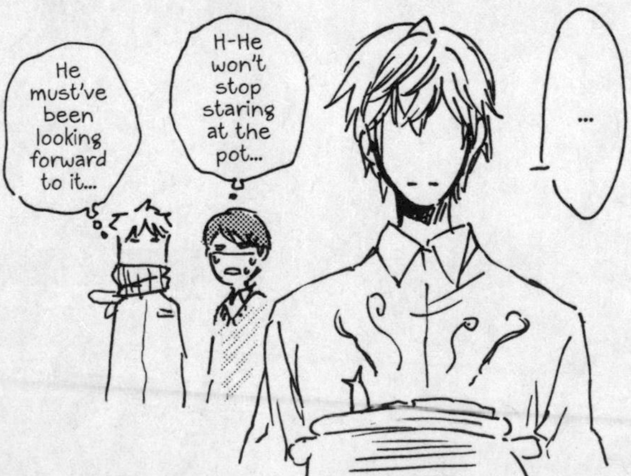
...
H-He won't stop staring at the pot...
He must've been looking forward to it...

Hitorijime
My Hero

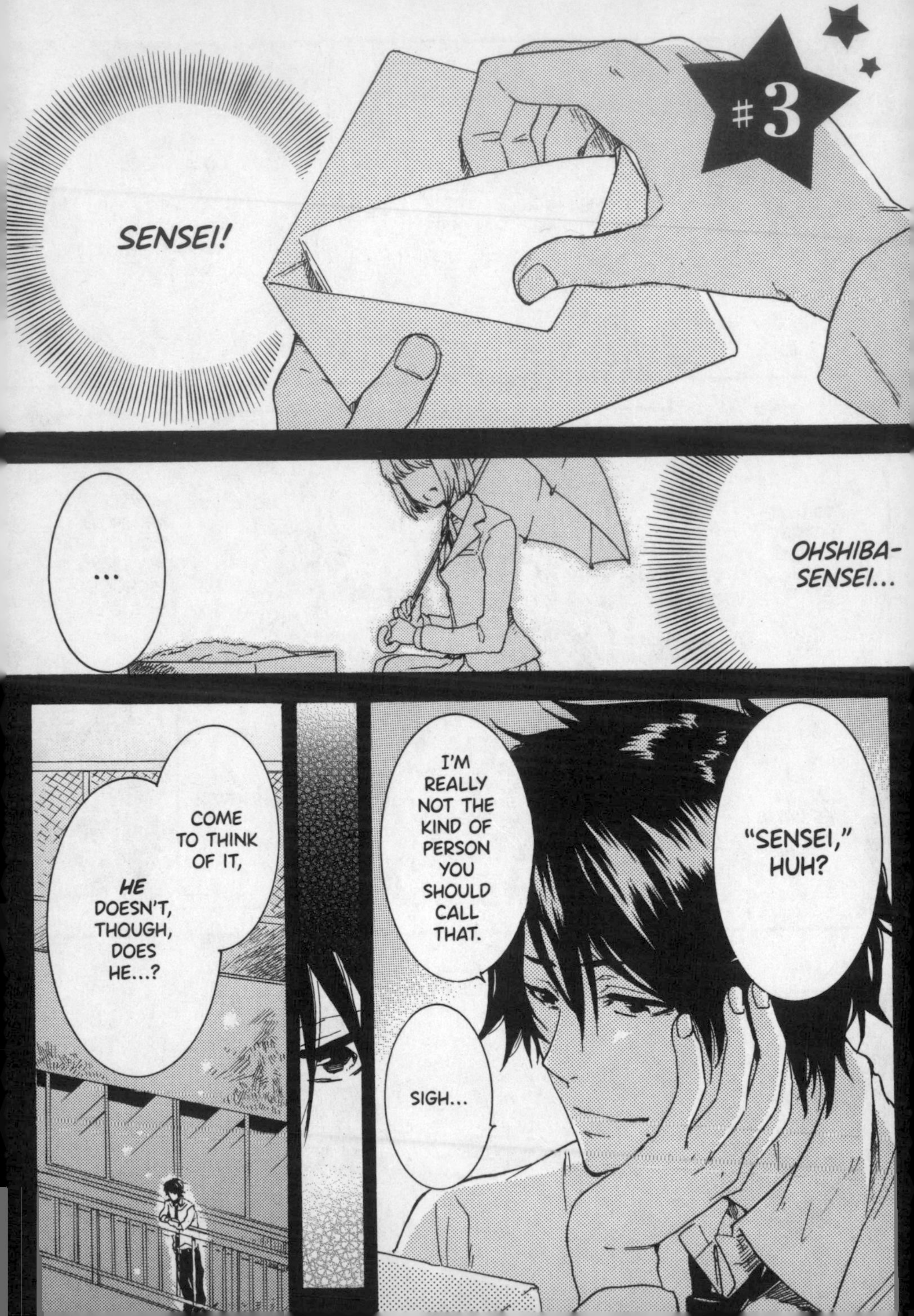
#3
SENSEI!
OHSHIBA-SENSEI...
...
"SENSEI," HUH?
I'M REALLY NOT THE KIND OF PERSON YOU SHOULD CALL THAT.
SIGH...
COME TO THINK OF IT,
HE DOESN'T, THOUGH, DOES HE...?

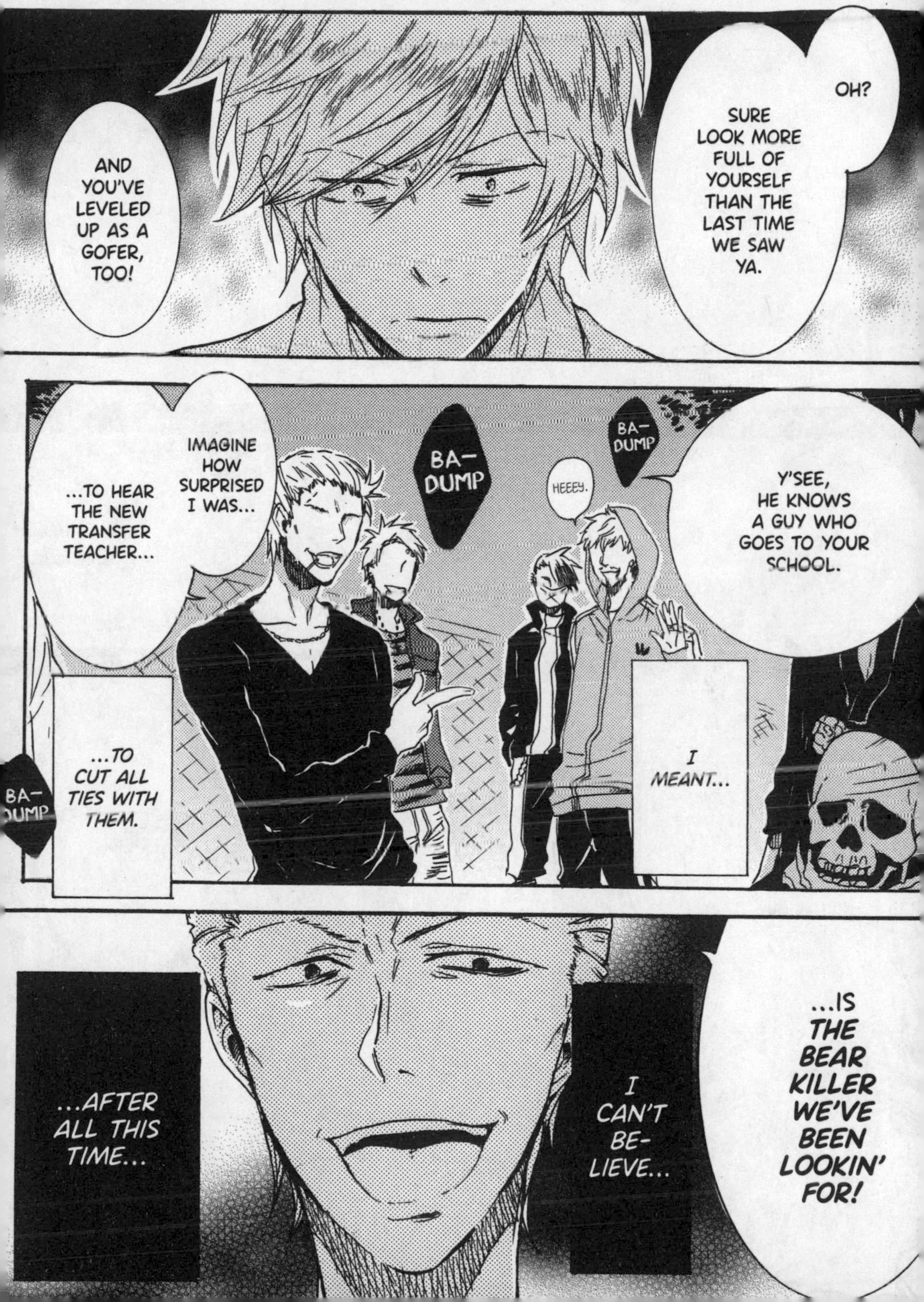
OH?
SURE LOOK MORE FULL OF YOURSELF THAN THE LAST TIME WE SAW YA.
AND YOU'VE LEVELED UP AS A GOFER, TOO!
Y'SEE, HE KNOWS A GUY WHO GOES TO YOUR SCHOOL.
BA-DUMP
HEEEY.
I MEANT...
BA-DUMP
IMAGINE HOW SURPRISED I WAS...
...TO HEAR THE NEW TRANSFER TEACHER...
...TO CUT ALL TIES WITH THEM.
BA-DUMP
...IS THE BEAR KILLER WE'VE BEEN LOOKIN' FOR!
I CAN'T BE-LIEVE...
...AFTER ALL THIS TIME...

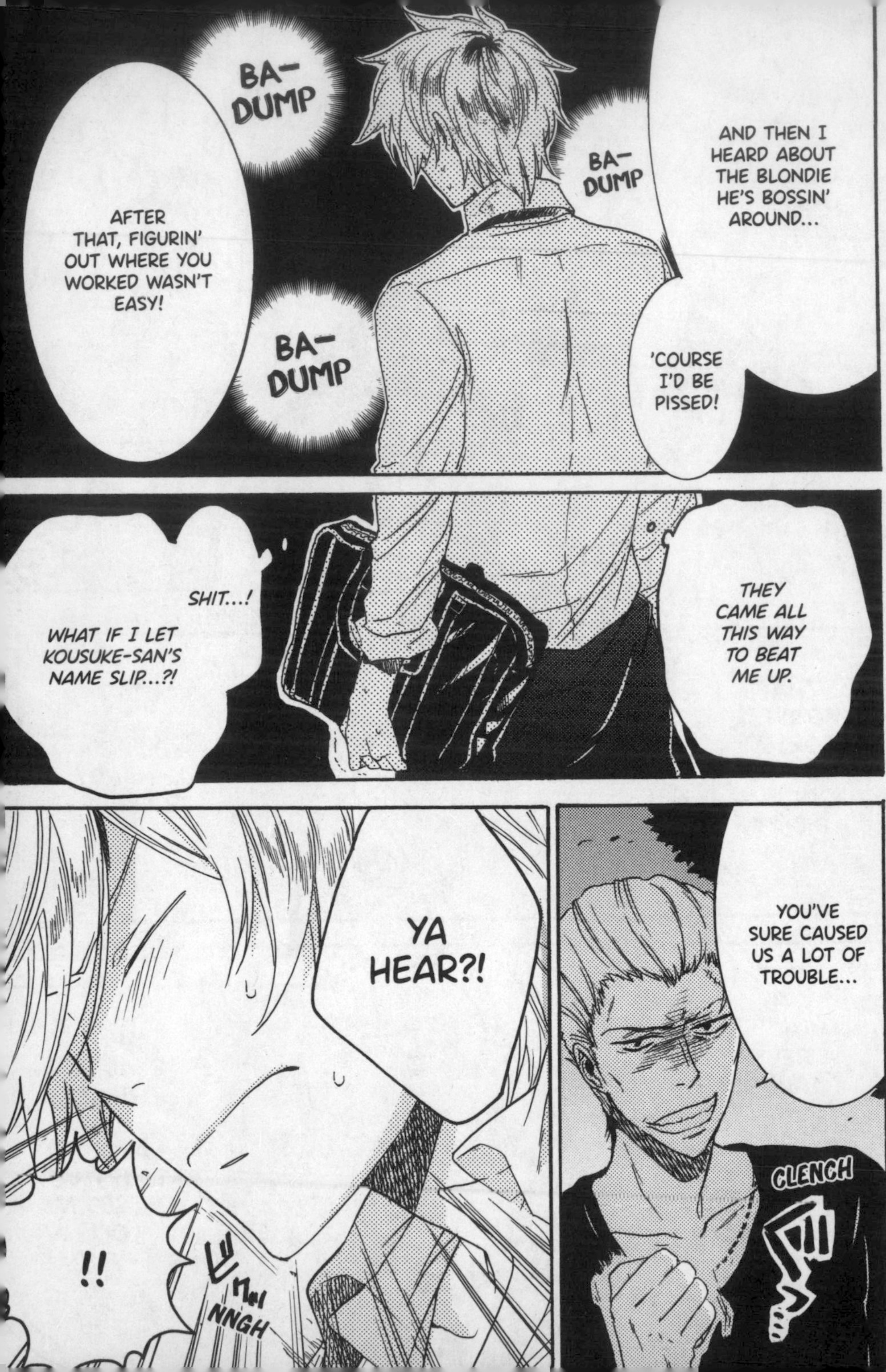
AND THEN I HEARD ABOUT THE BLONDIE HE'S BOSSIN' AROUND...
'COURSE I'D BE PISSED!
BA-DUMP
BA-DUMP
AFTER THAT, FIGURIN' OUT WHERE YOU WORKED WASN'T EASY!
BA-DUMP
THEY CAME ALL THIS WAY TO BEAT ME UP.
SHIT...!
WHAT IF I LET KOUSUKE-SAN'S NAME SLIP...?!
YOU'VE SURE CAUSED US A LOT OF TROUBLE...
CLENCH
YA HEAR?!
NNGH
!!

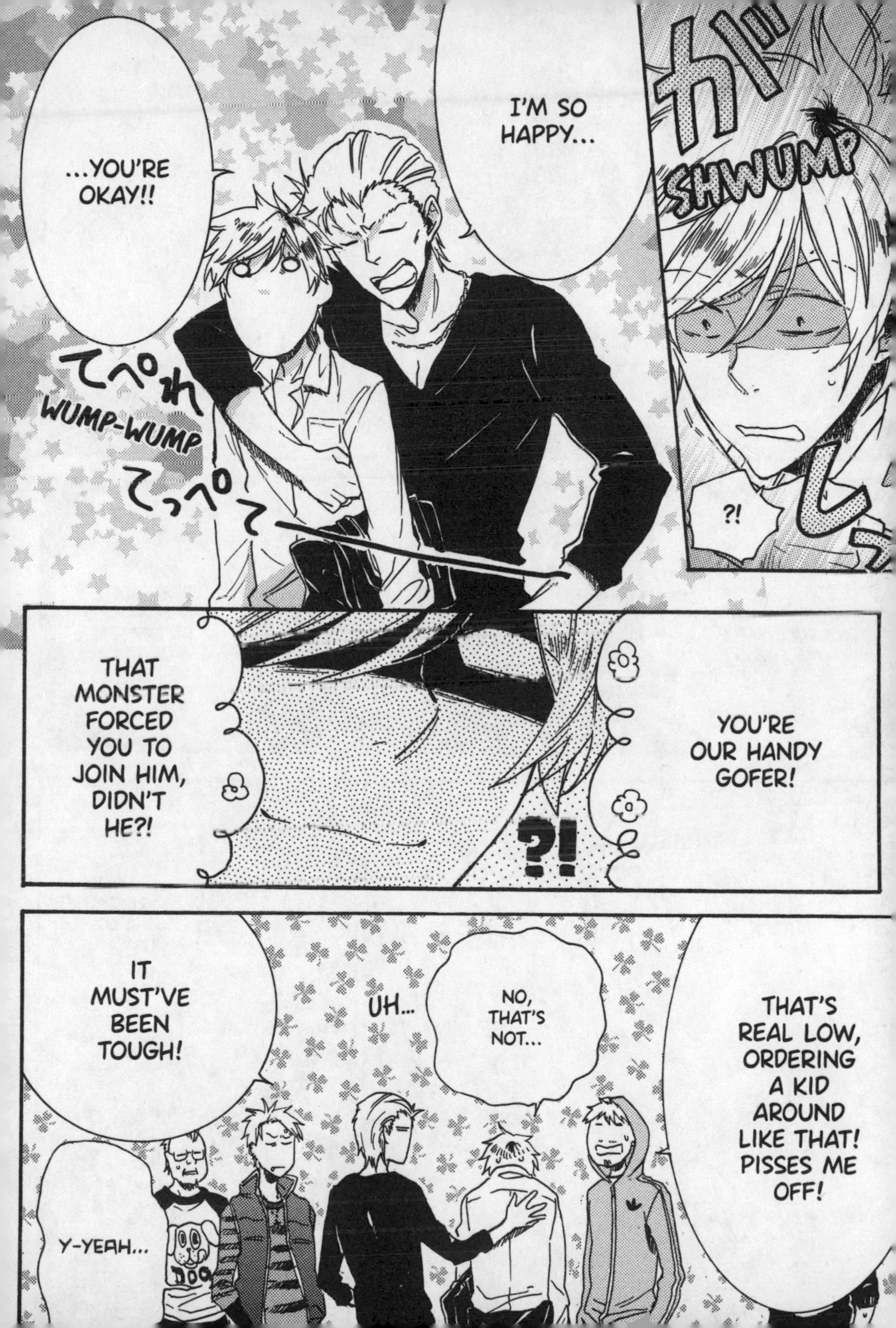
SHWUMP
?!
I'M SO HAPPY...
...YOU'RE OKAY!!
WUMP-WUMP
YOU'RE OUR HANDY GOFER!
?!
THAT MONSTER FORCED YOU TO JOIN HIM, DIDN'T HE?!
THAT'S REAL LOW, ORDERING A KID AROUND LIKE THAT! PISSES ME OFF!
NO, THAT'S NOT...
UH...
IT MUST'VE BEEN TOUGH!
Y-YEAH...

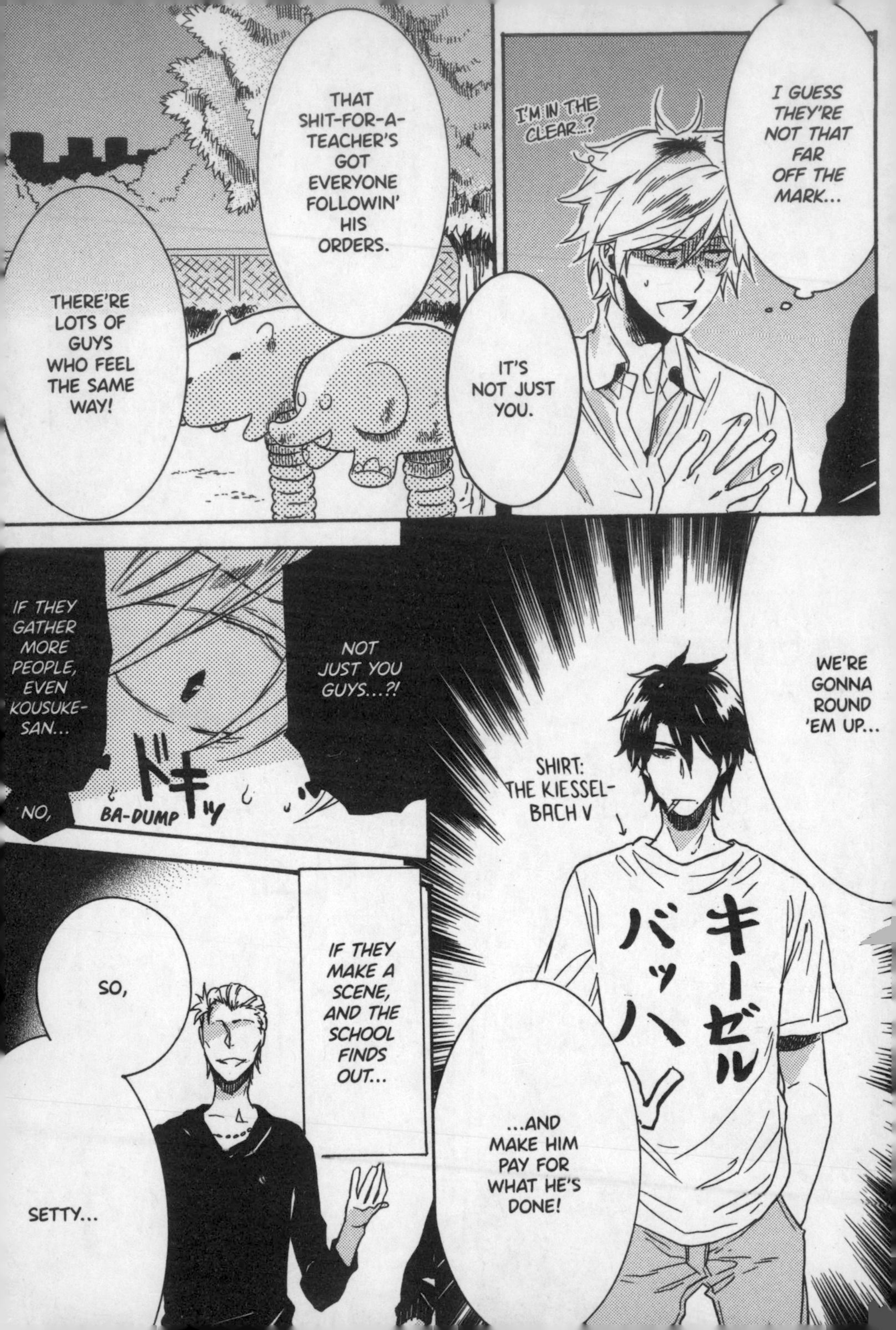

I GUESS THEY'RE NOT THAT FAR OFF THE MARK...
I'M IN THE CLEAR...?
IT'S NOT JUST YOU.
THAT SHIT-FOR-A-TEACHER'S GOT EVERYONE FOLLOWIN' HIS ORDERS.
THERE'RE LOTS OF GUYS WHO FEEL THE SAME WAY!
WE'RE GONNA ROUND 'EM UP...
SHIRT: THE KIESSEL-BACH V
キーゼルバッハV
...AND MAKE HIM PAY FOR WHAT HE'S DONE!
NOT JUST YOU GUYS...?!
IF THEY GATHER MORE PEOPLE, EVEN KOUSUKE-SAN...
NO,
ドキッ
BA-DUMP
IF THEY MAKE A SCENE, AND THE SCHOOL FINDS OUT...
SO,
SETTY...

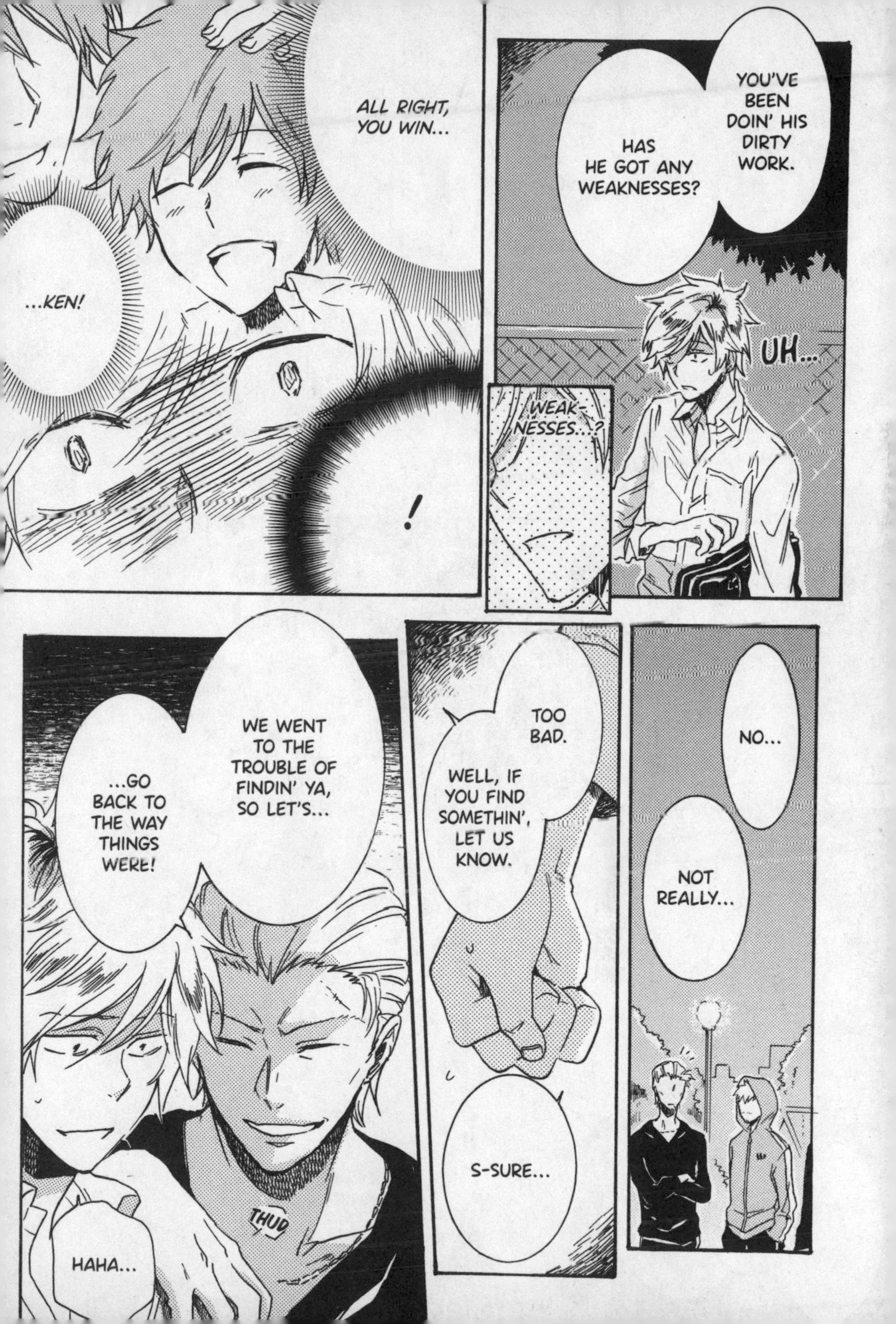
YOU'VE BEEN DOIN' HIS DIRTY WORK.
HAS HE GOT ANY WEAKNESSES?
UH...
WEAK-NESSES...?
ALL RIGHT, YOU WIN...
...KEN!
!
NO...
NOT REALLY...
TOO BAD.
WELL, IF YOU FIND SOMETHIN', LET US KNOW.
S-SURE...
WE WENT TO THE TROUBLE OF FINDIN' YA, SO LET'S...
...GO BACK TO THE WAY THINGS WERE!
THUD
HAHA...

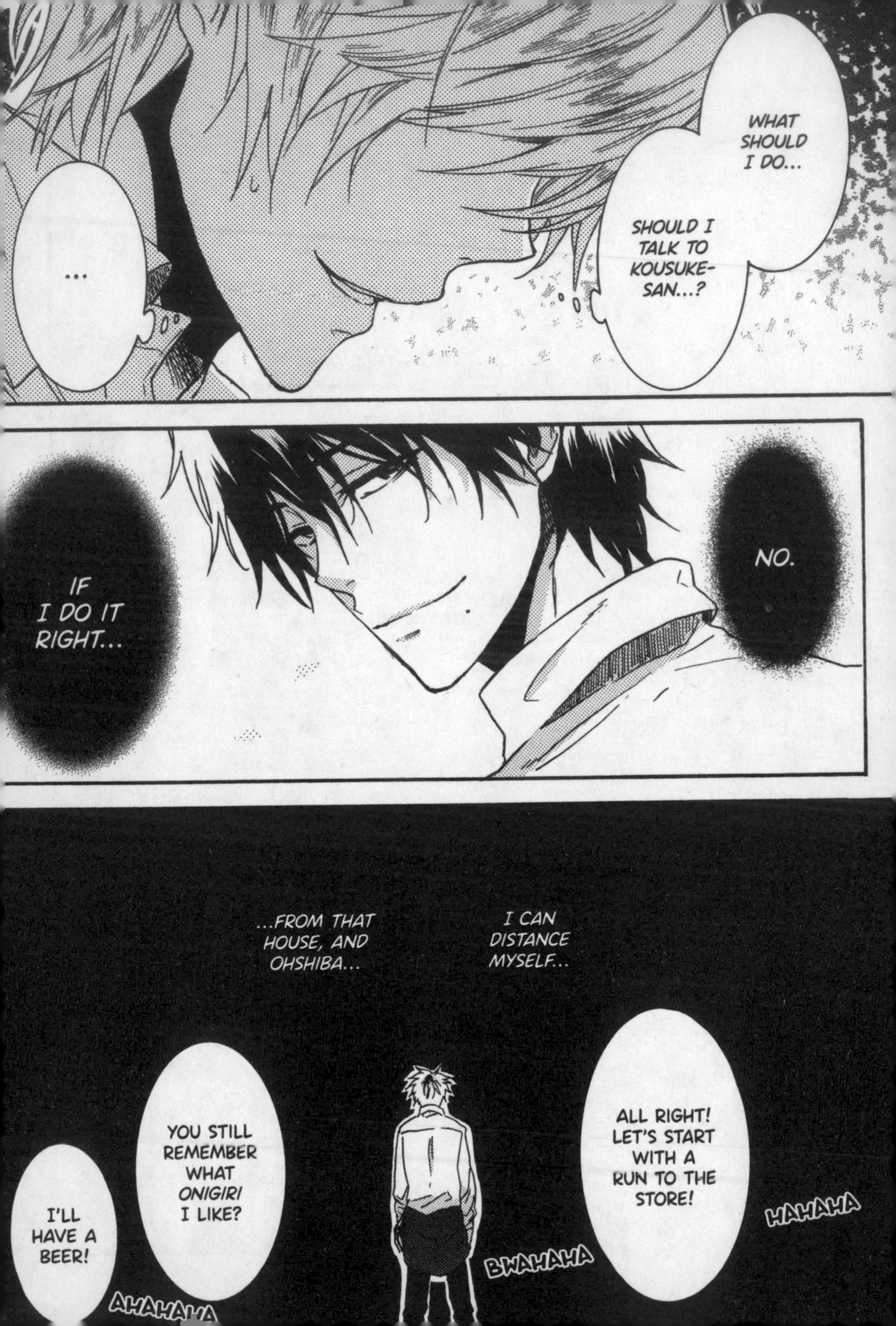
WHAT SHOULD I DO...
SHOULD I TALK TO KOUSUKE-SAN...?
...
NO.
IF I DO IT RIGHT...
I CAN DISTANCE MYSELF...
...FROM THAT HOUSE, AND OHSHIBA...
ALL RIGHT! LET'S START WITH A RUN TO THE STORE!
HAHAHA
BWAHAHA
YOU STILL REMEMBER WHAT ONIGIRI I LIKE?
I'LL HAVE A BEER!
AHAHAHA

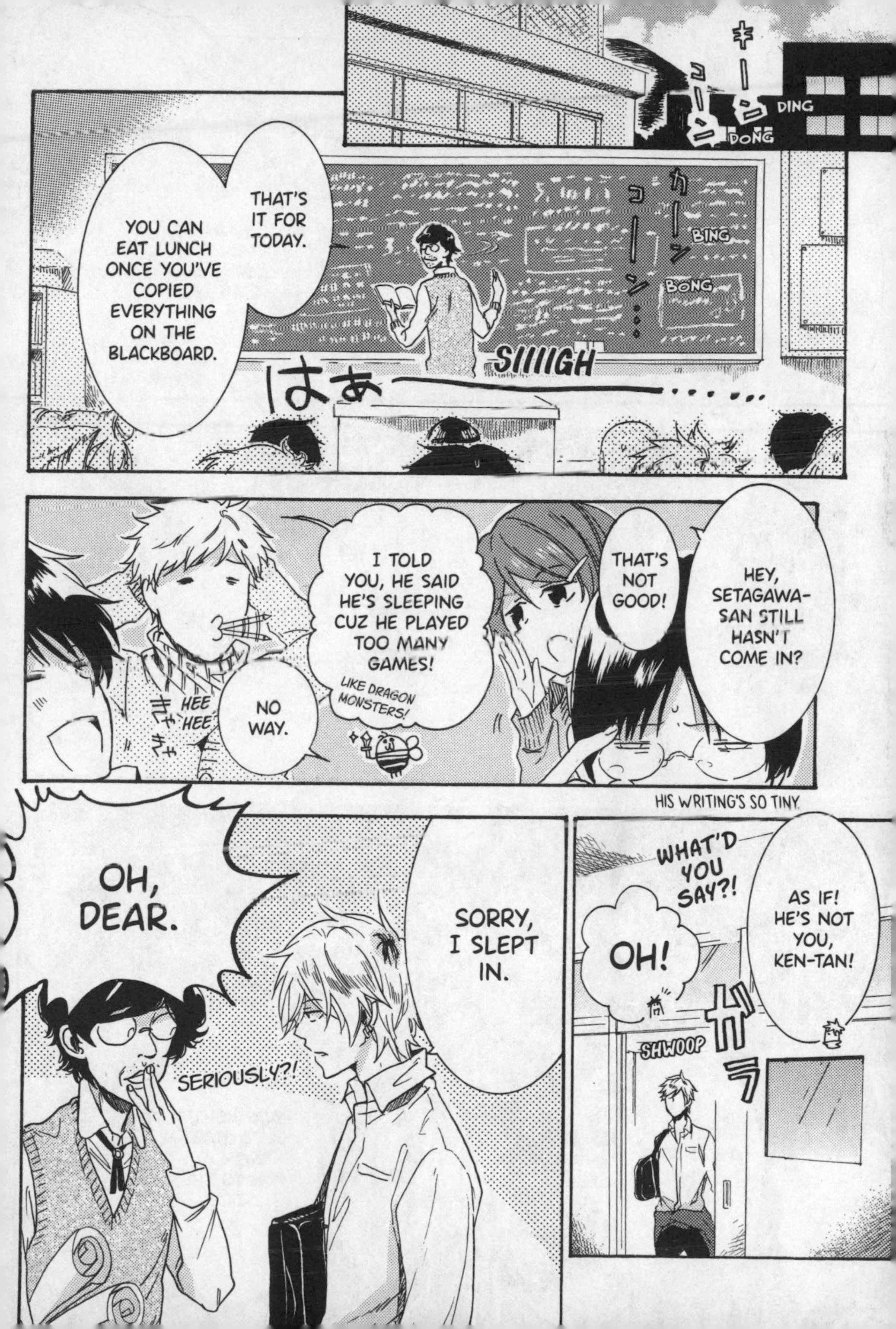
キーンコーン
DING
DONG
カーンコーン…
BING
BONG
THAT'S IT FOR TODAY.
YOU CAN EAT LUNCH ONCE YOU'VE COPIED EVERYTHING ON THE BLACKBOARD.
SIIIIGH
はあ——……
HEY, SETAGAWA-SAN STILL HASN'T COME IN?
THAT'S NOT GOOD!
I TOLD YOU, HE SAID HE'S SLEEPING CUZ HE PLAYED TOO MANY GAMES!
LIKE DRAGON MONSTERS!
NO WAY.
HEE HEE
きゃきゃ
HIS WRITING'S SO TINY.
AS IF! HE'S NOT YOU, KEN-TAN!
WHAT'D YOU SAY?!
OH!
SHWOOP
ガラ
SORRY, I SLEPT IN.
OH, DEAR.
SERIOUSLY?!

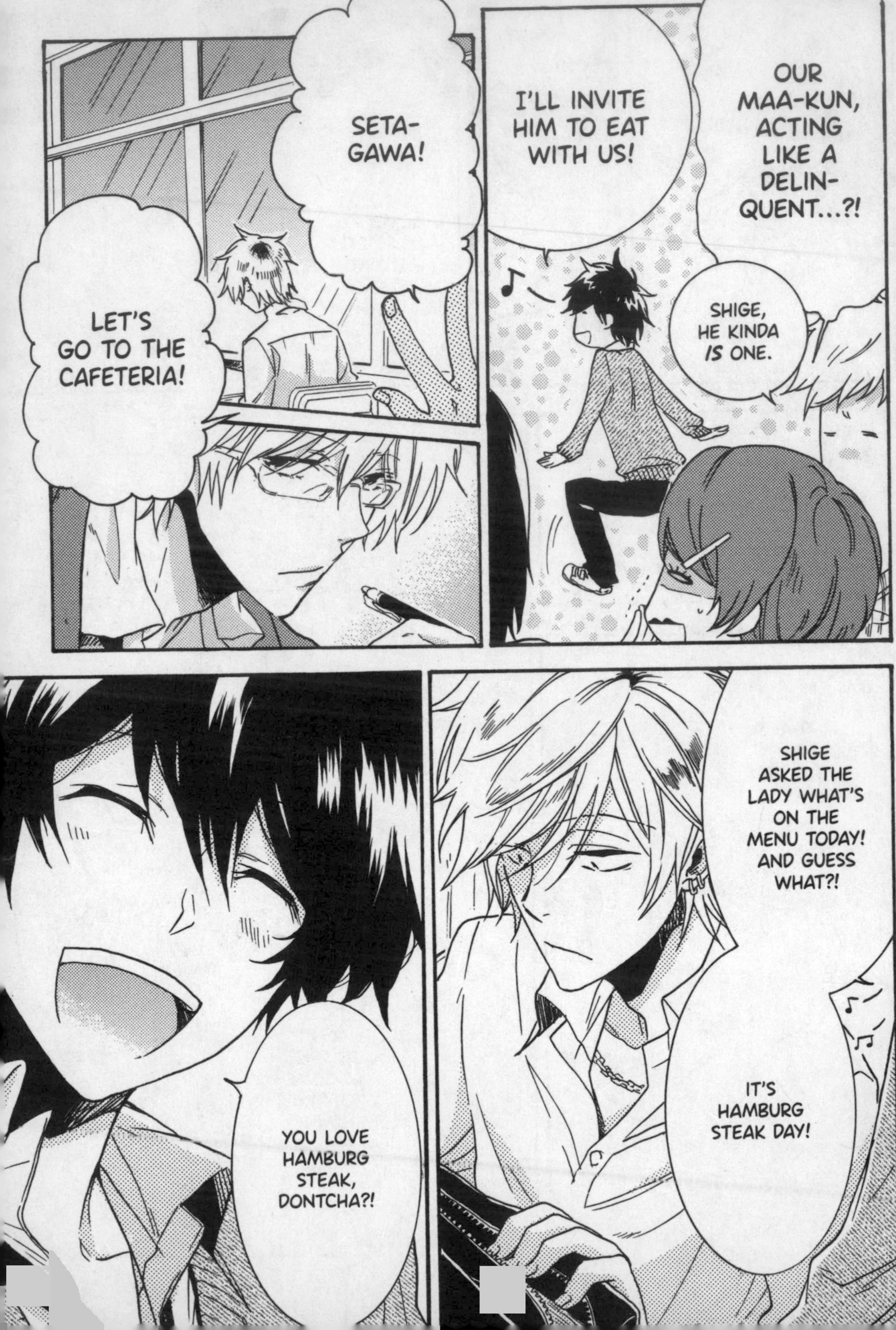
OUR MAA-KUN, ACTING LIKE A DELIN-QUENT...?!
I'LL INVITE HIM TO EAT WITH US!
SHIGE, HE KINDA *IS* ONE.
SETA-GAWA!
LET'S GO TO THE CAFETERIA!
SHIGE ASKED THE LADY WHAT'S ON THE MENU TODAY! AND GUESS WHAT?!
IT'S HAMBURG STEAK DAY!
YOU LOVE HAMBURG STEAK, DONTCHA?!

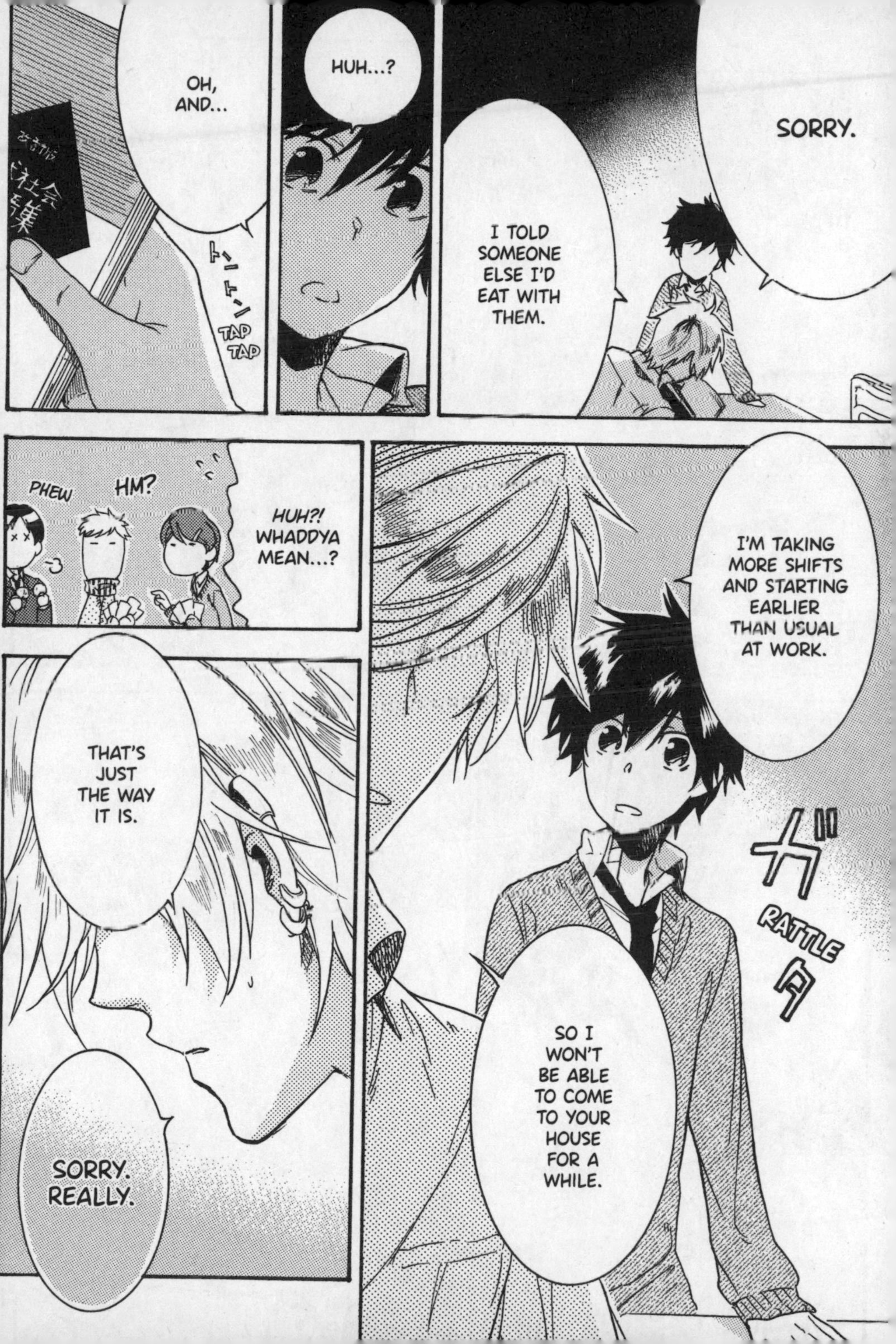
SORRY.
I TOLD SOMEONE ELSE I'D EAT WITH THEM.
HUH...?
OH, AND...
トントン
TAP TAP
I'M TAKING MORE SHIFTS AND STARTING EARLIER THAN USUAL AT WORK.
RATTLE
SO I WON'T BE ABLE TO COME TO YOUR HOUSE FOR A WHILE.
HUH?! WHADDYA MEAN...?
HM?
PHEW
THAT'S JUST THE WAY IT IS.
SORRY. REALLY.

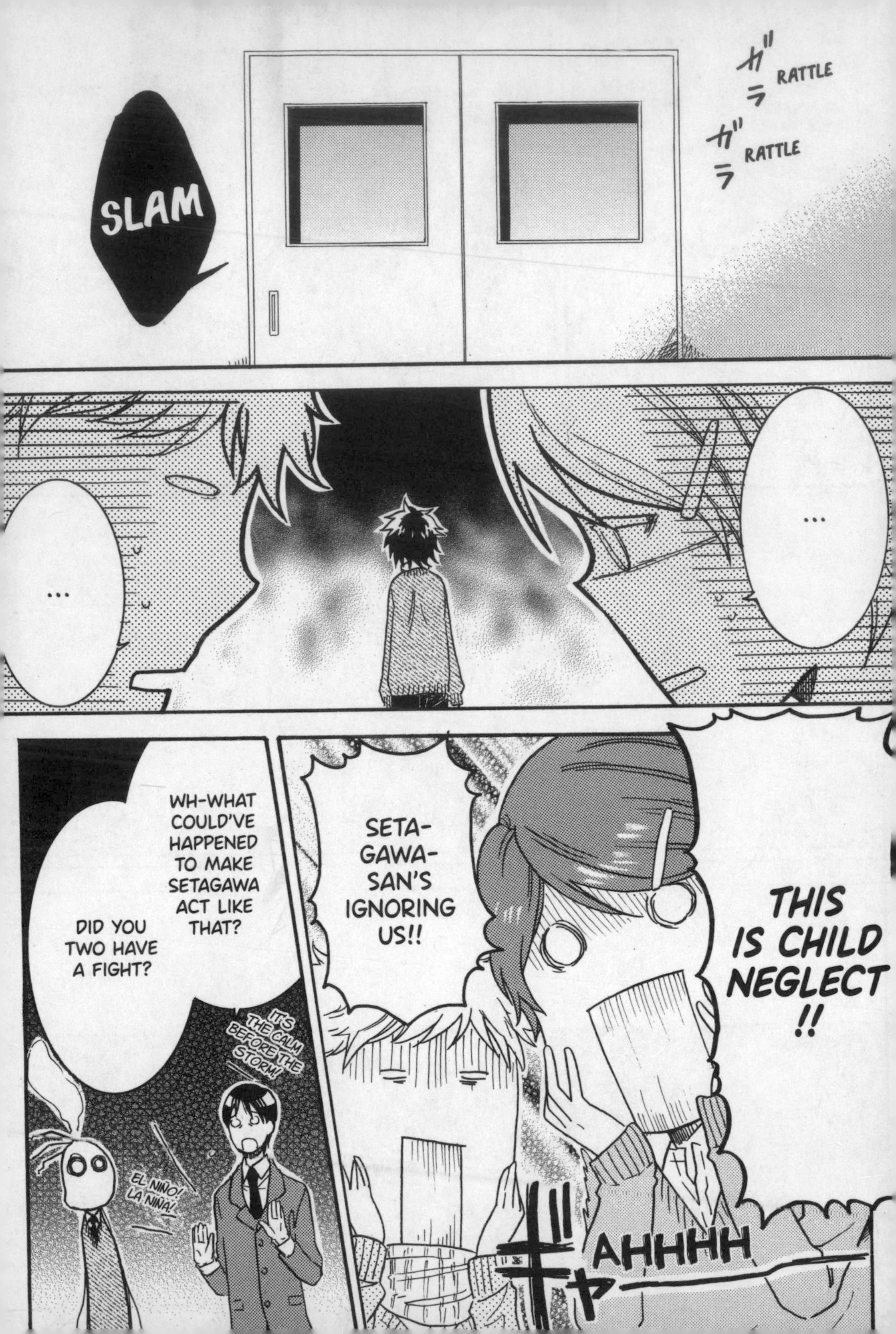
ガラ RATTLE
ガラ RATTLE
SLAM
...
...
THIS IS CHILD NEGLECT!!
SETA-GAWA-SAN'S IGNORING US!!
AHHHH
WH-WHAT COULD'VE HAPPENED TO MAKE SETAGAWA ACT LIKE THAT?
DID YOU TWO HAVE A FIGHT?
IT'S THE CALM BEFORE THE STORM!
EL NIÑO! LA NIÑA!

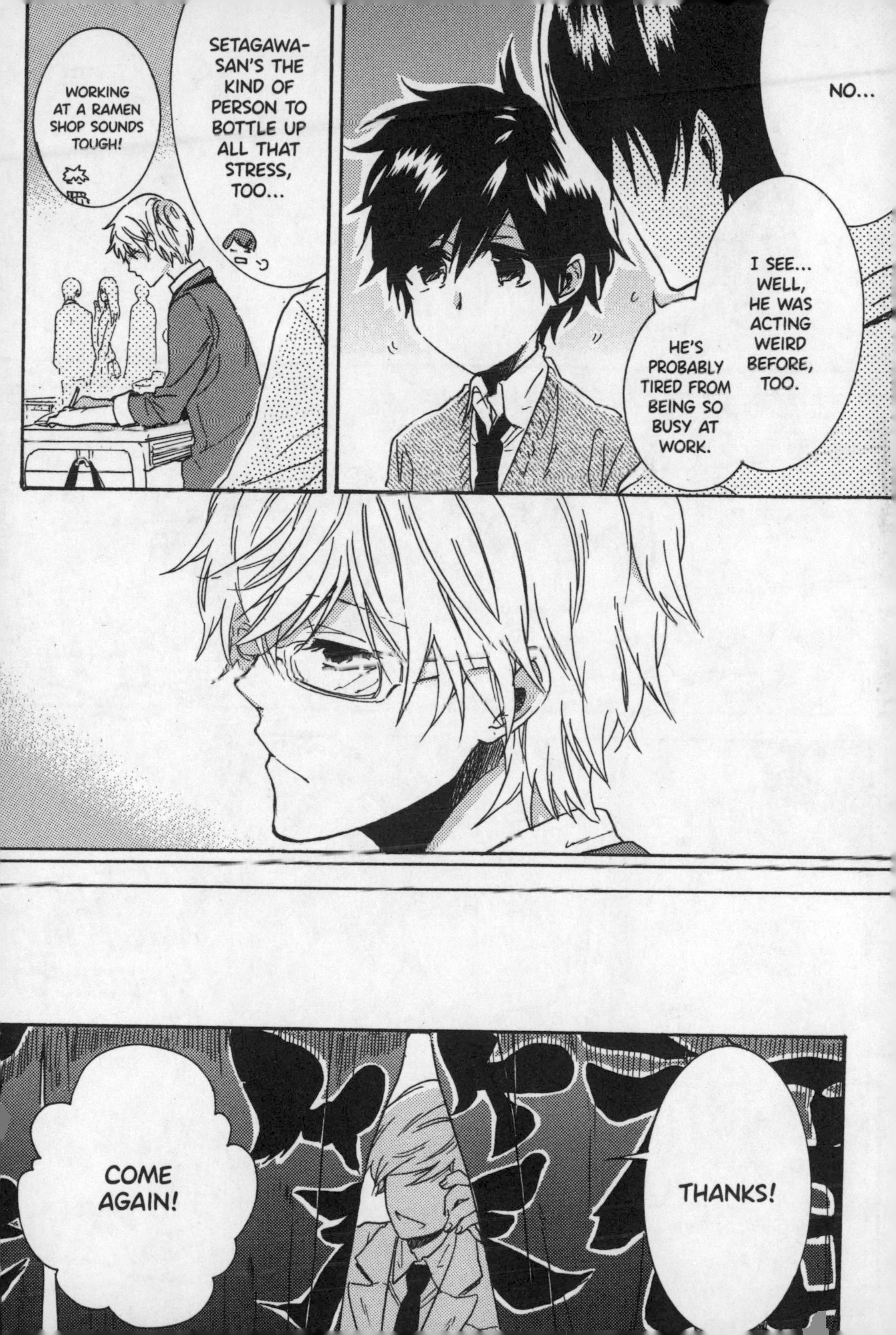
NO...
I SEE... WELL, HE WAS ACTING WEIRD BEFORE, TOO.
HE'S PROBABLY TIRED FROM BEING SO BUSY AT WORK.
SETAGAWA-SAN'S THE KIND OF PERSON TO BOTTLE UP ALL THAT STRESS, TOO...
WORKING AT A RAMEN SHOP SOUNDS TOUGH!
THANKS!
COME AGAIN!

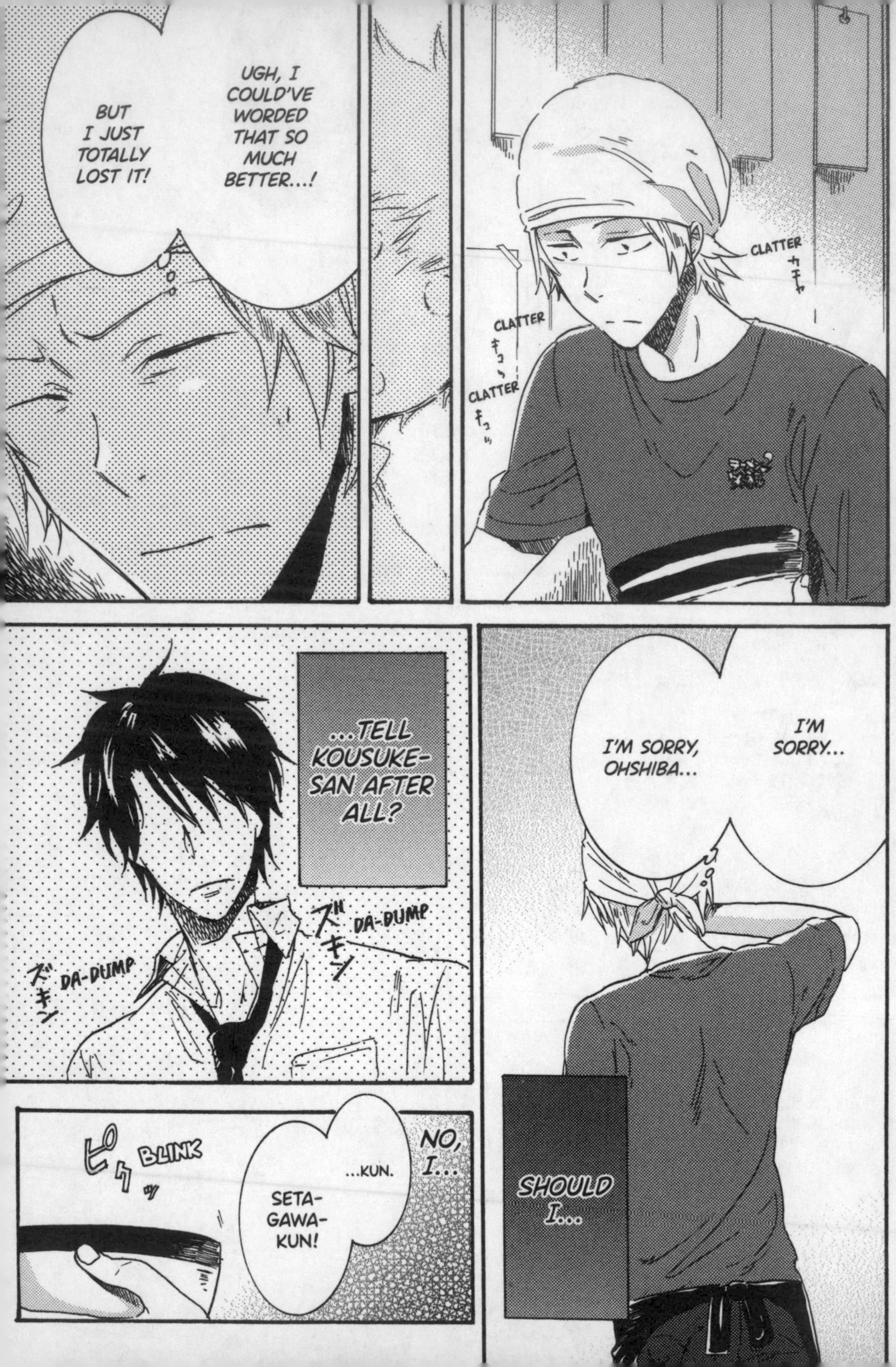
CLATTER
CLATTER
CLATTER
UGH, I COULD'VE WORDED THAT SO MUCH BETTER...!
BUT I JUST TOTALLY LOST IT!
I'M SORRY...
I'M SORRY, OHSHIBA...
SHOULD I...
...TELL KOUSUKE-SAN AFTER ALL?
DA-DUMP
DA-DUMP
NO, I...
...KUN.
SETA-GAWA-KUN!
BLINK

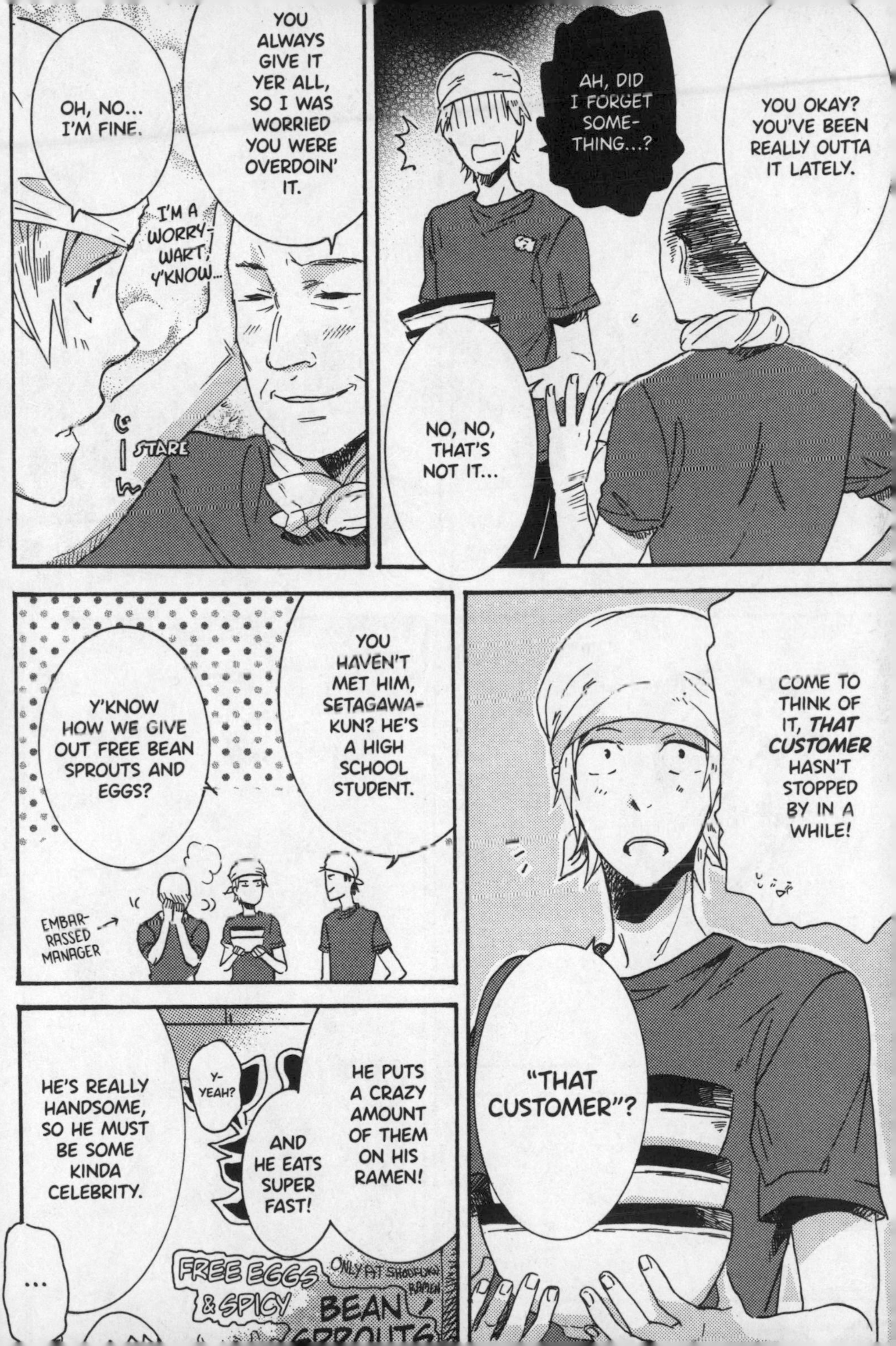
YOU OKAY? YOU'VE BEEN REALLY OUTTA IT LATELY.
AH, DID I FORGET SOME-THING...?
NO, NO, THAT'S NOT IT...
YOU ALWAYS GIVE IT YER ALL, SO I WAS WORRIED YOU WERE OVERDOIN' IT.
I'M A WORRY-WART, Y'KNOW...
OH, NO... I'M FINE.
STARE
COME TO THINK OF IT, *THAT CUSTOMER* HASN'T STOPPED BY IN A WHILE!
"THAT CUSTOMER"?
YOU HAVEN'T MET HIM, SETAGAWA-KUN? HE'S A HIGH SCHOOL STUDENT.
Y'KNOW HOW WE GIVE OUT FREE BEAN SPROUTS AND EGGS?
EMBARRASSED MANAGER
HE PUTS A CRAZY AMOUNT OF THEM ON HIS RAMEN!
Y-YEAH?
AND HE EATS SUPER FAST!
HE'S REALLY HANDSOME, SO HE MUST BE SOME KINDA CELEBRITY.
...
FREE EGGS & SPICY
BEAN
ONLY AT SHOUFUKU RAMEN

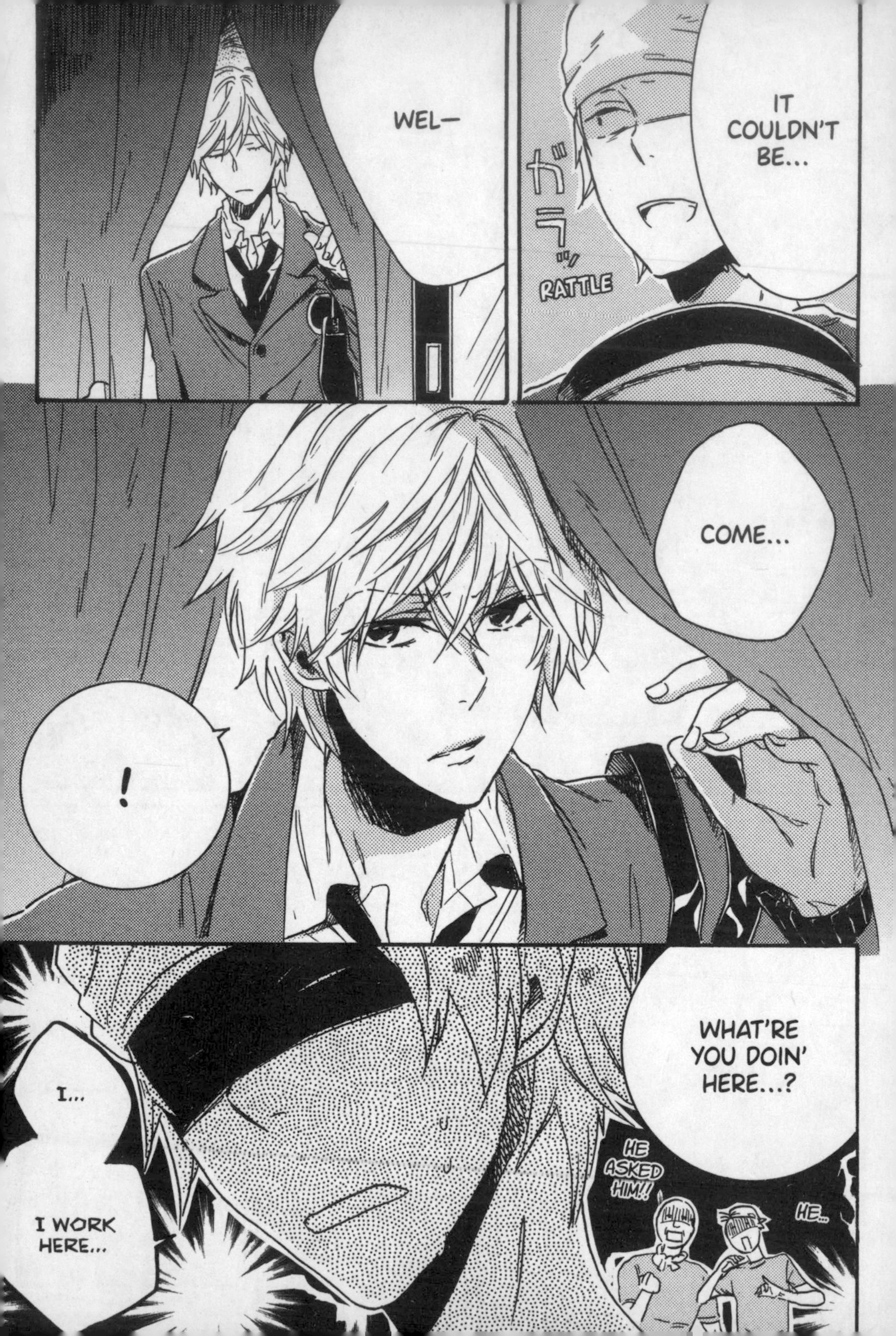
IT COULDN'T BE...
ガラッ
RATTLE
WEL—
COME...
!
WHAT'RE YOU DOIN' HERE...?
HE...
HE ASKED HIM!!
I...
I WORK HERE...

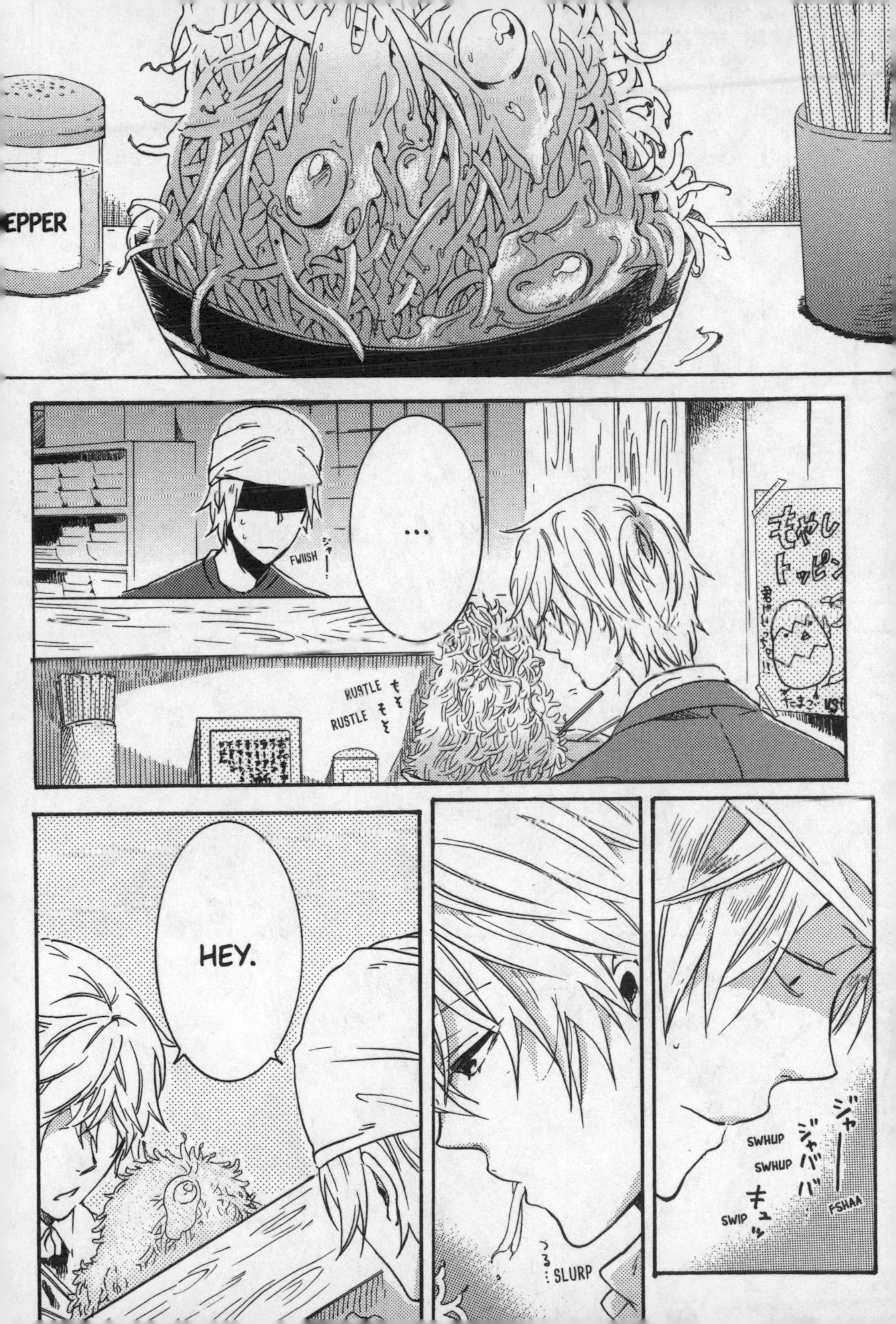
EPPER
...
ジャー
FWIISH
もそ もそ
RUSTLE
RUSTLE
ジャー
ジャババ
SWHUP
SWHUP
FSHAA
キュッ
SWIP
つる…
SLURP
HEY.

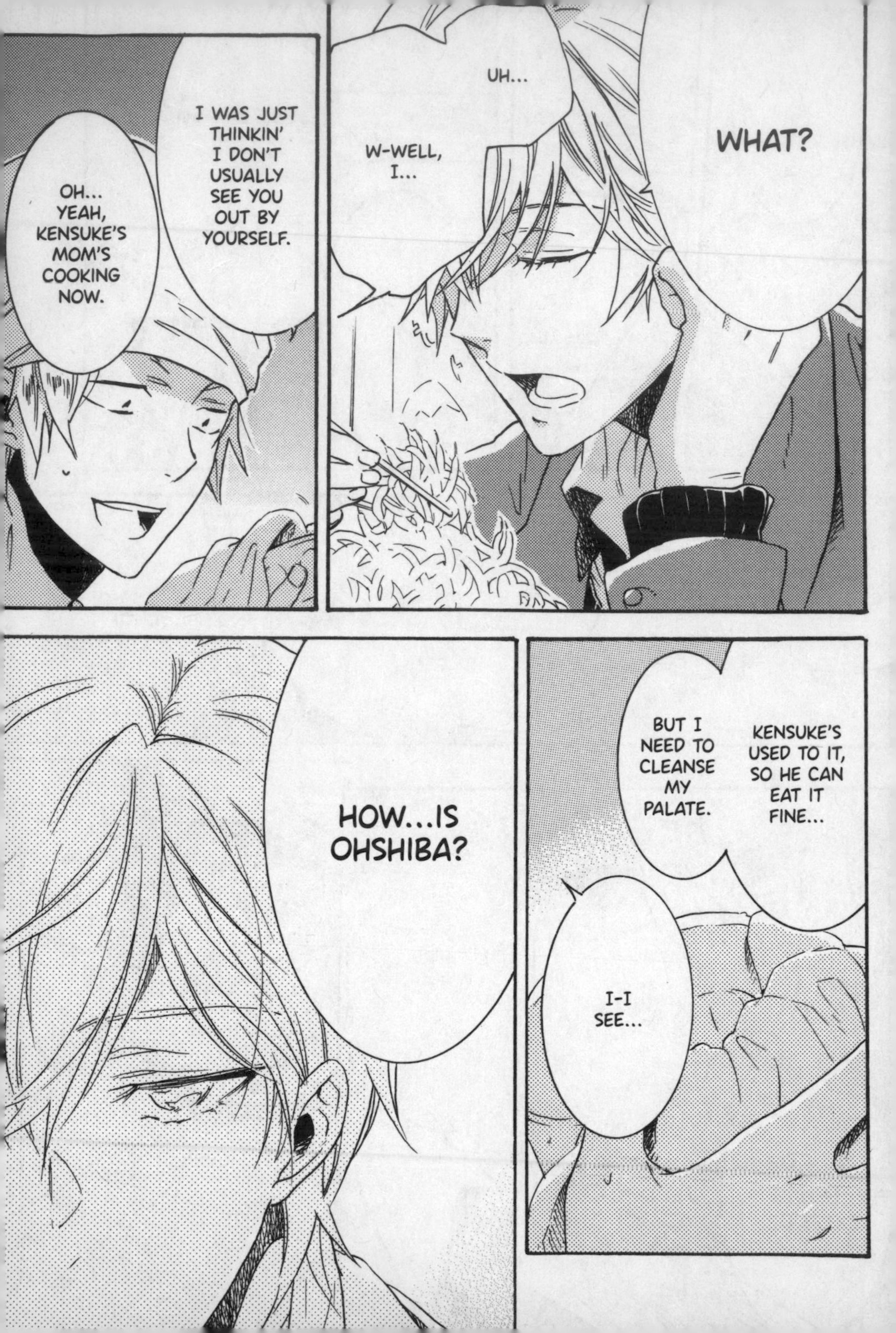
WHAT?
UH...
W-WELL, I...
I WAS JUST THINKIN' I DON'T USUALLY SEE YOU OUT BY YOURSELF.
OH... YEAH, KENSUKE'S MOM'S COOKING NOW.
KENSUKE'S USED TO IT, SO HE CAN EAT IT FINE...
BUT I NEED TO CLEANSE MY PALATE.
I-I SEE...
HOW...IS OHSHIBA?

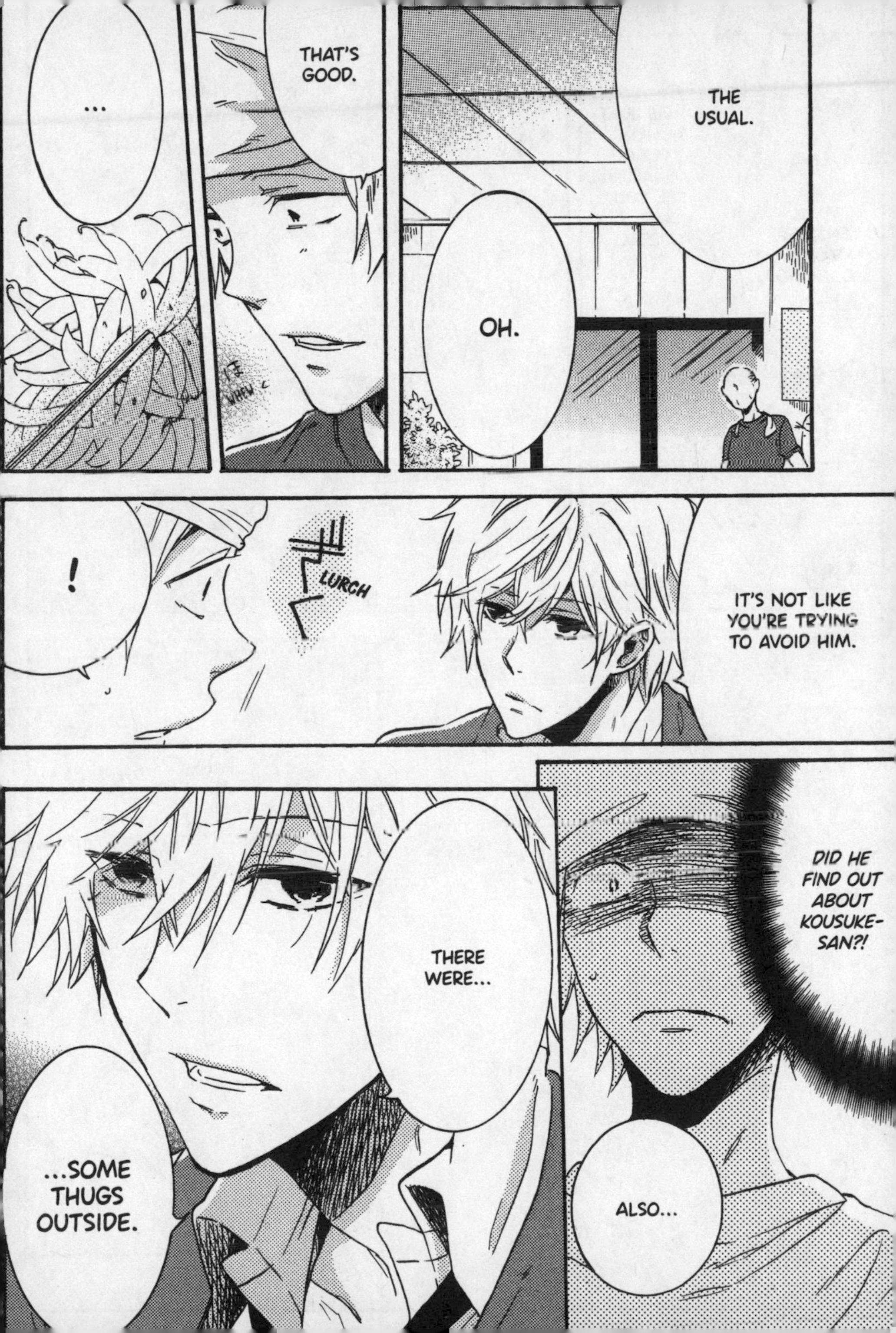
THE USUAL.
OH.
THAT'S GOOD.
...
IT'S NOT LIKE YOU'RE TRYING TO AVOID HIM.
LURCH
!
DID HE FIND OUT ABOUT KOUSUKE-SAN?!
ALSO...
THERE WERE...
...SOME THUGS OUTSIDE.

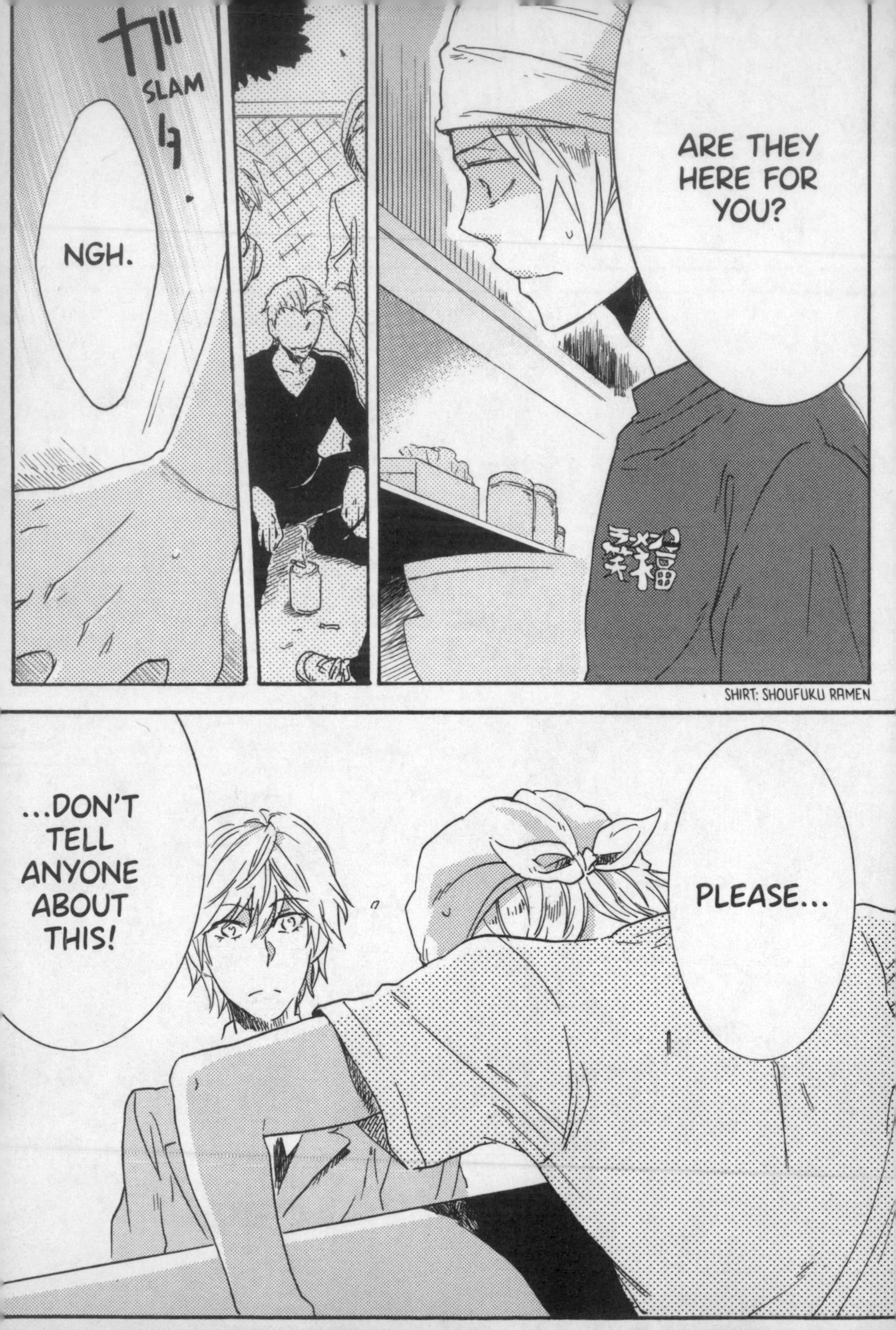
ARE THEY HERE FOR YOU?
ラーメン笑福
SHIRT: SHOUFUKU RAMEN
SLAM
NGH.
PLEASE...
...DON'T TELL ANYONE ABOUT THIS!

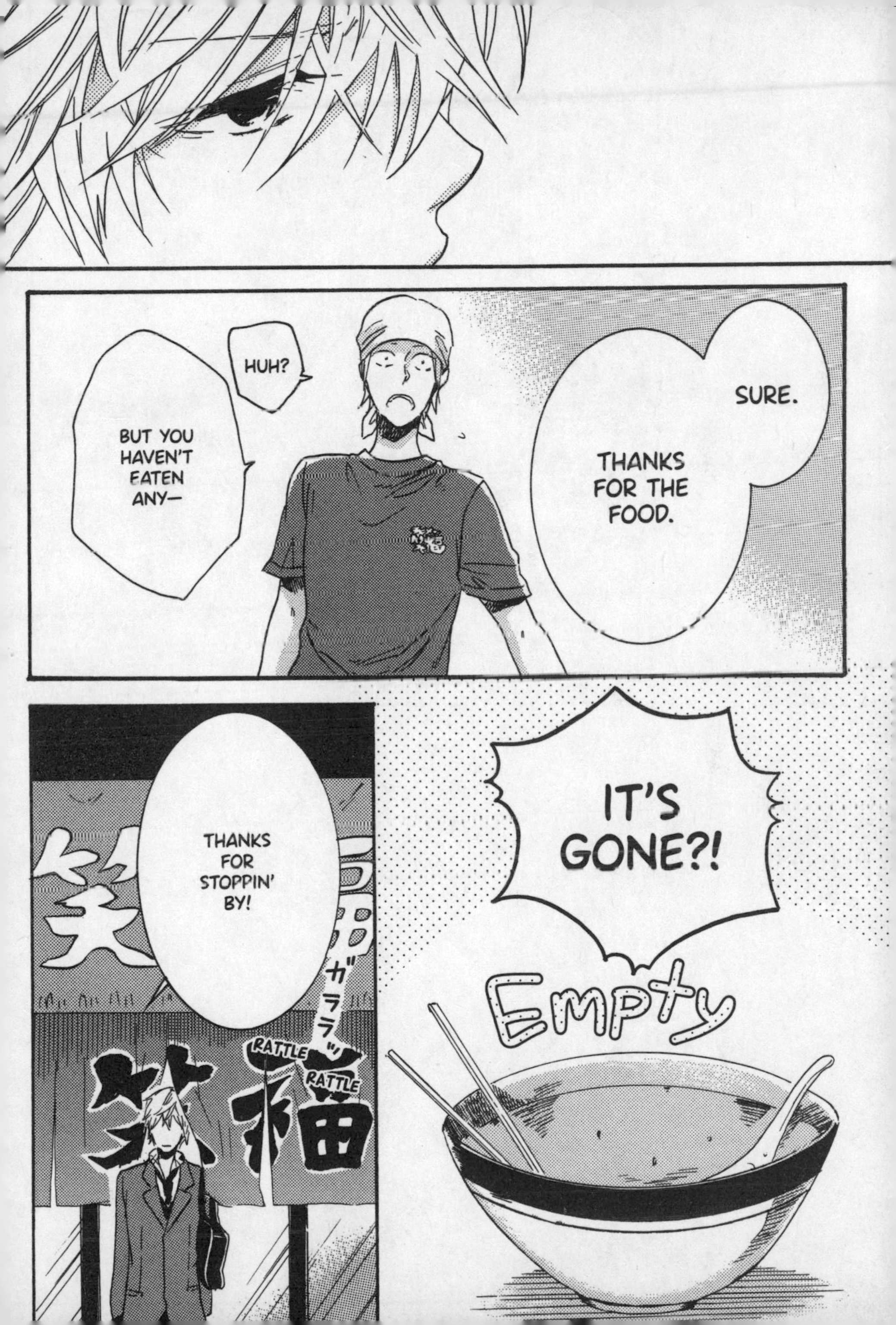
SURE.
THANKS FOR THE FOOD.
HUH?
BUT YOU HAVEN'T EATEN ANY—
IT'S GONE?!
Empty
THANKS FOR STOPPIN' BY!
ガララッ
RATTLE RATTLE

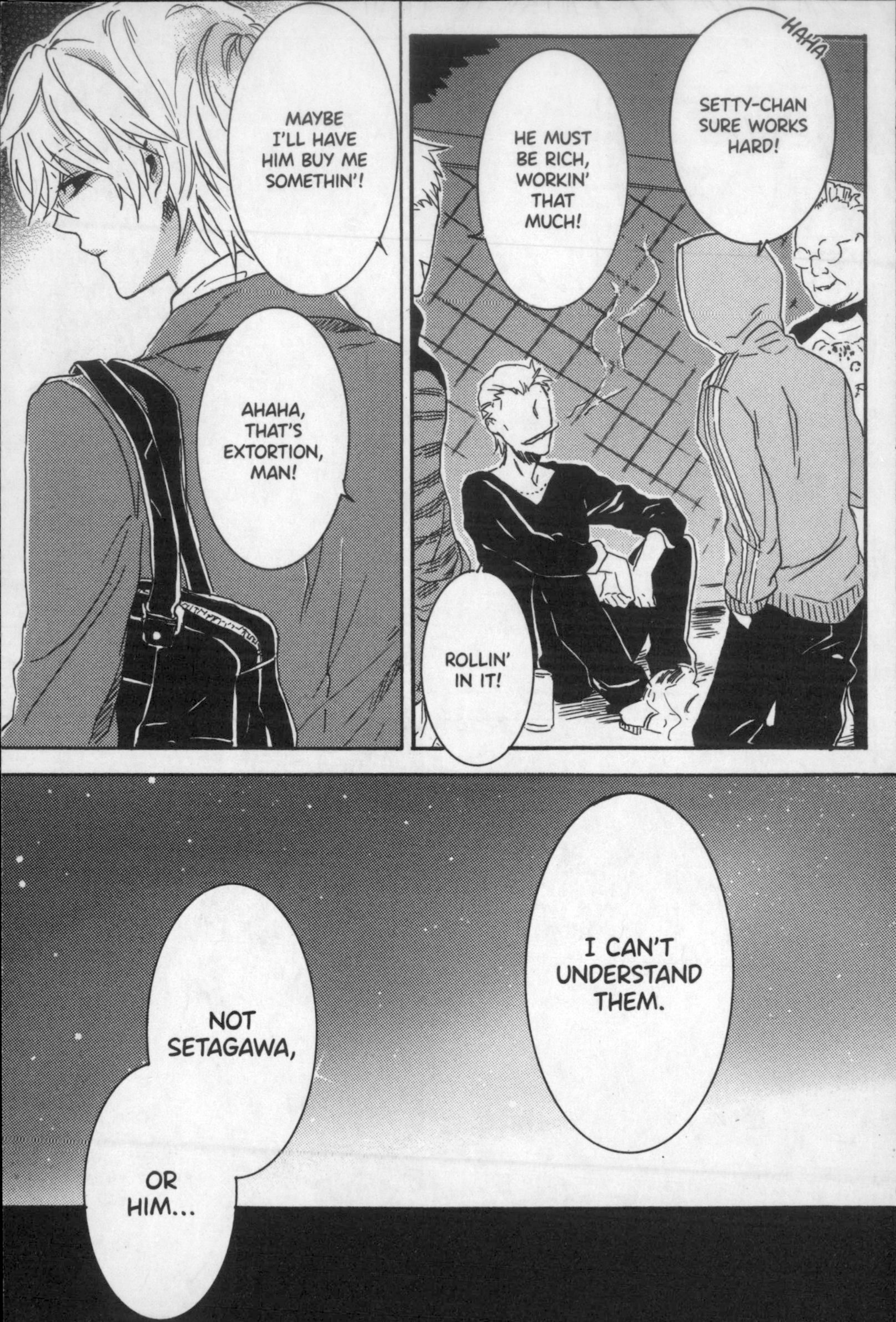
HAHA
SETTY-CHAN SURE WORKS HARD!
HE MUST BE RICH, WORKIN' THAT MUCH!
ROLLIN' IN IT!
MAYBE I'LL HAVE HIM BUY ME SOMETHIN'!
AHAHA, THAT'S EXTORTION, MAN!
I CAN'T UNDERSTAND THEM.
NOT SETAGAWA,
OR HIM...

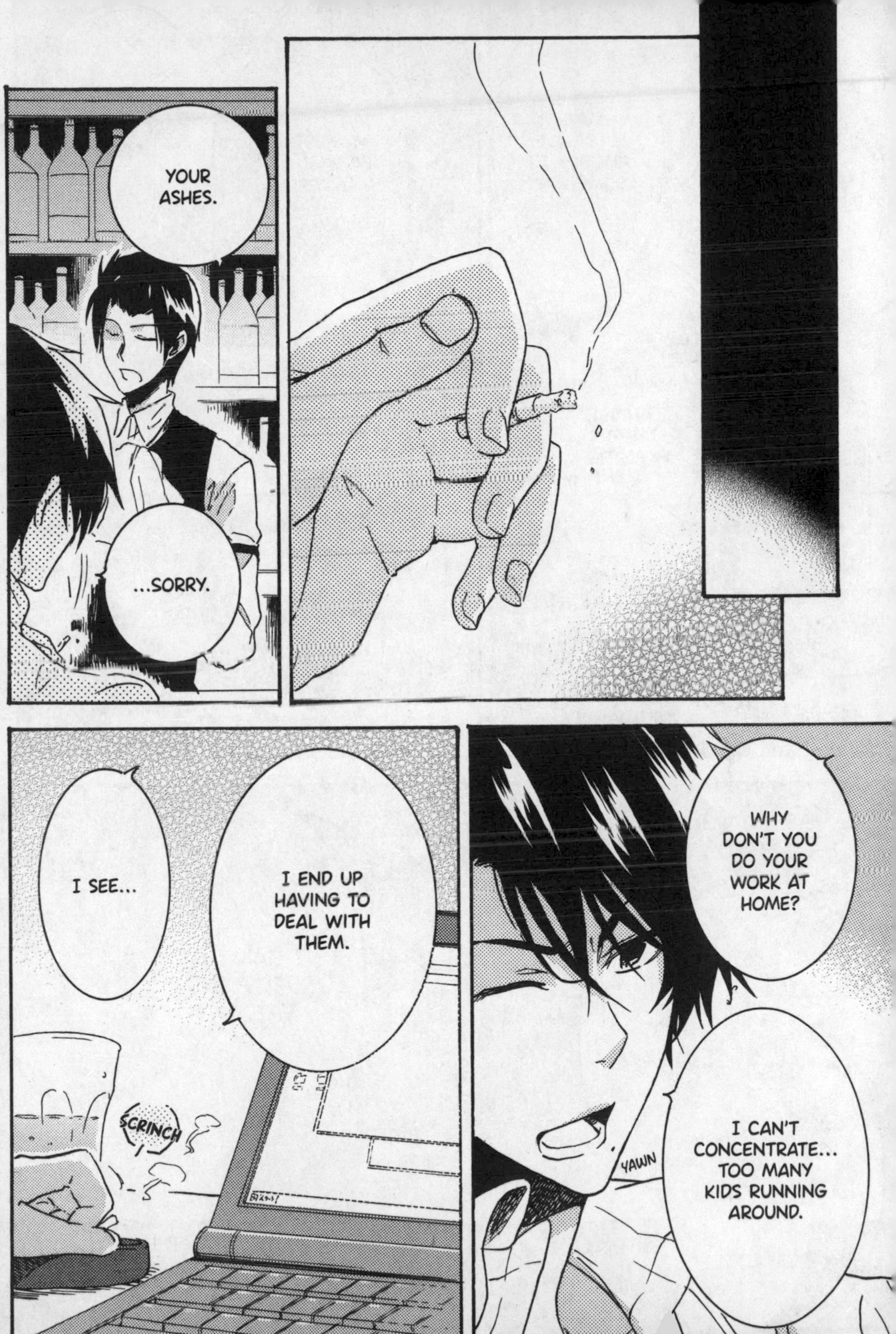
YOUR ASHES.
...SORRY.
WHY DON'T YOU DO YOUR WORK AT HOME?
YAWN
I CAN'T CONCENTRATE... TOO MANY KIDS RUNNING AROUND.
I END UP HAVING TO DEAL WITH THEM.
I SEE...
SCRINCH

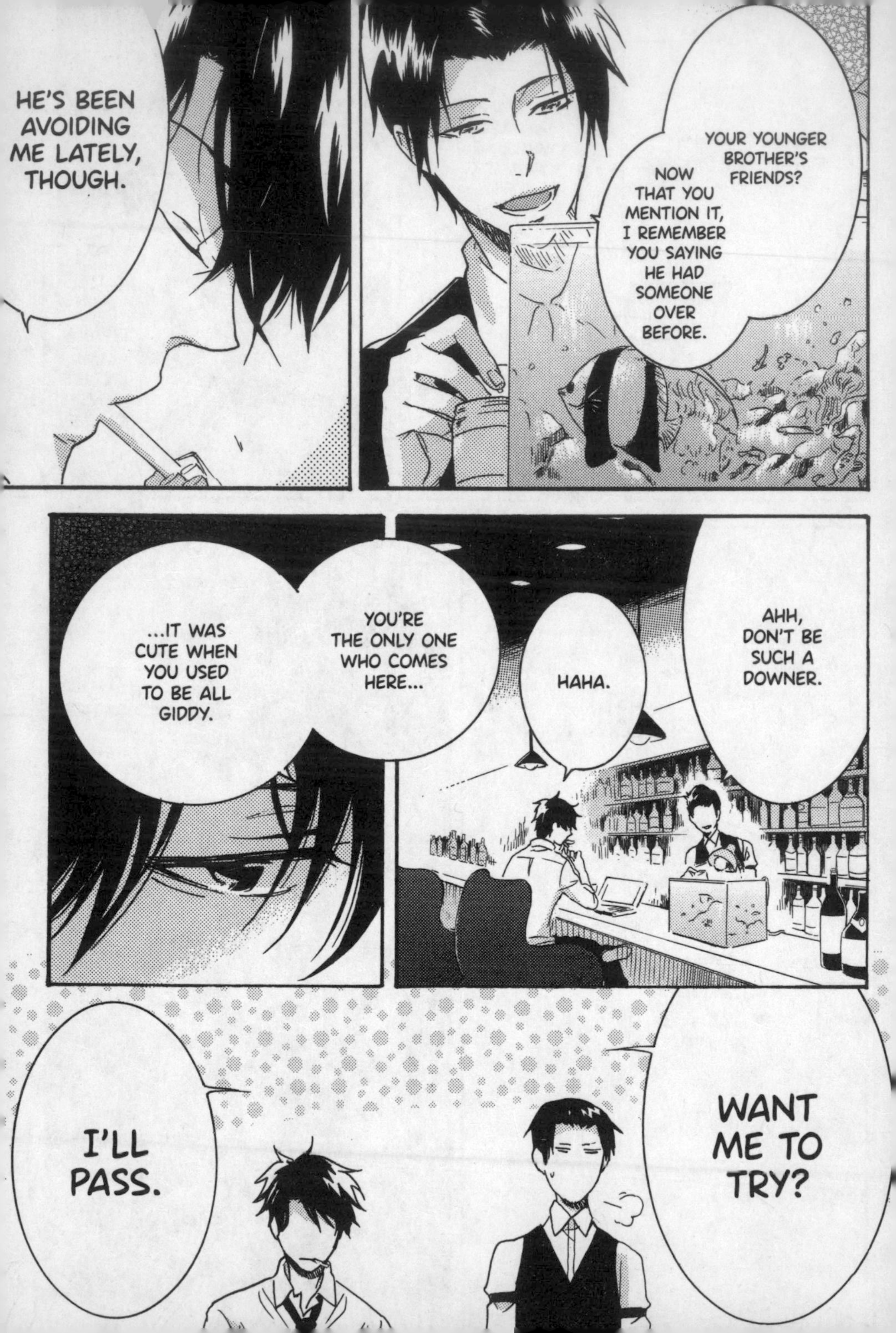
YOUR YOUNGER BROTHER'S FRIENDS?
NOW THAT YOU MENTION IT, I REMEMBER YOU SAYING HE HAD SOMEONE OVER BEFORE.
HE'S BEEN AVOIDING ME LATELY, THOUGH.
AHH, DON'T BE SUCH A DOWNER.
HAHA.
YOU'RE THE ONLY ONE WHO COMES HERE...
...IT WAS CUTE WHEN YOU USED TO BE ALL GIDDY.
WANT ME TO TRY?
I'LL PASS.

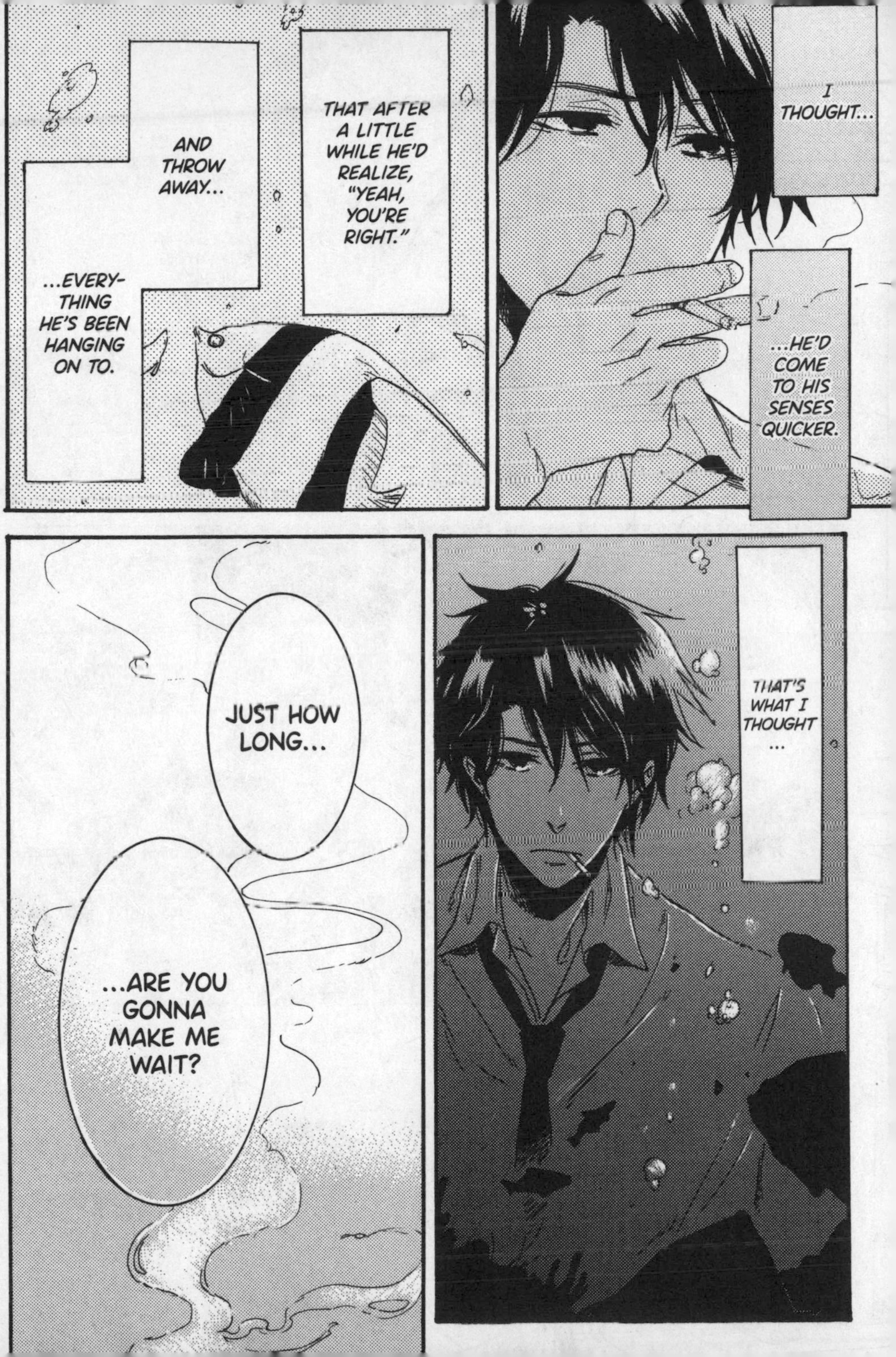
I THOUGHT...
...HE'D COME TO HIS SENSES QUICKER.
THAT AFTER A LITTLE WHILE HE'D REALIZE, "YEAH, YOU'RE RIGHT."
AND THROW AWAY...
...EVERY-THING HE'S BEEN HANGING ON TO.
THAT'S WHAT I THOUGHT...
JUST HOW LONG...
...ARE YOU GONNA MAKE ME WAIT?

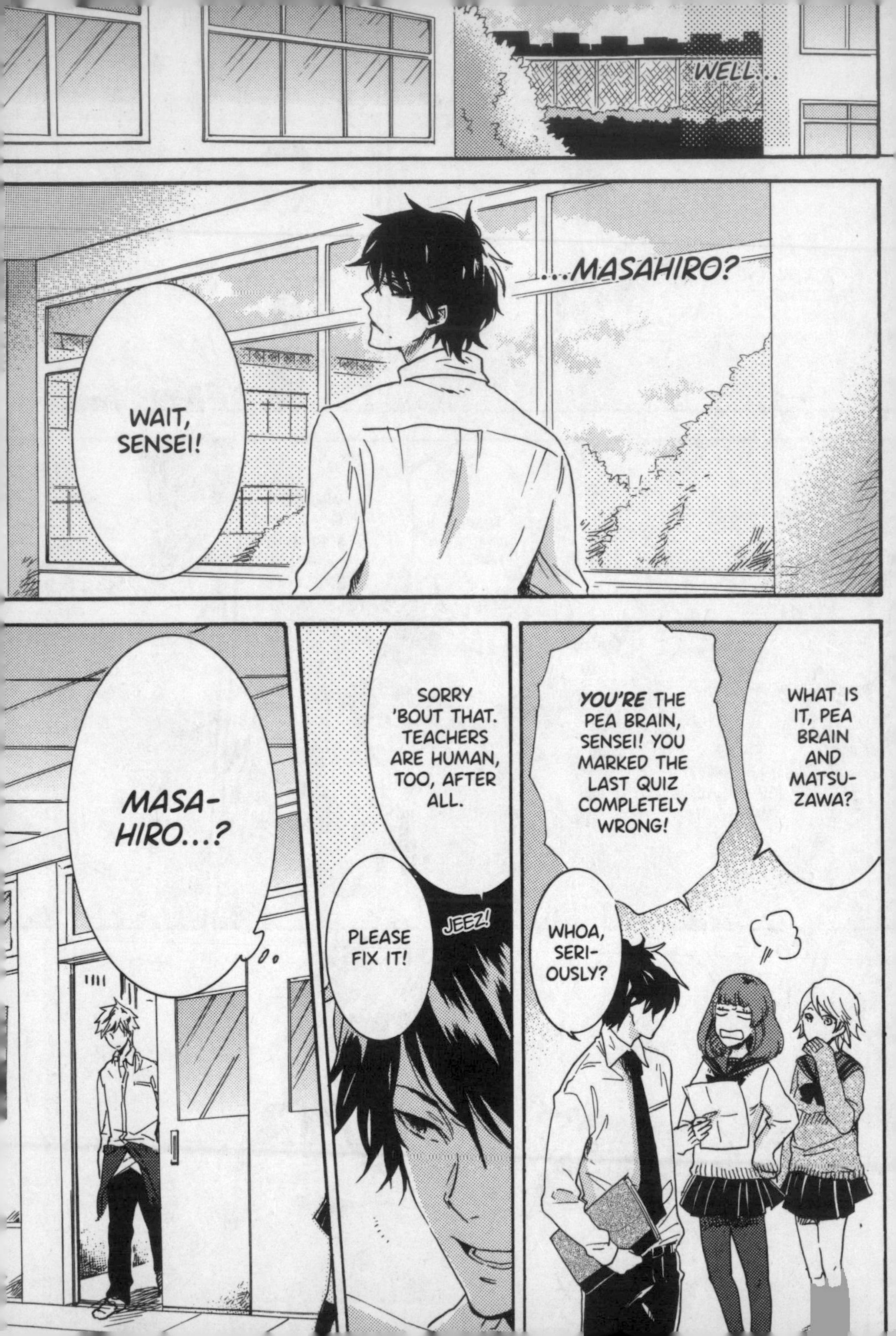
WELL...
...MASAHIRO?
WAIT, SENSEI!
WHAT IS IT, PEA BRAIN AND MATSU-ZAWA?
YOU'RE THE PEA BRAIN, SENSEI! YOU MARKED THE LAST QUIZ COMPLETELY WRONG!
WHOA, SERI-OUSLY?
SORRY 'BOUT THAT. TEACHERS ARE HUMAN, TOO, AFTER ALL.
JEEZ!
PLEASE FIX IT!
MASA-HIRO...?

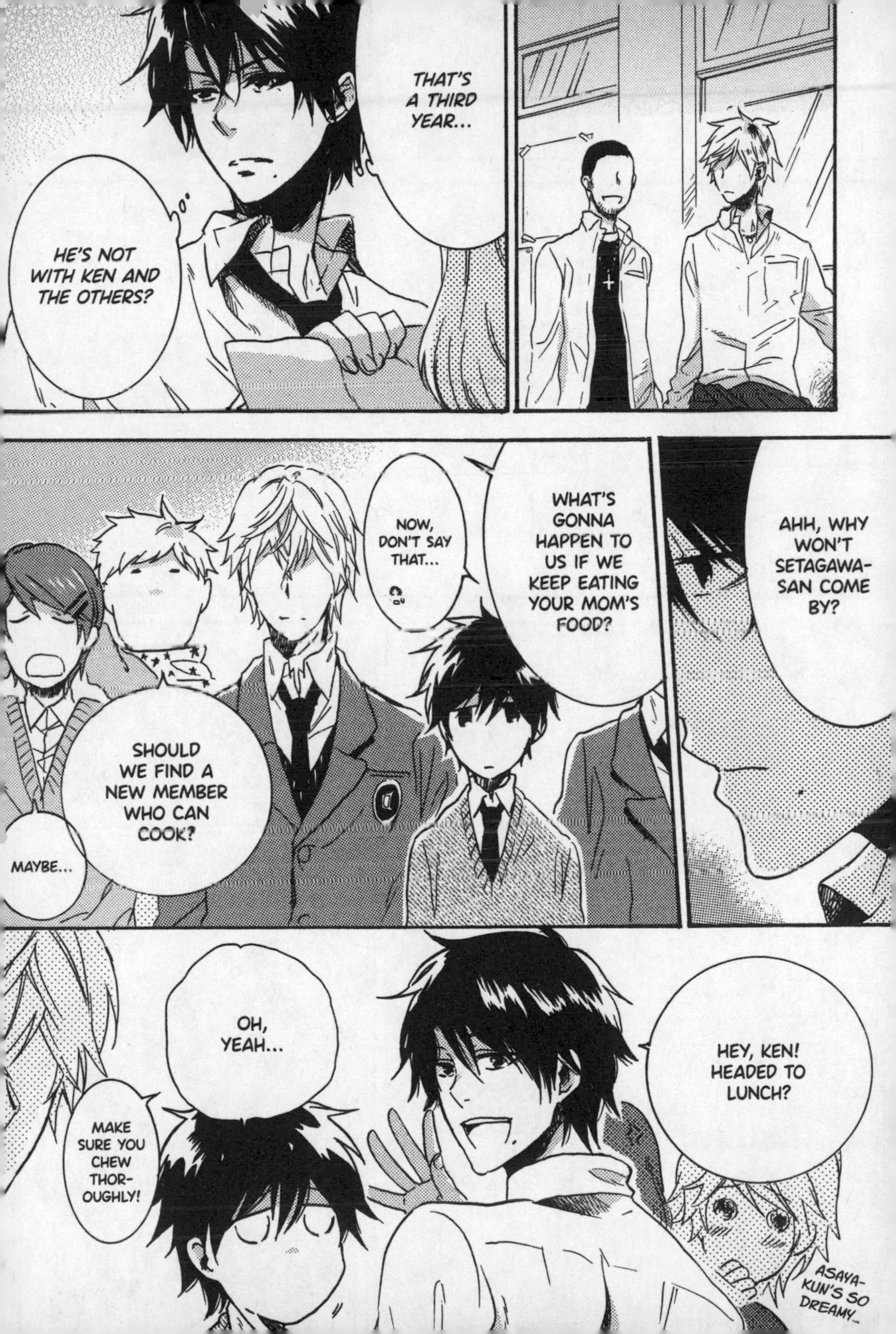
THAT'S A THIRD YEAR...
HE'S NOT WITH KEN AND THE OTHERS?
AHH, WHY WON'T SETAGAWA-SAN COME BY?
WHAT'S GONNA HAPPEN TO US IF WE KEEP EATING YOUR MOM'S FOOD?
NOW, DON'T SAY THAT...
SHOULD WE FIND A NEW MEMBER WHO CAN COOK?
MAYBE...
HEY, KEN! HEADED TO LUNCH?
ASAYA-KUN'S SO DREAMY...
OH, YEAH...
MAKE SURE YOU CHEW THOR-OUGHLY!

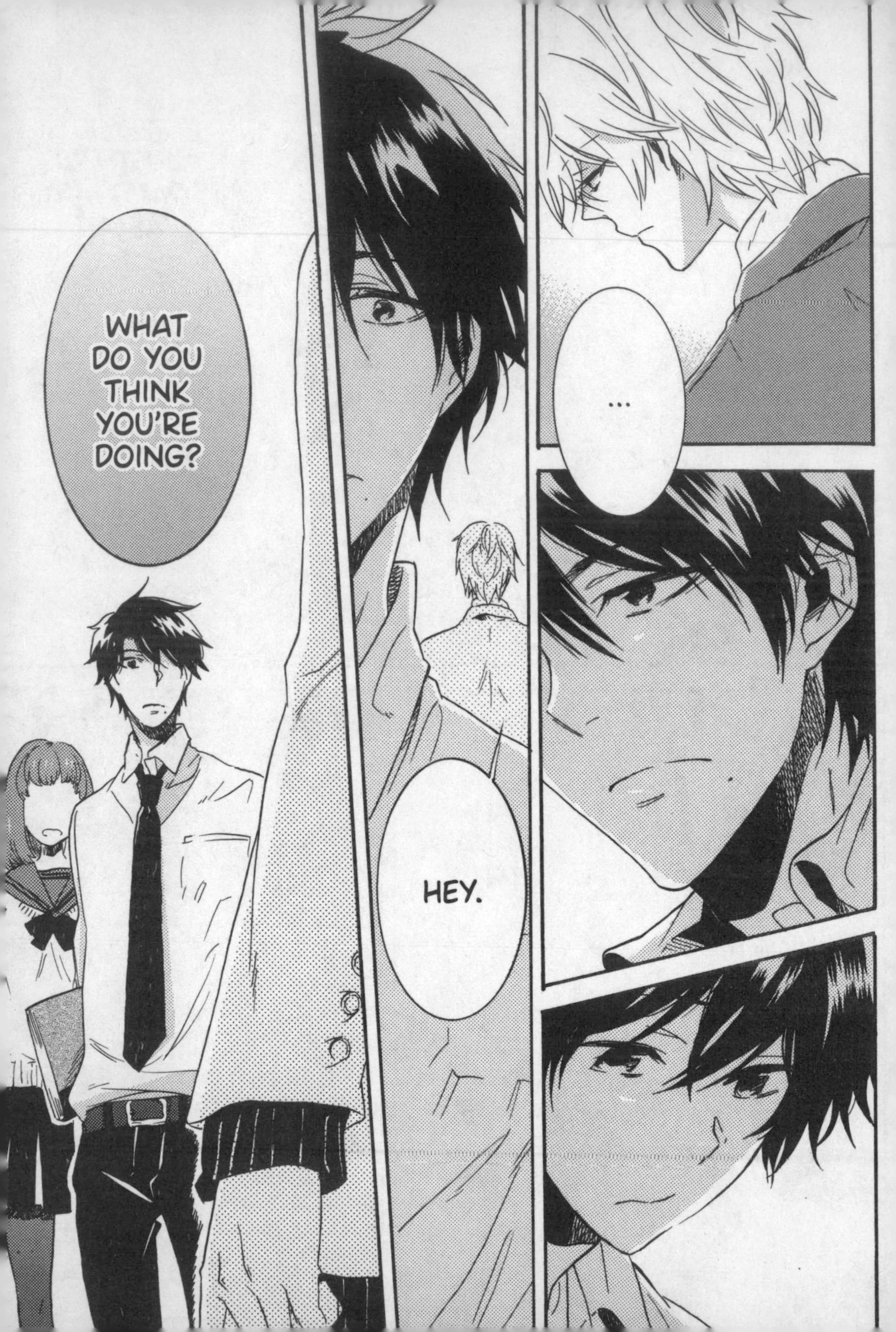
...
HEY.
WHAT DO YOU THINK YOU'RE DOING?

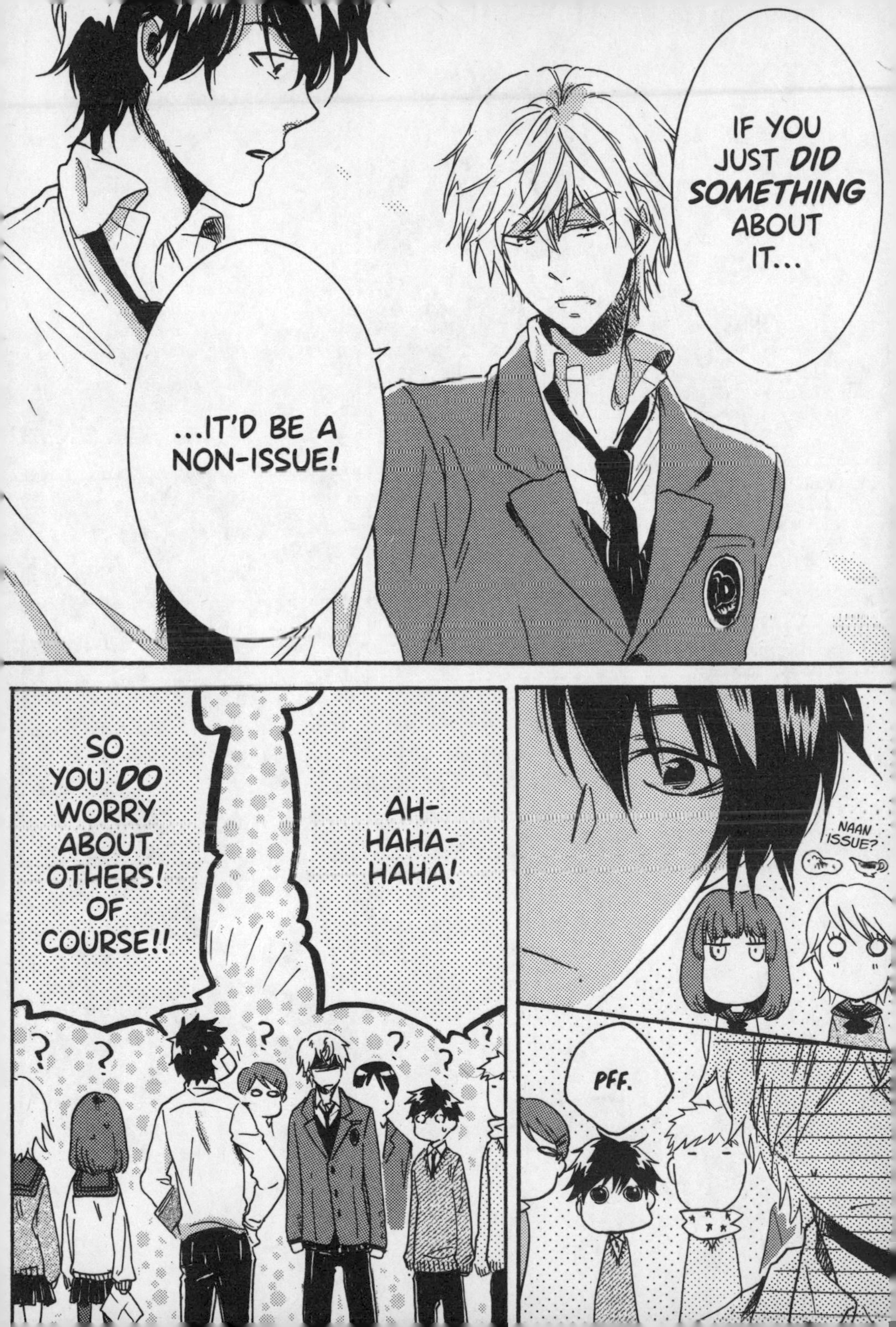
IF YOU JUST DID SOMETHING ABOUT IT...
...IT'D BE A NON-ISSUE!
NAAN ISSUE?
PFF.
AH-HAHA-HAHA!
SO YOU DO WORRY ABOUT OTHERS! OF COURSE!!

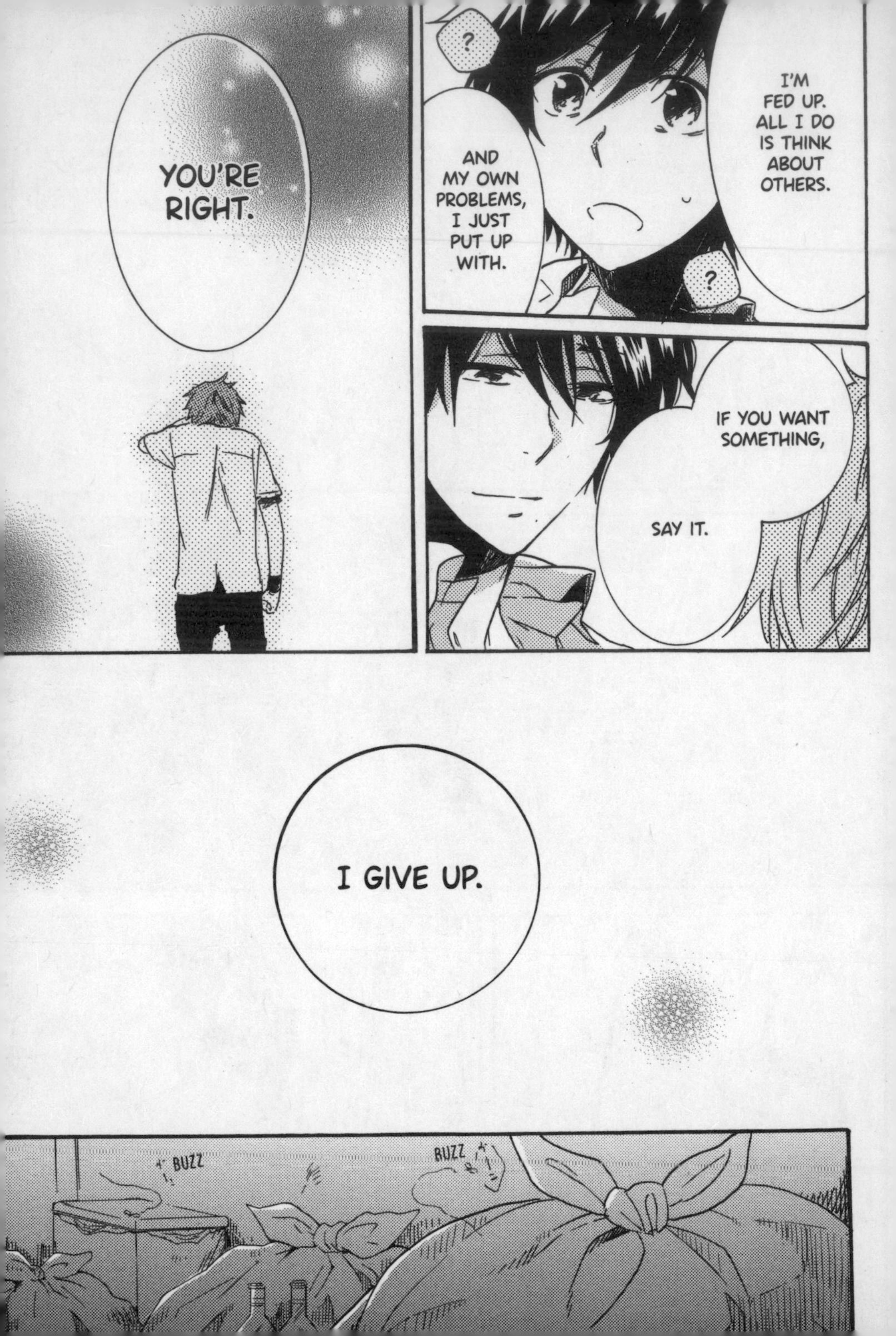
?
I'M FED UP. ALL I DO IS THINK ABOUT OTHERS.
AND MY OWN PROBLEMS, I JUST PUT UP WITH.
?
IF YOU WANT SOMETHING,
SAY IT.
YOU'RE RIGHT.
I GIVE UP.
BUZZ
BUZZ

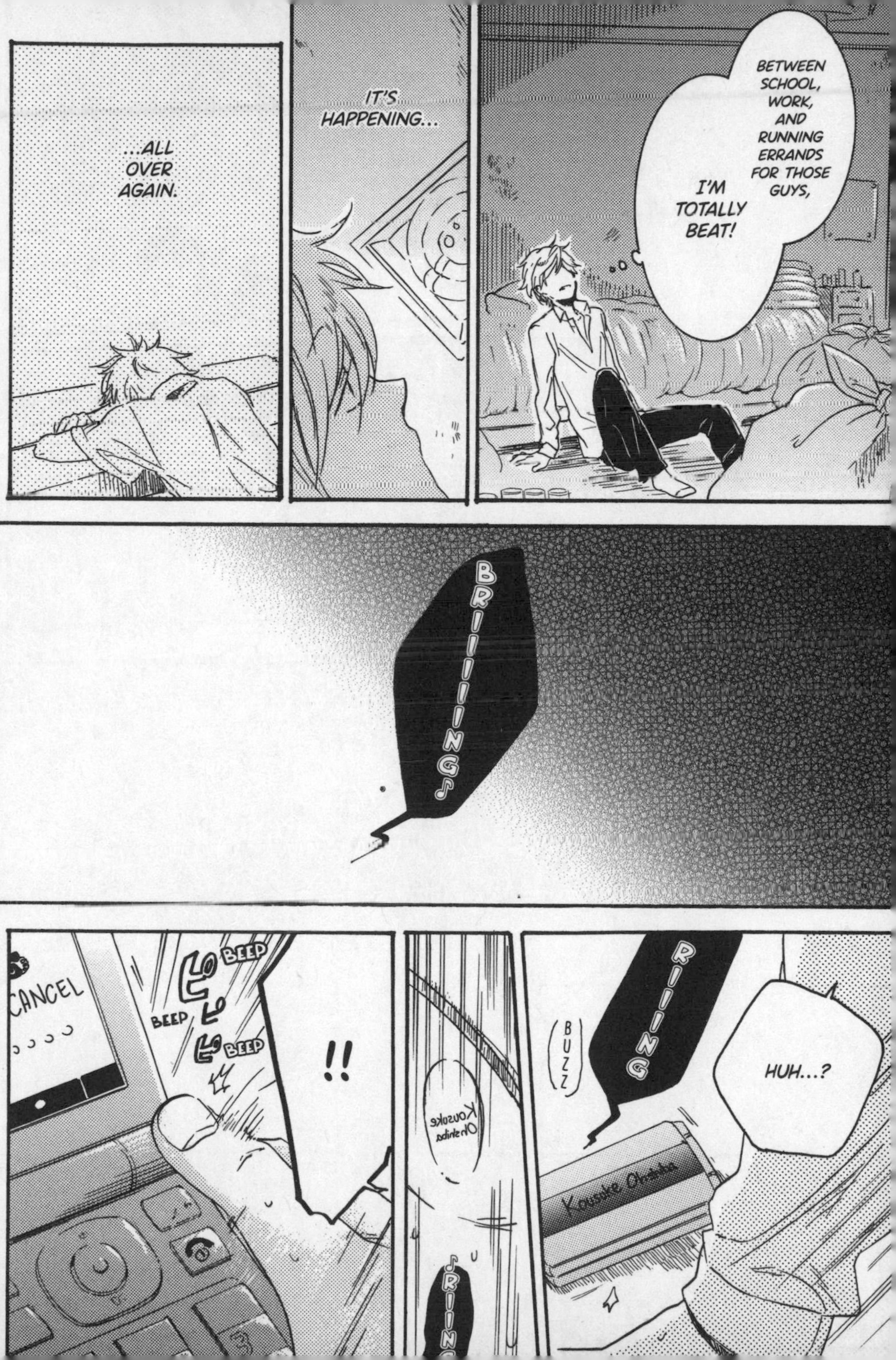
BETWEEN SCHOOL, WORK, AND RUNNING ERRANDS FOR THOSE GUYS,
I'M TOTALLY BEAT!
IT'S HAPPENING...
...ALL OVER AGAIN.
BRIIIIIING♪
HUH...?
RIIING
BUZZ
Kousuke Ohshiba
!!
BEEP
BEEP
BEEP
CANCEL

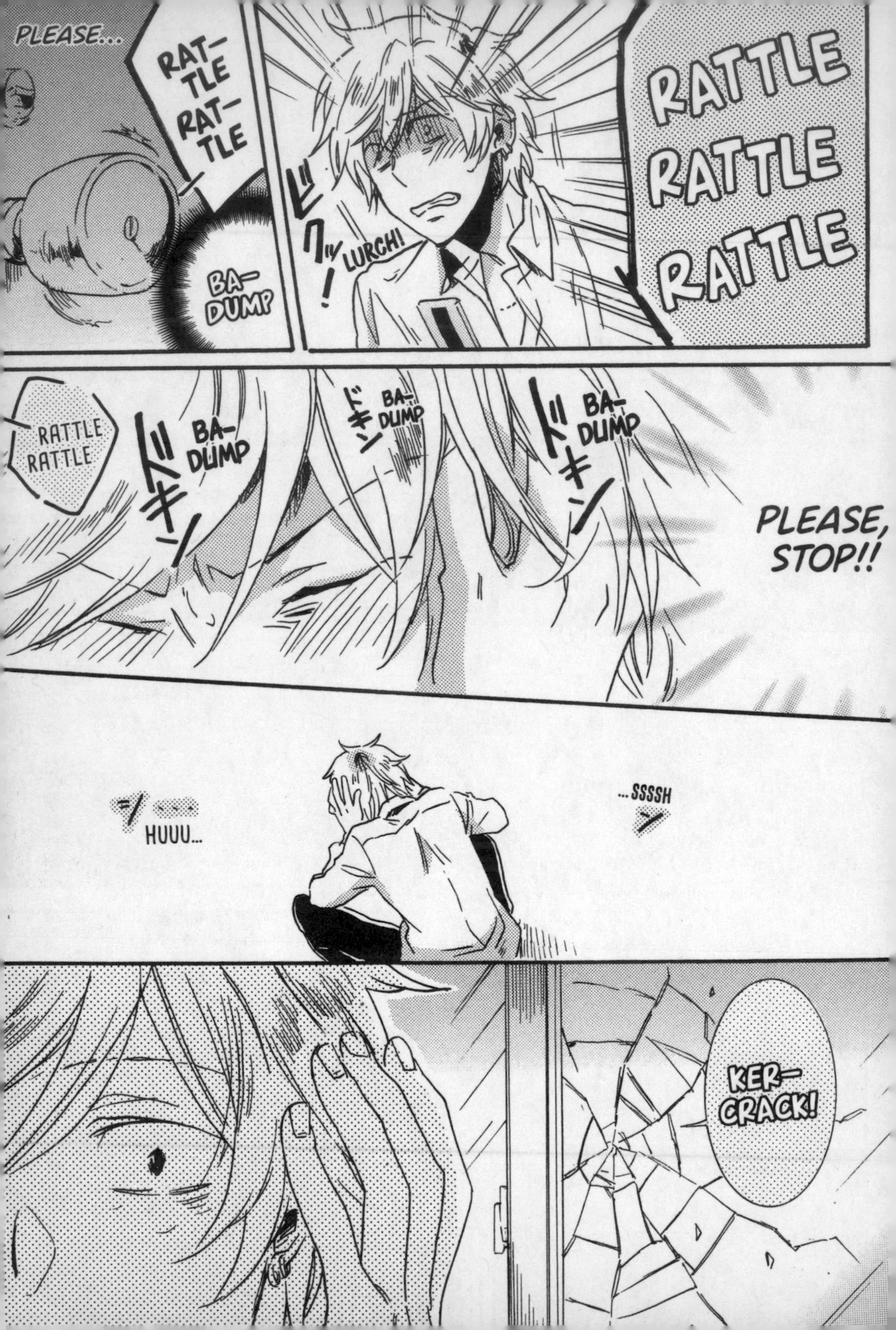
RATTLE RATTLE RATTLE
ビクッ!
LURCH!
PLEASE...
RAT-TLE RAT-TLE
BA-DUMP
PLEASE, STOP!!
ドキン
BA-DUMP
ドキン
BA-DUMP
ドキン
BA-DUMP
RATTLE RATTLE
...SSSSH
HUUU...
KER-CRACK!

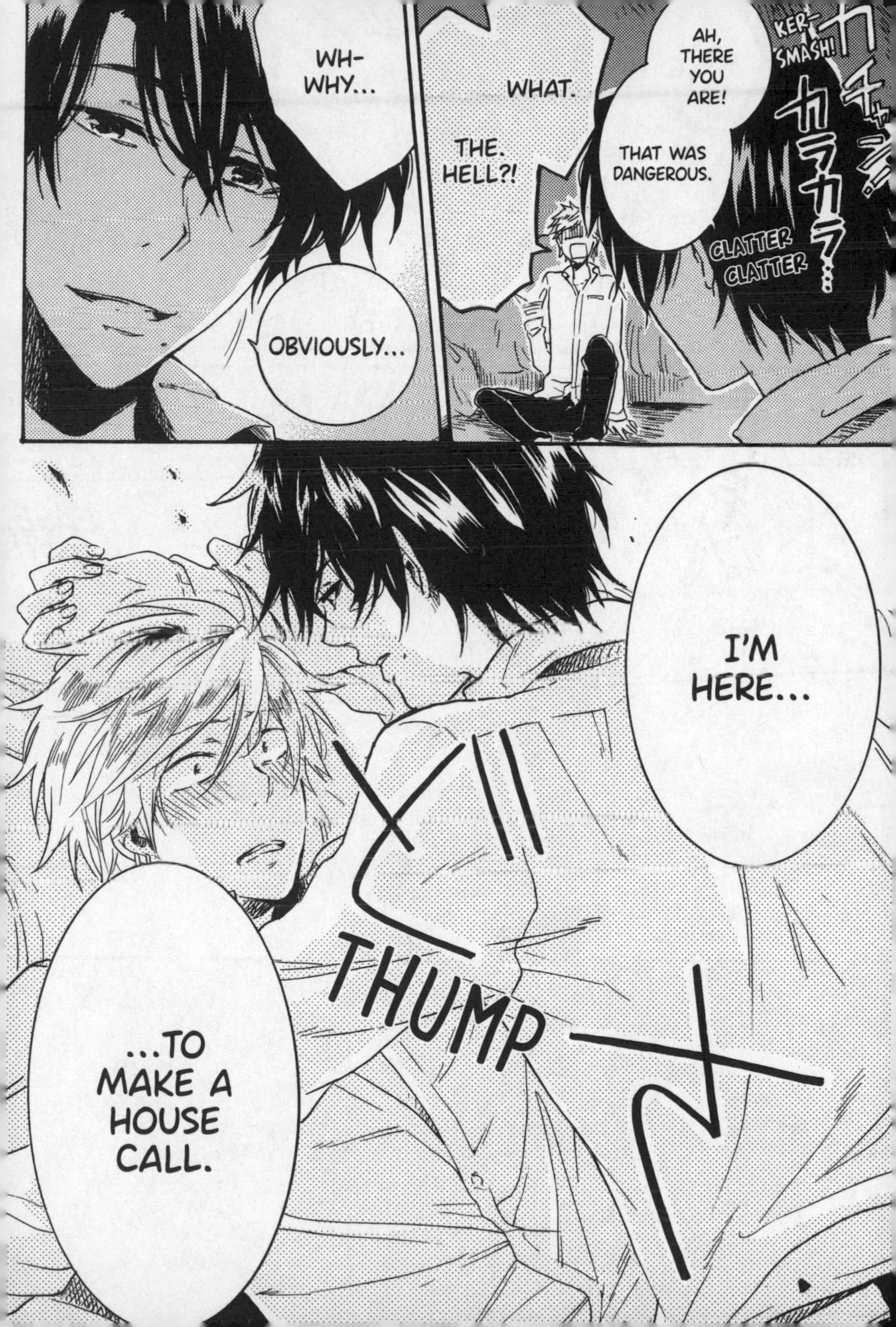

KER-SMASH!
AH, THERE YOU ARE!
THAT WAS DANGEROUS.
CLATTER CLATTER
WHAT. THE. HELL?!
WH-WHY...
OBVIOUSLY...
I'M HERE...
THUMP
...TO MAKE A HOUSE CALL.

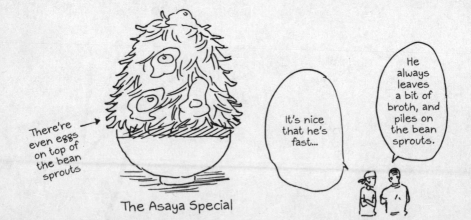

He always leaves a bit of broth, and piles on the bean sprouts.
It's nice that he's fast...
There're even eggs on top of the bean sprouts
The Asaya Special

Hitorijime
My Hero

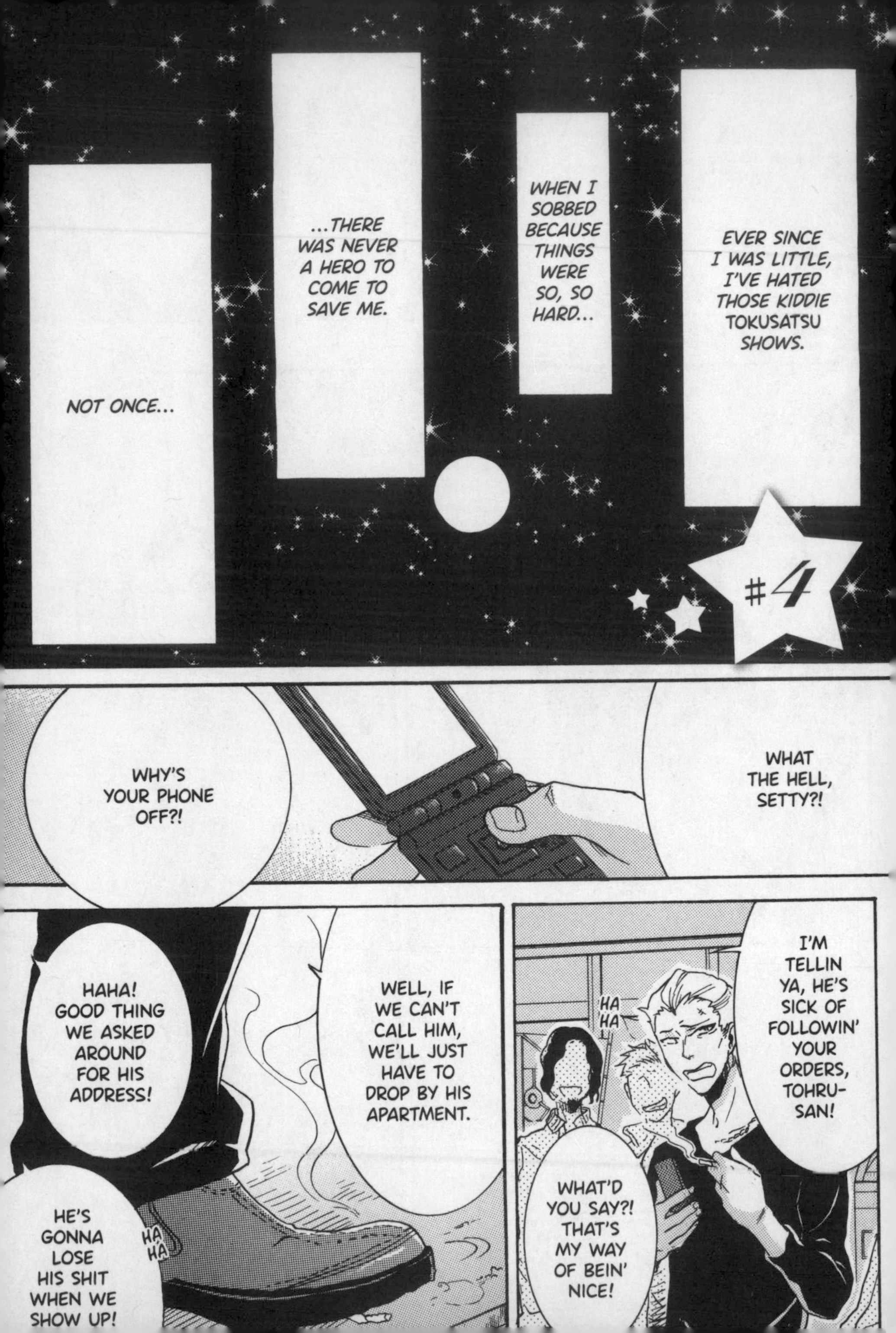
EVER SINCE I WAS LITTLE, I'VE HATED THOSE KIDDIE TOKUSATSU SHOWS.
WHEN I SOBBED BECAUSE THINGS WERE SO, SO HARD...
...THERE WAS NEVER A HERO TO COME TO SAVE ME.
NOT ONCE...
#4
WHAT THE HELL, SETTY?!
WHY'S YOUR PHONE OFF?!
I'M TELLIN YA, HE'S SICK OF FOLLOWIN' YOUR ORDERS, TOHRU-SAN!
HA HA
WHAT'D YOU SAY?! THAT'S MY WAY OF BEIN' NICE!
WELL, IF WE CAN'T CALL HIM, WE'LL JUST HAVE TO DROP BY HIS APARTMENT.
HAHA! GOOD THING WE ASKED AROUND FOR HIS ADDRESS!
HA HA
HE'S GONNA LOSE HIS SHIT WHEN WE SHOW UP!

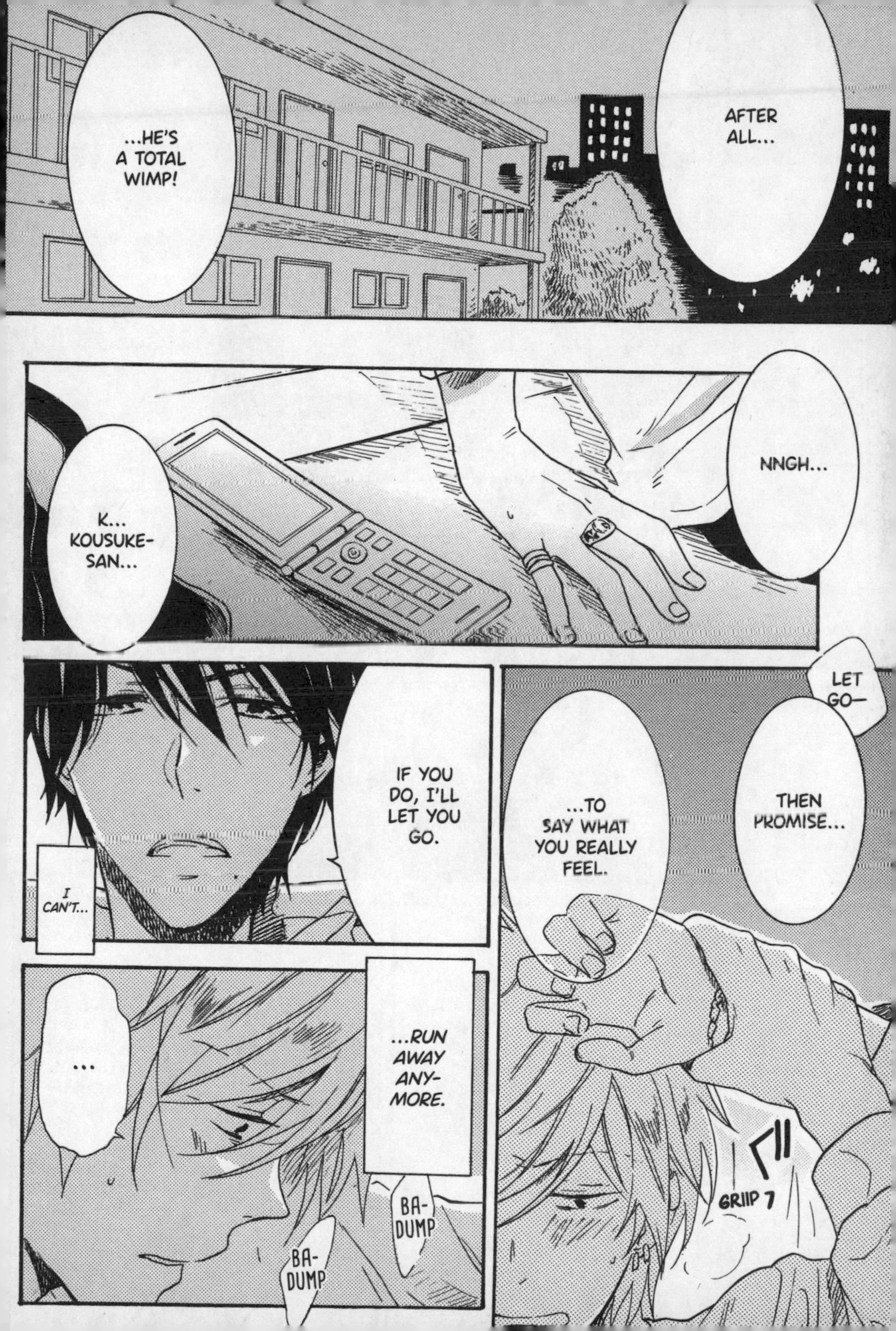
AFTER ALL...
...HE'S A TOTAL WIMP!
NNGH...
K... KOUSUKE-SAN...
LET GO—
THEN PROMISE...
...TO SAY WHAT YOU REALLY FEEL.
GRIIP
IF YOU DO, I'LL LET YOU GO.
I CAN'T...
...RUN AWAY ANYMORE.
...
BA-DUMP
BA-DUMP

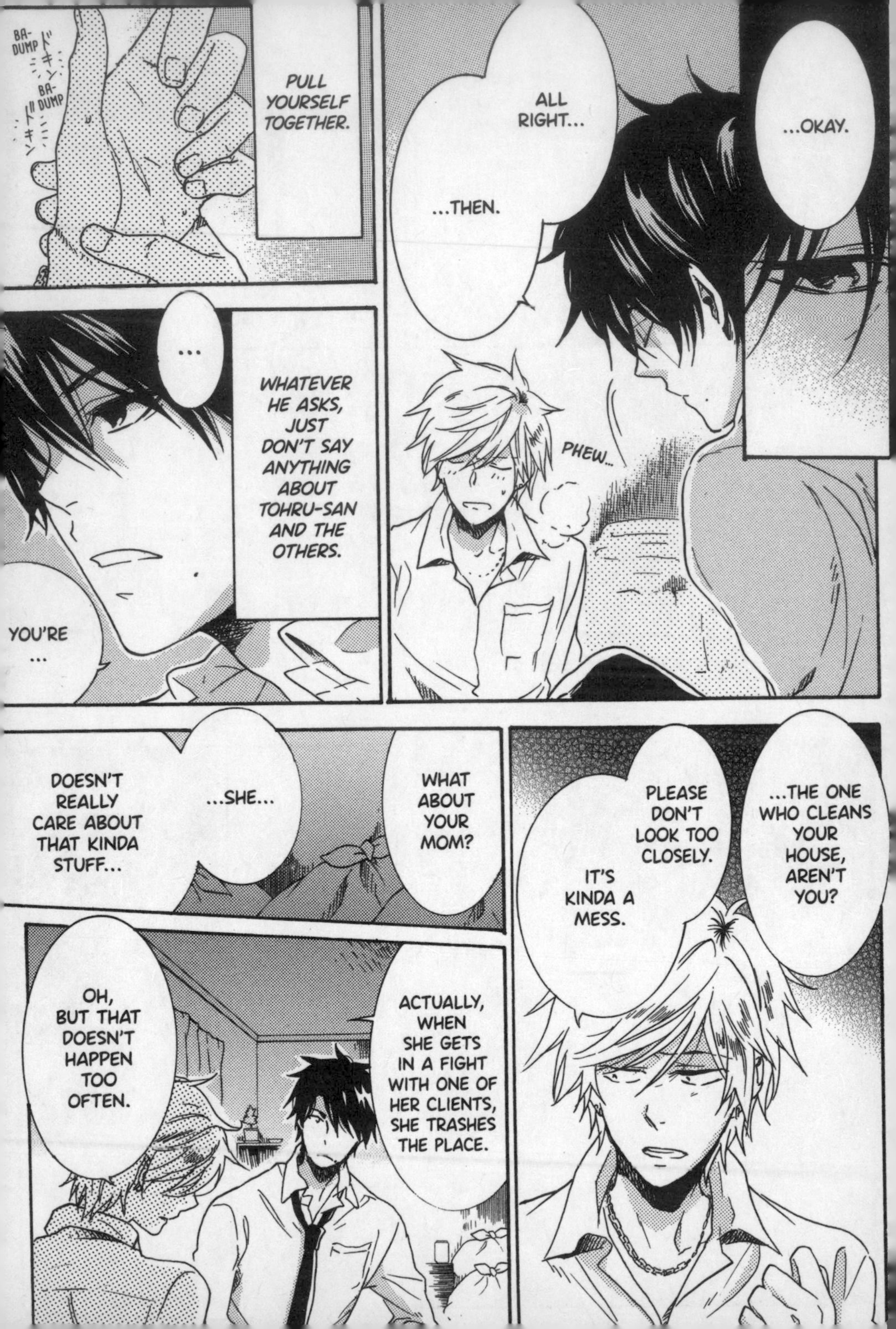
...OKAY.
ALL RIGHT...
...THEN.
PHEW...
PULL YOURSELF TOGETHER.
BA-DUMP ドキン
BA-DUMP ドキン
...
WHATEVER HE ASKS, JUST DON'T SAY ANYTHING ABOUT TOHRU-SAN AND THE OTHERS.
YOU'RE ...
...THE ONE WHO CLEANS YOUR HOUSE, AREN'T YOU?
PLEASE DON'T LOOK TOO CLOSELY.
IT'S KINDA A MESS.
WHAT ABOUT YOUR MOM?
...SHE...
DOESN'T REALLY CARE ABOUT THAT KINDA STUFF...
ACTUALLY, WHEN SHE GETS IN A FIGHT WITH ONE OF HER CLIENTS, SHE TRASHES THE PLACE.
OH, BUT THAT DOESN'T HAPPEN TOO OFTEN.

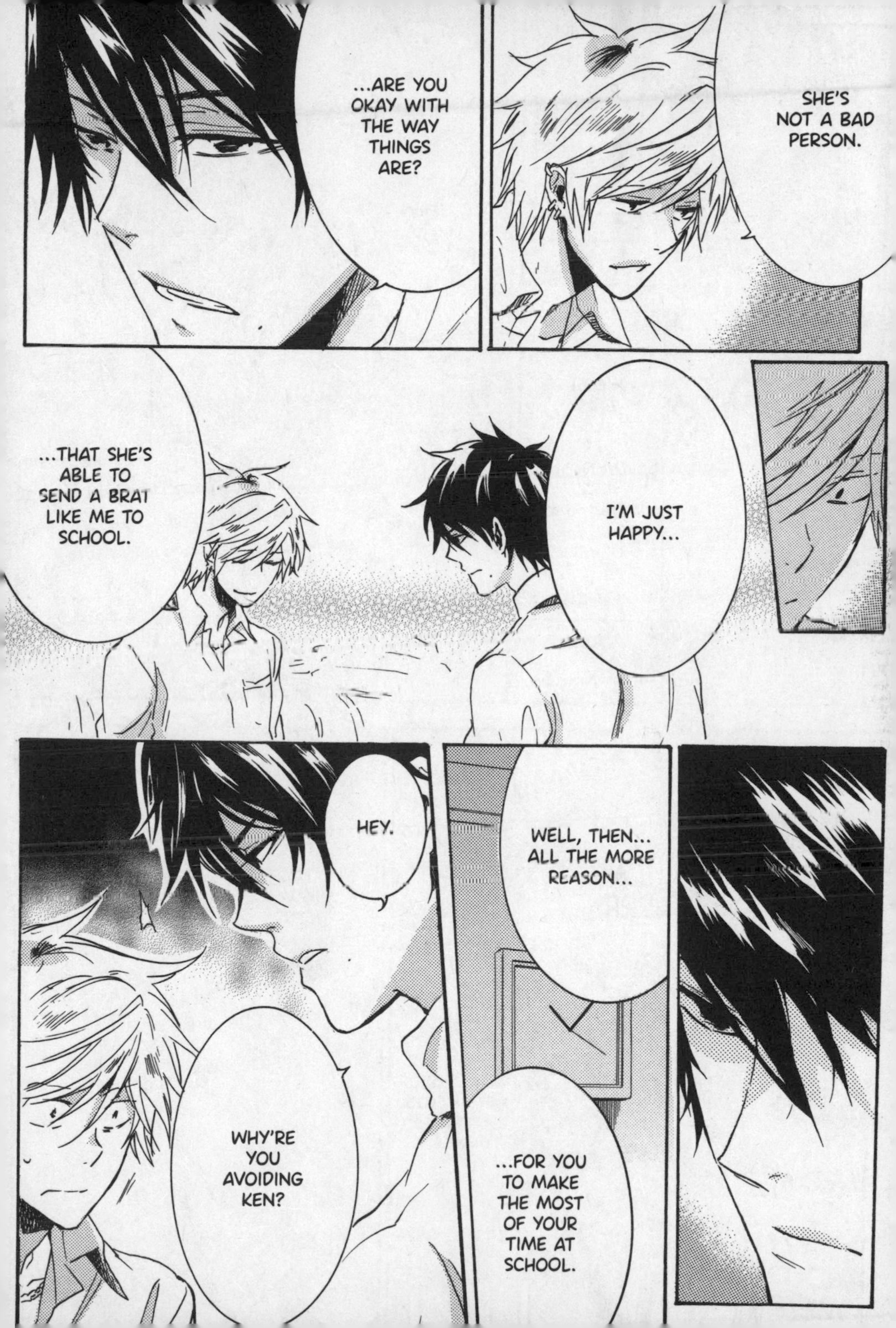
SHE'S NOT A BAD PERSON.
...ARE YOU OKAY WITH THE WAY THINGS ARE?
I'M JUST HAPPY...
...THAT SHE'S ABLE TO SEND A BRAT LIKE ME TO SCHOOL.
WELL, THEN... ALL THE MORE REASON...
...FOR YOU TO MAKE THE MOST OF YOUR TIME AT SCHOOL.
HEY.
WHY'RE YOU AVOIDING KEN?

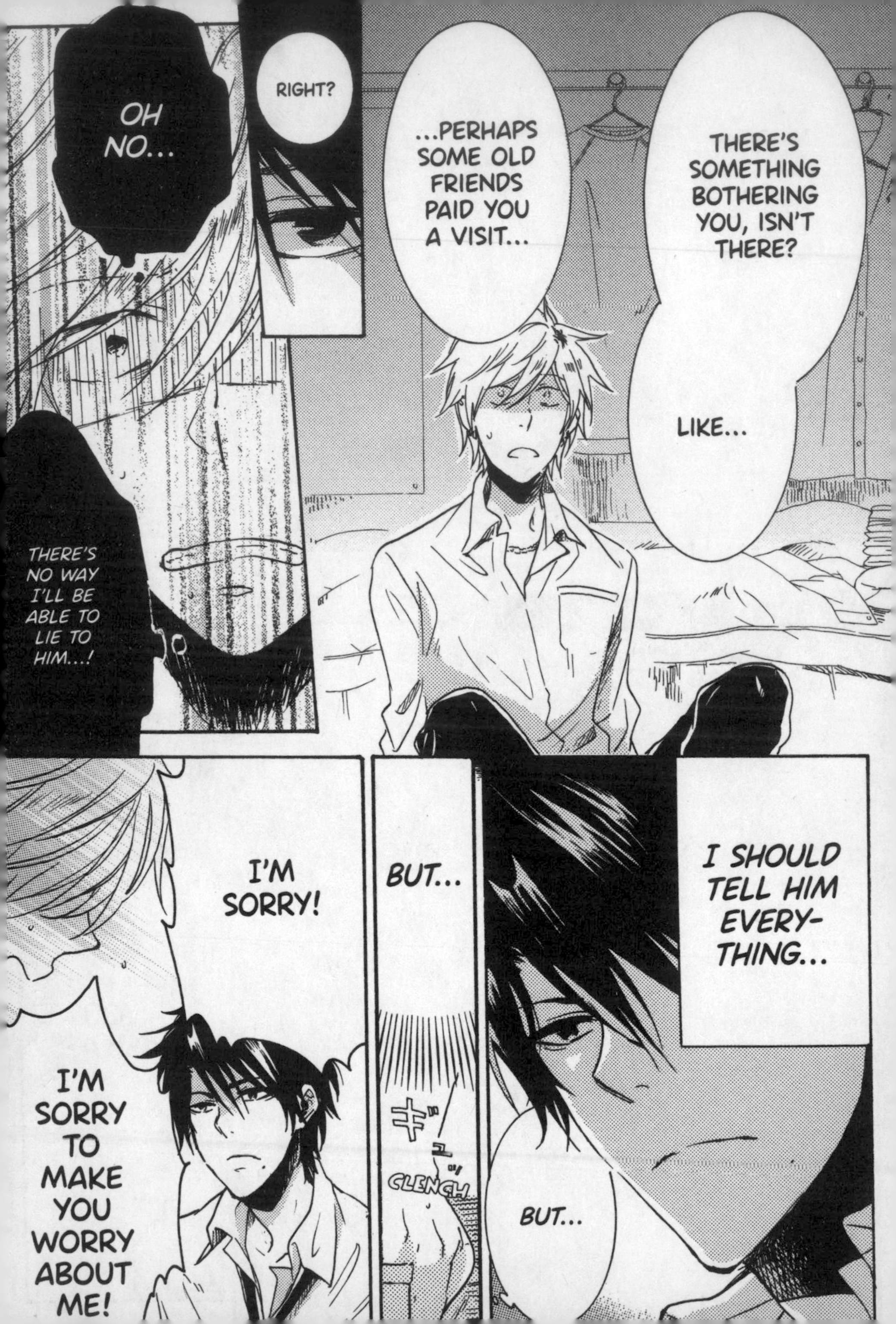
THERE'S SOMETHING BOTHERING YOU, ISN'T THERE?
LIKE...
...PERHAPS SOME OLD FRIENDS PAID YOU A VISIT...
RIGHT?
OH NO...
THERE'S NO WAY I'LL BE ABLE TO LIE TO HIM...!
I SHOULD TELL HIM EVERY-THING...
BUT...
BUT...
CLENCH
I'M SORRY!
I'M SORRY TO MAKE YOU WORRY ABOUT ME!

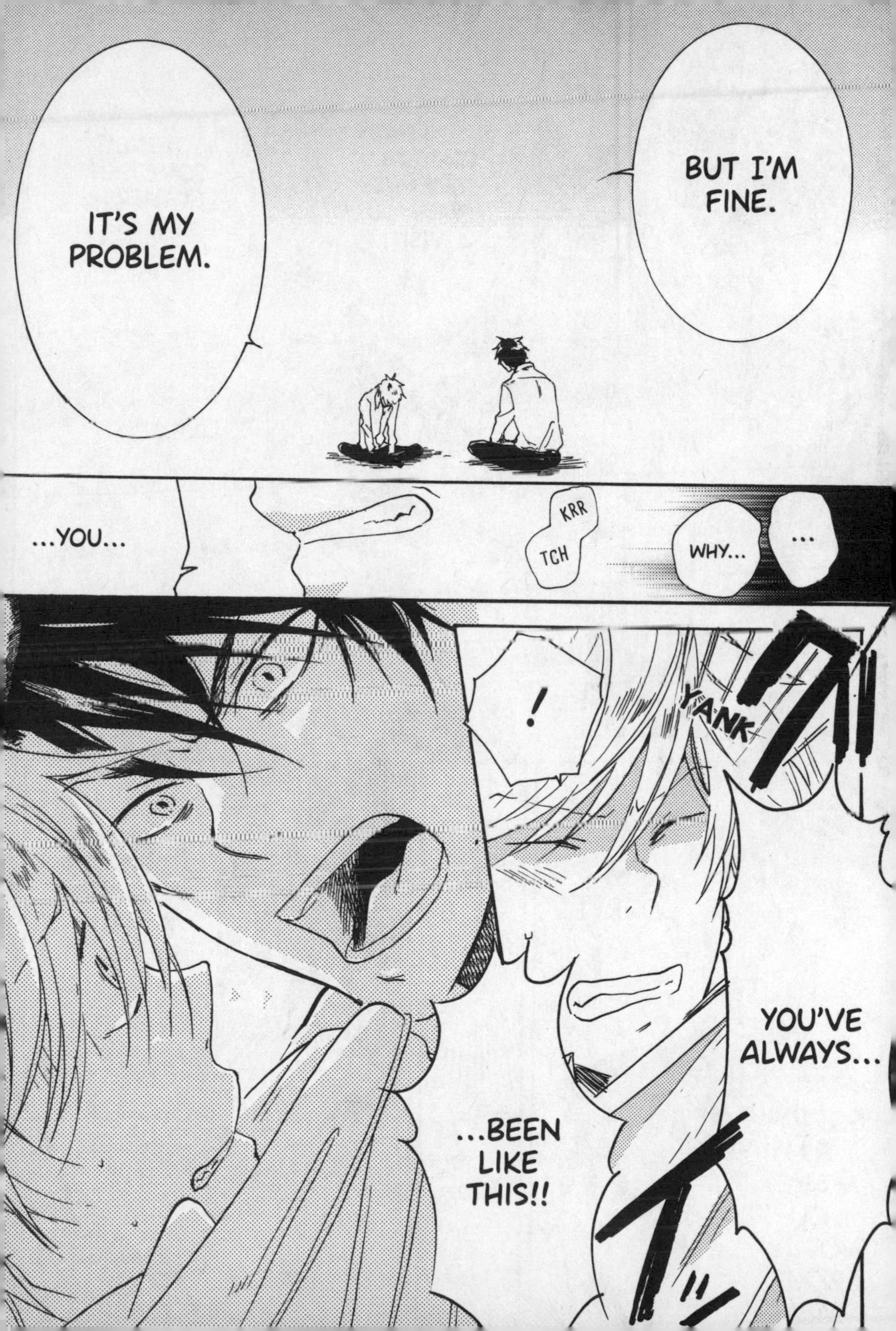
BUT I'M FINE.
IT'S MY PROBLEM.
...
WHY...
KRR
TCH
...YOU...
!
YANK
YOU'VE ALWAYS...
...BEEN LIKE THIS!!

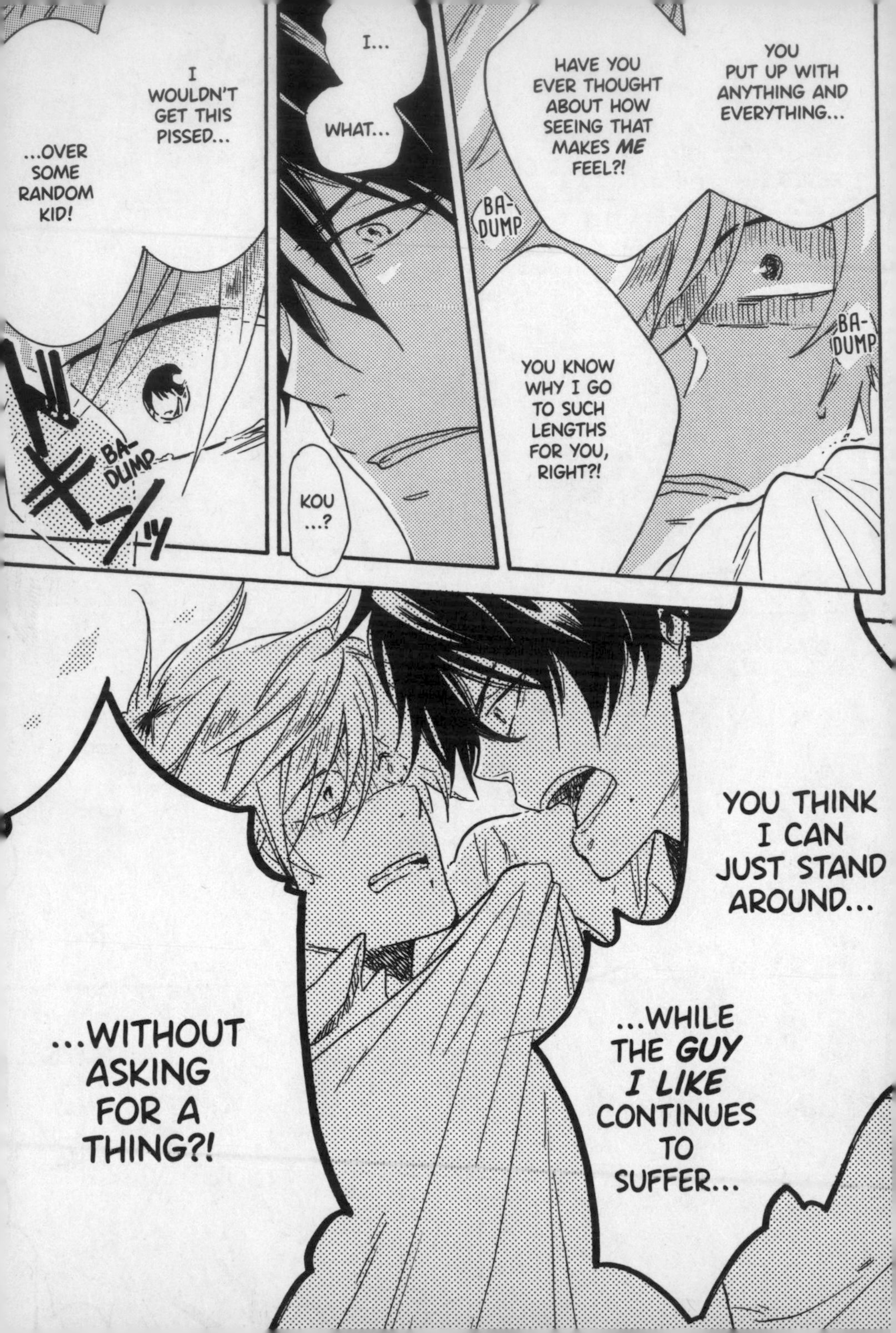
YOU PUT UP WITH ANYTHING AND EVERYTHING...
HAVE YOU EVER THOUGHT ABOUT HOW SEEING THAT MAKES *ME* FEEL?!
BA-DUMP
BA-DUMP
YOU KNOW WHY I GO TO SUCH LENGTHS FOR YOU, RIGHT?!
I...
WHAT...
KOU ...?
I WOULDN'T GET THIS PISSED...
...OVER SOME RANDOM KID!
BA-DUMP
YOU THINK I CAN JUST STAND AROUND...
...WHILE THE *GUY I LIKE* CONTINUES TO SUFFER...
...WITHOUT ASKING FOR A THING?!

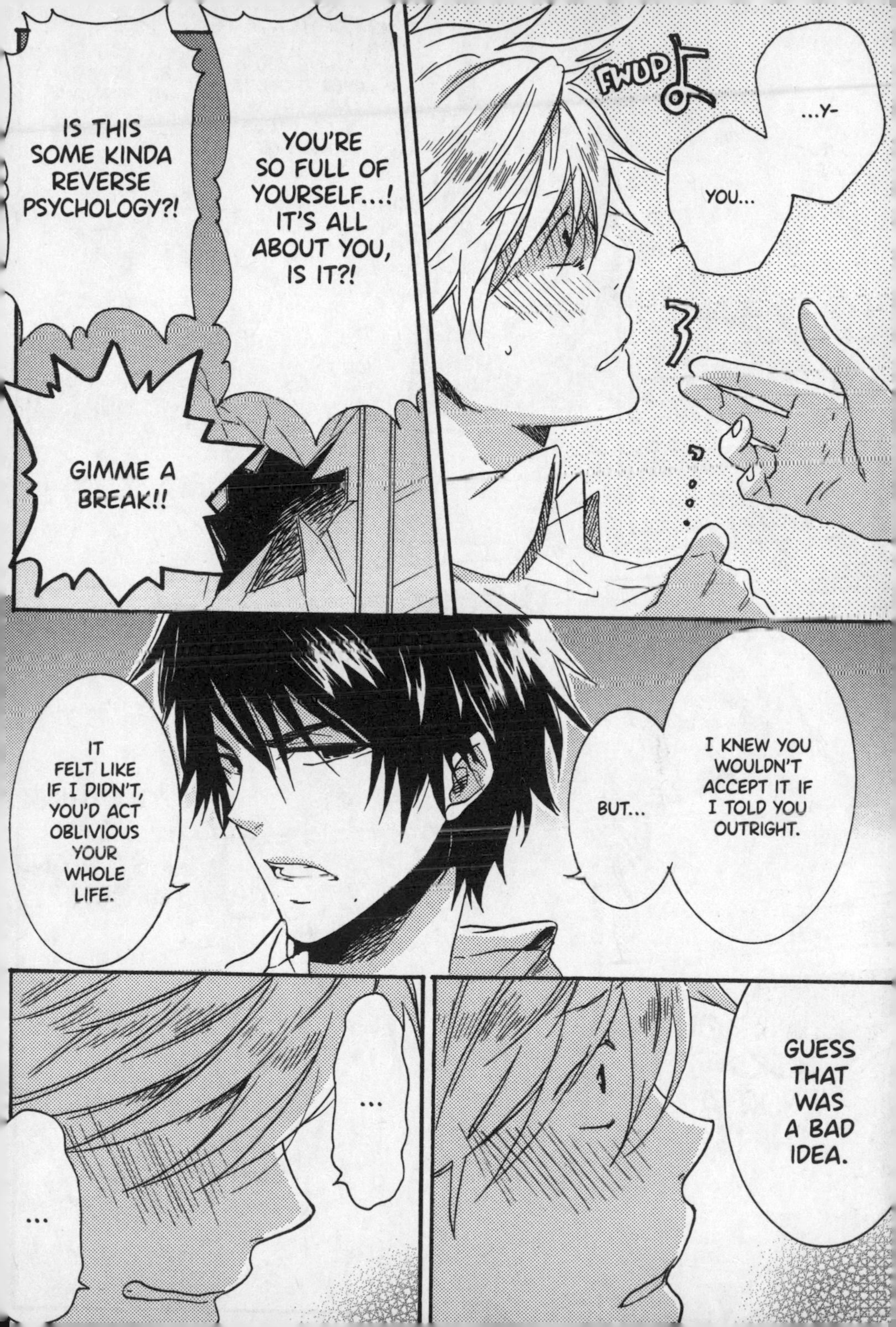
FWUP
...Y-
YOU...
YOU'RE SO FULL OF YOURSELF...! IT'S ALL ABOUT YOU, IS IT?!
IS THIS SOME KINDA REVERSE PSYCHOLOGY?!
GIMME A BREAK!!
I KNEW YOU WOULDN'T ACCEPT IT IF I TOLD YOU OUTRIGHT.
BUT...
IT FELT LIKE IF I DIDN'T, YOU'D ACT OBLIVIOUS YOUR WHOLE LIFE.
GUESS THAT WAS A BAD IDEA.
...
...

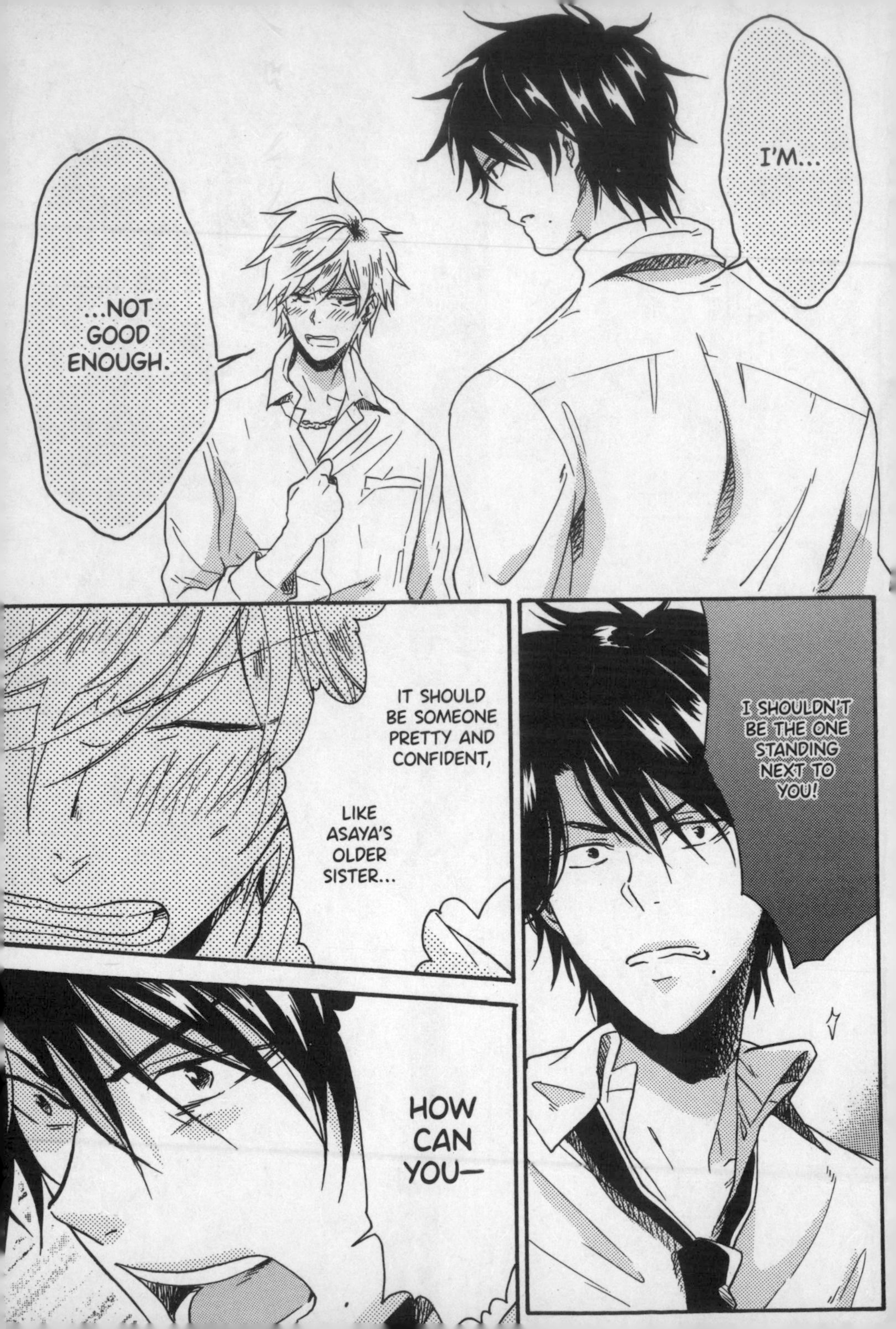
I'M...
...NOT GOOD ENOUGH.
I SHOULDN'T BE THE ONE STANDING NEXT TO YOU!
IT SHOULD BE SOMEONE PRETTY AND CONFIDENT,
LIKE ASAYA'S OLDER SISTER...
HOW CAN YOU—

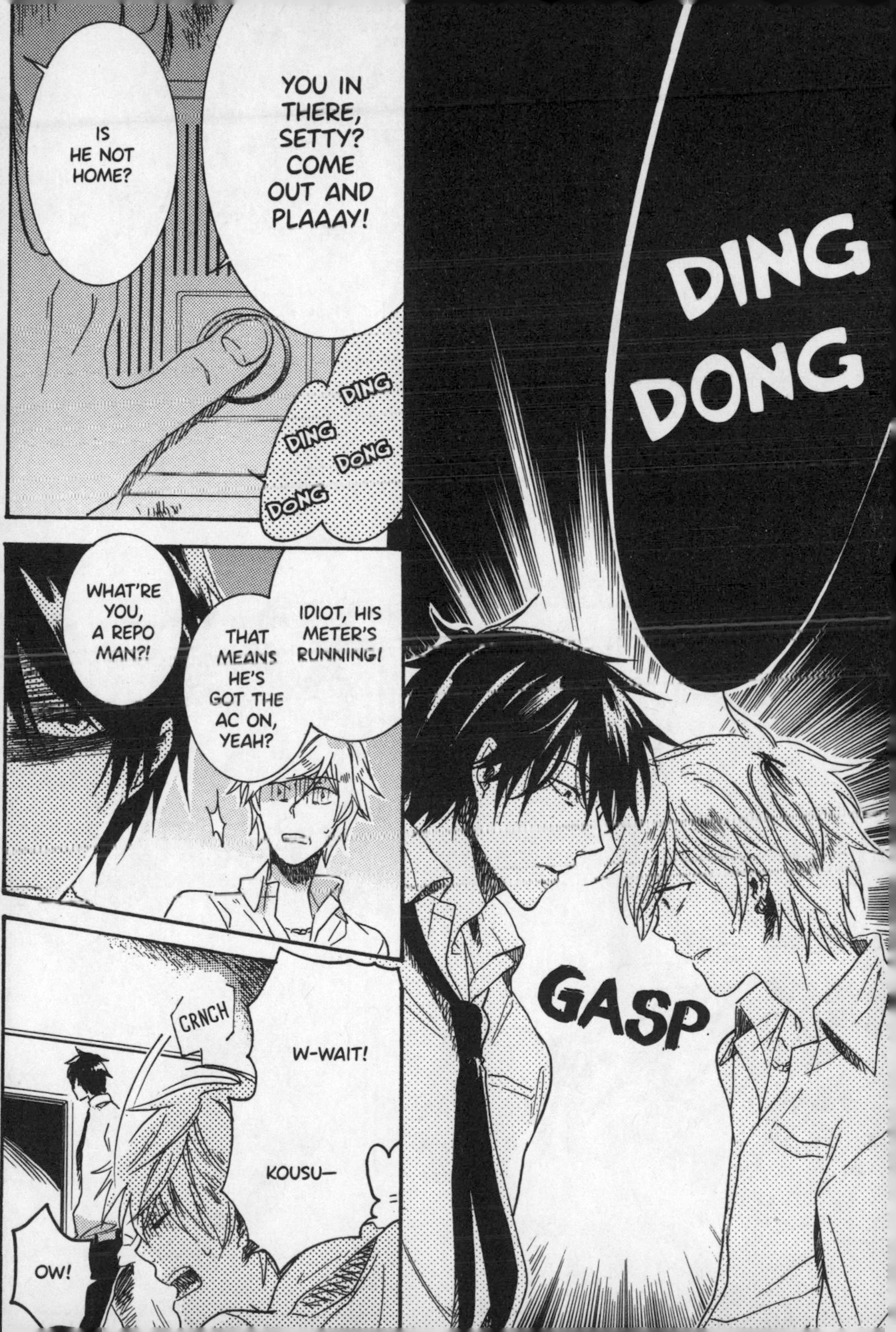
DING DONG
GASP
YOU IN THERE, SETTY? COME OUT AND PLAAAY!
IS HE NOT HOME?
DING DING DONG DONG
IDIOT, HIS METER'S RUNNING!
THAT MEANS HE'S GOT THE AC ON, YEAH?
WHAT'RE YOU, A REPO MAN?!
W-WAIT!
CRNCH
KOUSU–
OW!

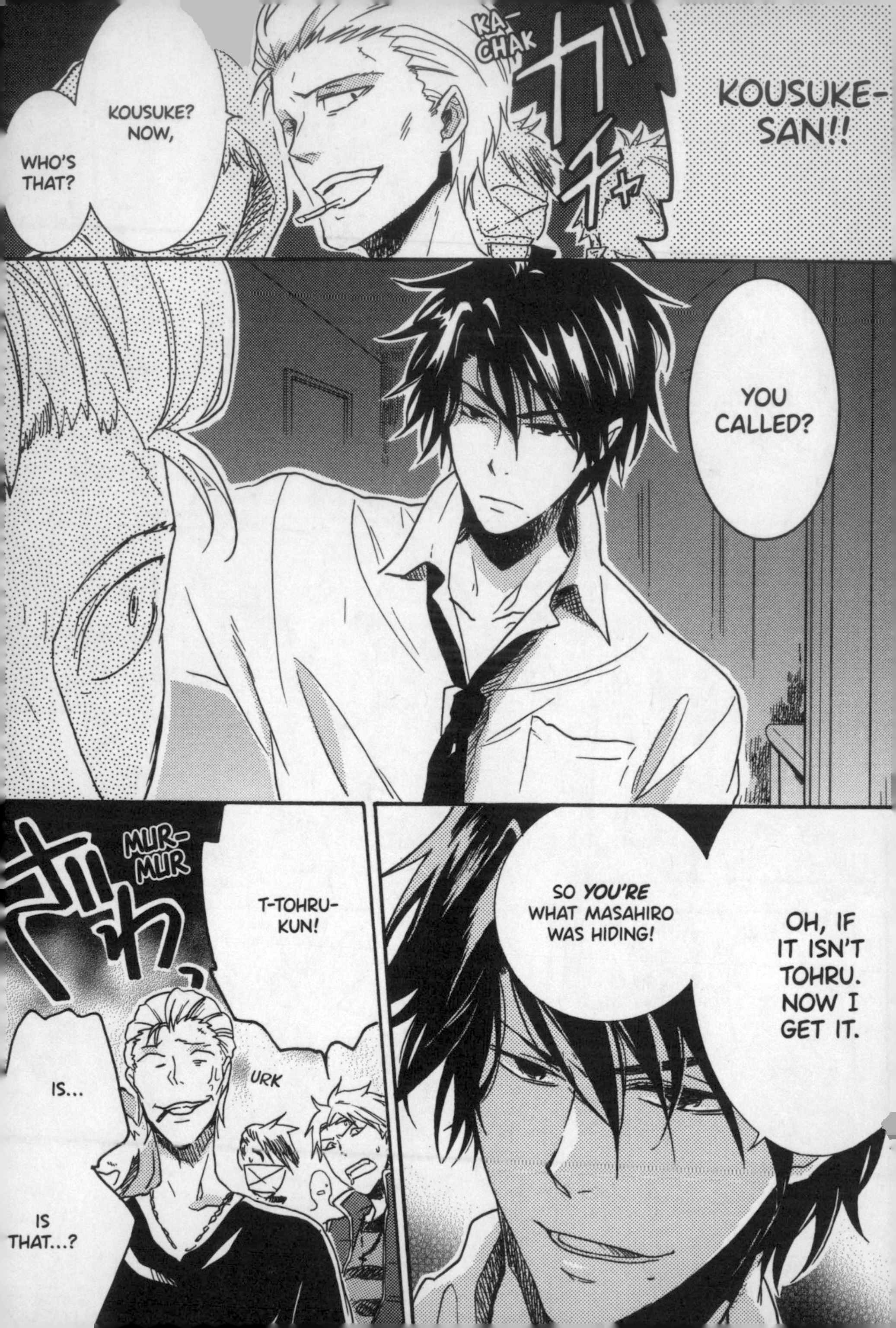
KOUSUKE-SAN!!
KA-CHAK
KOUSUKE? NOW,
WHO'S THAT?
YOU CALLED?
OH, IF IT ISN'T TOHRU. NOW I GET IT.
SO *YOU'RE* WHAT MASAHIRO WAS HIDING!
T-TOHRU-KUN!
MUR-MUR
URK
IS...
IS THAT...?

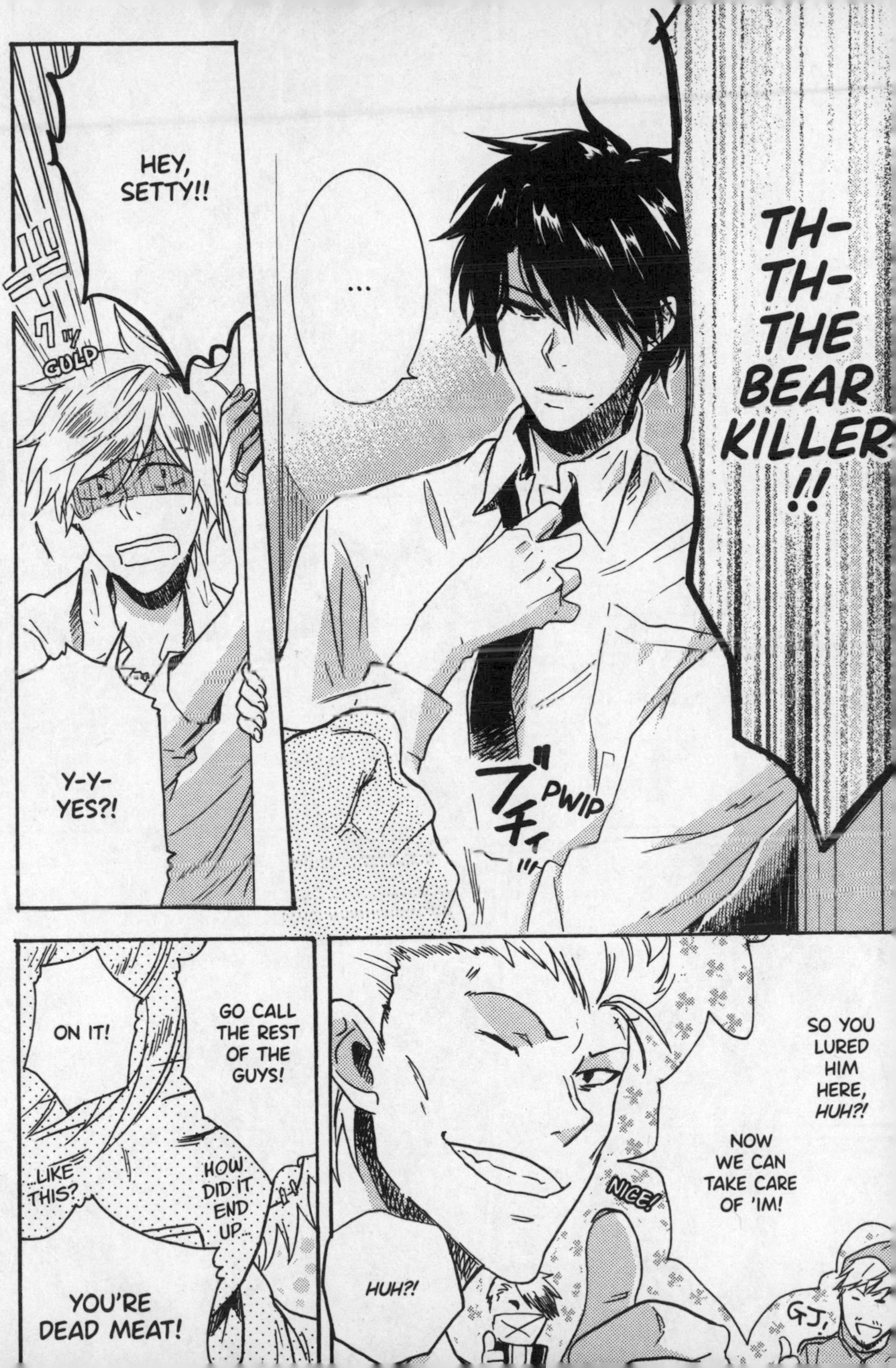
TH-TH-THE BEAR KILLER!!
...
PWIP
HEY, SETTY!!
GULP
Y-Y-YES?!
SO YOU LURED HIM HERE, HUH?!
NOW WE CAN TAKE CARE OF 'IM!
NICE!
GJ,
HUH?!
GO CALL THE REST OF THE GUYS!
ON IT!
HOW DID IT END UP...
...LIKE THIS?
YOU'RE DEAD MEAT!

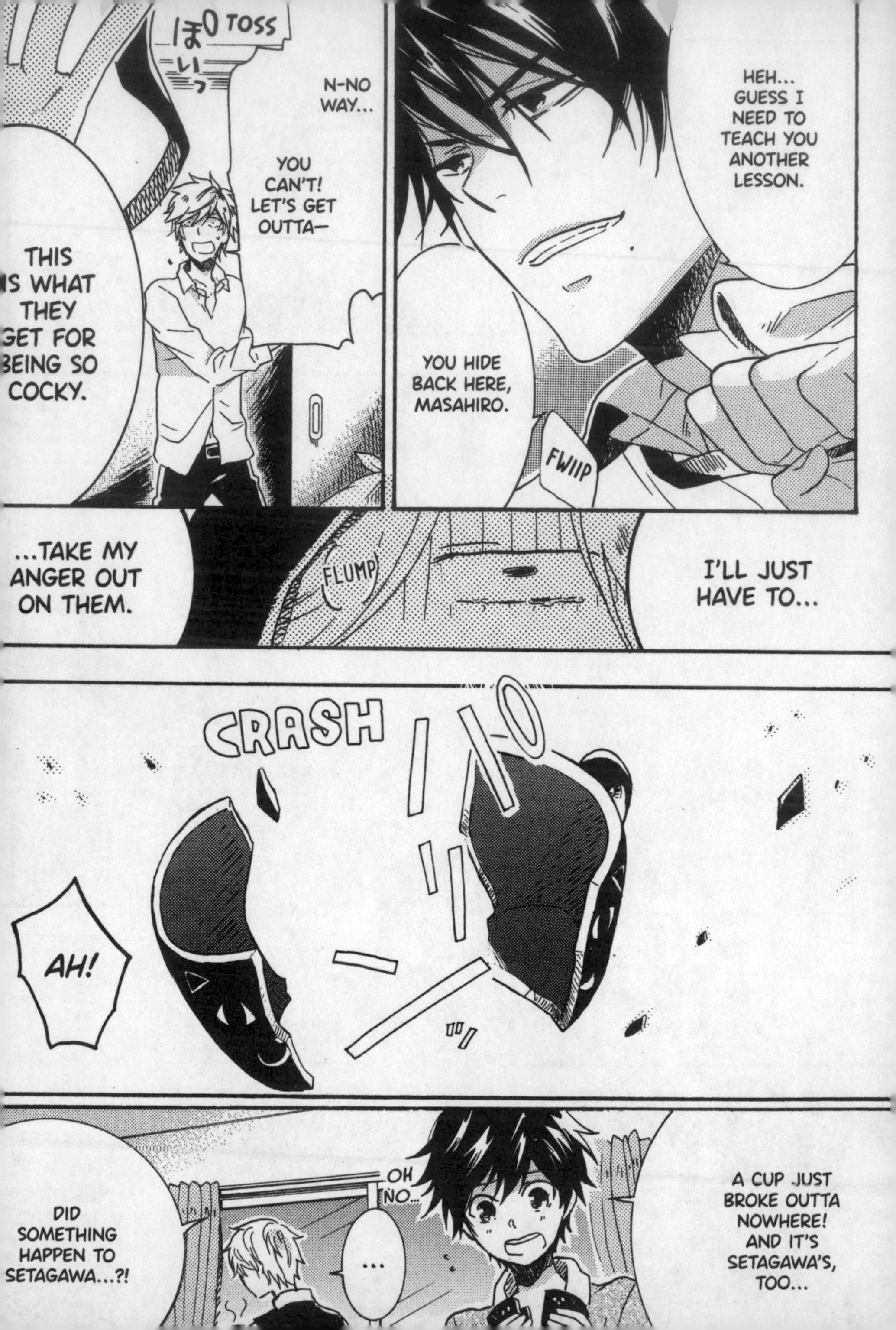
HEH... GUESS I NEED TO TEACH YOU ANOTHER LESSON.
YOU HIDE BACK HERE, MASAHIRO.
FWIIP
TOSS
N-NO WAY...
YOU CAN'T! LET'S GET OUTTA—
THIS S WHAT THEY GET FOR BEING SO COCKY.
I'LL JUST HAVE TO...
FLUMP
...TAKE MY ANGER OUT ON THEM.
CRASH
AH!
A CUP JUST BROKE OUTTA NOWHERE! AND IT'S SETAGAWA'S, TOO...
OH NO...
...
DID SOMETHING HAPPEN TO SETAGAWA...?!

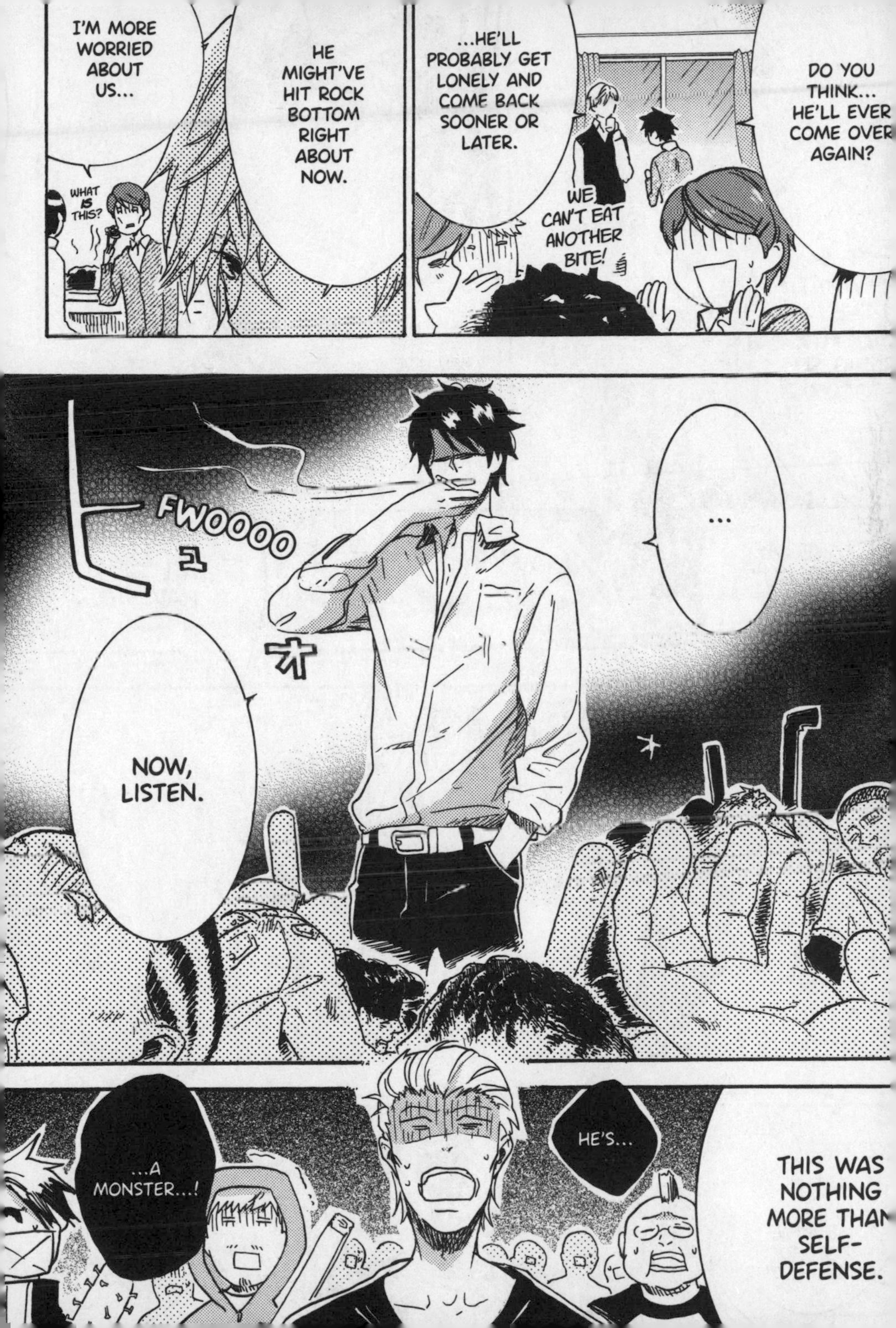
DO YOU THINK... HE'LL EVER COME OVER AGAIN?
...HE'LL PROBABLY GET LONELY AND COME BACK SOONER OR LATER.
WE CAN'T EAT ANOTHER BITE!
HE MIGHT'VE HIT ROCK BOTTOM RIGHT ABOUT NOW.
I'M MORE WORRIED ABOUT US...
WHAT IS THIS?
...
FWOOOO
NOW, LISTEN.
THIS WAS NOTHING MORE THAN SELF-DEFENSE.
HE'S...
...A MONSTER...!

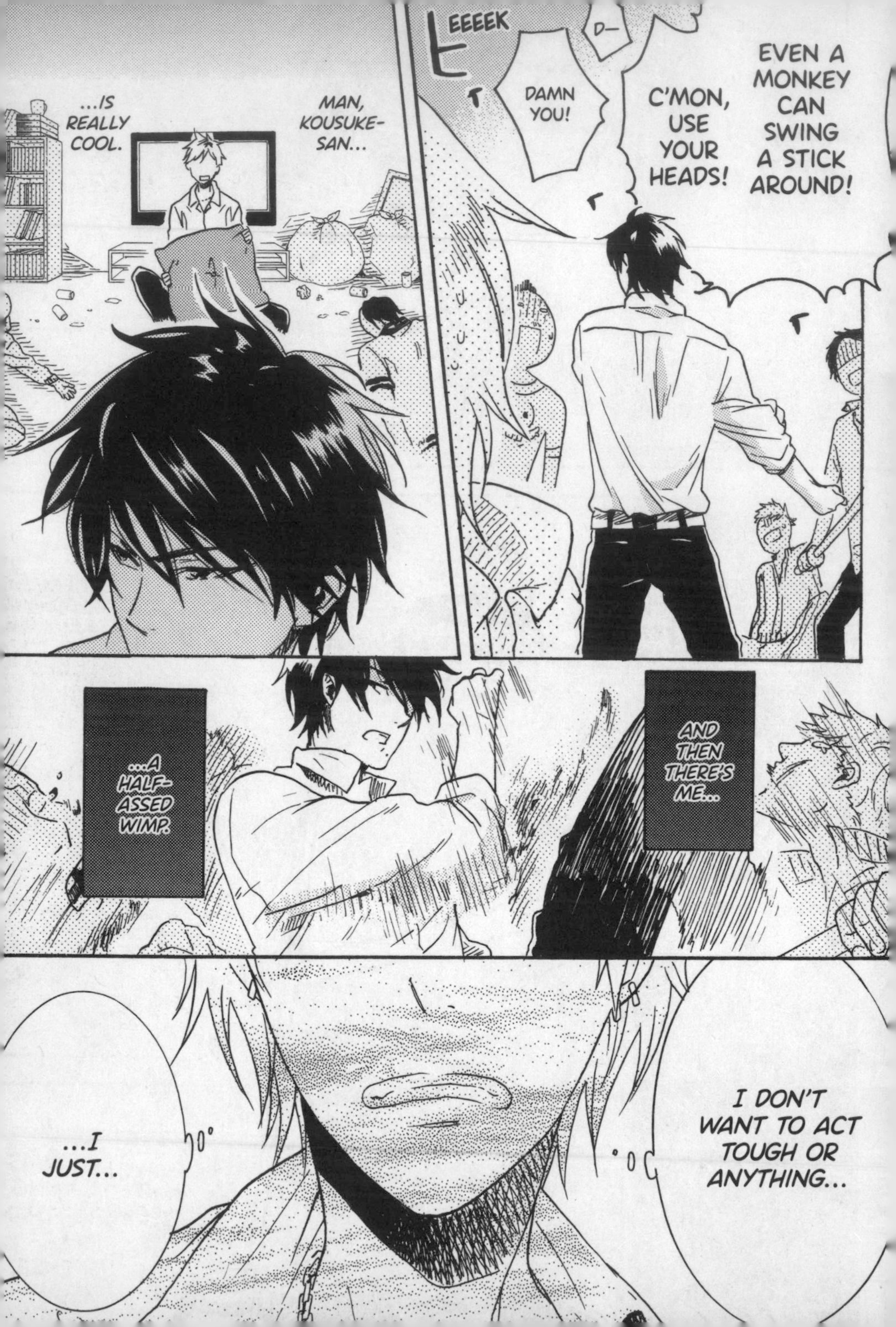
EVEN A MONKEY CAN SWING A STICK AROUND!
C'MON, USE YOUR HEADS!
D—
DAMN YOU!
EEEEK
MAN, KOUSUKE-SAN...
...IS REALLY COOL.
AND THEN THERE'S ME...
...A HALF-ASSED WIMP.
I DON'T WANT TO ACT TOUGH OR ANYTHING...
...I JUST...

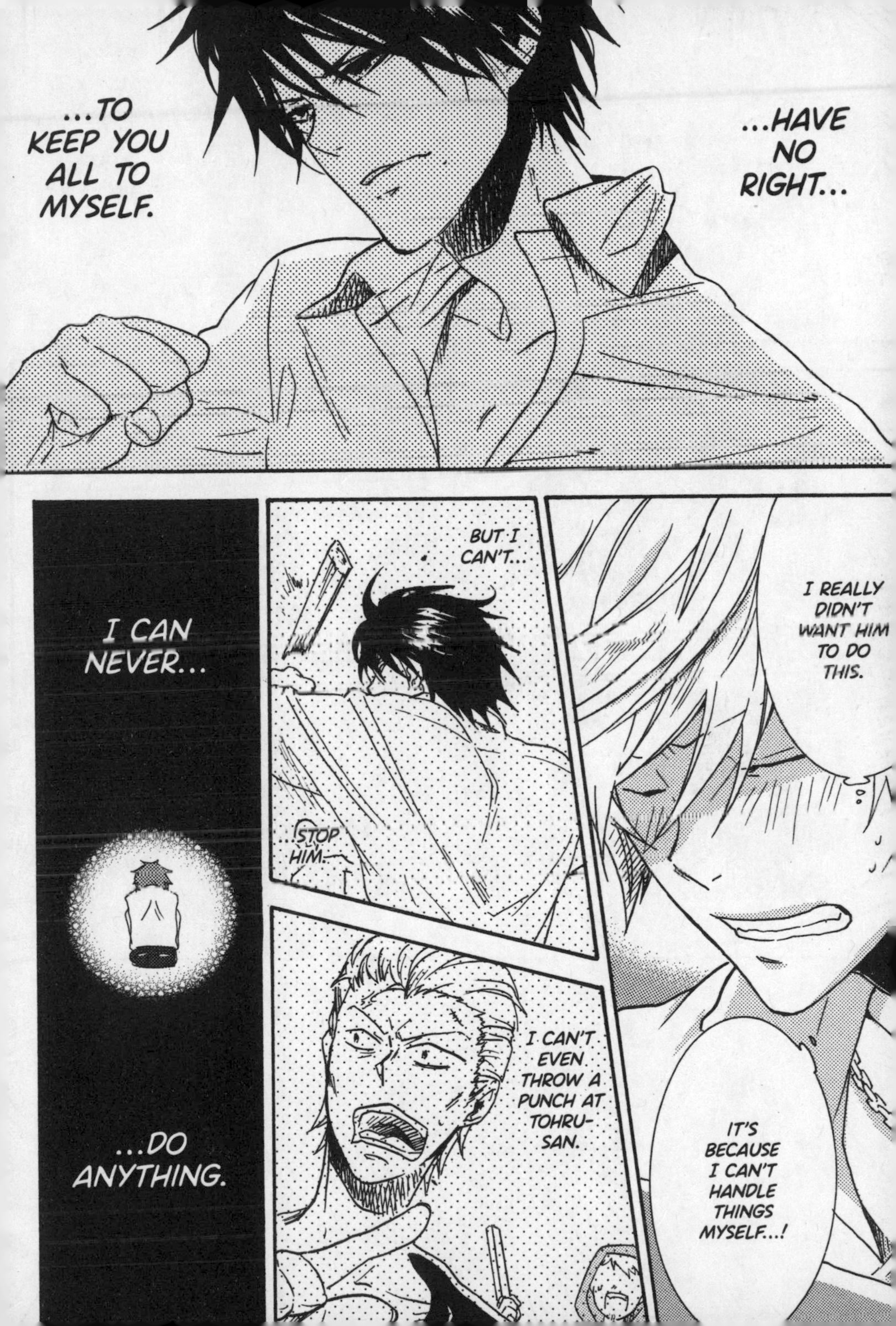
...HAVE NO RIGHT...
...TO KEEP YOU ALL TO MYSELF.
I REALLY DIDN'T WANT HIM TO DO THIS.
IT'S BECAUSE I CAN'T HANDLE THINGS MYSELF...!
BUT I CAN'T...
...STOP HIM...
I CAN'T EVEN THROW A PUNCH AT TOHRU-SAN.
I CAN NEVER...
...DO ANYTHING.

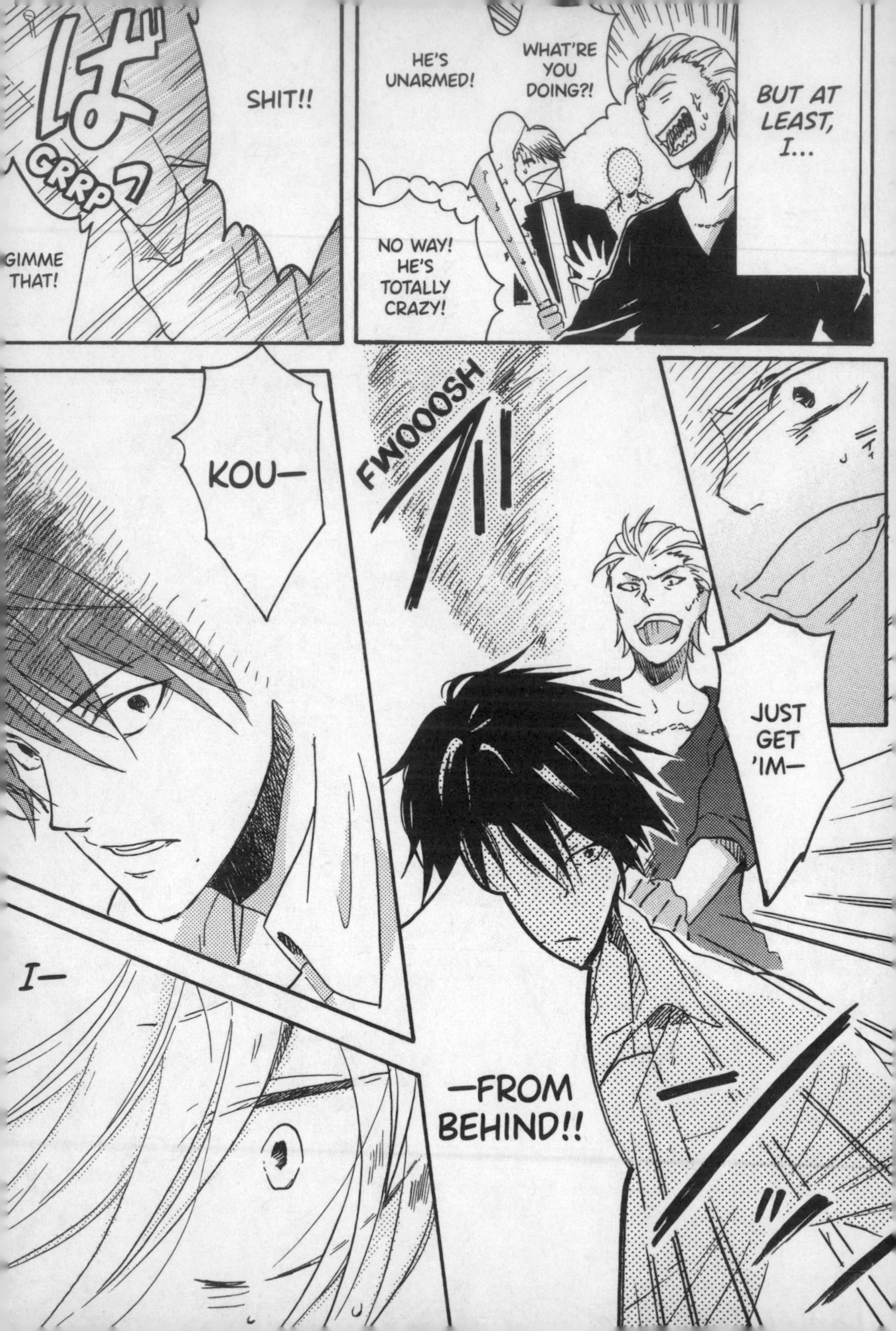
BUT AT LEAST, I...
WHAT'RE YOU DOING?!
HE'S UNARMED!
NO WAY! HE'S TOTALLY CRAZY!
GRRP
SHIT!!
GIMME THAT!
JUST GET 'IM—
FWOOOSH
—FROM BEHIND!!
KOU—
I—

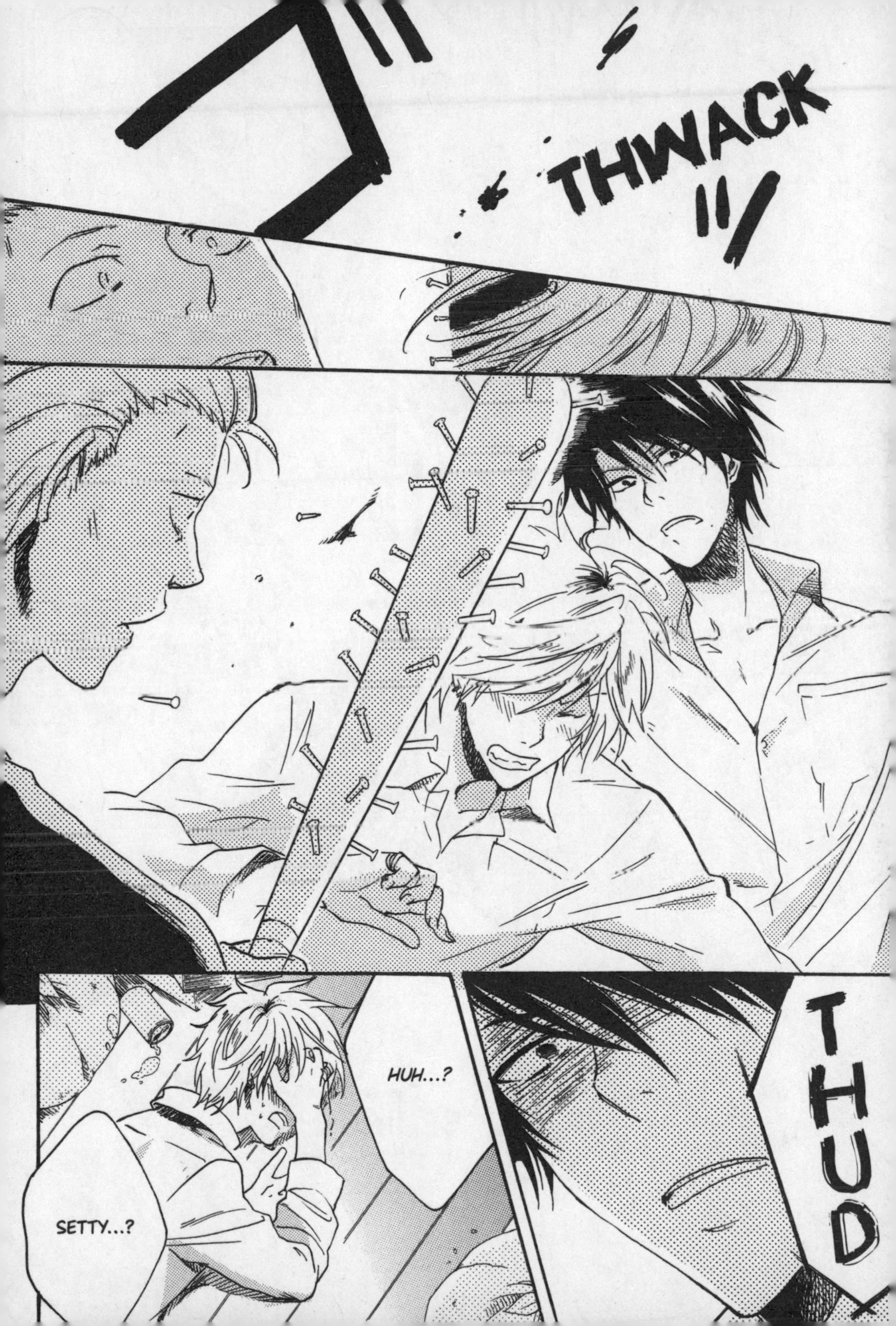
THWACK
THUD
HUH...?
SETTY...?

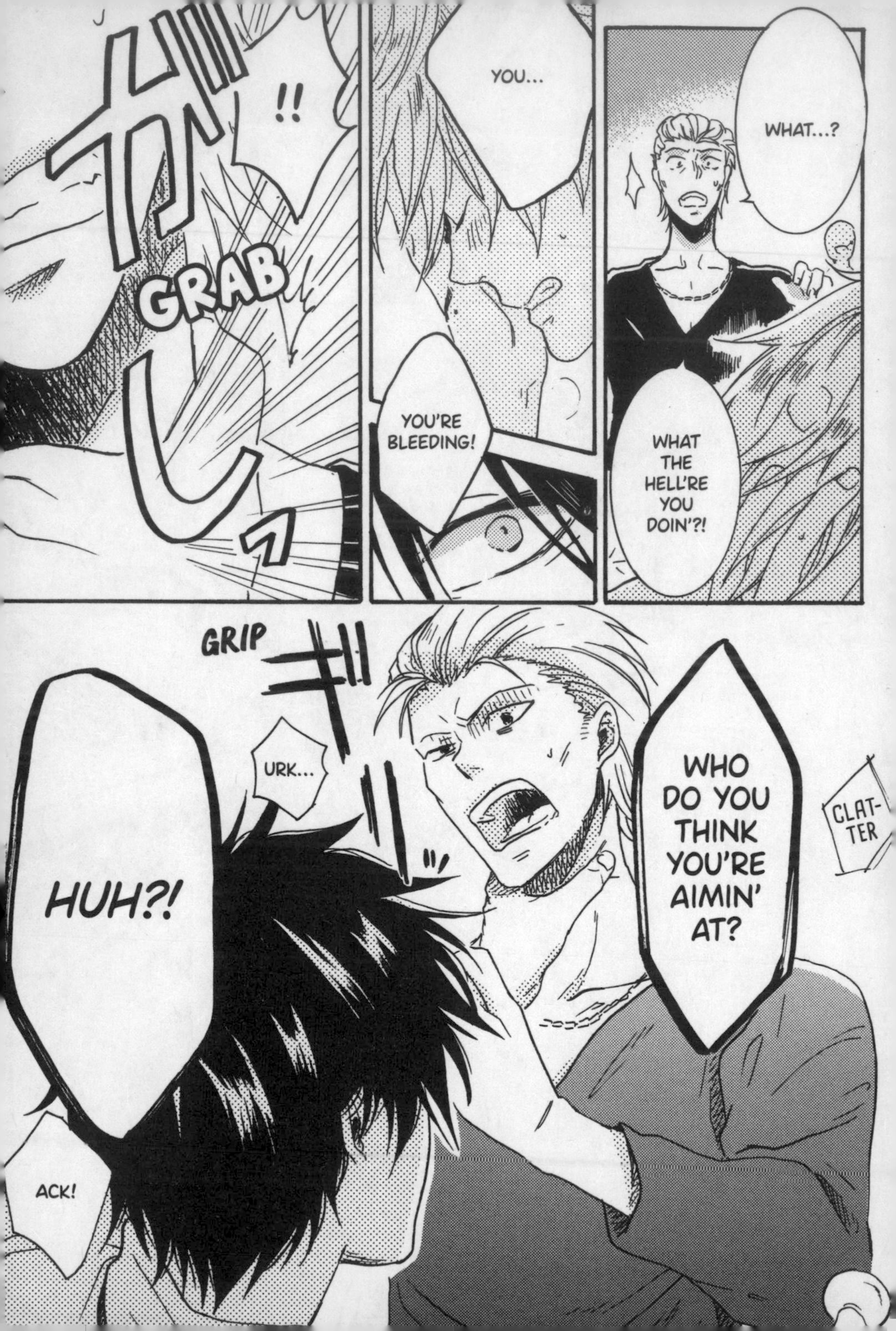
WHAT...?
WHAT THE HELL'RE YOU DOIN'?!
YOU...
YOU'RE BLEEDING!
!!
GRAB
CLAT-TER
WHO DO YOU THINK YOU'RE AIMIN' AT?
GRIP
URK...
HUH?!
ACK!

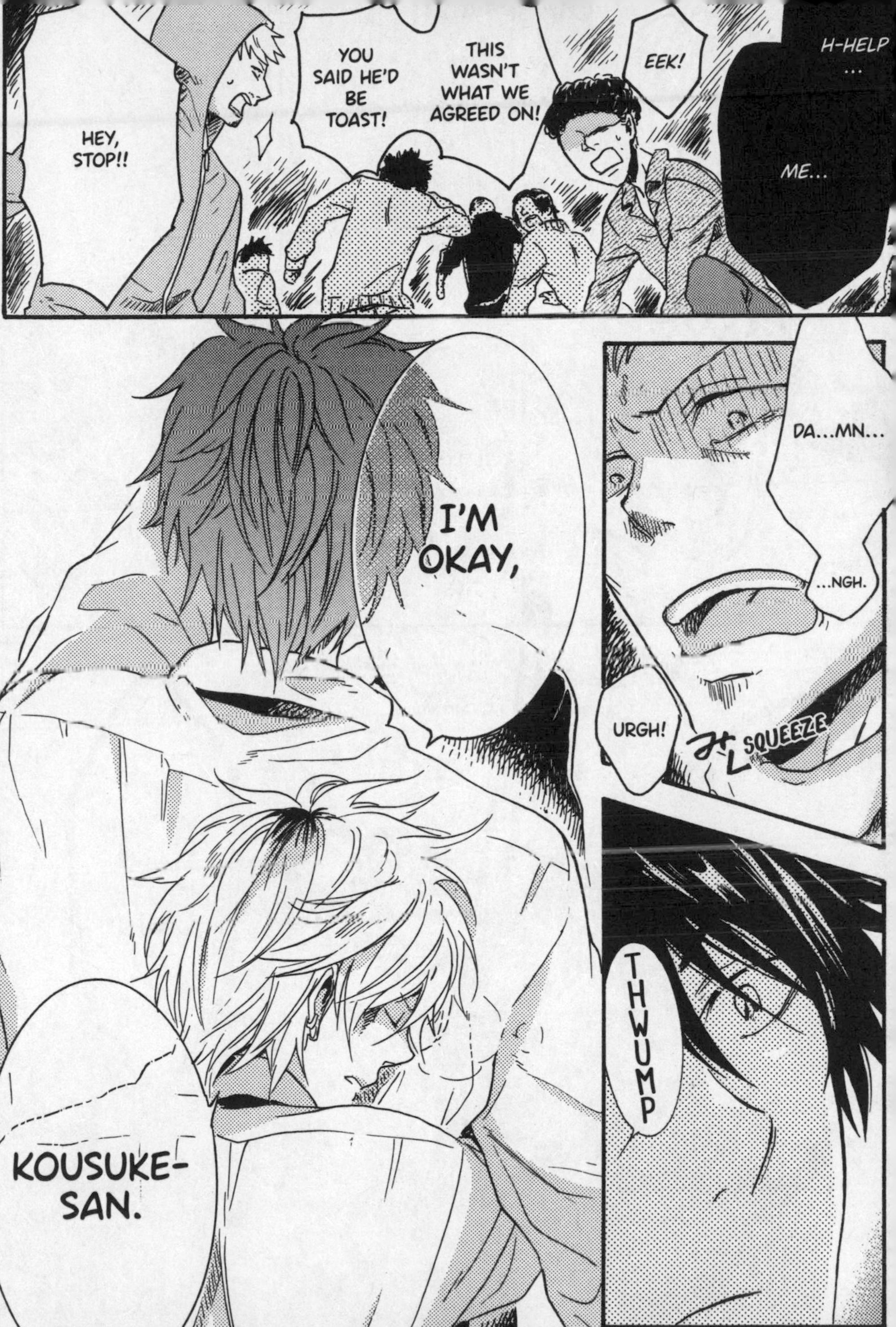
H-HELP ... ME...
EEK!
THIS WASN'T WHAT WE AGREED ON!
YOU SAID HE'D BE TOAST!
HEY, STOP!!
DA...MN...
...NGH.
URGH!
SQUEEZE
THWUMP
I'M OKAY,
KOUSUKE-SAN.

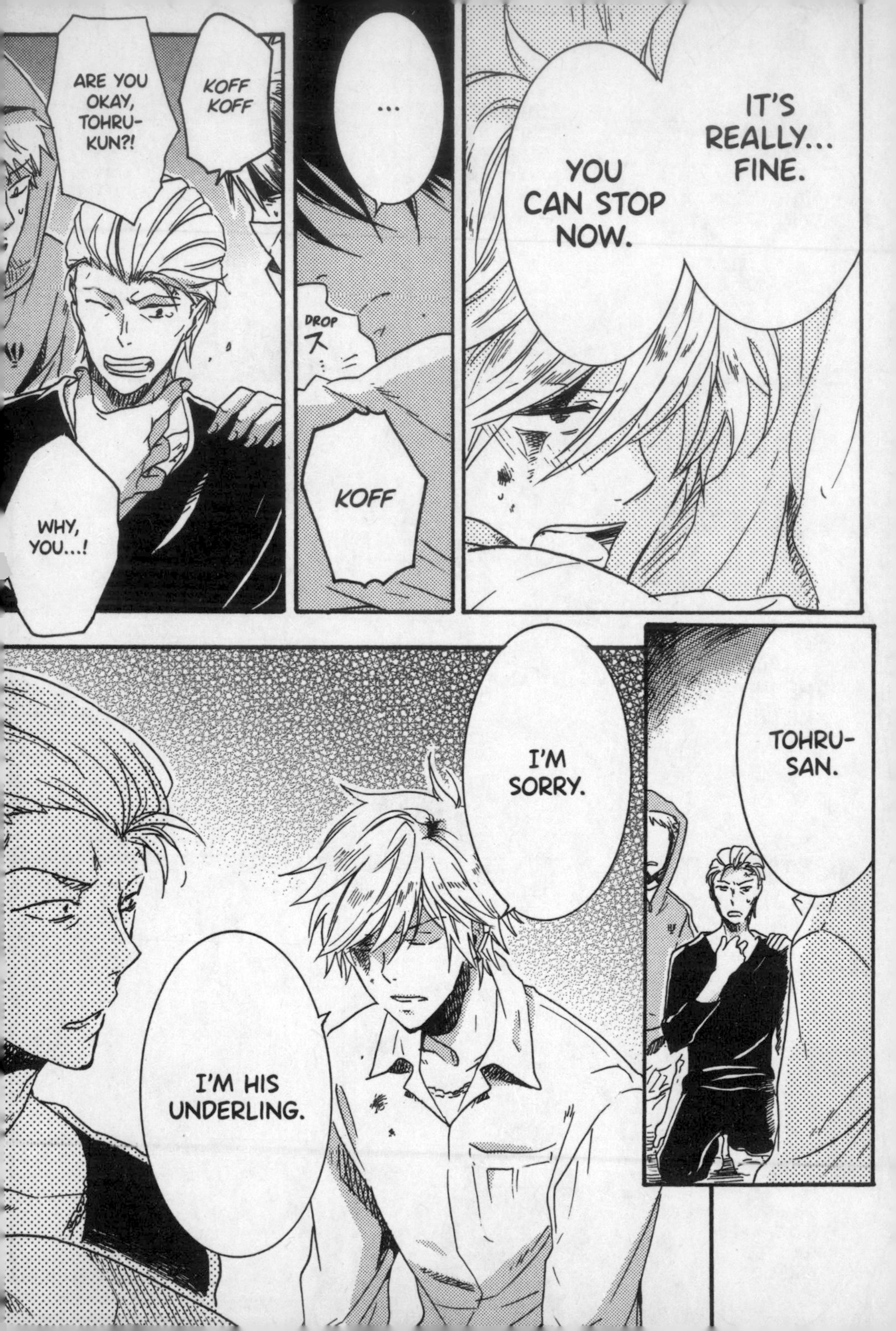
IT'S REALLY... FINE.
YOU CAN STOP NOW.
...
DROP ス
KOFF
KOFF KOFF
ARE YOU OKAY, TOHRU-KUN?!
WHY, YOU...!
TOHRU-SAN.
I'M SORRY.
I'M HIS UNDERLING.

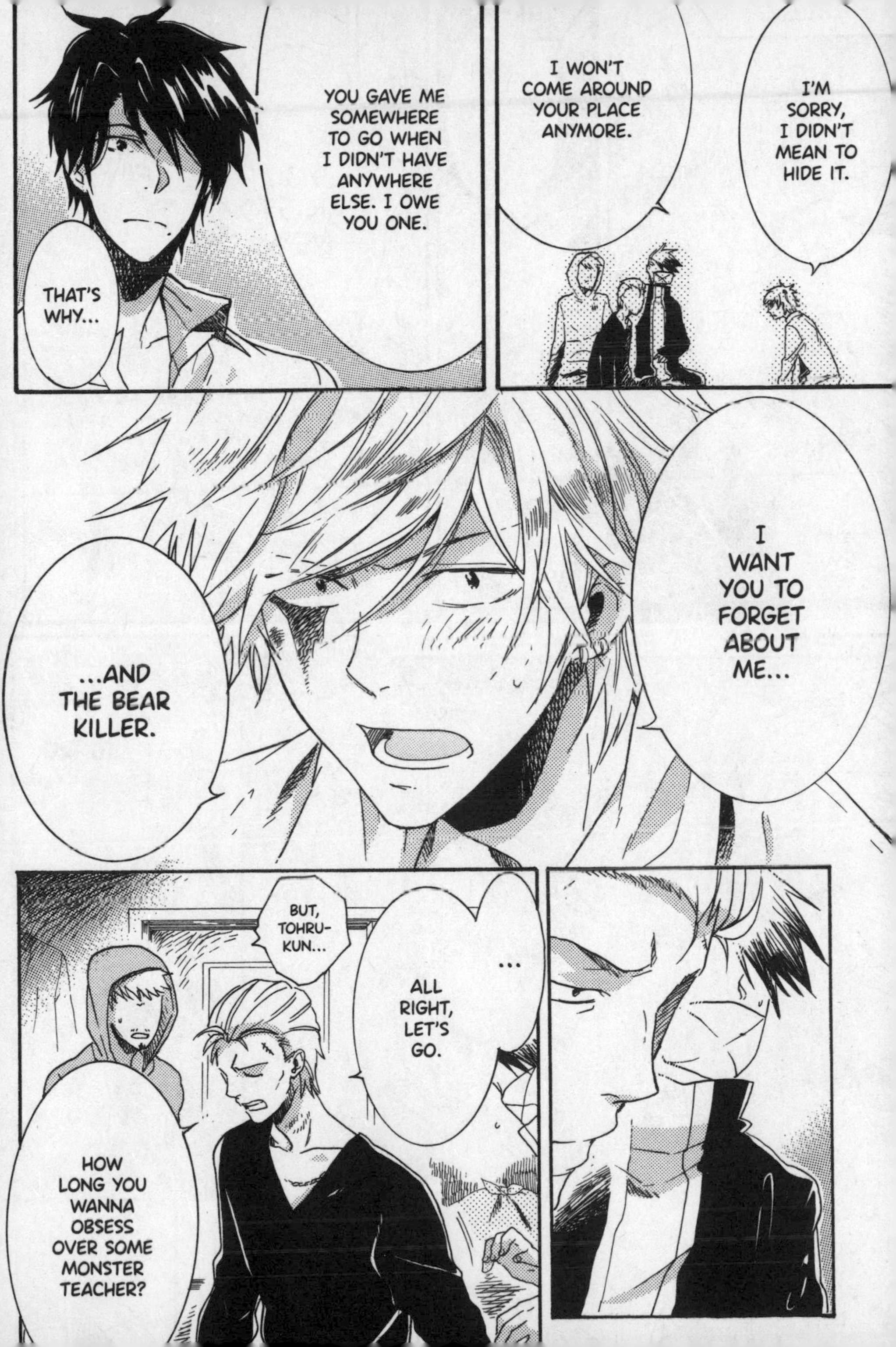
I'M SORRY, I DIDN'T MEAN TO HIDE IT.
I WON'T COME AROUND YOUR PLACE ANYMORE.
YOU GAVE ME SOMEWHERE TO GO WHEN I DIDN'T HAVE ANYWHERE ELSE. I OWE YOU ONE.
THAT'S WHY...
I WANT YOU TO FORGET ABOUT ME...
...AND THE BEAR KILLER.
... ALL RIGHT, LET'S GO.
BUT, TOHRU-KUN...
HOW LONG YOU WANNA OBSESS OVER SOME MONSTER TEACHER?

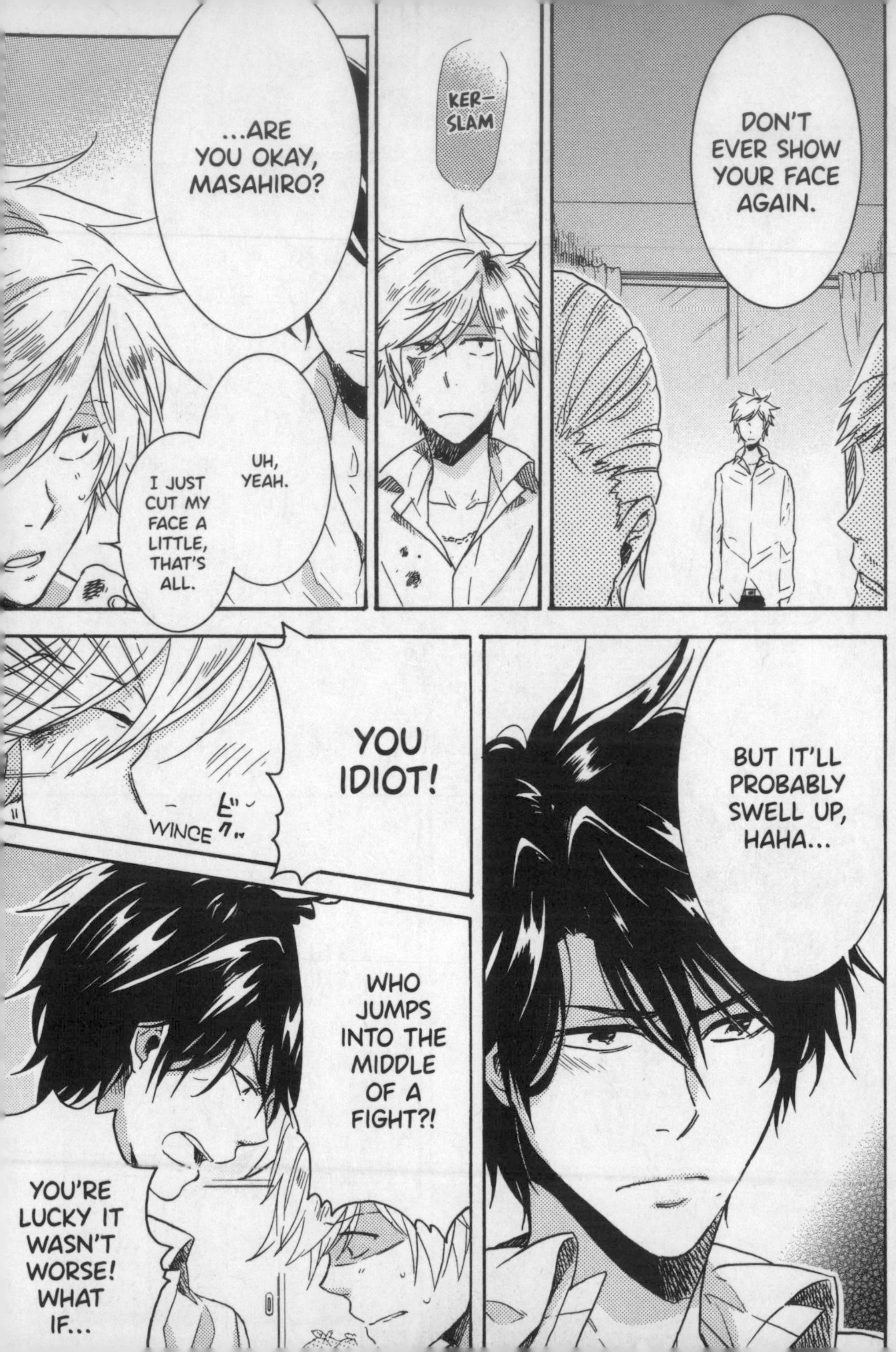
DON'T EVER SHOW YOUR FACE AGAIN.
KER-SLAM
...ARE YOU OKAY, MASAHIRO?
UH, YEAH.
I JUST CUT MY FACE A LITTLE, THAT'S ALL.
BUT IT'LL PROBABLY SWELL UP, HAHA...
YOU IDIOT!
WINCE
WHO JUMPS INTO THE MIDDLE OF A FIGHT?!
YOU'RE LUCKY IT WASN'T WORSE! WHAT IF...

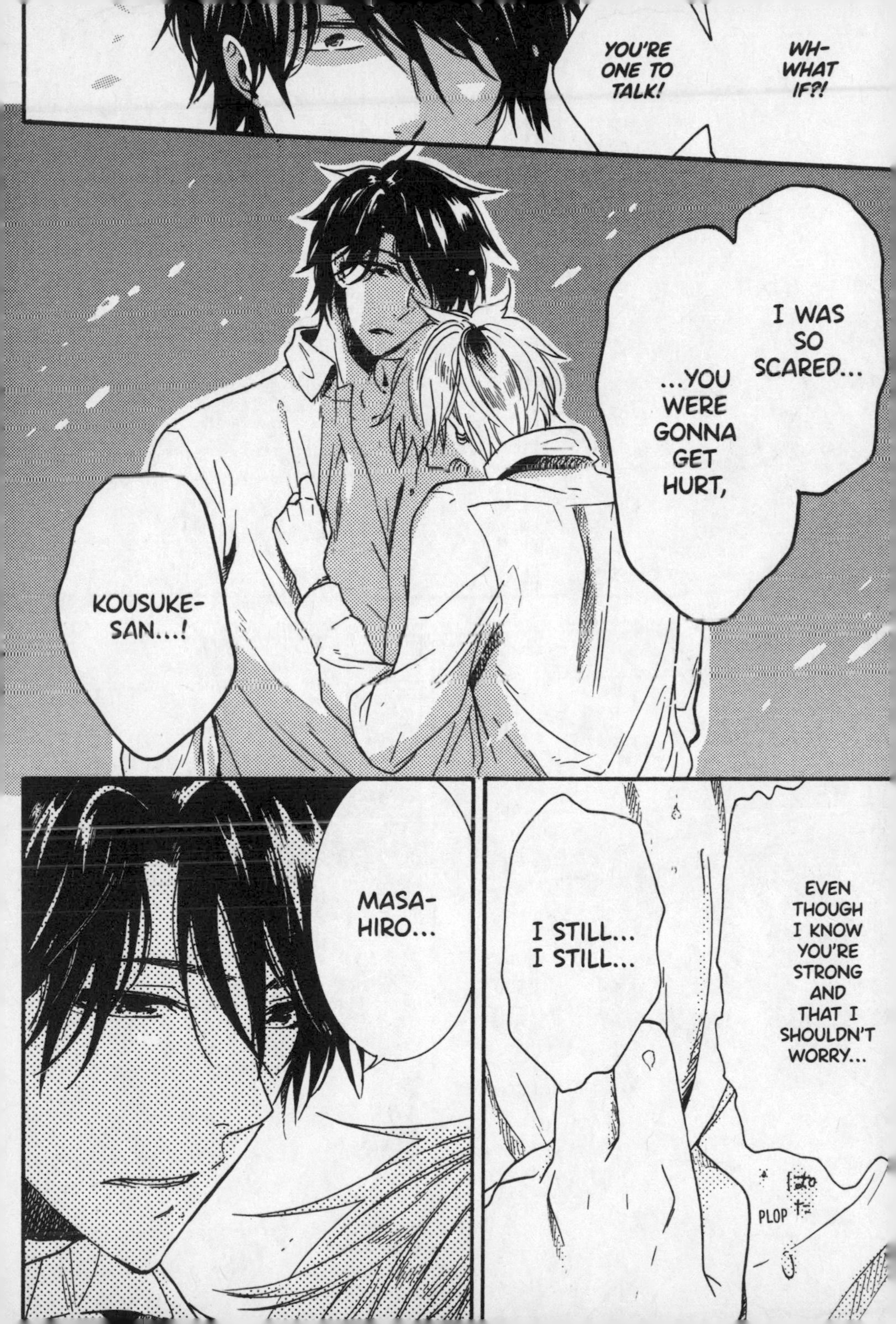
WH- WHAT IF?!
YOU'RE ONE TO TALK!
I WAS SO SCARED...
...YOU WERE GONNA GET HURT,
KOUSUKE-SAN...!
EVEN THOUGH I KNOW YOU'RE STRONG AND THAT I SHOULDN'T WORRY...
I STILL... I STILL...
PLOP
MASA-HIRO...

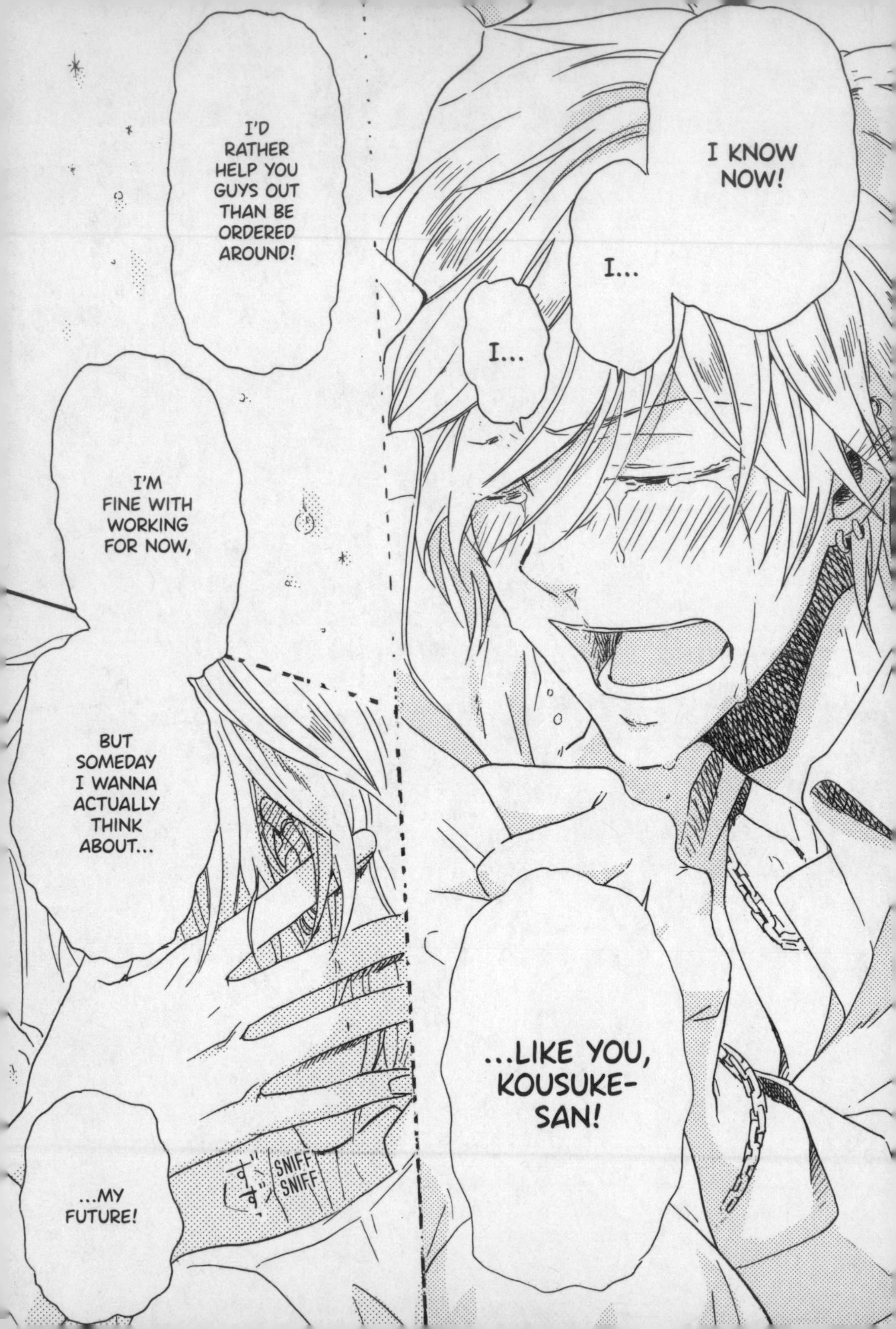

I KNOW NOW!
I...
I...
...LIKE YOU, KOUSUKE-SAN!
I'D RATHER HELP YOU GUYS OUT THAN BE ORDERED AROUND!
I'M FINE WITH WORKING FOR NOW,
BUT SOMEDAY I WANNA ACTUALLY THINK ABOUT...
SNIFF SNIFF
...MY FUTURE!

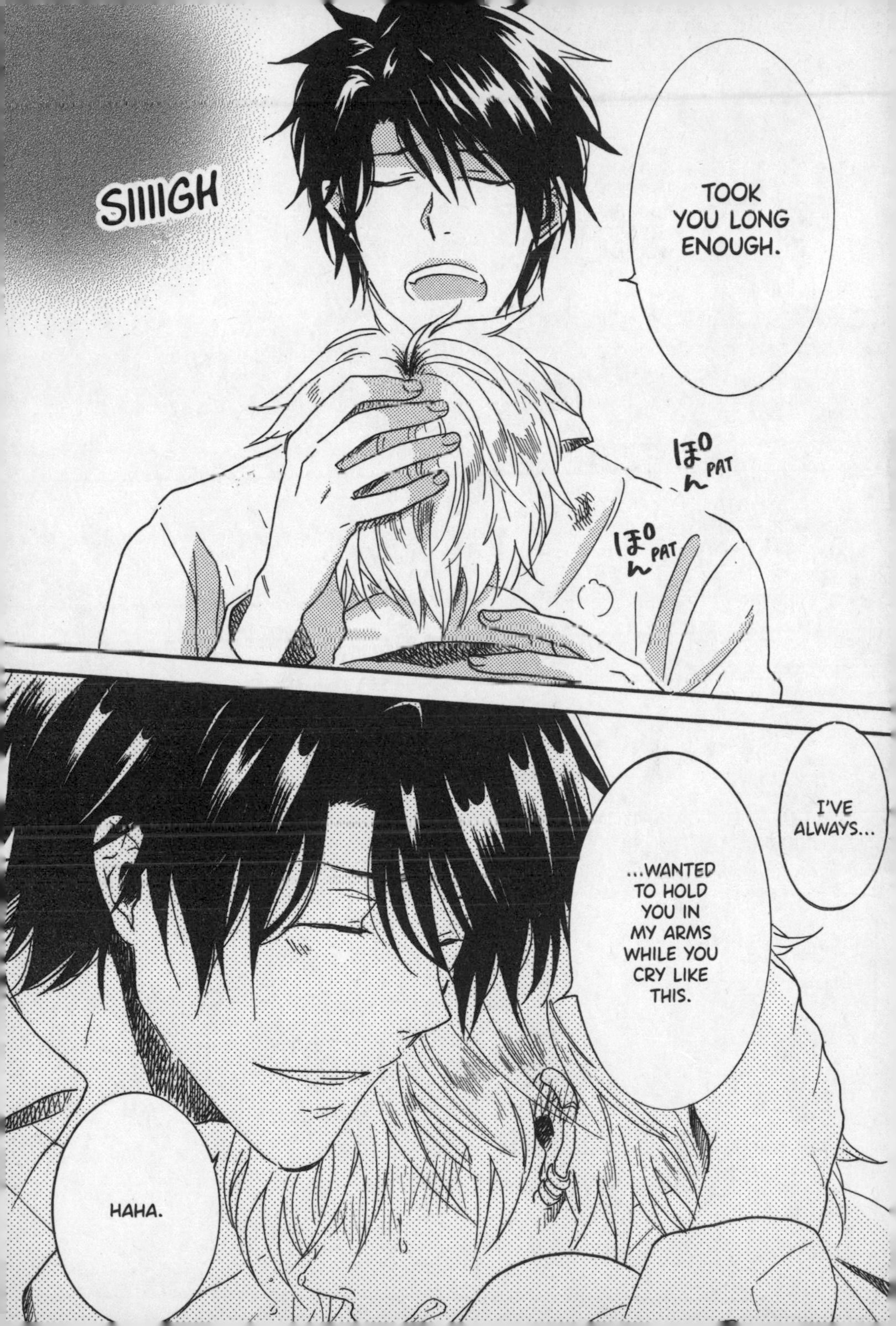
TOOK YOU LONG ENOUGH.
SIIIIGH
ぽん PAT
ぽん PAT
I'VE ALWAYS...
...WANTED TO HOLD YOU IN MY ARMS WHILE YOU CRY LIKE THIS.
HAHA.

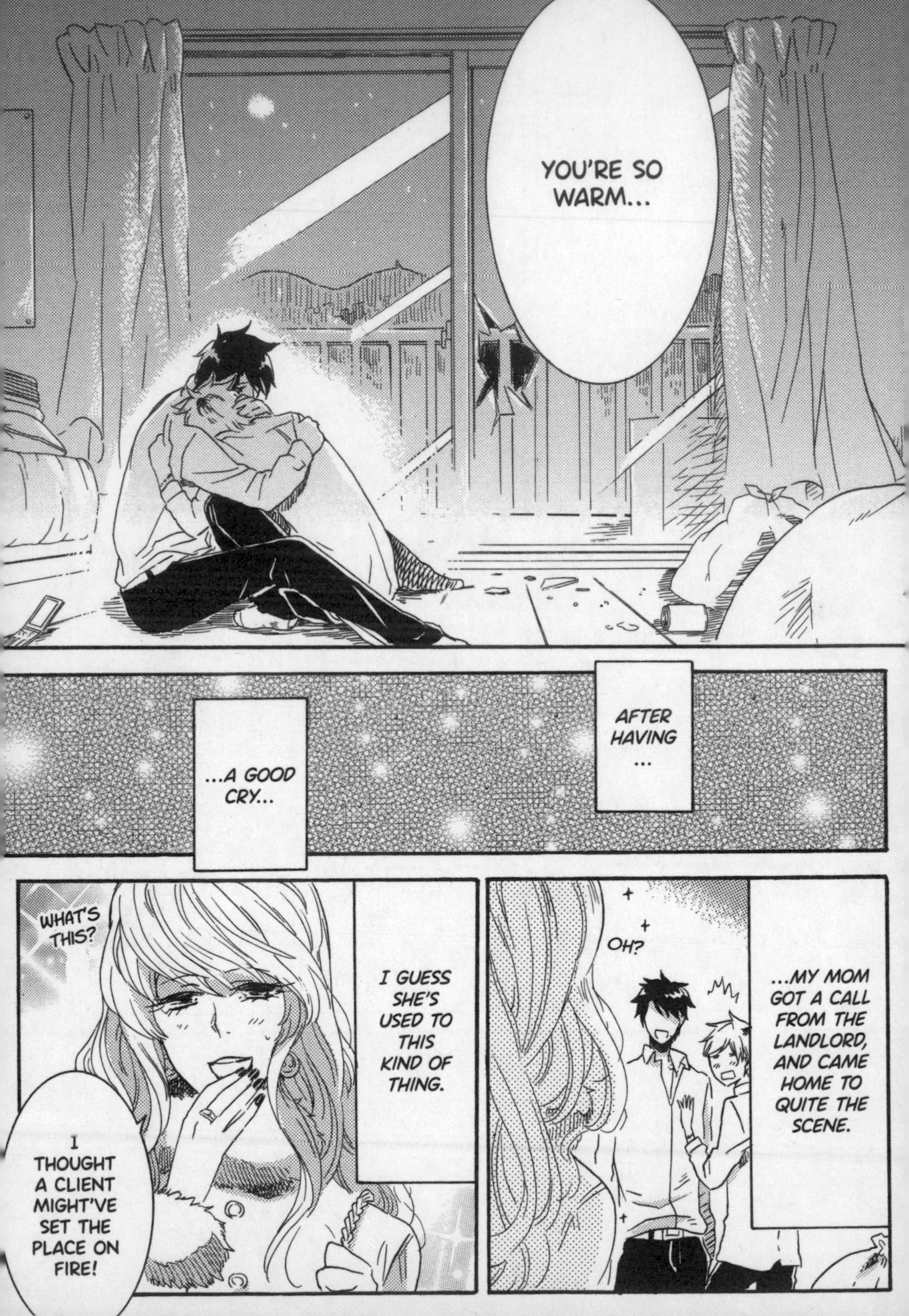
YOU'RE SO WARM...
AFTER HAVING ...
...A GOOD CRY...
...MY MOM GOT A CALL FROM THE LANDLORD, AND CAME HOME TO QUITE THE SCENE.
OH?
I GUESS SHE'S USED TO THIS KIND OF THING.
WHAT'S THIS?
I THOUGHT A CLIENT MIGHT'VE SET THE PLACE ON FIRE!

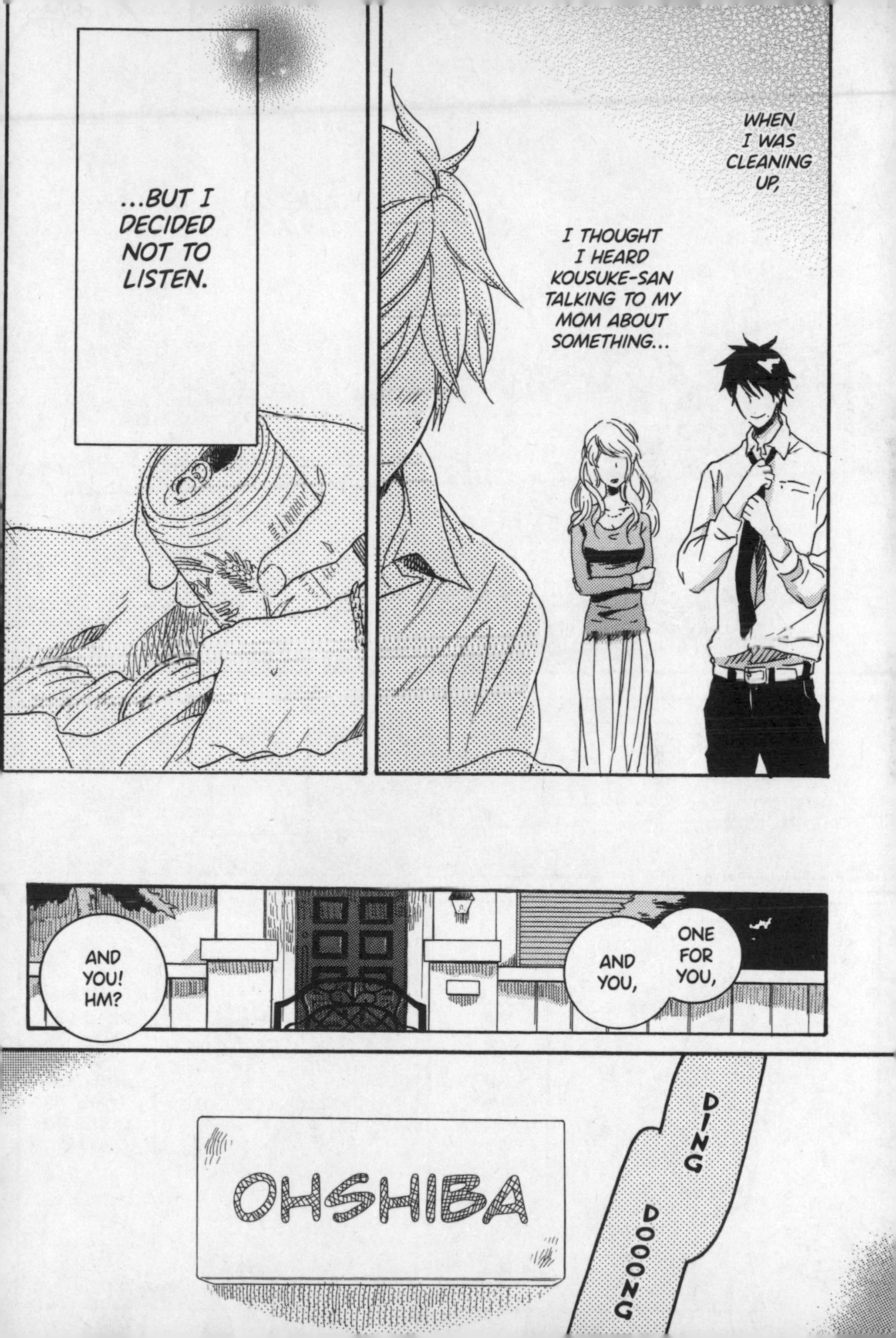
WHEN I WAS CLEANING UP,
I THOUGHT I HEARD KOUSUKE-SAN TALKING TO MY MOM ABOUT SOMETHING...
...BUT I DECIDED NOT TO LISTEN.
ONE FOR YOU,
AND YOU,
AND YOU! HM?
DING DOOOONG
OHSHIBA

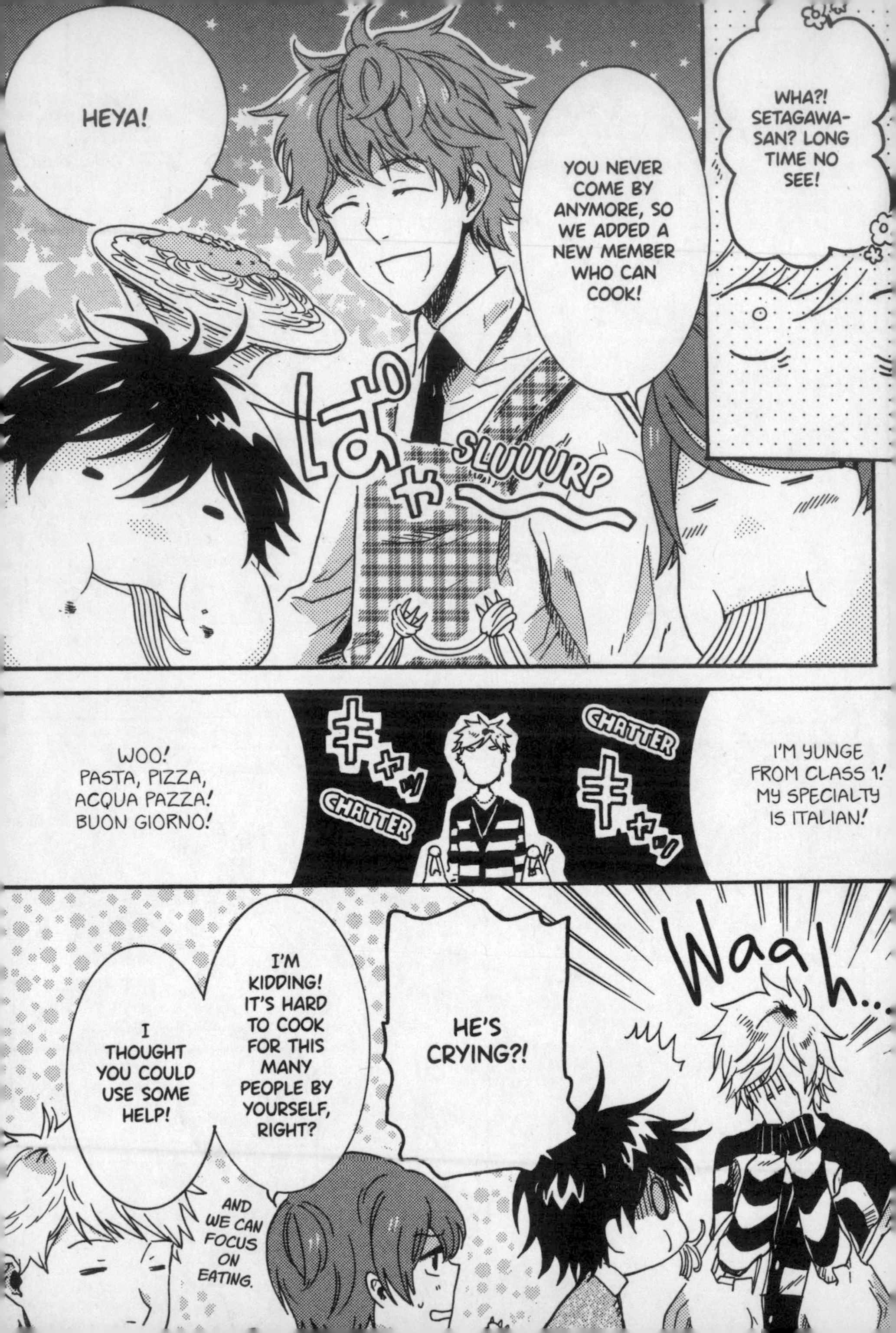
WHA?! SETAGAWA-SAN? LONG TIME NO SEE!
HEYA!
YOU NEVER COME BY ANYMORE, SO WE ADDED A NEW MEMBER WHO CAN COOK!
SLUUURP
I'M YUNGE FROM CLASS 1! MY SPECIALTY IS ITALIAN!
CHATTER
CHATTER
WOO! PASTA, PIZZA, ACQUA PAZZA! BUON GIORNO!
Waah...
HE'S CRYING?!
I'M KIDDING! IT'S HARD TO COOK FOR THIS MANY PEOPLE BY YOURSELF, RIGHT?
I THOUGHT YOU COULD USE SOME HELP!
AND WE CAN FOCUS ON EATING.

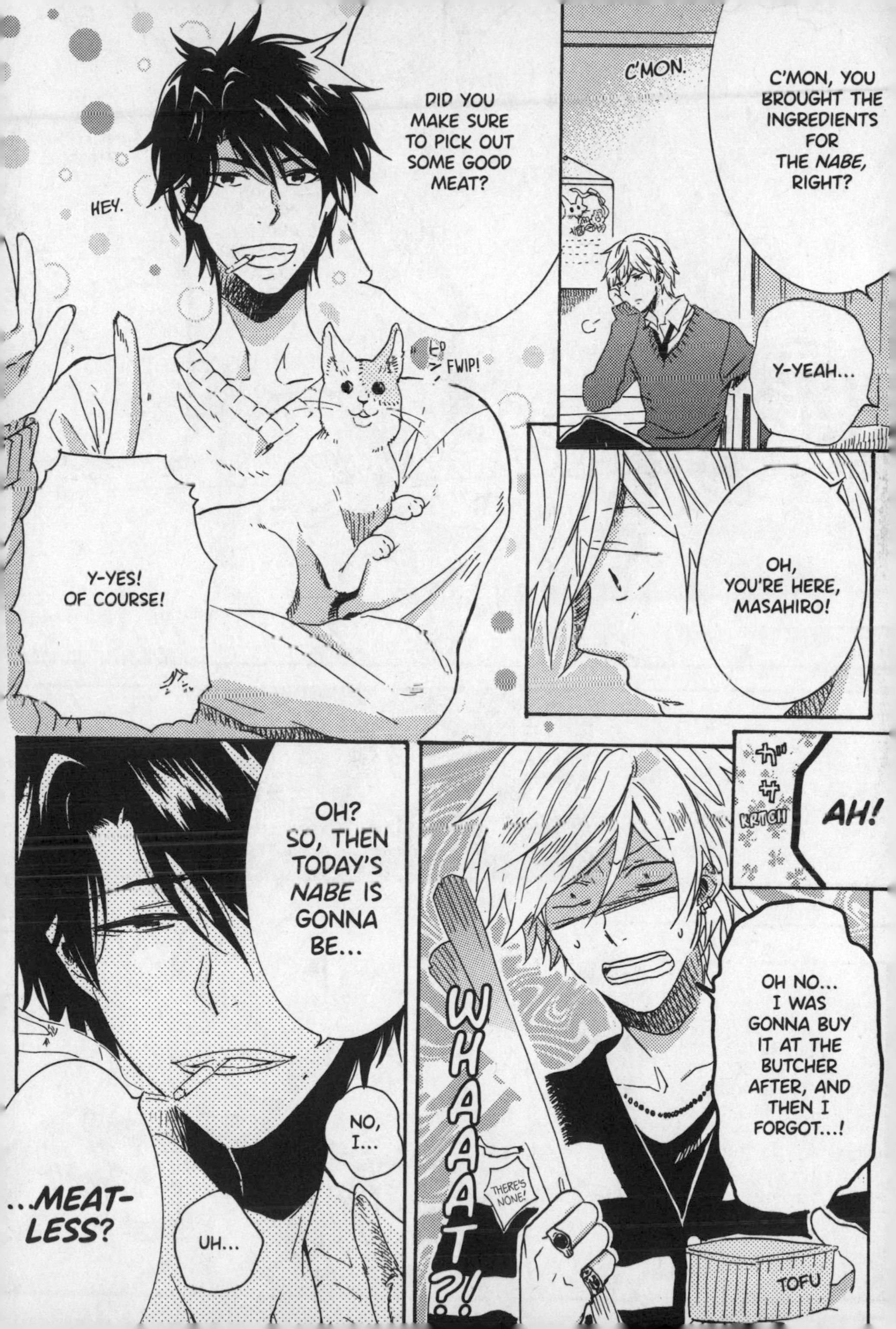
C'MON.
C'MON, YOU BROUGHT THE INGREDIENTS FOR THE *NABE*, RIGHT?
Y-YEAH...
OH, YOU'RE HERE, MASAHIRO!
HEY.
DID YOU MAKE SURE TO PICK OUT SOME GOOD MEAT?
FWIP!
Y-YES! OF COURSE!
AH!
KRTCH
OH NO... I WAS GONNA BUY IT AT THE BUTCHER AFTER, AND THEN I FORGOT...!
WHAAAAT?!
THERE'S NONE!
TOFU
OH? SO, THEN TODAY'S *NABE* IS GONNA BE...
NO, I...
UH...
...MEAT-LESS?

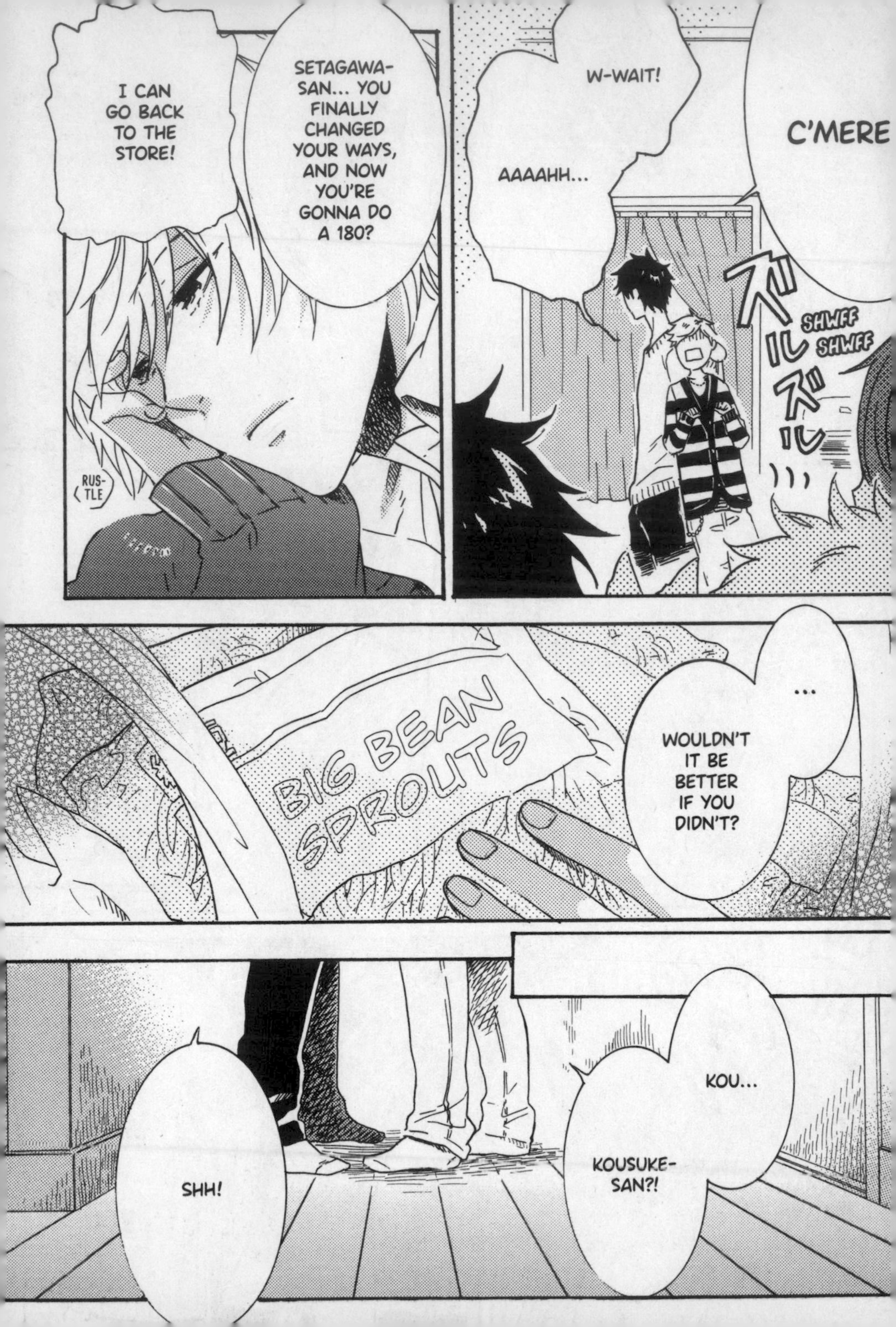
C'MERE
W-WAIT!
AAAAHH...
SHWFF SHWFF
SETAGAWA-SAN... YOU FINALLY CHANGED YOUR WAYS, AND NOW YOU'RE GONNA DO A 180?
I CAN GO BACK TO THE STORE!
RUS-TLE
...
WOULDN'T IT BE BETTER IF YOU DIDN'T?
BIG BEAN SPROUTS
KOU...
KOUSUKE-SAN?!
SHH!

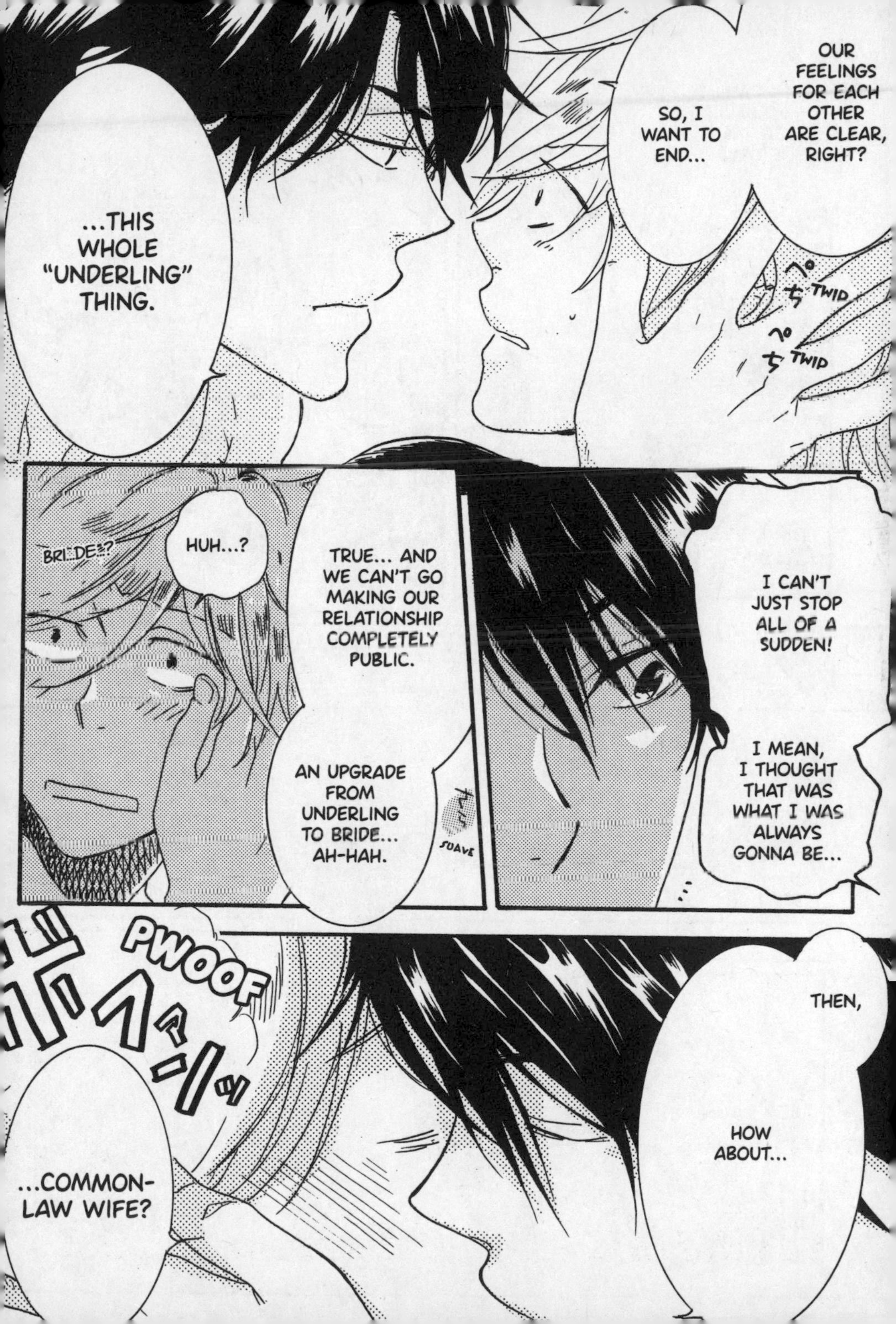
OUR FEELINGS FOR EACH OTHER ARE CLEAR, RIGHT?
SO, I WANT TO END...
TWID
TWID
...THIS WHOLE "UNDERLING" THING.
I CAN'T JUST STOP ALL OF A SUDDEN!
I MEAN, I THOUGHT THAT WAS WHAT I WAS ALWAYS GONNA BE...
...
TRUE... AND WE CAN'T GO MAKING OUR RELATIONSHIP COMPLETELY PUBLIC.
AN UPGRADE FROM UNDERLING TO BRIDE... AH-HAH.
SUAVE
HUH...?
BRIDE?
THEN,
HOW ABOUT...
PWOOF
...COMMON-LAW WIFE?

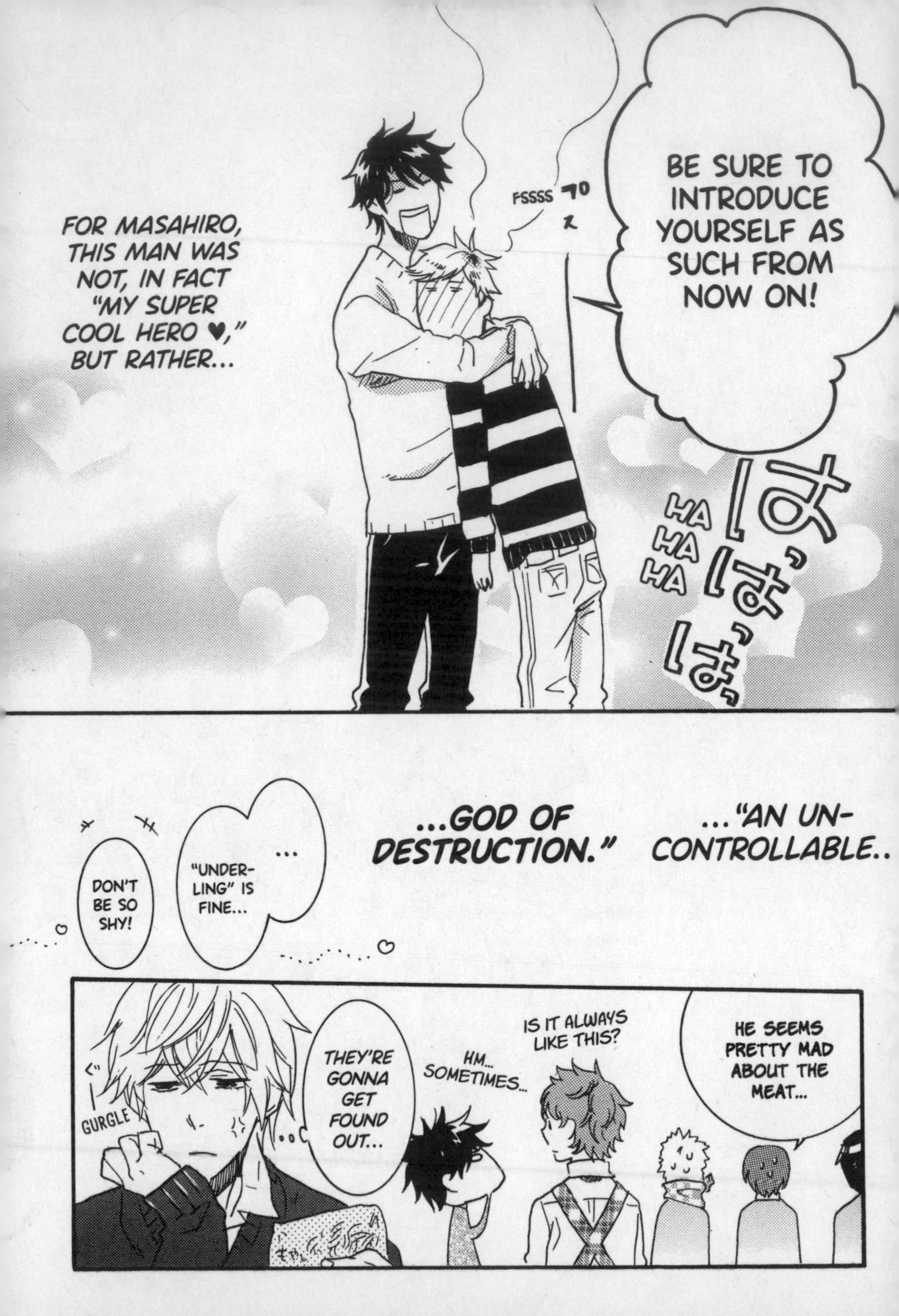
BE SURE TO INTRODUCE YOURSELF AS SUCH FROM NOW ON!
HA HA HA
FSSSS
FOR MASAHIRO, THIS MAN WAS NOT, IN FACT "MY SUPER COOL HERO ♥," BUT RATHER...
..."AN UN-CONTROLLABLE..
...GOD OF DESTRUCTION."
...
"UNDER-LING" IS FINE...
DON'T BE SO SHY!
HE SEEMS PRETTY MAD ABOUT THE MEAT...
IS IT ALWAYS LIKE THIS?
HM... SOMETIMES...
THEY'RE GONNA GET FOUND OUT...
GURGLE

Sweet Memory

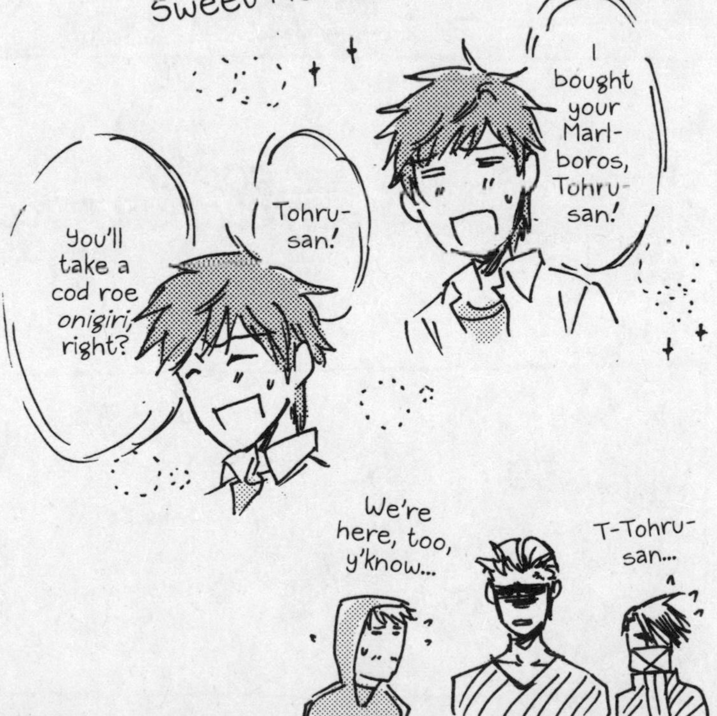
I bought your Marlboros, Tohru-san!
Tohru-san!
You'll take a cod roe *onigiri*, right?
T-Tohru-san...
We're here, too, y'know...

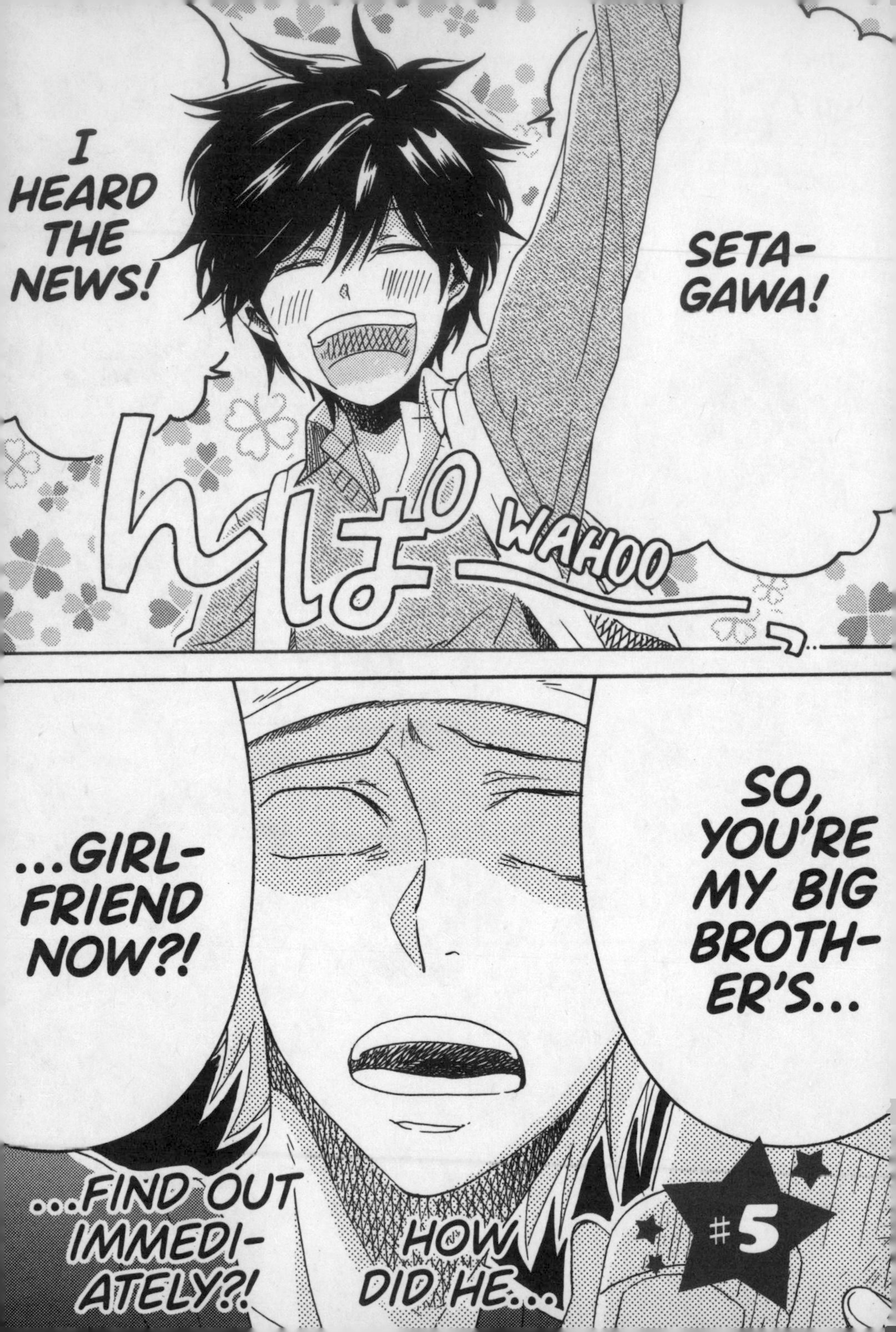
SETA-GAWA!
I HEARD THE NEWS!
んぱ
WAHOO
SO, YOU'RE MY BIG BROTH-ER'S...
...GIRL-FRIEND NOW?!
HOW DID HE...
...FIND OUT IMMEDI-ATELY?!
#5

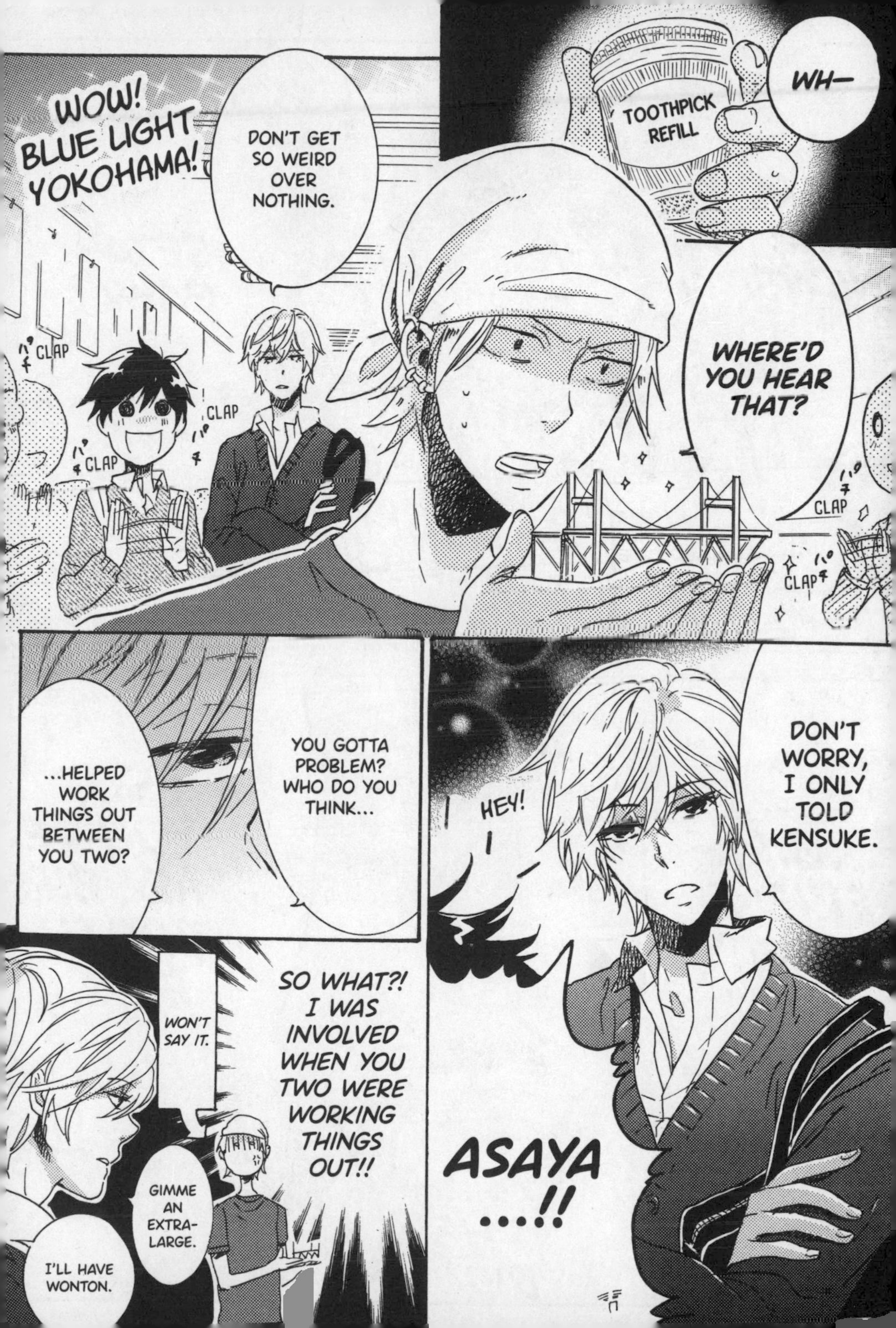
WH—
TOOTHPICK REFILL
WHERE'D YOU HEAR THAT?
CLAP
CLAP
CLAP
CLAP
CLAP
DON'T GET SO WEIRD OVER NOTHING.
WOW! BLUE LIGHT YOKOHAMA!
DON'T WORRY, I ONLY TOLD KENSUKE.
HEY!
ASAYA ...!!
YOU GOTTA PROBLEM? WHO DO YOU THINK...
...HELPED WORK THINGS OUT BETWEEN YOU TWO?
SO WHAT?! I WAS INVOLVED WHEN YOU TWO WERE WORKING THINGS OUT!!
WON'T SAY IT.
GIMME AN EXTRA-LARGE.
I'LL HAVE WONTON.

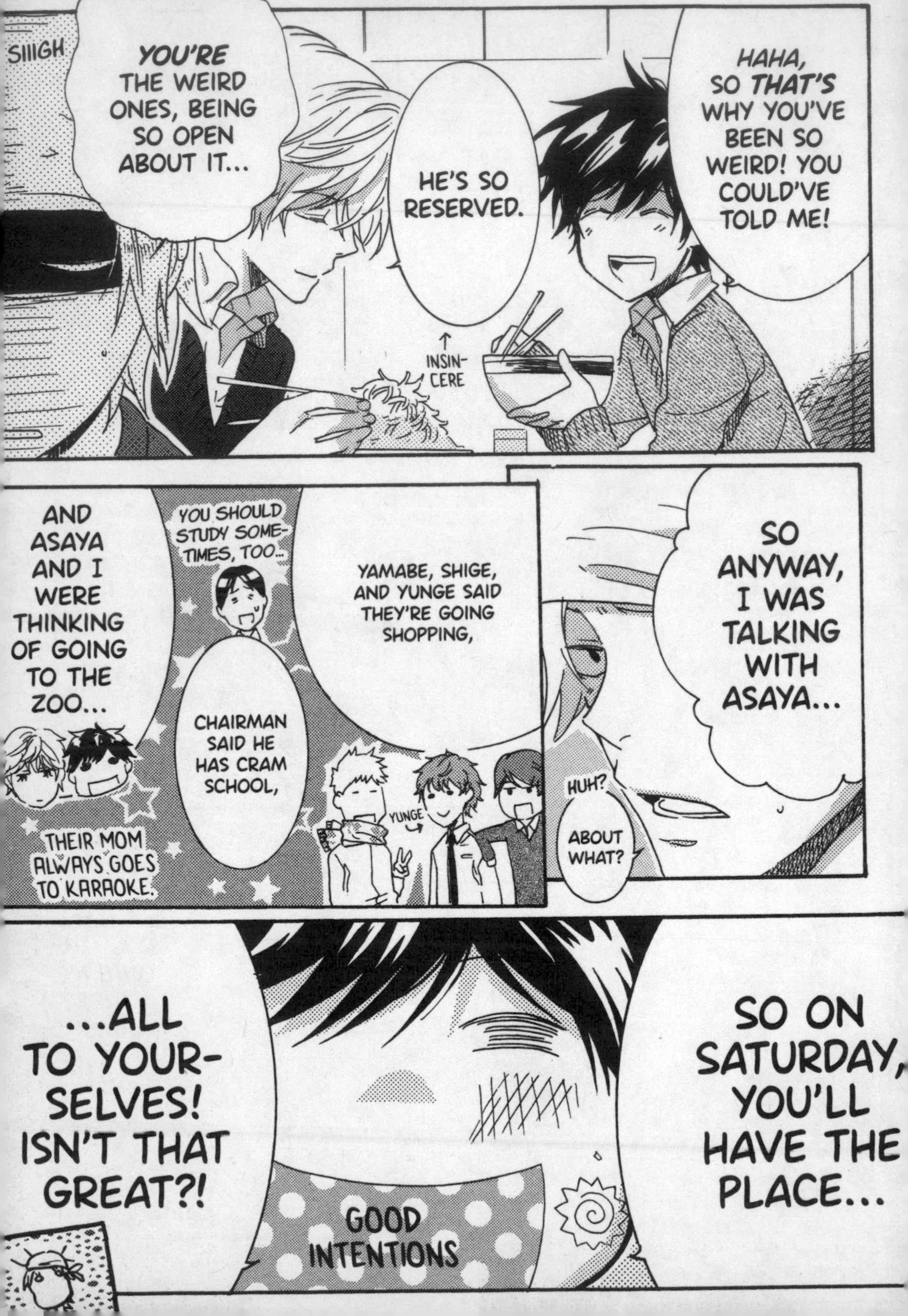
HAHA, SO THAT'S WHY YOU'VE BEEN SO WEIRD! YOU COULD'VE TOLD ME!
HE'S SO RESERVED.
INSIN-CERE
SIIIGH
YOU'RE THE WEIRD ONES, BEING SO OPEN ABOUT IT...
SO ANYWAY, I WAS TALKING WITH ASAYA...
HUH?
ABOUT WHAT?
YAMABE, SHIGE, AND YUNGE SAID THEY'RE GOING SHOPPING,
YUNGE
YOU SHOULD STUDY SOME-TIMES, TOO...
CHAIRMAN SAID HE HAS CRAM SCHOOL,
AND ASAYA AND I WERE THINKING OF GOING TO THE ZOO...
THEIR MOM ALWAYS GOES TO KARAOKE.
SO ON SATURDAY, YOU'LL HAVE THE PLACE...
GOOD INTENTIONS
...ALL TO YOUR-SELVES! ISN'T THAT GREAT?!

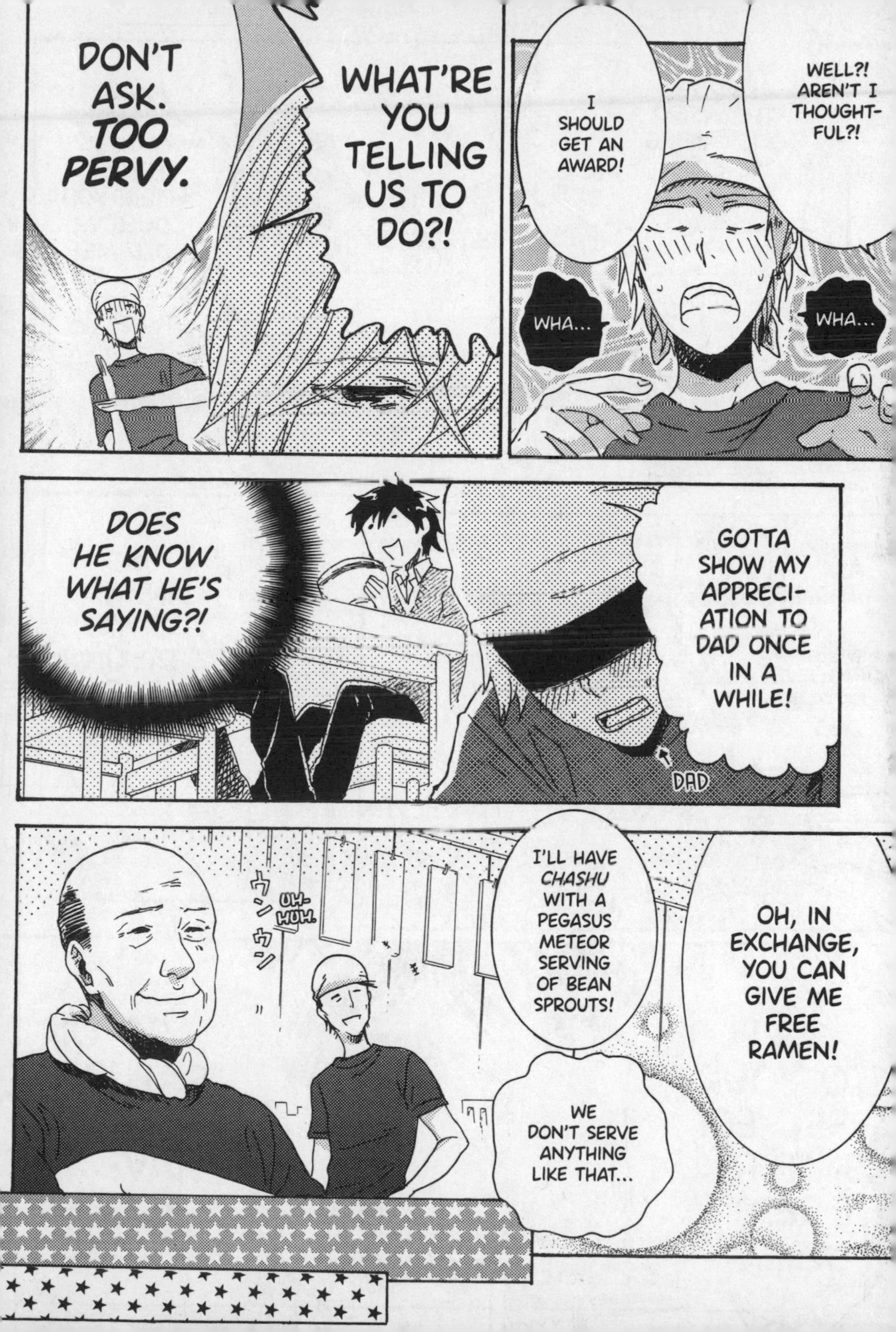

WELL?! AREN'T I THOUGHTFUL?!
I SHOULD GET AN AWARD!
WHA...
WHA...
WHAT'RE YOU TELLING US TO DO?!
DON'T ASK. TOO PERVY.
GOTTA SHOW MY APPRECIATION TO DAD ONCE IN A WHILE!
DAD
DOES HE KNOW WHAT HE'S SAYING?!
OH, IN EXCHANGE, YOU CAN GIVE ME FREE RAMEN!
I'LL HAVE *CHASHU* WITH A PEGASUS METEOR SERVING OF BEAN SPROUTS!
WE DON'T SERVE ANYTHING LIKE THAT...
ウンウン
UH-HUH.

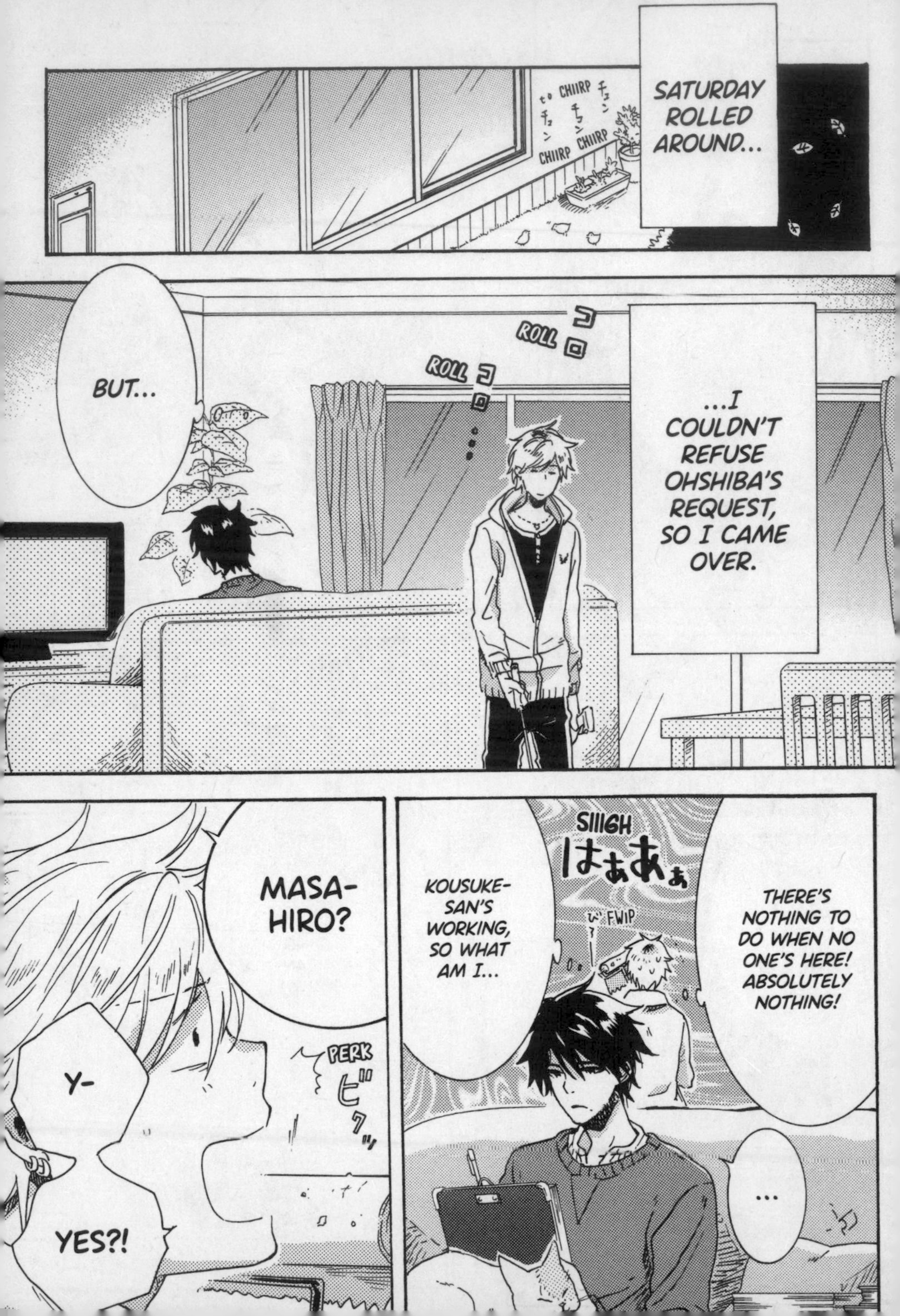
SATURDAY ROLLED AROUND...
CHIIRP CHIIRP
CHIIRP CHIIRP
...I COULDN'T REFUSE OHSHIBA'S REQUEST, SO I CAME OVER.
ROLL
ROLL
BUT...
THERE'S NOTHING TO DO WHEN NO ONE'S HERE! ABSOLUTELY NOTHING!
SIIGH
KOUSUKE-SAN'S WORKING, SO WHAT AM I...
FWIP
...
MASA-HIRO?
PERK
Y-
YES?!

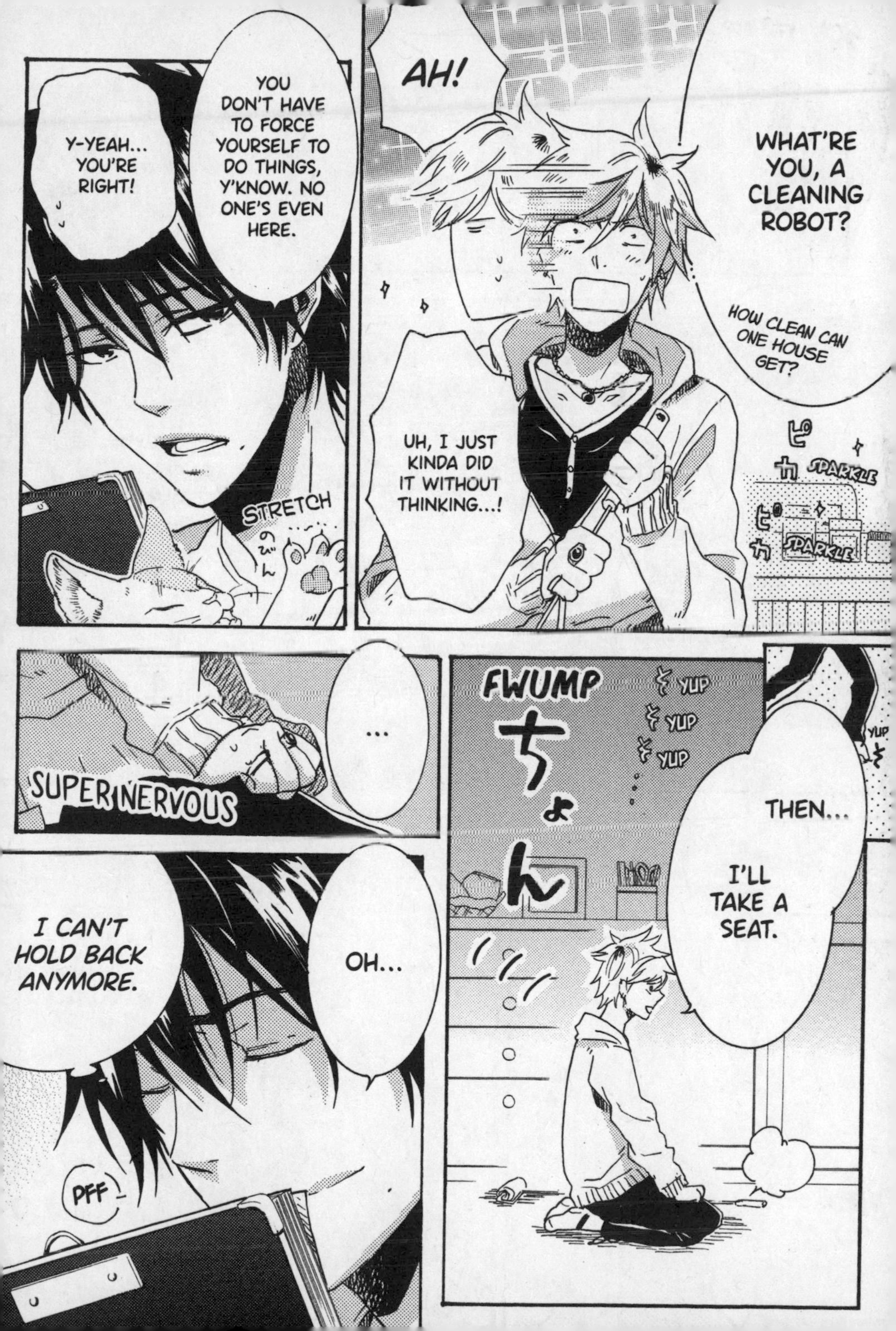
AH!
WHAT'RE YOU, A CLEANING ROBOT?
HOW CLEAN CAN ONE HOUSE GET?
UH, I JUST KINDA DID IT WITHOUT THINKING...!
ピカ SPARKLE
ピカ SPARKLE
YOU DON'T HAVE TO FORCE YOURSELF TO DO THINGS, Y'KNOW. NO ONE'S EVEN HERE.
Y-YEAH... YOU'RE RIGHT!
STRETCH
のびーん
YUP
THEN...
I'LL TAKE A SEAT.
FWUMP
ちょん
YUP
YUP
YUP
...
SUPER NERVOUS
OH...
I CAN'T HOLD BACK ANYMORE.
PFF

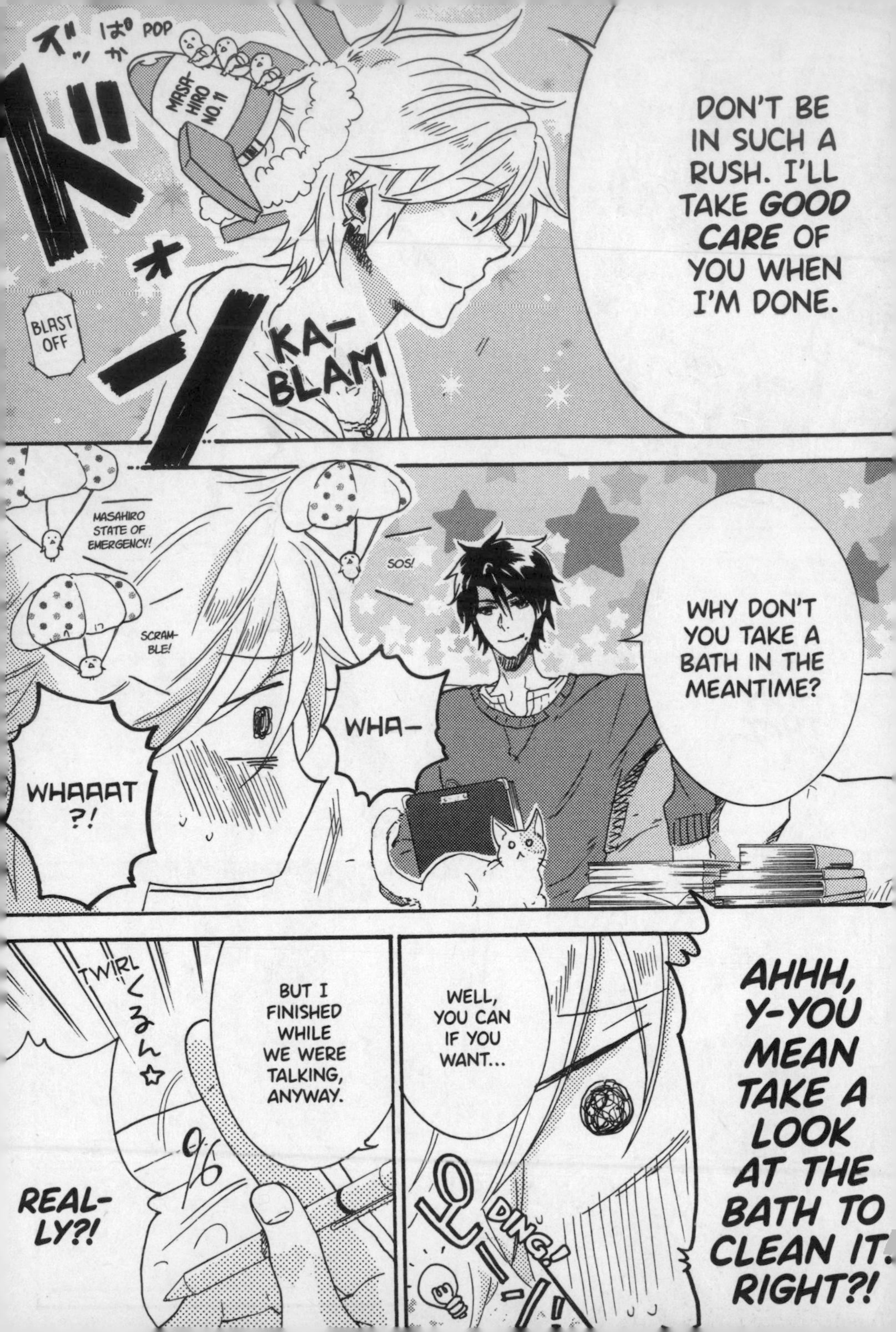
DON'T BE IN SUCH A RUSH. I'LL TAKE GOOD CARE OF YOU WHEN I'M DONE.
POP
MASA-HIRO NO.11
BLAST OFF
KA-BLAM
WHY DON'T YOU TAKE A BATH IN THE MEANTIME?
WHA-
SOS!
MASAHIRO STATE OF EMERGENCY!
SCRAM-BLE!
WHAAAT?!
AHHH, Y-YOU MEAN TAKE A LOOK AT THE BATH TO CLEAN IT. RIGHT?!
WELL, YOU CAN IF YOU WANT...
DING!
BUT I FINISHED WHILE WE WERE TALKING, ANYWAY.
TWIRL くるん☆
REAL-LY?!

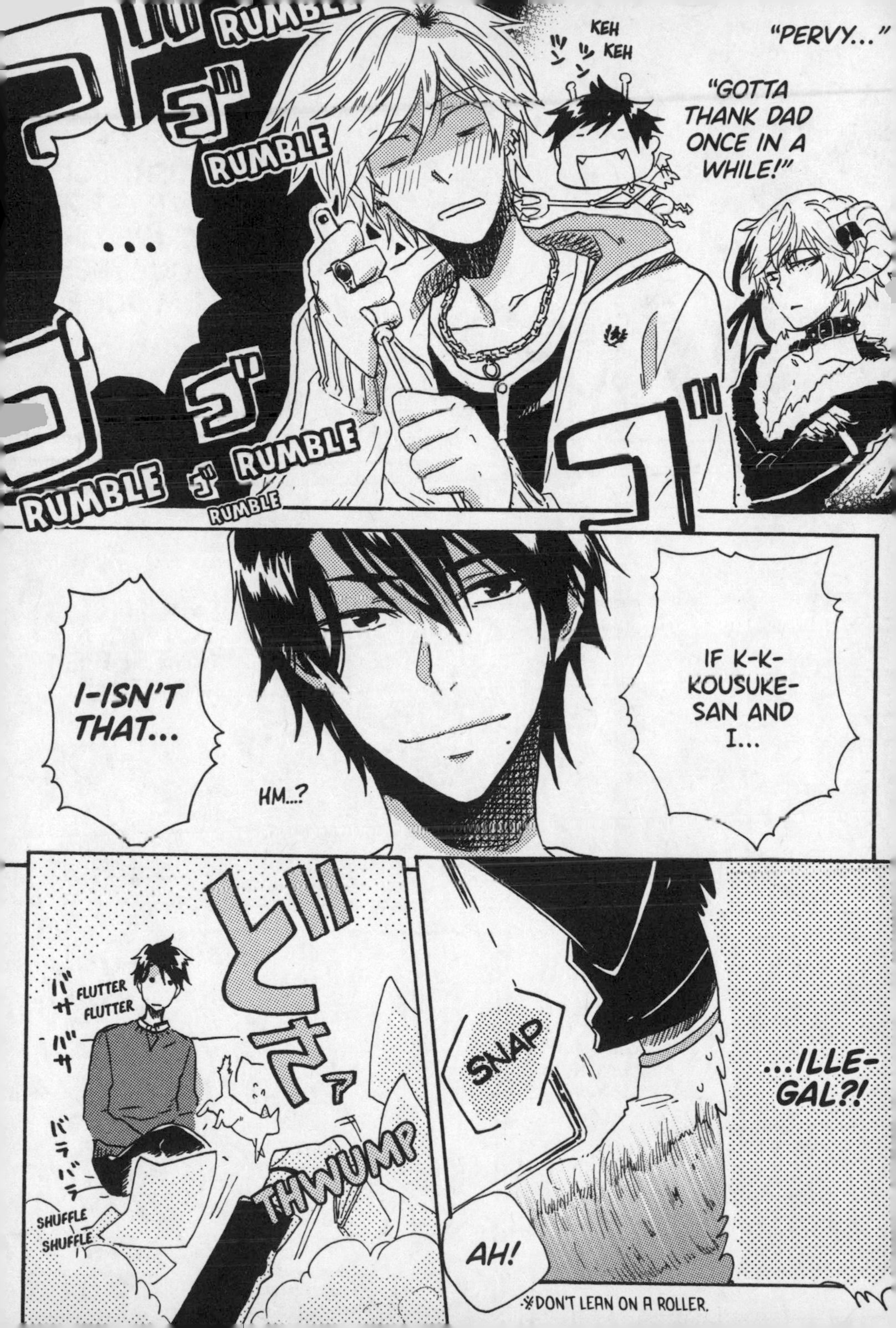
"PERVY..."
"GOTTA THANK DAD ONCE IN A WHILE!"
KEH KEH
RUMBLE RUMBLE
...
RUMBLE RUMBLE
RUMBLE RUMBLE
IF K-K-KOUSUKE-SAN AND I...
HM...?
I-ISN'T THAT...
...ILLE-GAL?!
SNAP
AH!
THWUMP
FLUTTER FLUTTER
SHUFFLE SHUFFLE
※DON'T LEAN ON A ROLLER.

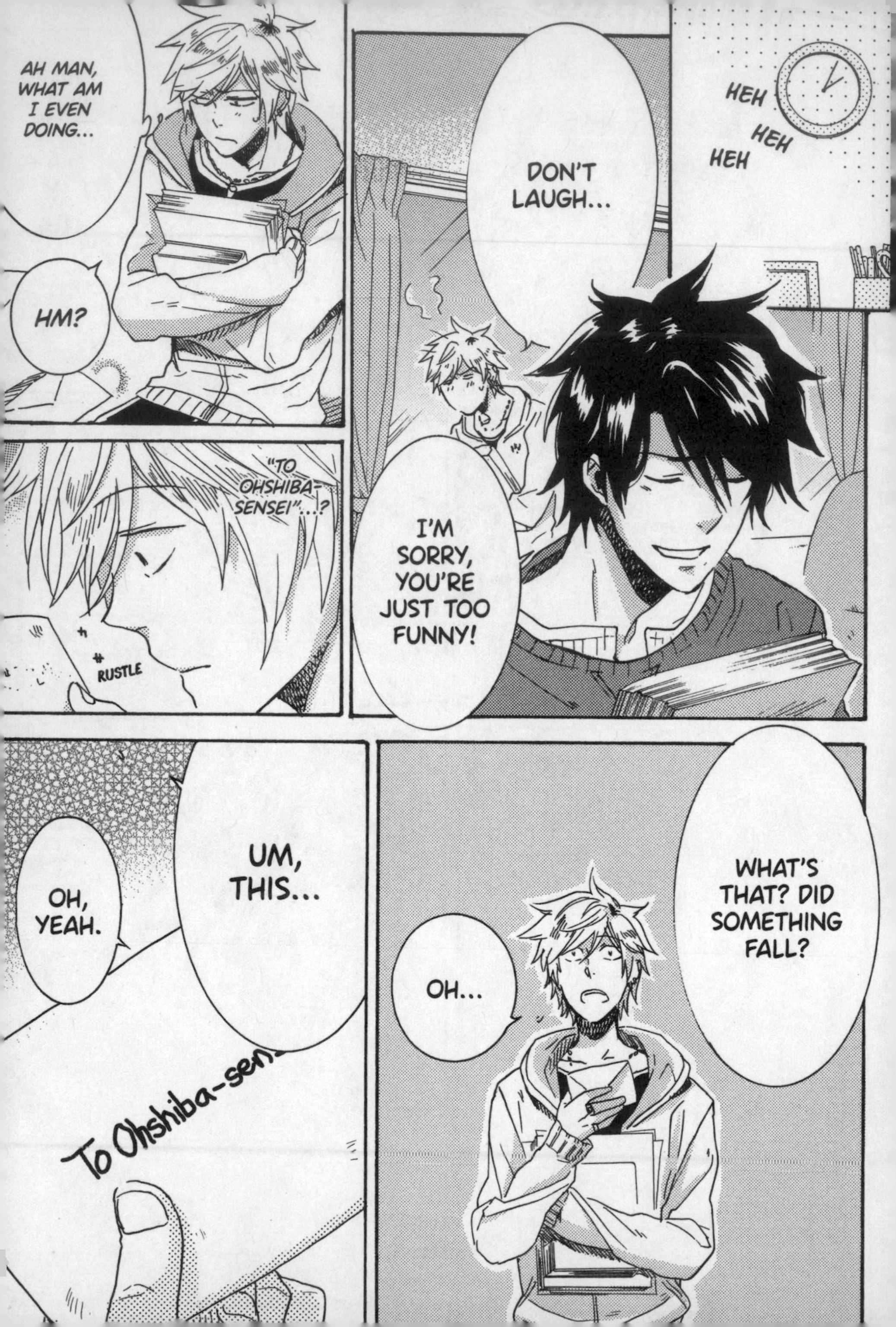
HEH
HEH
HEH
DON'T LAUGH...
I'M SORRY, YOU'RE JUST TOO FUNNY!
AH MAN, WHAT AM I EVEN DOING...
HM?
"TO OHSHIBA-SENSEI"...?
RUSTLE
WHAT'S THAT? DID SOMETHING FALL?
OH...
UM, THIS...
OH, YEAH.
To Ohshiba-sen

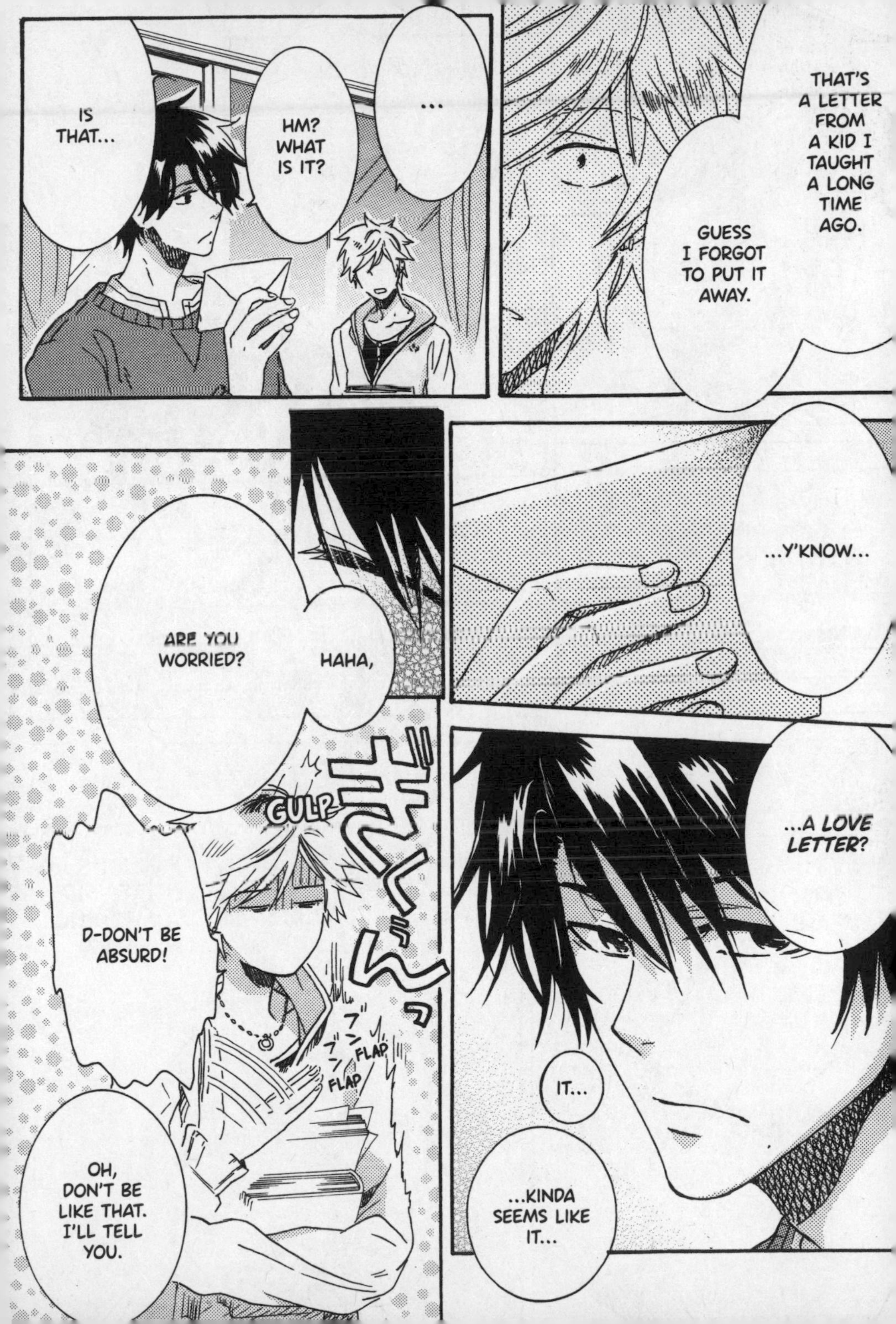
IS THAT...
HM? WHAT IS IT?
...
THAT'S A LETTER FROM A KID I TAUGHT A LONG TIME AGO.
GUESS I FORGOT TO PUT IT AWAY.
...Y'KNOW...
...A LOVE LETTER?
IT...
...KINDA SEEMS LIKE IT...
HAHA,
ARE YOU WORRIED?
GULP
ぎくぅっ
D-DON'T BE ABSURD!
FLAP
FLAP
OH, DON'T BE LIKE THAT. I'LL TELL YOU.

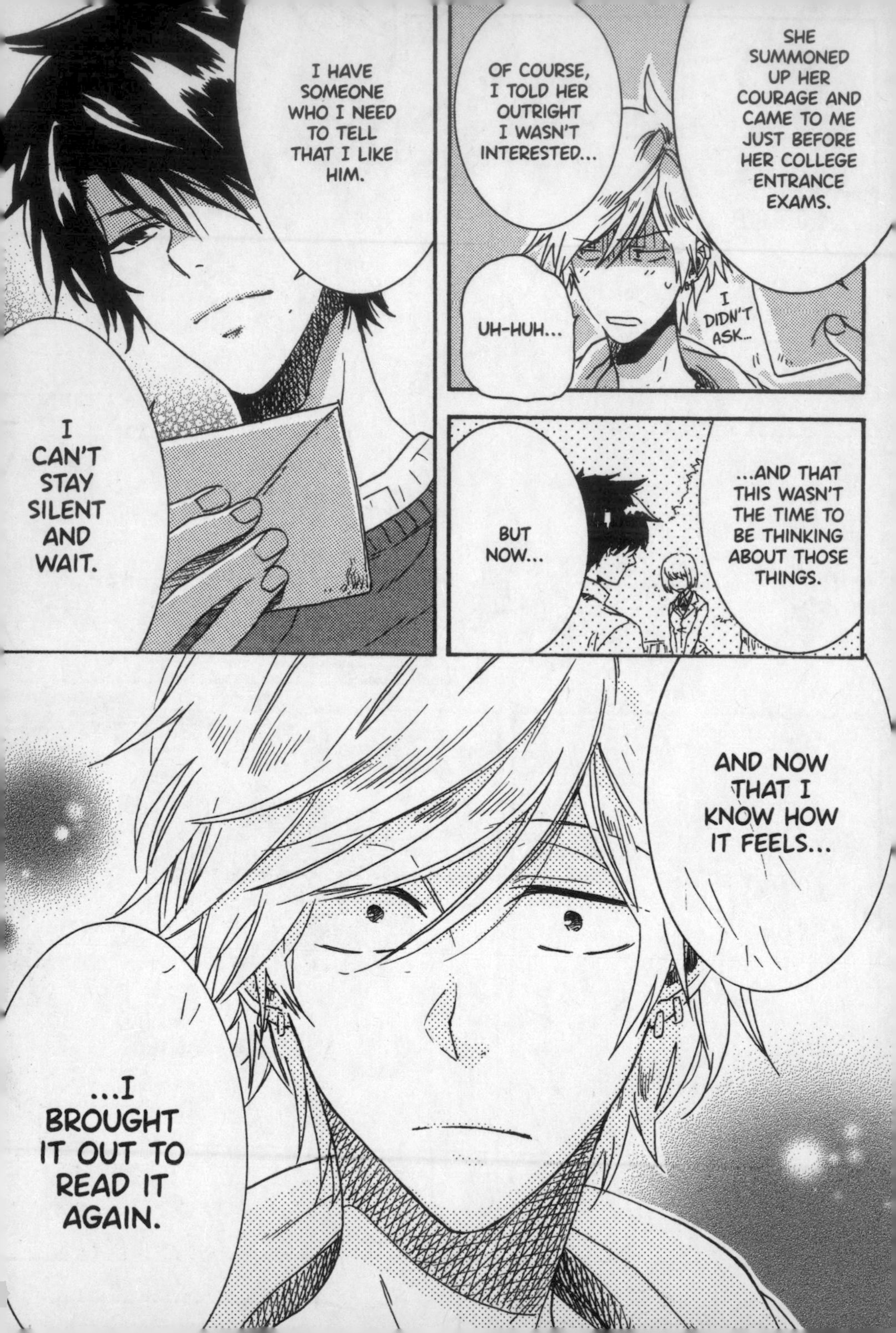
SHE SUMMONED UP HER COURAGE AND CAME TO ME JUST BEFORE HER COLLEGE ENTRANCE EXAMS.
OF COURSE, I TOLD HER OUTRIGHT I WASN'T INTERESTED...
I DIDN'T ASK...
UH-HUH...
...AND THAT THIS WASN'T THE TIME TO BE THINKING ABOUT THOSE THINGS.
BUT NOW...
I HAVE SOMEONE WHO I NEED TO TELL THAT I LIKE HIM.
I CAN'T STAY SILENT AND WAIT.
AND NOW THAT I KNOW HOW IT FEELS...
...I BROUGHT IT OUT TO READ IT AGAIN.

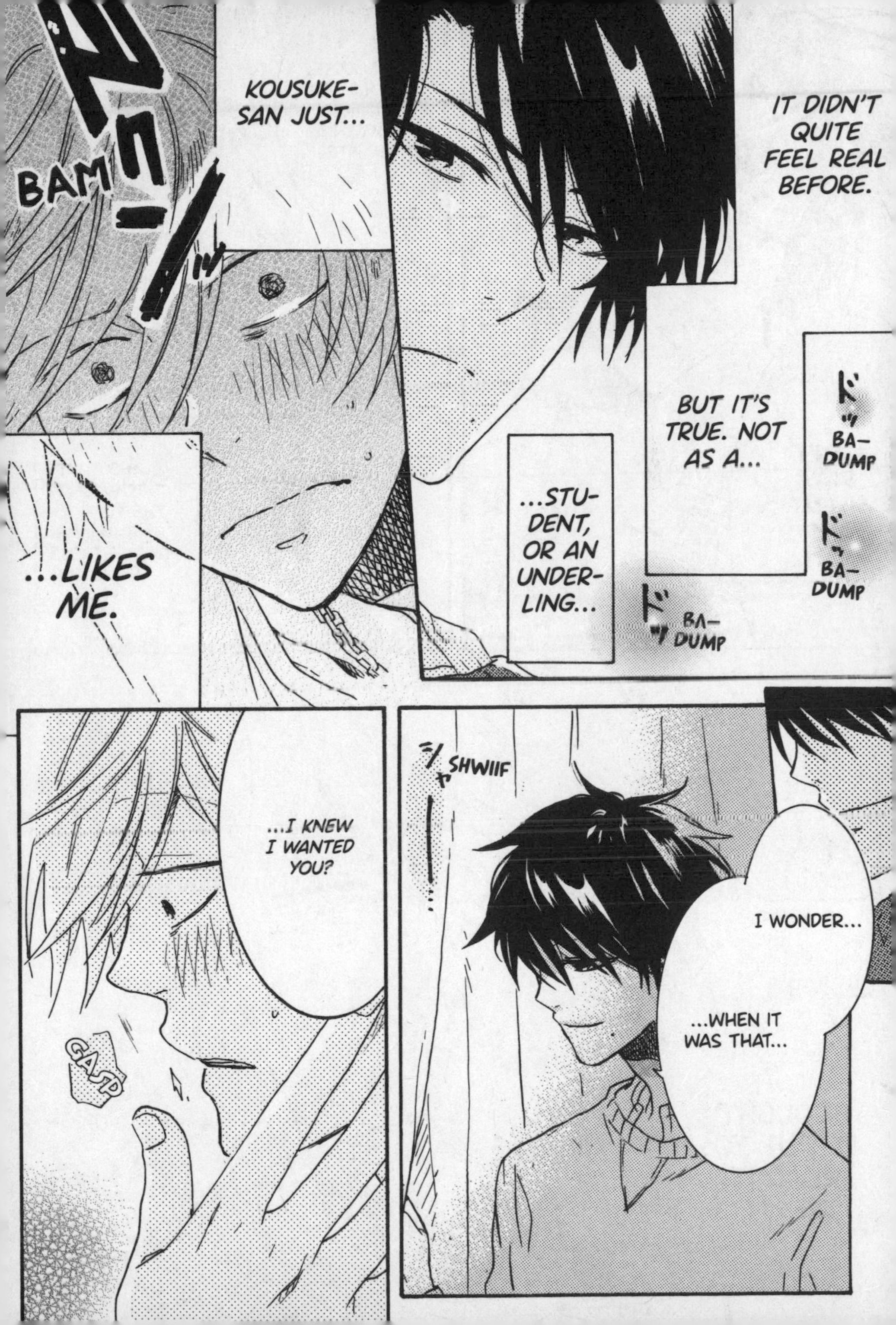
IT DIDN'T QUITE FEEL REAL BEFORE.
BUT IT'S TRUE. NOT AS A...
BA-DUMP
BA-DUMP
...STU-DENT, OR AN UNDER-LING...
BA-DUMP
KOUSUKE-SAN JUST...
BAM
...LIKES ME.
SHWIIF
I WONDER...
...WHEN IT WAS THAT...
...I KNEW I WANTED YOU?
GASP

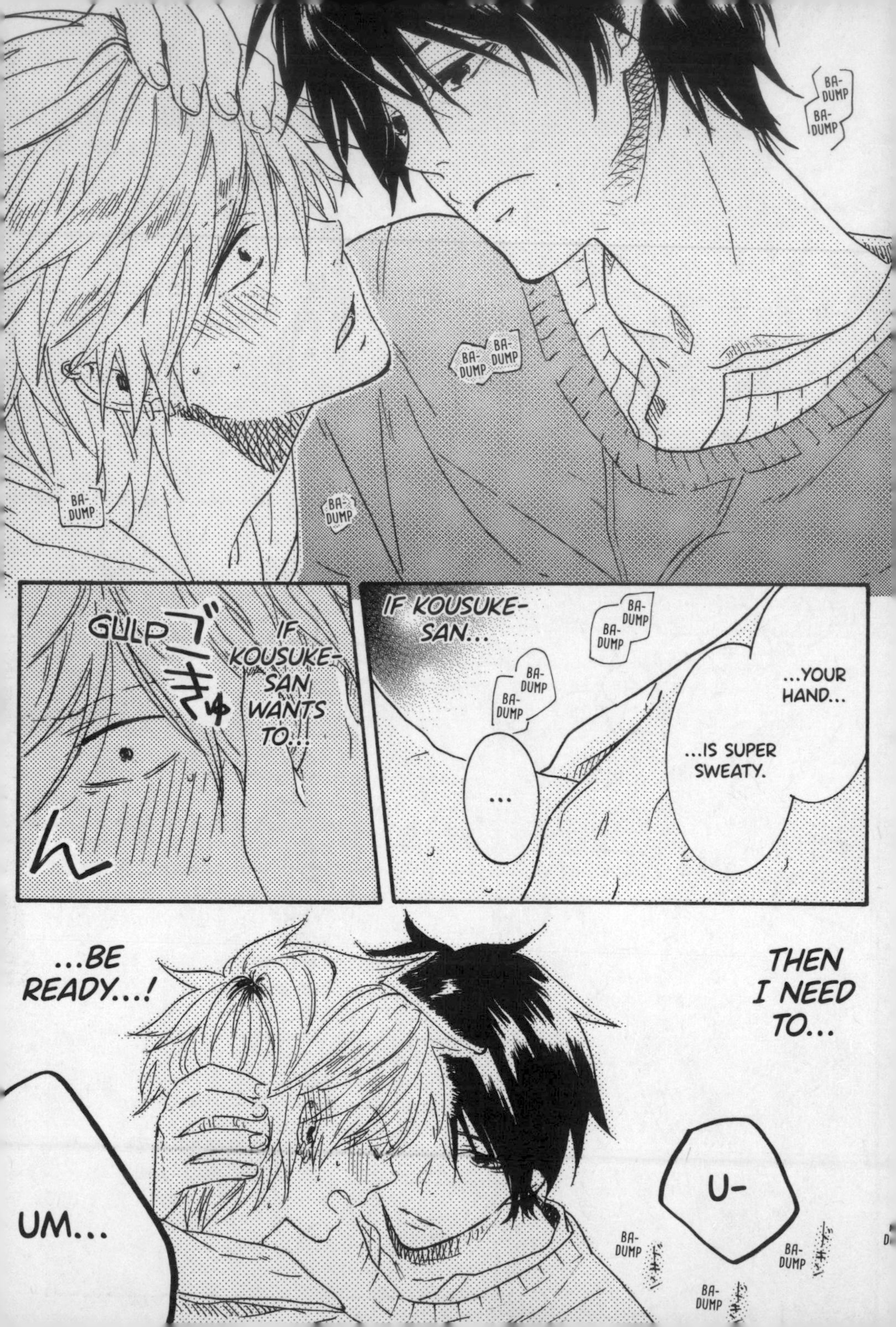
BA-DUMP
BA-DUMP
BA-DUMP
BA-DUMP
BA-DUMP
BA-DUMP
IF KOUSUKE-SAN...
BA-DUMP
BA-DUMP
BA-DUMP
BA-DUMP
...YOUR HAND...
...IS SUPER SWEATY.
...
IF KOUSUKE-SAN WANTS TO...
GULP ゴきゅ
ん
THEN I NEED TO...
U-
...BE READY...!
UM...
BA-DUMP
BA-DUMP
BA-DUMP

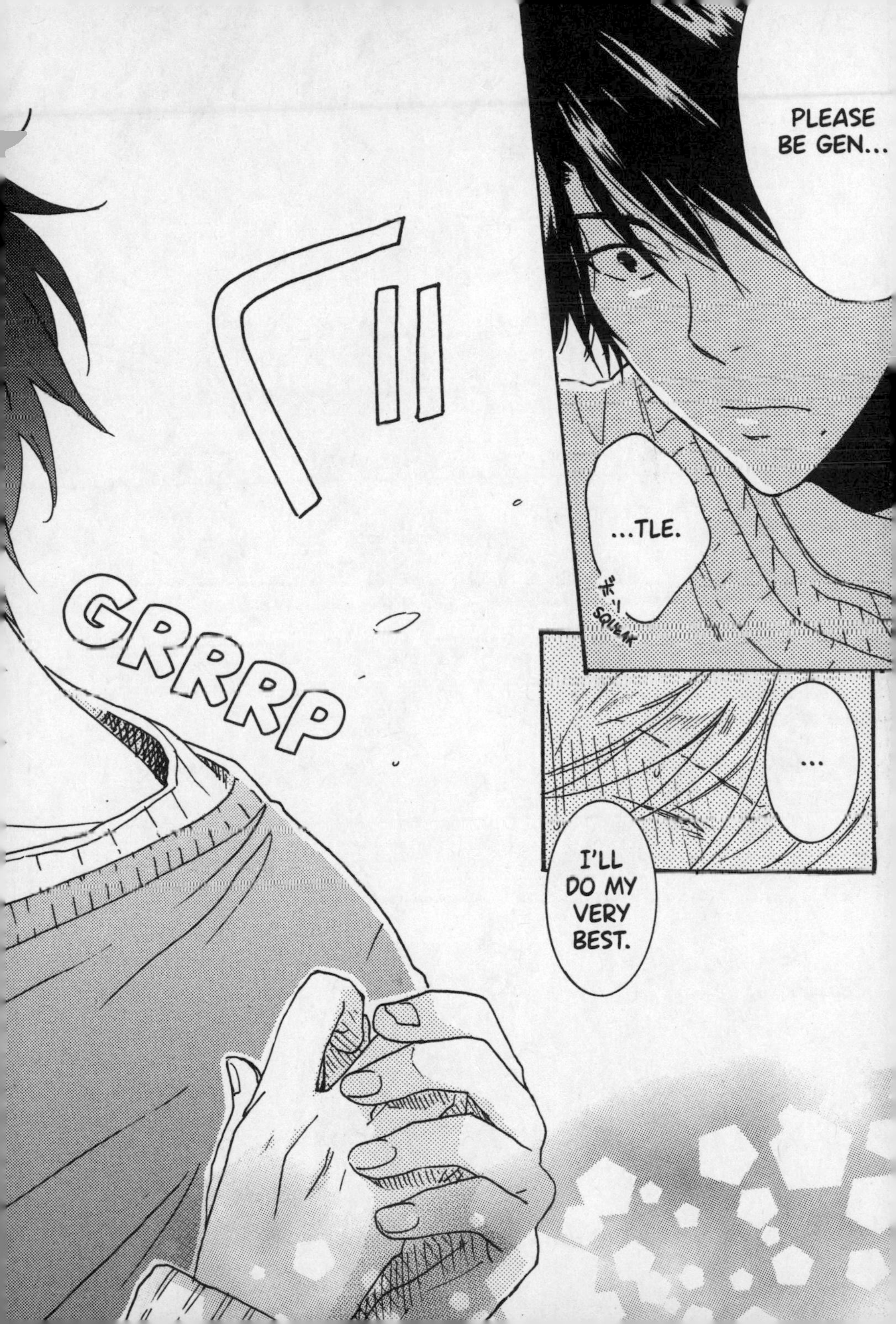
PLEASE BE GEN...
...TLE.
ボッ
SQUEAK
...
I'LL DO MY VERY BEST.
GRRRP

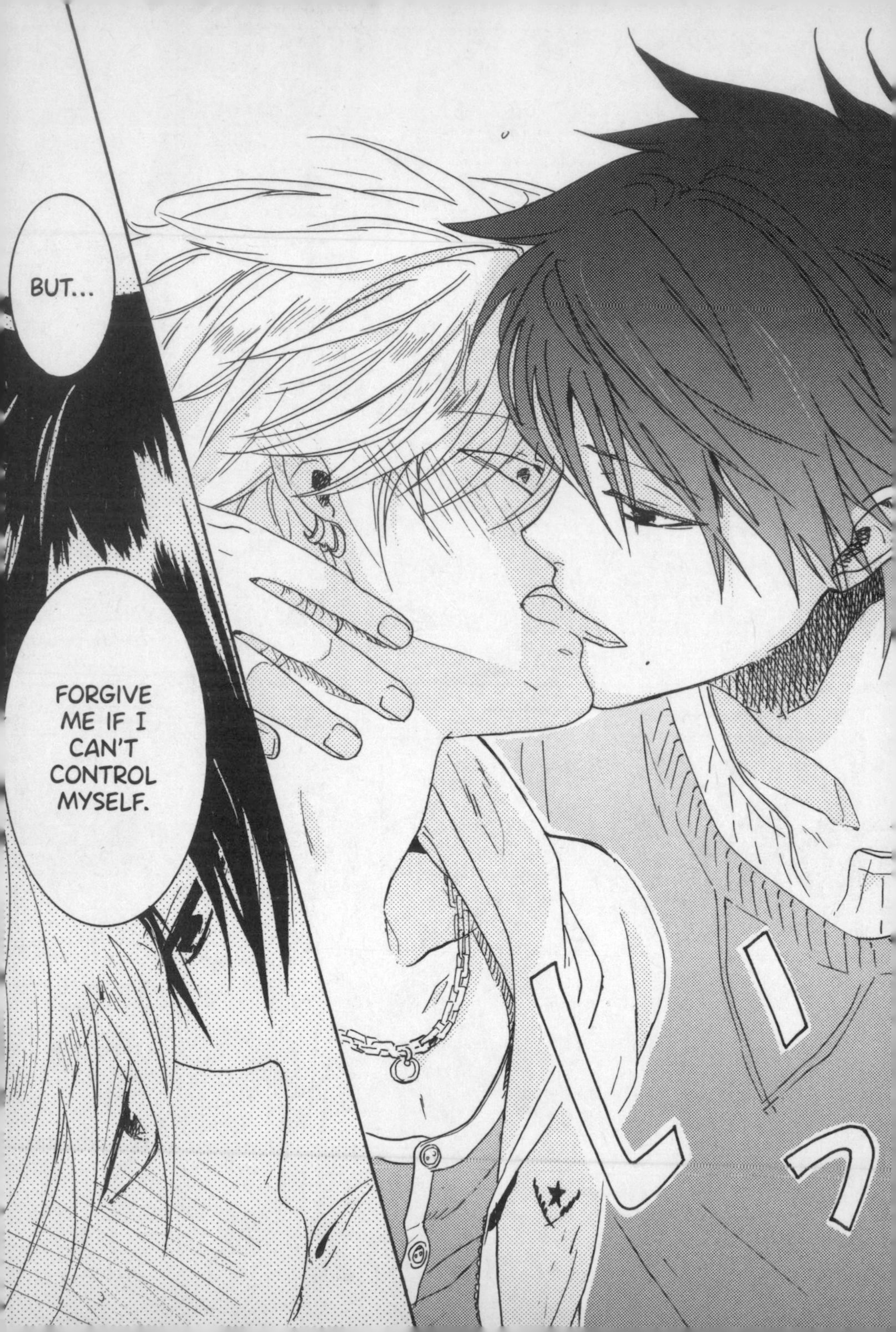
BUT...
FORGIVE ME IF I CAN'T CONTROL MYSELF.

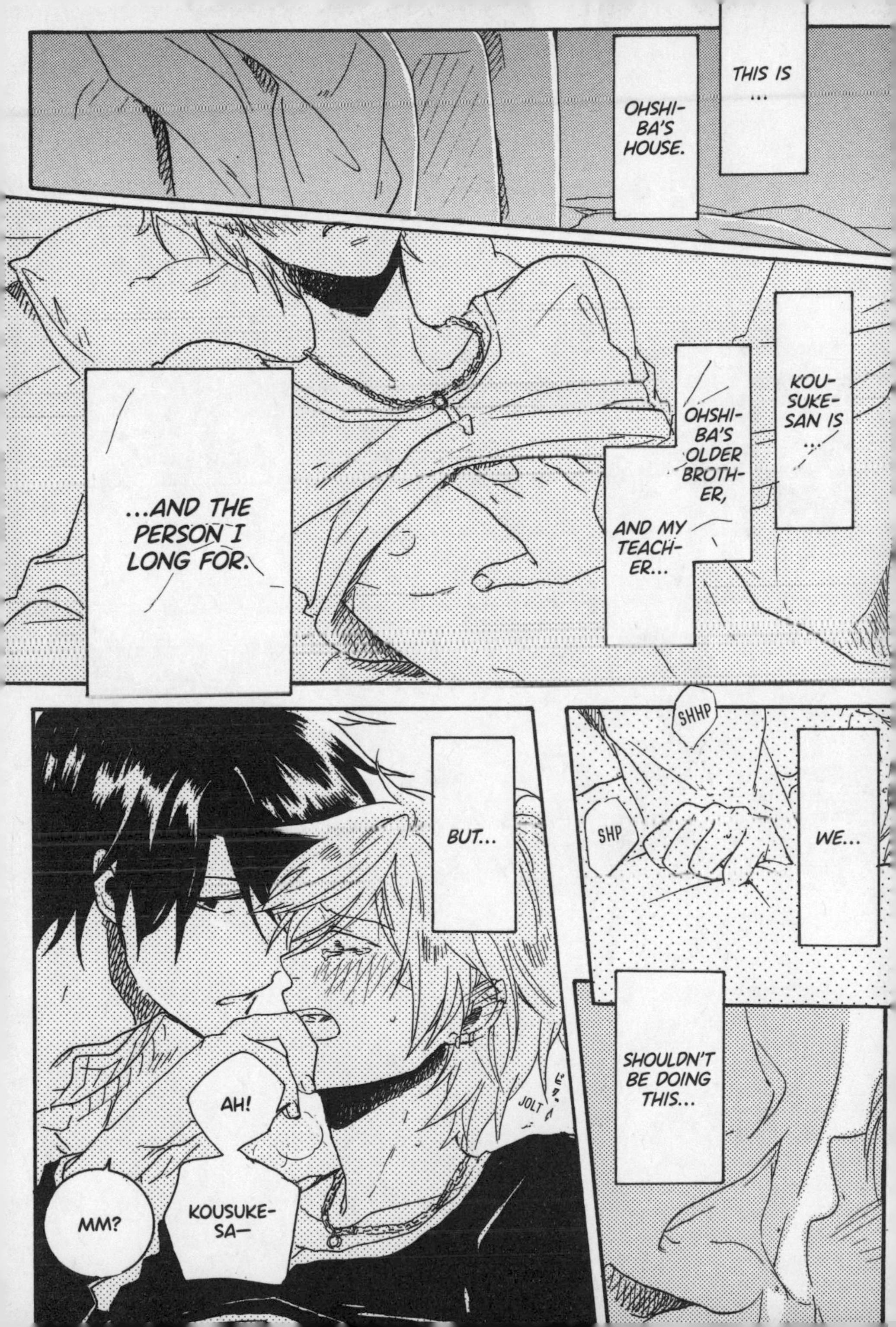
THIS IS ...
OHSHIBA'S HOUSE.
KOUSUKE-SAN IS ...
OHSHIBA'S OLDER BROTHER,
AND MY TEACHER...
...AND THE PERSON I LONG FOR.
SHHP
WE...
SHP
SHOULDN'T BE DOING THIS...
BUT...
JOLT
AH!
KOUSUKE-SA—
MM?

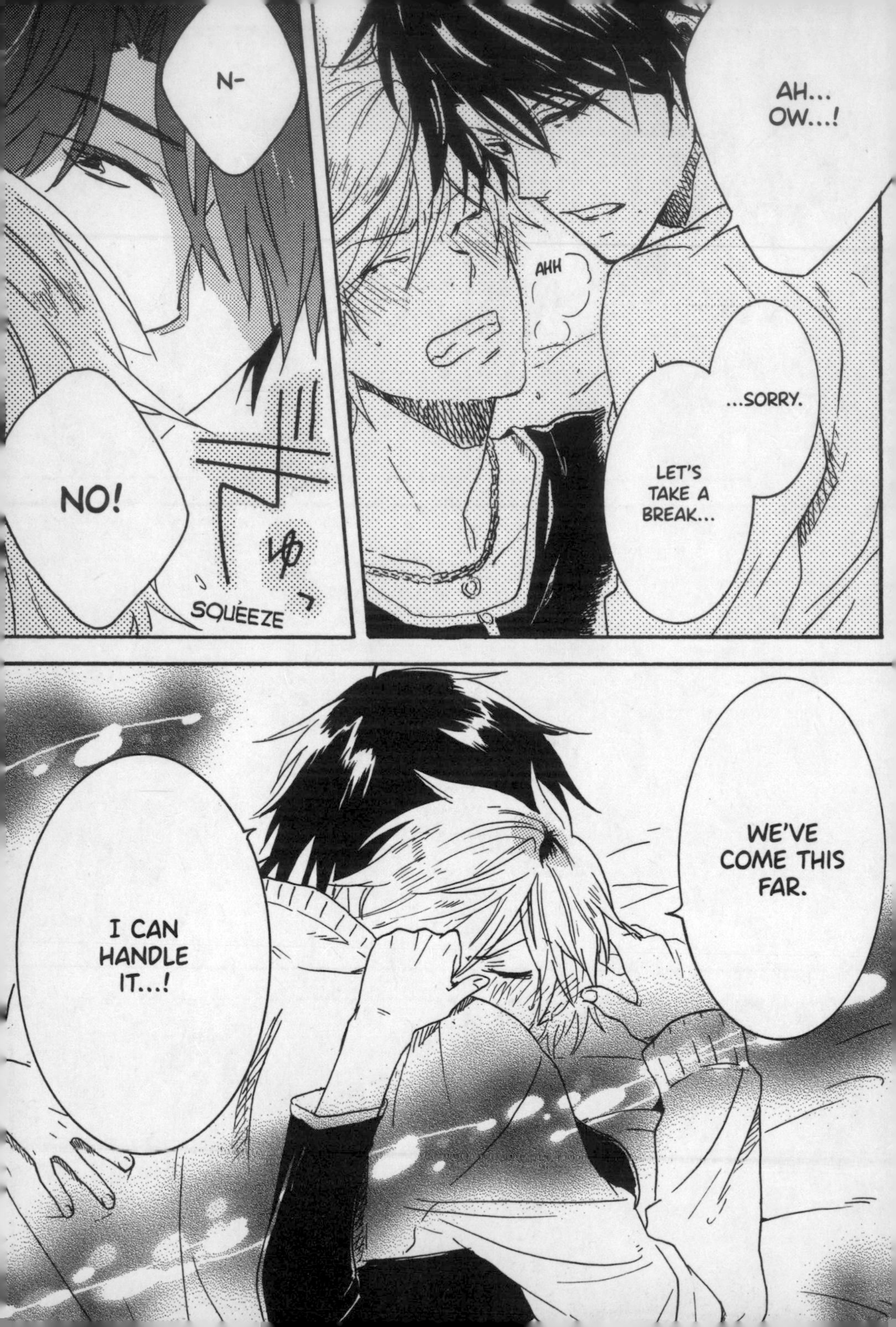
AH... OW...!
AHH
...SORRY.
LET'S TAKE A BREAK...
N-
NO!
SQUEEZE
WE'VE COME THIS FAR.
I CAN HANDLE IT...!

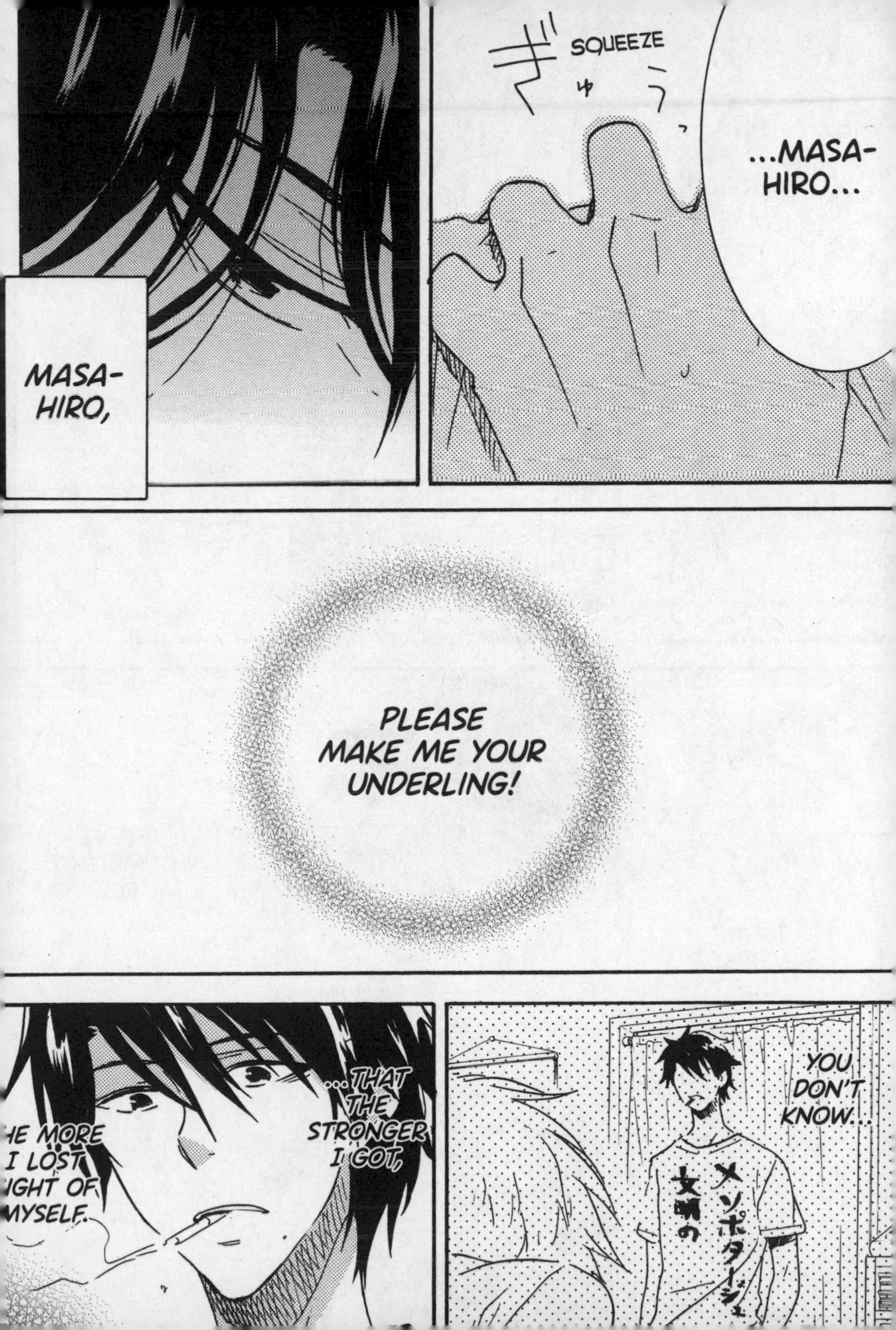

ぎゅうっ
SQUEEZE
...MASA-HIRO...
MASA-HIRO,
PLEASE MAKE ME YOUR UNDERLING!
YOU DON'T KNOW...
メソポタージュ文明の
...THAT THE STRONGER I GOT,
HE MORE I LOST IGHT OF MYSELF.

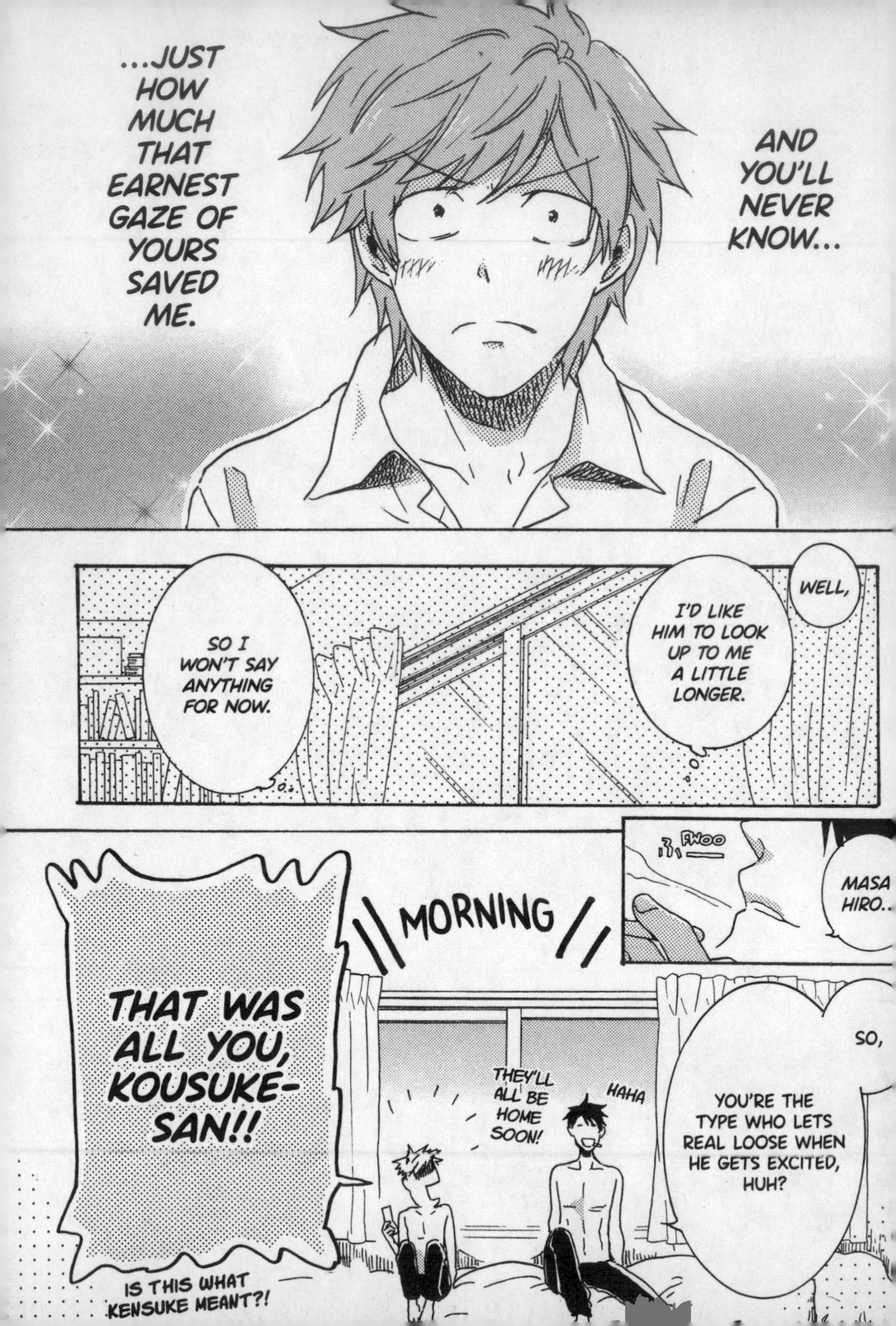
AND YOU'LL NEVER KNOW...
...JUST HOW MUCH THAT EARNEST GAZE OF YOURS SAVED ME.
WELL,
I'D LIKE HIM TO LOOK UP TO ME A LITTLE LONGER.
SO I WON'T SAY ANYTHING FOR NOW.
FWOO
MASA HIRO...
SO,
YOU'RE THE TYPE WHO LETS REAL LOOSE WHEN HE GETS EXCITED, HUH?
HAHA
THEY'LL ALL BE HOME SOON!
MORNING
THAT WAS ALL YOU, KOUSUKE-SAN!!
IS THIS WHAT KENSUKE MEANT?!

Hitorijime
My Hero

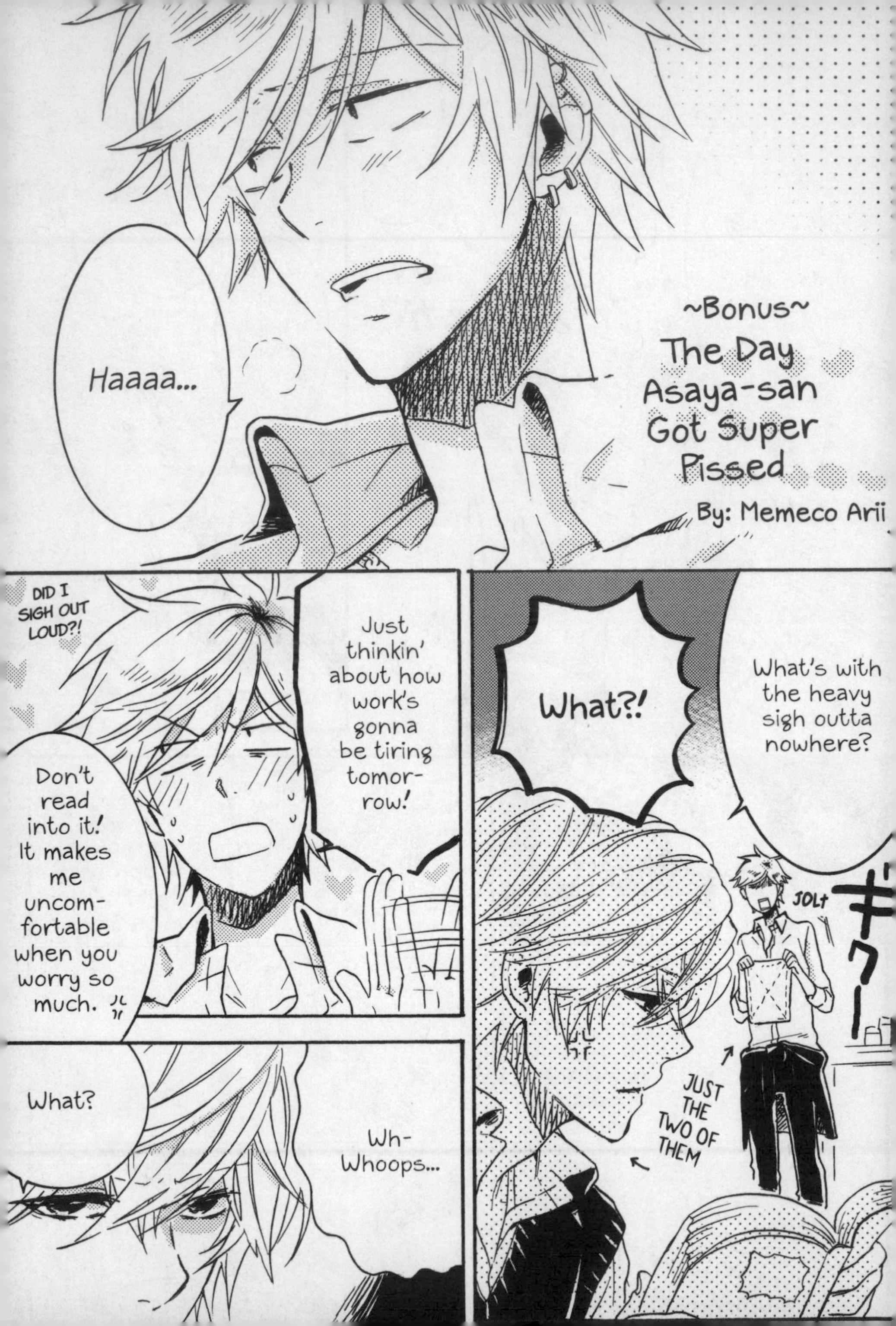
~Bonus~
The Day Asaya-san Got Super Pissed
By: Memeco Arii
Haaaa...
What's with the heavy sigh outta nowhere?
What?!
JOLT
ギクー
JUST THE TWO OF THEM
Just thinkin' about how work's gonna be tiring tomorrow!
Don't read into it! It makes me uncomfortable when you worry so much.
DID I SIGH OUT LOUD?!
Wh-Whoops...
What?

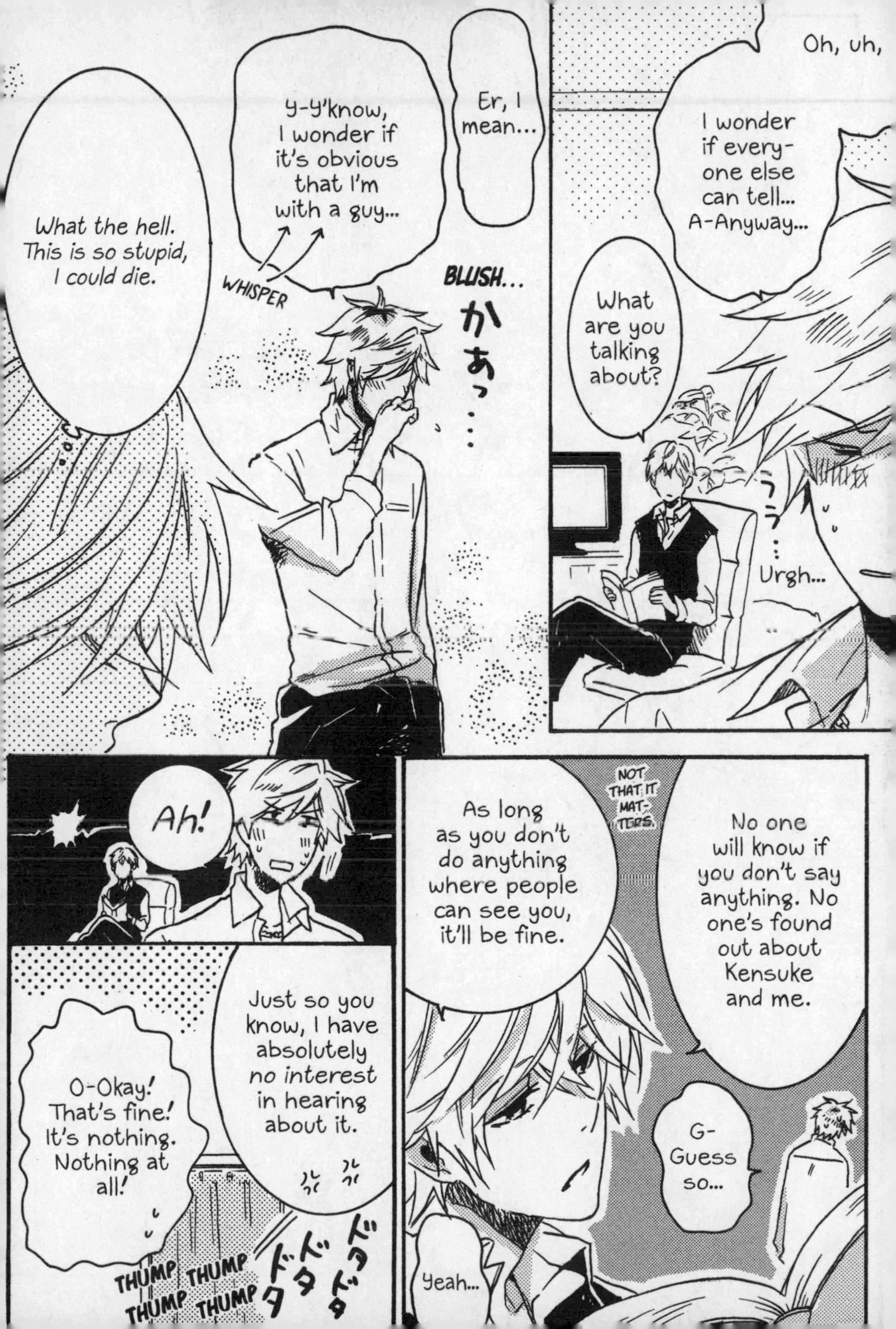
Oh, uh,
I wonder if every-one else can tell... A-Anyway...
What are you talking about?
Urgh...
Er, I mean...
Y-Y'know, I wonder if it's obvious that I'm with a guy...
WHISPER
BLUSH... かあっ…
What the hell. This is so stupid, I could die.
No one will know if you don't say anything. No one's found out about Kensuke and me.
NOT THAT IT MAT-TERS.
As long as you don't do anything where people can see you, it'll be fine.
G-Guess so...
Yeah...
Ah!
Just so you know, I have absolutely *no interest* in hearing about it.
O-Okay! That's fine! It's nothing. Nothing at all!
THUMP THUMP THUMP THUMP
ドタドタドタドタ

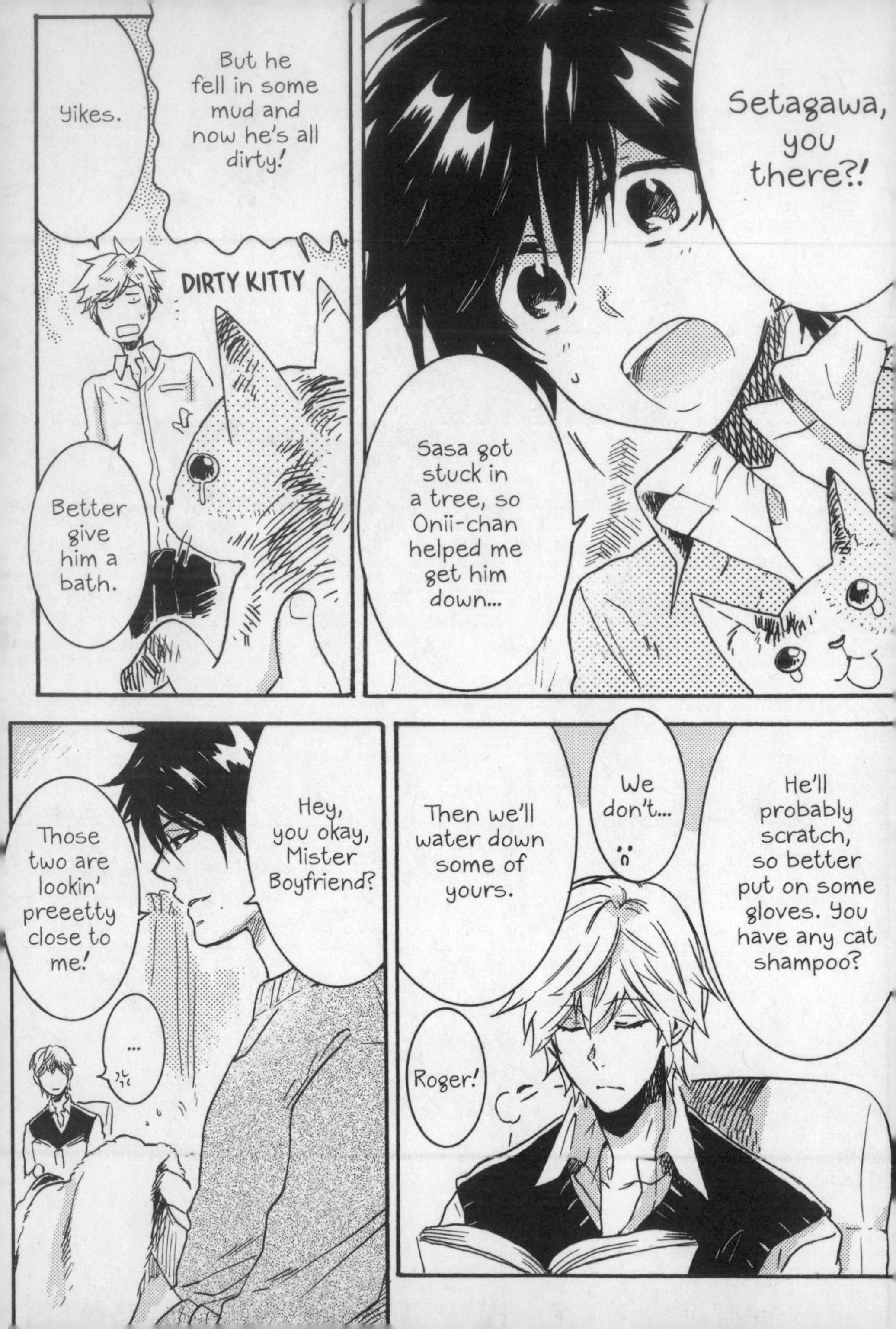
Setagawa, you there?!
Sasa got stuck in a tree, so Onii-chan helped me get him down...
But he fell in some mud and now he's all dirty!
Yikes.
DIRTY KITTY
Better give him a bath.
He'll probably scratch, so better put on some gloves. You have any cat shampoo?
We don't...
Then we'll water down some of yours.
Roger!
Hey, you okay, Mister Boyfriend?
Those two are lookin' preeetty close to me!
...

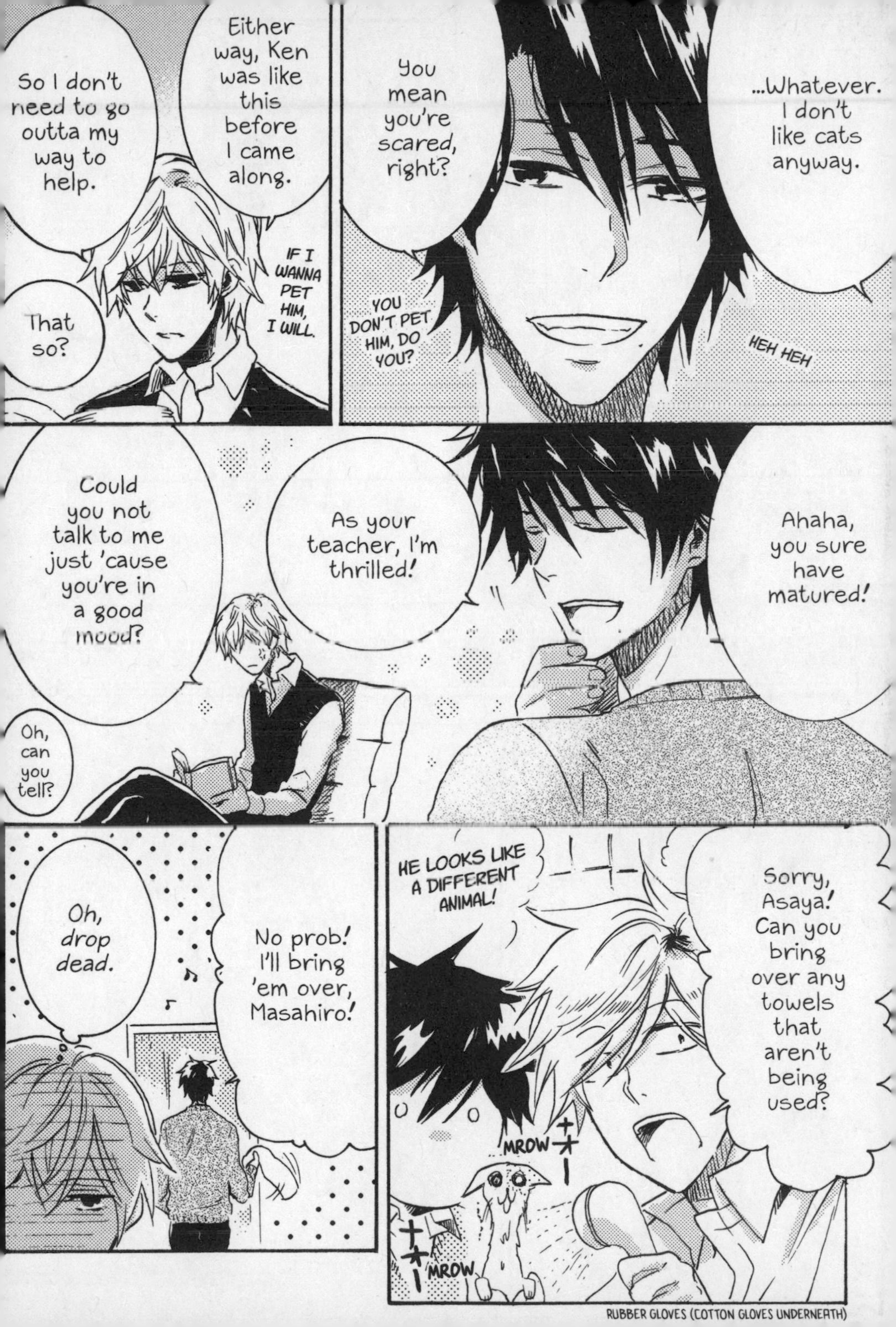

...Whatever. I don't like cats anyway.
You mean you're scared, right?
KEH HEH
YOU DON'T PET HIM, DO YOU?
Either way, Ken was like this before I came along.
So I don't need to go outta my way to help.
IF I WANNA PET HIM, I WILL.
That so?
Ahaha, you sure have matured!
As your teacher, I'm thrilled!
Could you not talk to me just 'cause you're in a good mood?
Oh, can you tell?
Sorry, Asaya! Can you bring over any towels that aren't being used?
HE LOOKS LIKE A DIFFERENT ANIMAL!
MROW
MROW
RUBBER GLOVES (COTTON GLOVES UNDERNEATH)
No prob! I'll bring 'em over, Masahiro!
Oh, drop dead.

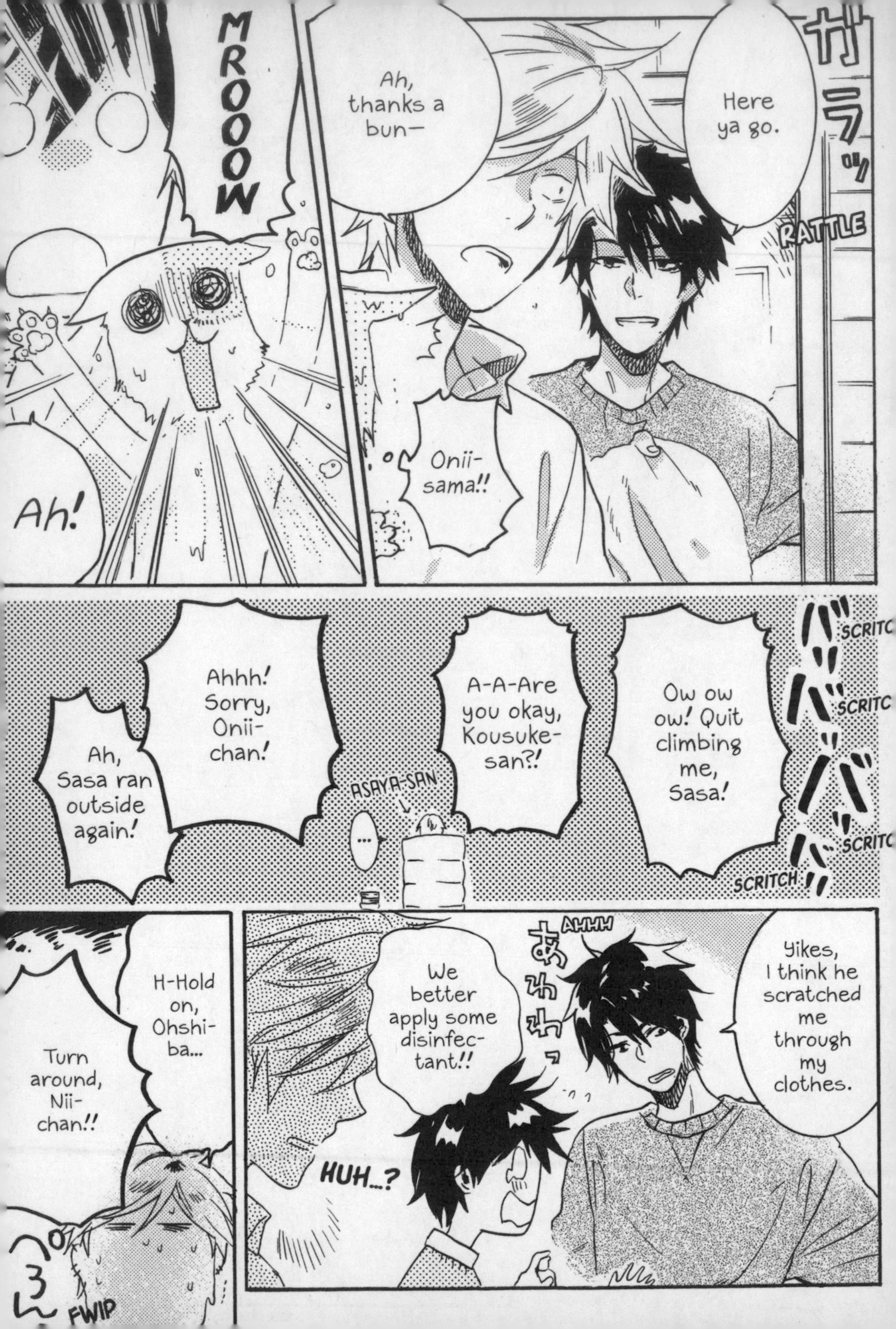
ガラッ
RATTLE
Here ya go.
Ah, thanks a bun—
Onii-sama!!
MROOOW
Ah!
SCRITCH
Ow ow ow! Quit climbing me, Sasa!
A-A-Are you okay, Kousuke-san?!
ASAYA-SAN
...
Ahhh! Sorry, Onii-chan!
Ah, Sasa ran outside again!
Yikes, I think he scratched me through my clothes.
あわわっ
AHHH
We better apply some disinfectant!!
HUH...?
H-Hold on, Ohshiba...
Turn around, Nii-chan!!
FWIP

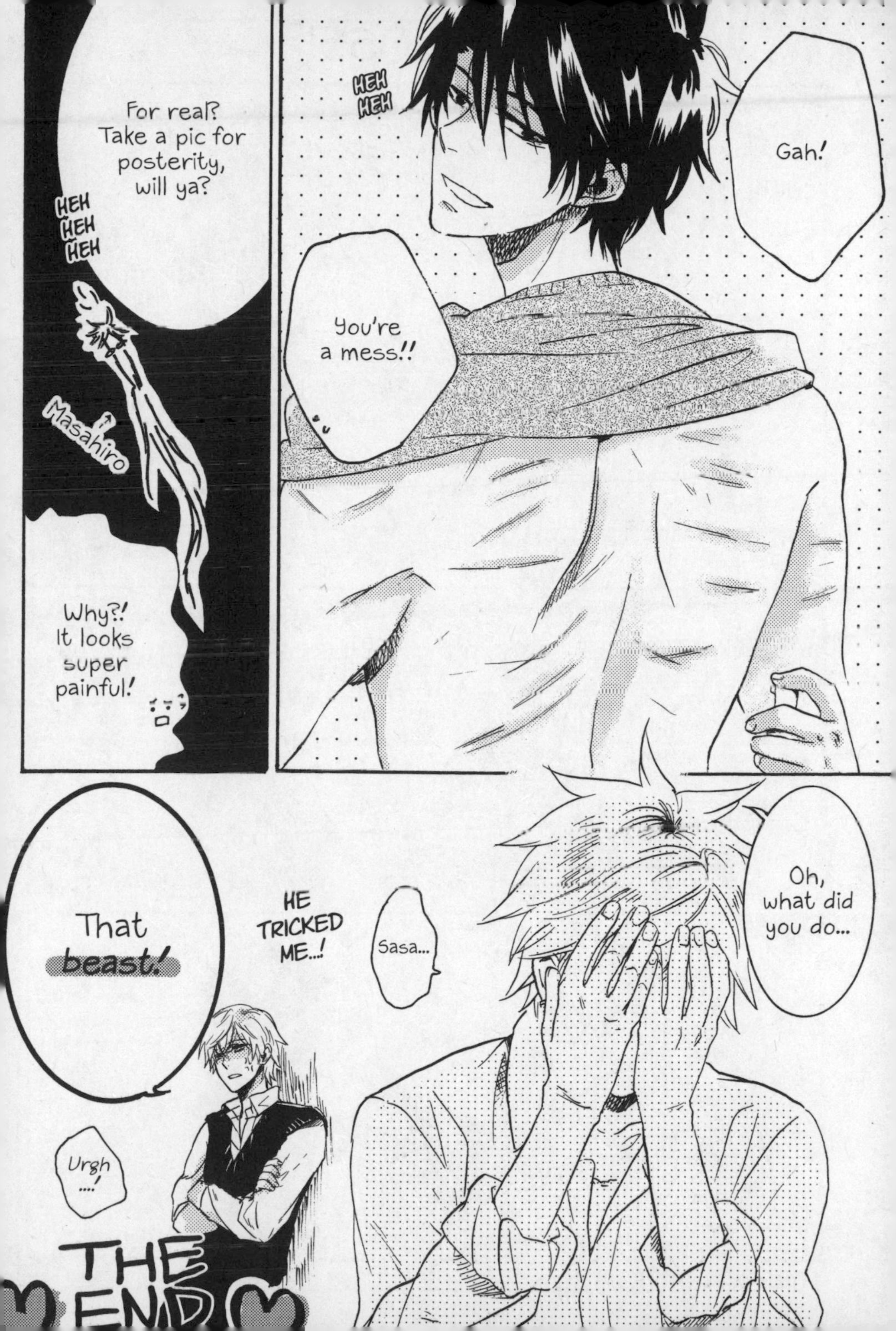
Gah!
HEH HEH
You're a mess!!
For real? Take a pic for posterity, will ya?
HEH HEH HEH
Masahiro
Why?! It looks super painful!
Oh, what did you do...
Sasa...
HE TRICKED ME...!
That beast!
Urgh...!
THE END

CHEAP GOSSIP

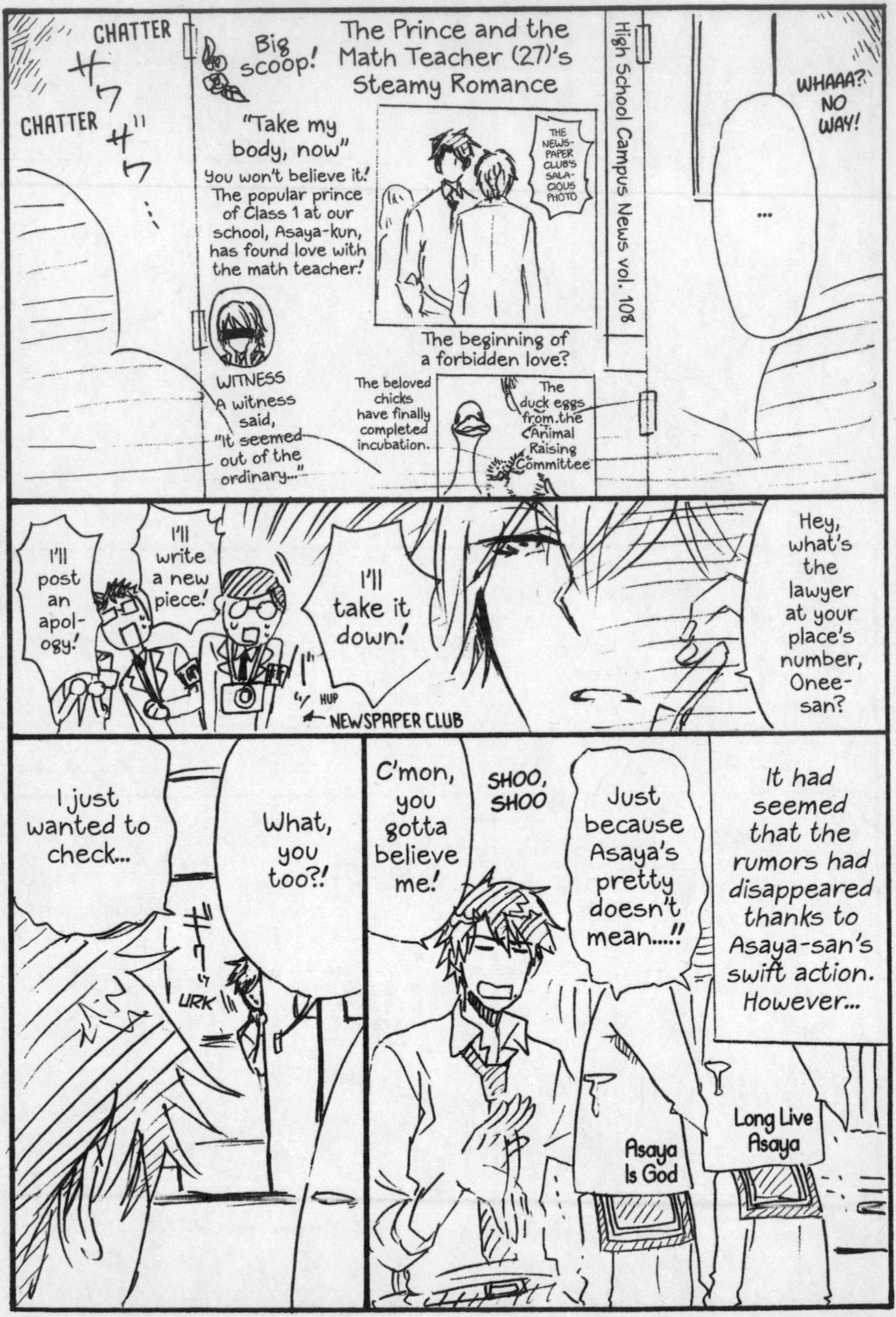
WHAAA? NO WAY!
...
High School Campus News vol. 108
The Prince and the Math Teacher (27)'s Steamy Romance
Big scoop!
"Take my body, now"
You won't believe it! The popular prince of Class 1 at our school, Asaya-kun, has found love with the math teacher!
THE NEWSPAPER CLUB'S SALACIOUS PHOTO
The beginning of a forbidden love?
The duck eggs from the Animal Raising Committee
The beloved chicks have finally completed incubation.
WITNESS
A witness said, "It seemed out of the ordinary..."
CHATTER
CHATTER
Hey, what's the lawyer at your place's number, Onee-san?
I'll take it down!
I'll write a new piece!
I'll post an apology!
HUP
NEWSPAPER CLUB
It had seemed that the rumors had disappeared thanks to Asaya-san's swift action. However...
Just because Asaya's pretty doesn't mean....!!
SHOO, SHOO
C'mon, you gotta believe me!
Long Live Asaya
Asaya Is God
What, you too?!
I just wanted to check...
URK

ONII-CHAN WAS A LITTLE HURT.

A JEALOUS HEART

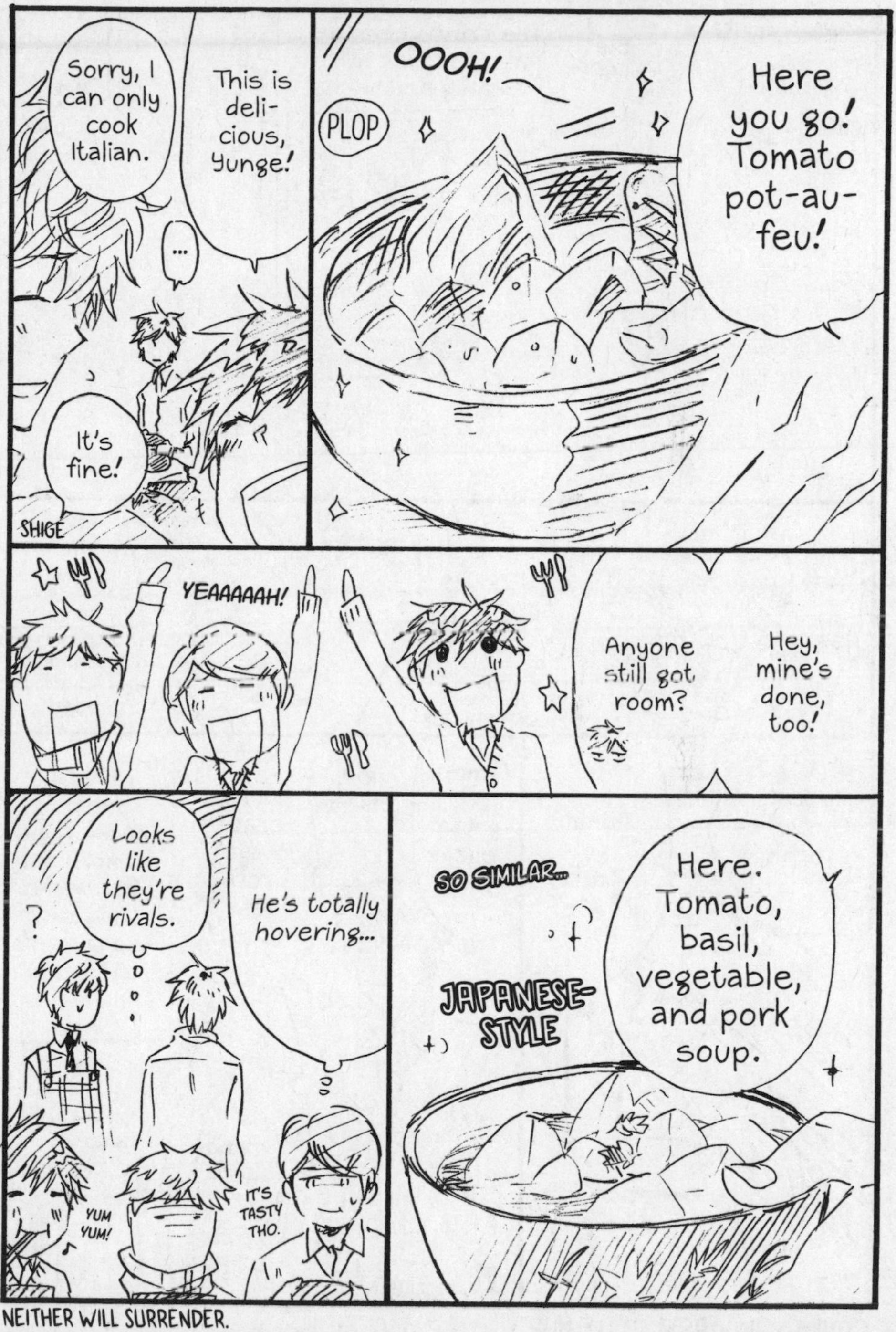
Here you go! Tomato pot-au-feu!
OOOH!
PLOP
This is delicious, Yunge!
Sorry, I can only cook Italian.
...
It's fine!
SHIGE
Hey, mine's done, too!
Anyone still got room?
YEAAAAAH!
Here. Tomato, basil, vegetable, and pork soup.
SO SIMILAR...
JAPANESE-STYLE
He's totally hovering...
Looks like they're rivals.
?
IT'S TASTY THO.
YUM YUM!

NEITHER WILL SURRENDER.

Hitorijime
My Hero

FIRST
RUN

Hitorijime My Hero #1 → gateau magazine vol. 3
Hitorijime My Hero #2 → gateau magazine vol. 4
Hitorijime My Hero #3 → gateau magazine vol. 7
Hitorijime My Hero #4 + #5 → gateau magazine vol. 8

Exciting Afterword

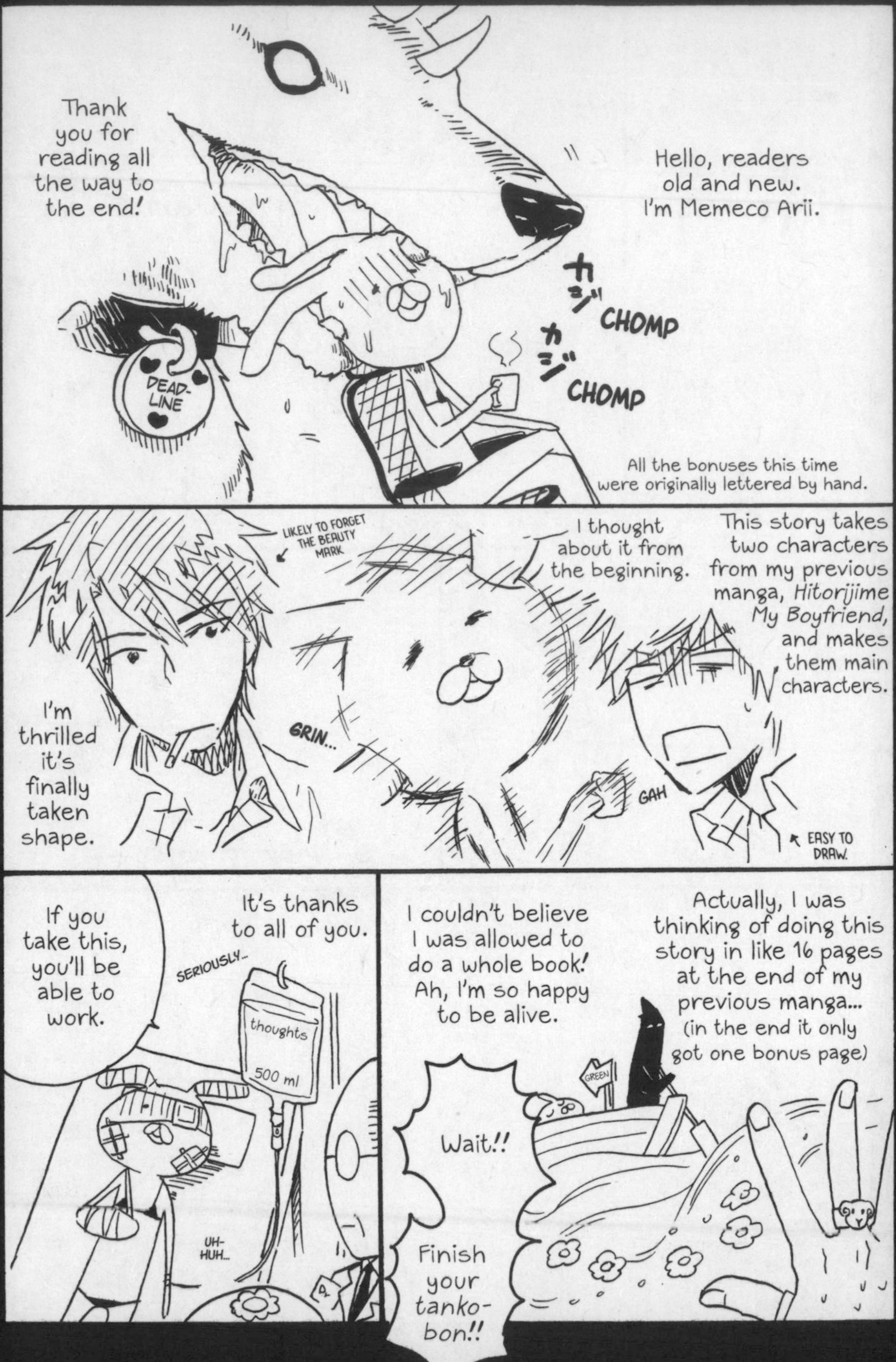
Hello, readers old and new. I'm Memeco Arii.
Thank you for reading all the way to the end!
カジ CHOMP
カジ CHOMP
DEAD-LINE
All the bonuses this time were originally lettered by hand.
This story takes two characters from my previous manga, *Hitorijime My Boyfriend,* and makes them main characters.
I thought about it from the beginning.
LIKELY TO FORGET THE BEAUTY MARK
I'm thrilled it's finally taken shape.
GRIN...
GAH
EASY TO DRAW.
Actually, I was thinking of doing this story in like 16 pages at the end of my previous manga... (in the end it only got one bonus page)
I couldn't believe I was allowed to do a whole book! Ah, I'm so happy to be alive.
GREEN
Wait!!
Finish your tankobon!!
It's thanks to all of you.
If you take this, you'll be able to work.
SERIOUSLY...
thoughts
500 ml
UH-HUH...

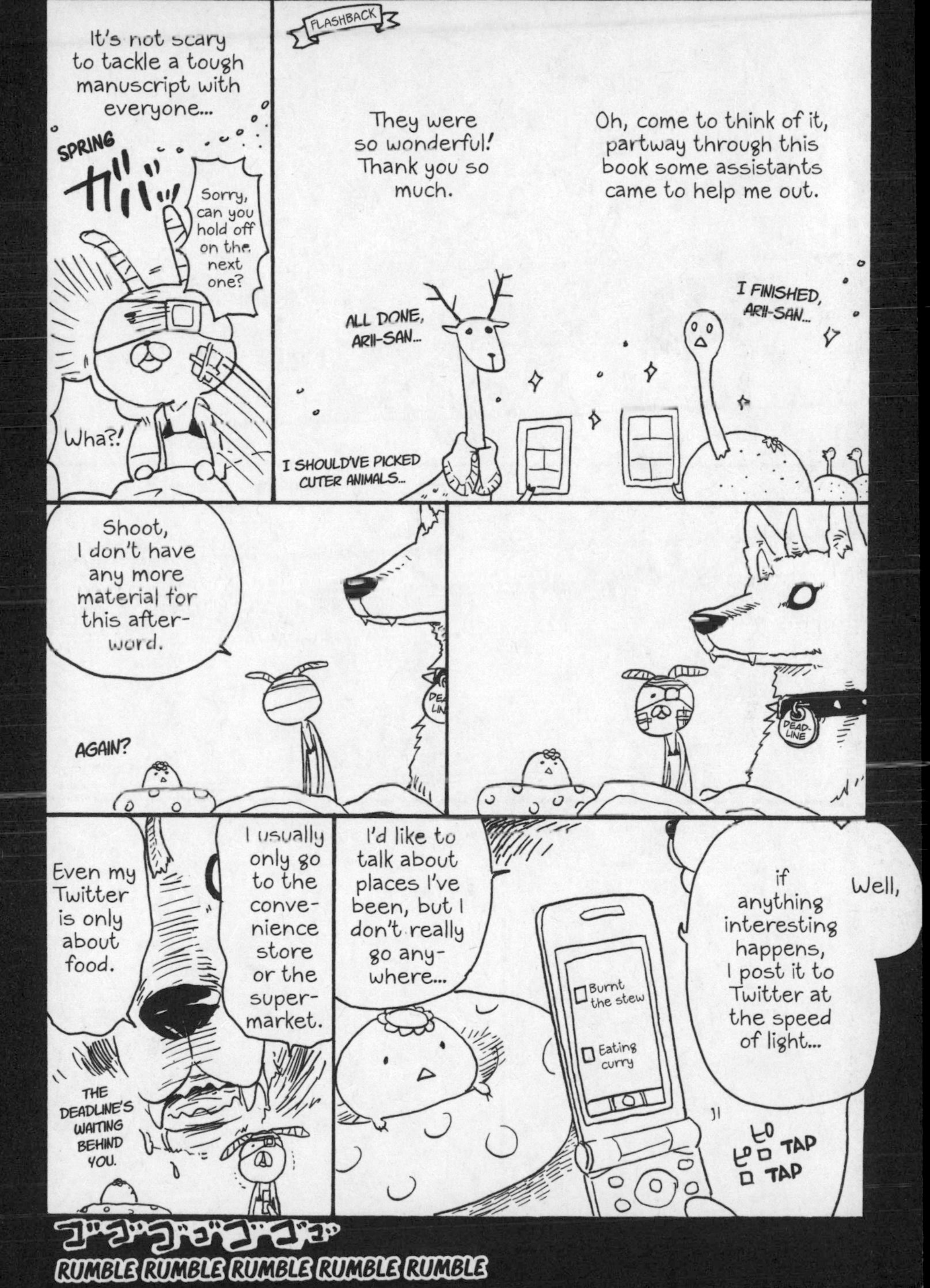
FLASHBACK
Oh, come to think of it, partway through this book some assistants came to help me out.
They were so wonderful! Thank you so much.
I FINISHED, ARII-SAN...
ALL DONE, ARII-SAN...
I SHOULD'VE PICKED CUTER ANIMALS...
It's not scary to tackle a tough manuscript with everyone...
SPRING
Sorry, can you hold off on the next one?
Wha?!
DEADLINE
Shoot, I don't have any more material for this afterword.
AGAIN?
DEADLINE
Well,
if anything interesting happens, I post it to Twitter at the speed of light...
Burnt the stew
Eating curry
TAP
TAP
I'd like to talk about places I've been, but I don't really go anywhere...
I usually only go to the convenience store or the supermarket.
Even my Twitter is only about food.
THE DEADLINE'S WAITING BEHIND YOU.
RUMBLE RUMBLE RUMBLE RUMBLE RUMBLE

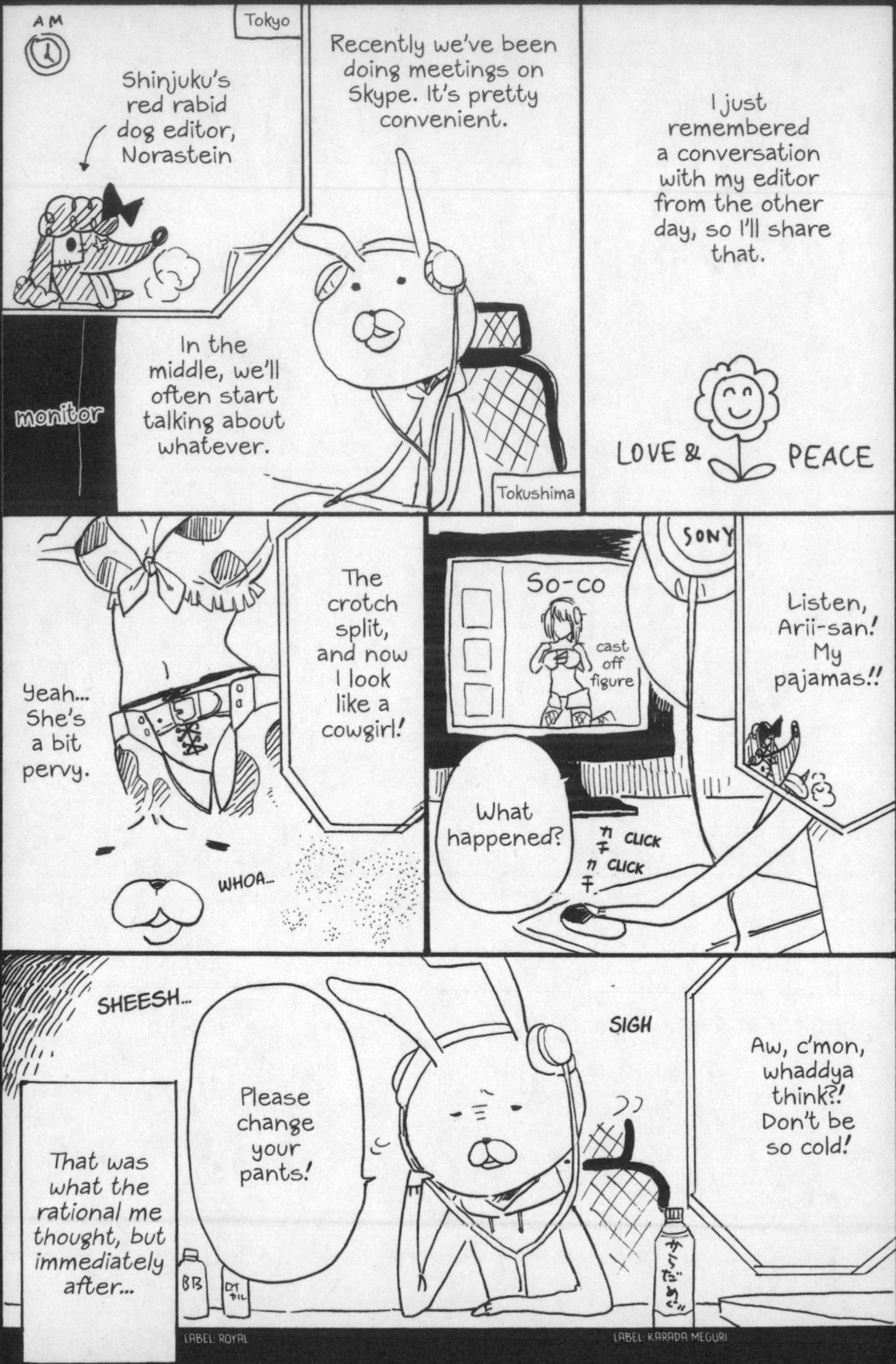
I just remembered a conversation with my editor from the other day, so I'll share that.
LOVE & PEACE
Recently we've been doing meetings on Skype. It's pretty convenient.
Tokyo
AM
Shinjuku's red rabid dog editor, Norastein
In the middle, we'll often start talking about whatever.
monitor
Tokushima
Listen, Arii-san! My pajamas!!
SONY
So-co
cast off figure
What happened?
CLICK
CLICK
The crotch split, and now I look like a cowgirl!
Yeah... She's a bit pervy.
WHOA...
Aw, c'mon, whaddya think?! Don't be so cold!
SIGH
Please change your pants!
SHEESH...
That was what the rational me thought, but immediately after...
LABEL: ROYAL
LABEL: KARADA MEGURI

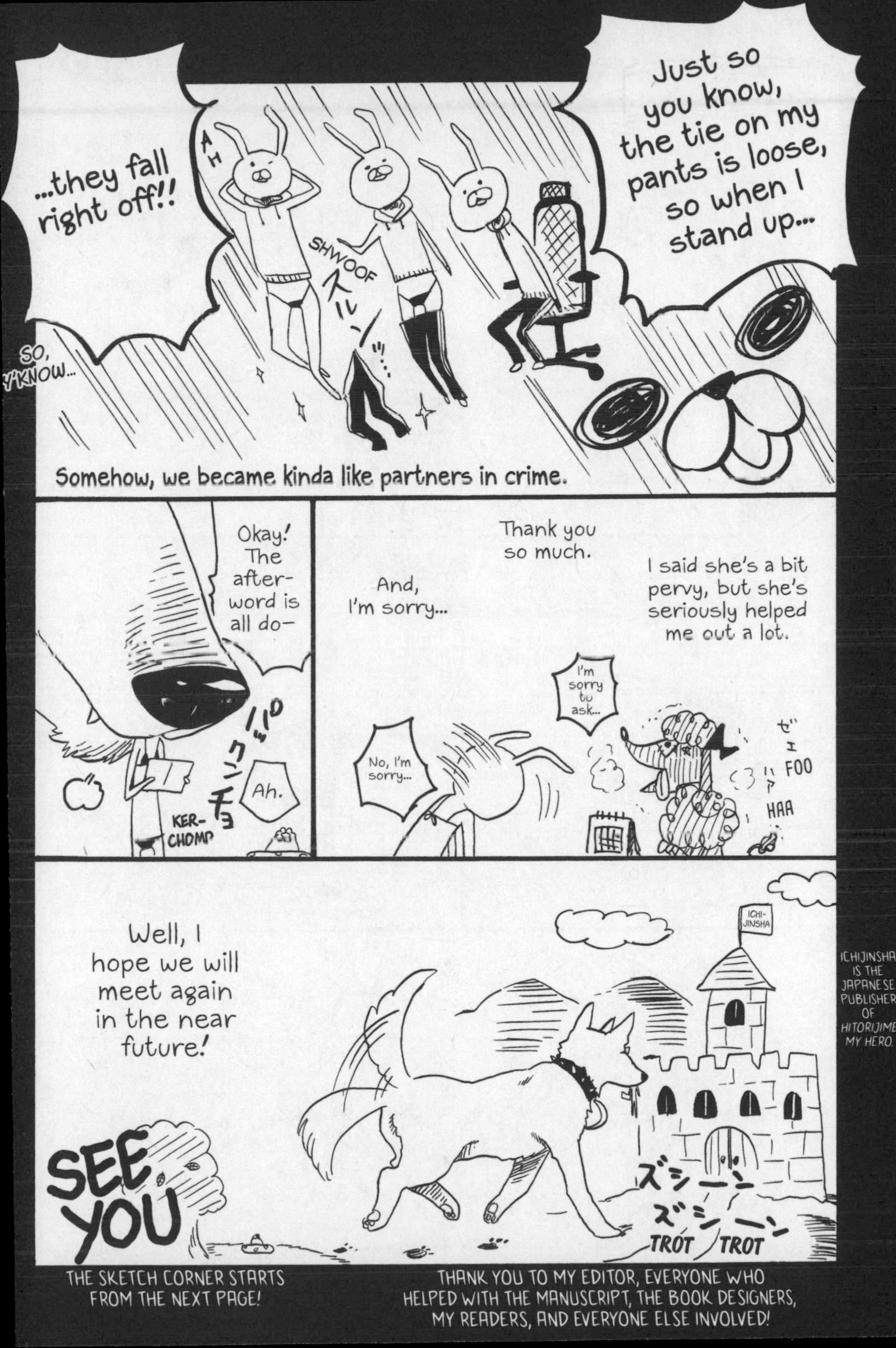
Just so you know, the tie on my pants is loose, so when I stand up...
...they fall right off!!
AH
SHWOOF
Somehow, we became kinda like partners in crime.
Thank you so much.
I said she's a bit pervy, but she's seriously helped me out a lot.
And, I'm sorry...
I'm sorry to ask...
No, I'm sorry...
FOO
HAA
Okay! The after-word is all do-
Ah.
KER-CHOMP
Well, I hope we will meet again in the near future!
ICHI-JINSHA
SEE YOU
TROT
TROT

SO, Y'KNOW...

ICHIJINSHA IS THE JAPANESE PUBLISHER OF HITORIJIME MY HERO.

THANK YOU TO MY EDITOR, EVERYONE WHO HELPED WITH THE MANUSCRIPT, THE BOOK DESIGNERS, MY READERS, AND EVERYONE ELSE INVOLVED!

THE SKETCH CORNER STARTS FROM THE NEXT PAGE!

Design Appendix

The Rough(ish)-Draft Display Corner

With the grief-filled author's comments

(1) Unnecessarily dramatic

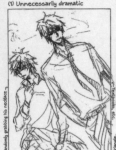

Randomly grabbing his necklace
Textbooks, etc.

(2) Screams "sexual harassment"

Triangle

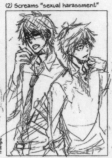

Sketch of the *tankobon* cover.
The composition for the two of them is hard!
Onii-chan is tall, so the difference in their height gives me problems when they're standing together.

Sketch of (4)'s opening image.
I couldn't decide between (3) and (2) for the front cover, but I went with (2).
I may have worried about it, but Masahiro-kun has a pretty worried look, too. Poor guy...

(3) "This old man is tormenting me"

(4) On the way home from shopping

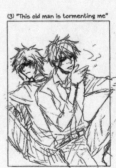

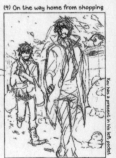

Kou has a present in his left pocket.

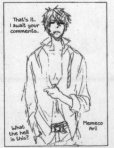

That's it. I await your comments.
What the hell is this?
Memeco Arii

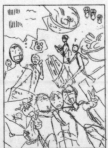

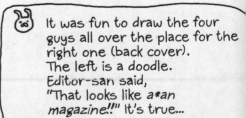

It was fun to draw the four guys all over the place for the right one (back cover).
The left is a doodle.
Editor-san said, "That looks like *a*an magazine!!*" It's true...

Doodles I drew on the last page of the storyboards I submitted to Editor-san (I was so busy I didn't have time to do 2 and 5)

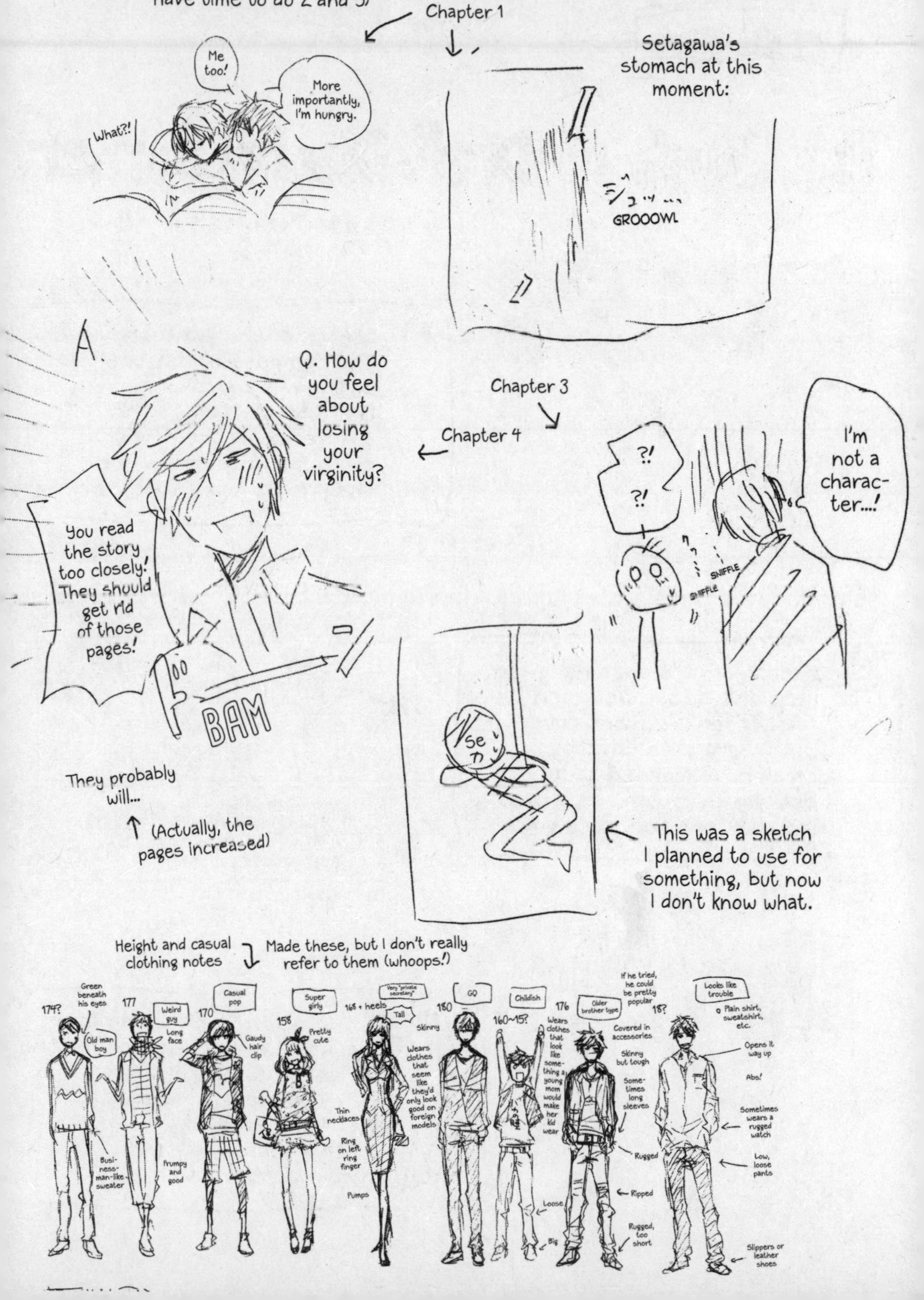

Chapter 1
Setagawa's stomach at this moment:
GROOOWL
Me too!
More importantly, I'm hungry.
What?!
Chapter 3
I'm not a charac-ter...!
?! ?!
SNIFFLE
SNIFFLE
Chapter 4
Q. How do you feel about losing your virginity?
A.
You read the story too closely! They should get rid of those pages!
BAM
They probably will...
(Actually, the pages increased)
Se
This was a sketch I planned to use for something, but now I don't know what.
Height and casual clothing notes
Made these, but I don't really refer to them (whoops!)
174?
Green beneath his eyes
Old man boy
Busi-ness-man-like sweater
177
Weird guy
Long face
Frumpy and good
170
Casual pop
Gaudy hair clip
158
Super girly
Pretty cute
168 + heels
Very "private secretary"
Tall
Thin necklaces
Ring on left ring finger
Pumps
Wears clothes that seem like they'd only look good on foreign models
180
GQ
Skinny
160~15?
Childish
Wears clothes that look like some-thing a young mom would make her kid wear
Loose
Big
176
Older brother type
If he tried, he could be pretty popular
Covered in accessories
Skinny but tough
Some-times long sleeves
Rugged
Ripped
Rugged, too short
18?
Looks like trouble
o Plain shirt, sweatshirt, etc.
Opens it way up
Abs!
Sometimes wears a rugged watch
Low, loose pants
Slippers or leather shoes

Hitorijime My Hero

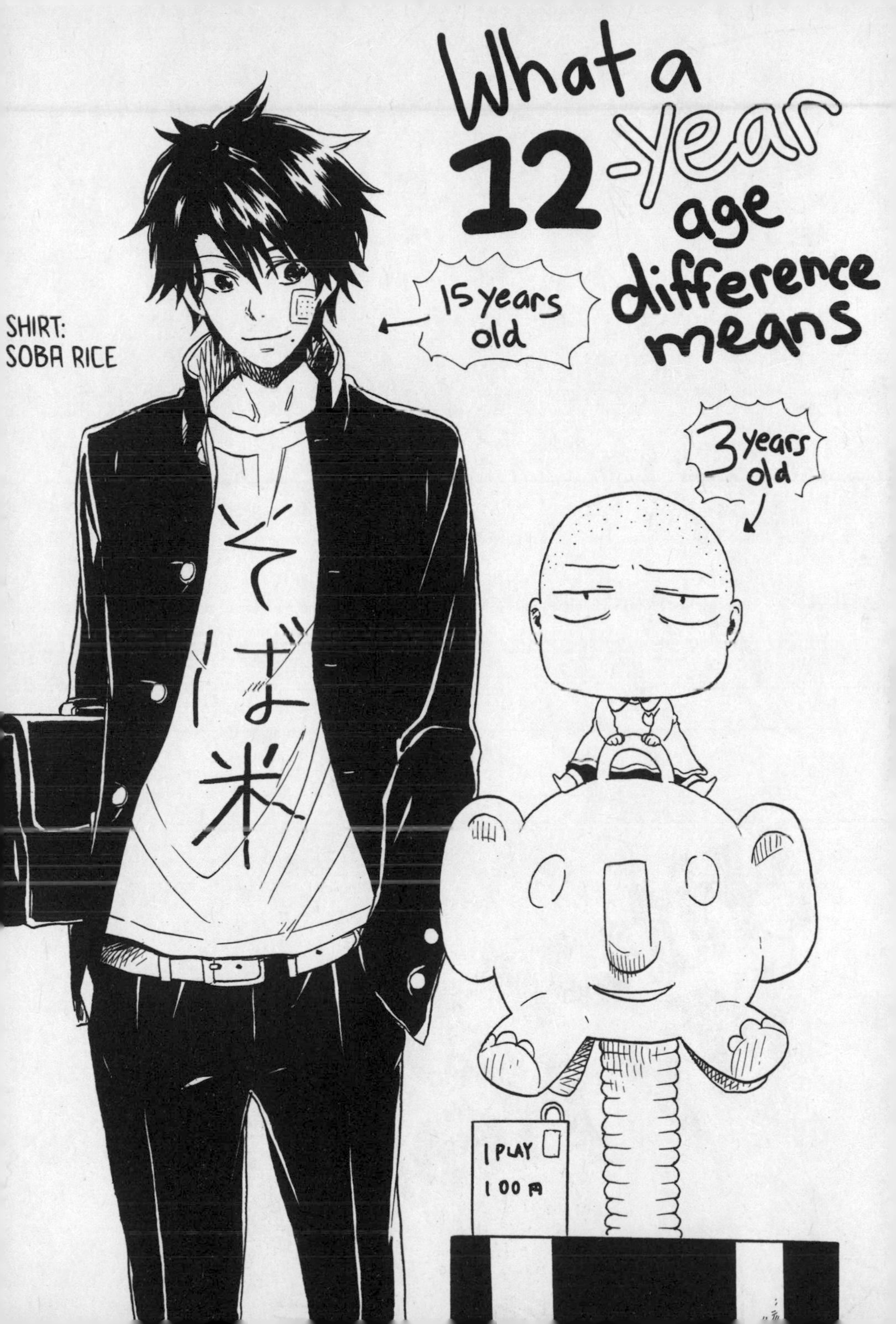
What a 12-year age difference means
SHIRT: SOBA RICE
15 years old
3 years old
そば米
1 PLAY
100円

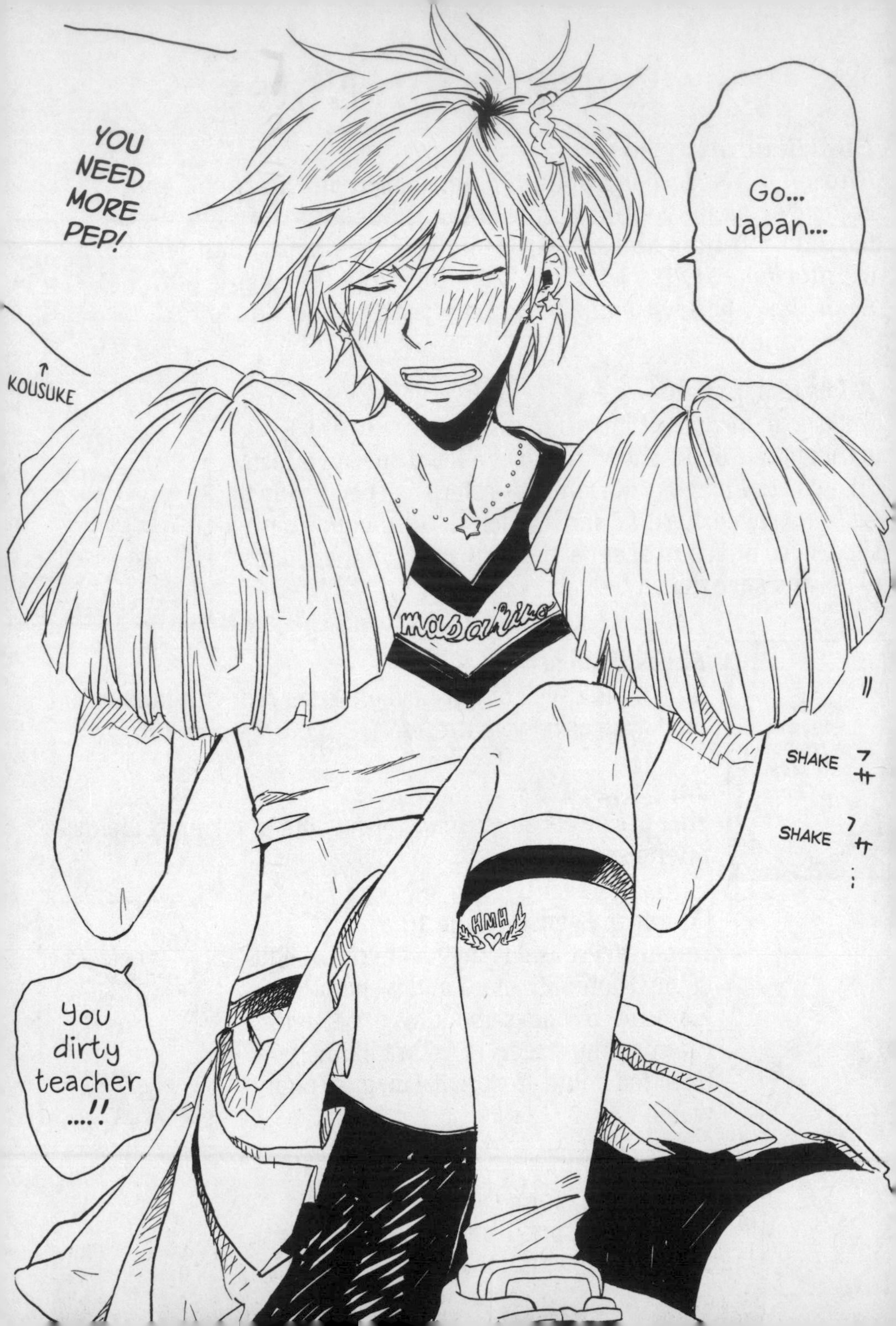
Go... Japan...
YOU NEED MORE PEP!
KOUSUKE
masahiro
SHAKE
SHAKE
HMH
You dirty teacher ...!!

Translation Notes

Hitorijime My Hero

Hitorijime My Hero is a spinoff comic based on *Hitorijime My Boyfriend,* a one-volume comic about the relationship between Kensuke Ohshiba and Asaya Hasekura. Many of the characters in *Hitorijime My Hero* know each other from the events of *Hitorijime My Boyfriend,* including Masahiro and Kousuke.

***Tokusatsu*, page 3**

Tokusatsu, meaning "special filming," refers to any live-action movie or TV show that uses a lot of special effects (like *Power Rangers*). Masahiro is referring specifically to *tokusatsu* superhero TV shows such as *Ultraman,* where a superhero or group of superheros always foil the villains' plans and save the day.

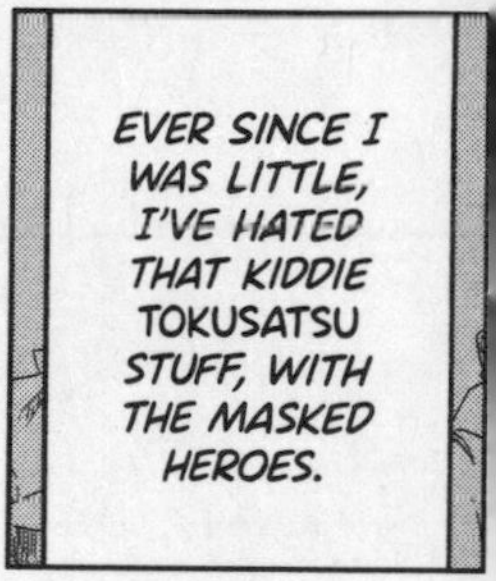
EVER SINCE I WAS LITTLE, I'VE HATED THAT KIDDIE TOKUSATSU STUFF, WITH THE MASKED HEROES.

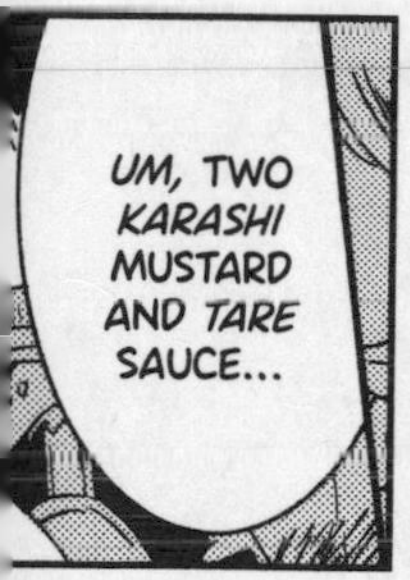
UM, TWO KARASHI MUSTARD AND TARE SAUCE...

***Karashi*, page 4**

Karashi is a type of mustard often served with Japanese food such as *oden, natto,* etc.

***Tare*, page 4**

Tare is a sweet sauce made of soy and other ingredients, often used in grilling.

Yomawari-sensei, page 16

Yomawari-sensei is the nickname of educator Osamu Mizutani and is the title of his series of books about his experiences roaming the streets at night talking to troubled youth. *Yomawari* means "night watch."

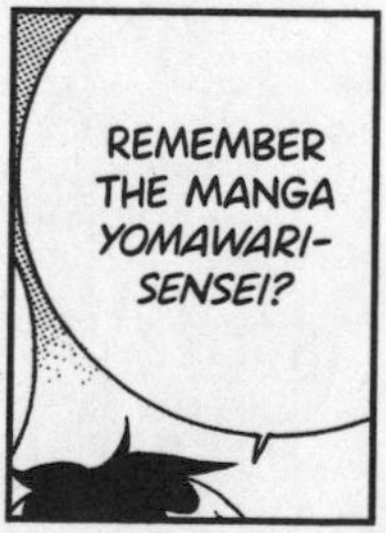
REMEMBER THE MANGA YOMAWARI-SENSEI?

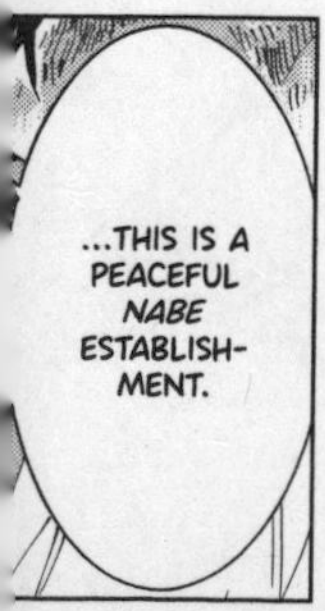
...THIS IS A PEACEFUL NABE ESTABLISH-MENT.

***Nabe*, page 16**

Nabe is short for *nabemono,* a kind of Japanese hot pot. It's considered a family dish, as it's meant for groups.

***Shirataki*, page 20**
Shirataki ("white waterfall") noodles are made from konjac yams, and are named for their appearance.

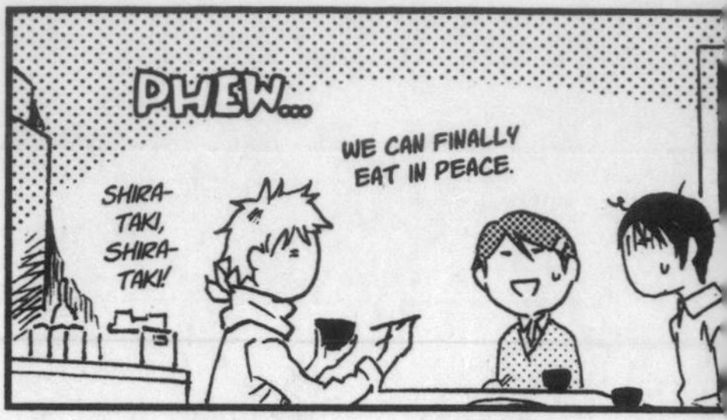
WE CAN FINALLY EAT IN PEACE.
PHEW...
SHIRA-TAKI, SHIRA-TAKI!

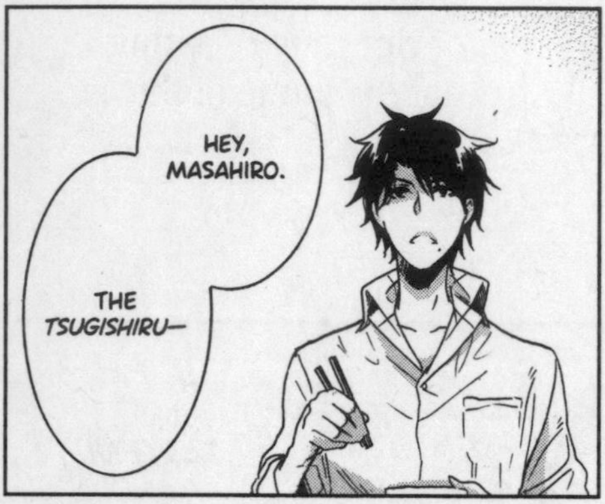
HEY, MASAHIRO.
THE TSUGISHIRU—

***Tsugishiru*, page 21**
Tsugishiru is a spicy soup with tofu.

***Imo-kenpi*, page 25**
Imo-kenpi is a popular snack made from candied sweet potato that resembles a French fry, but is crunchy like a chip.

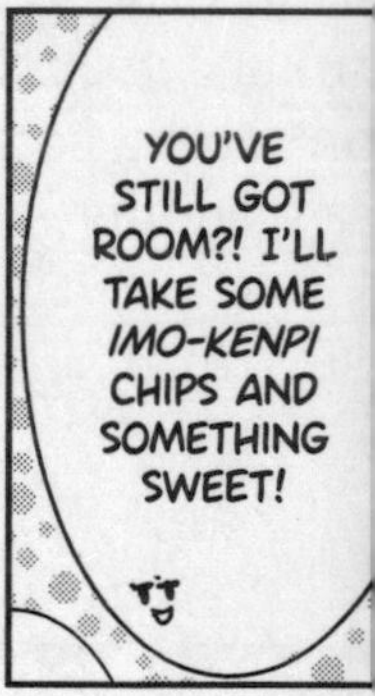
YOU'VE STILL GOT ROOM?! I'LL TAKE SOME *IMO-KENPI* CHIPS AND SOMETHING SWEET!

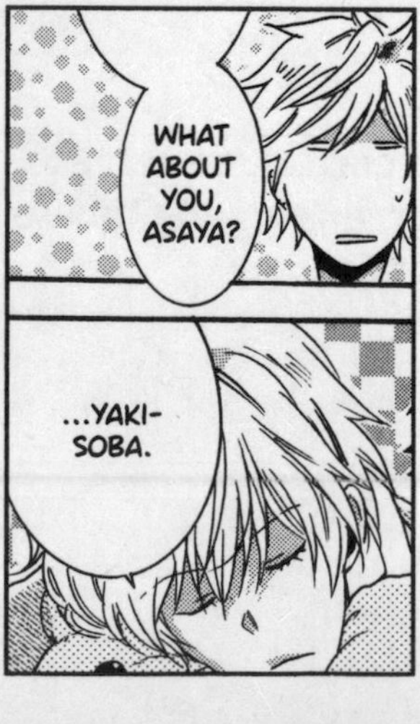
WHAT ABOUT YOU, ASAYA?
...YAKI-SOBA.

***Yakisoba*, page 25**
Yakisoba is a Japanese stir-fried noodle dish that usually contains vegetable, carrots, and chicken.

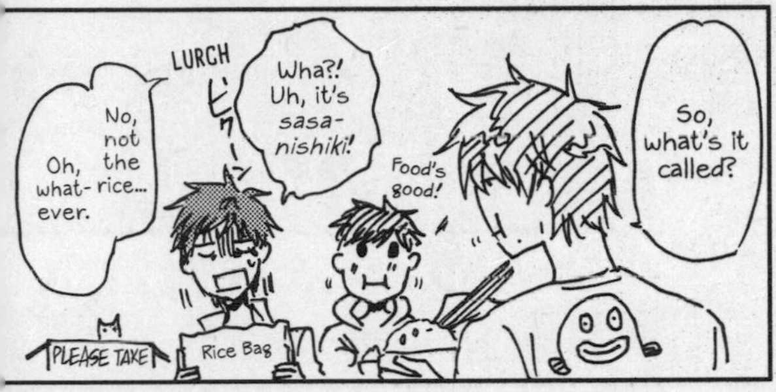
So, what's it called?
Food's good!
Wha?! Uh, it's sasa-nishiki!
LURCH
No, not the rice... Oh, whatever.
PLEASE TAKE
Rice Bag

***Sasanishiki*, page 35**
Sasanishiki is a type of rice from Sendai, Japan. Masahiro thinks Kousuke is asking what type of rice they're eating, not the name of the cat.

***Sekihan*, page 42**
Sekihan is a dish made from sticky rice and adzuki beans, often served on special occasions such as weddings and holidays.

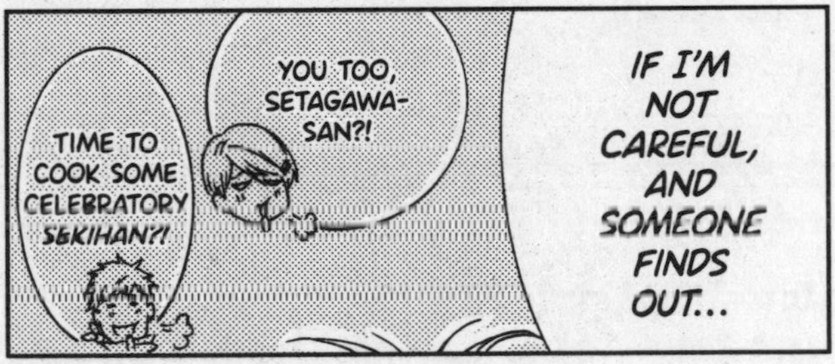
IF I'M NOT CAREFUL, AND SOMEONE FINDS OUT...
YOU TOO, SETAGAWA-SAN?!
TIME TO COOK SOME CELEBRATORY SEKIHAN?!

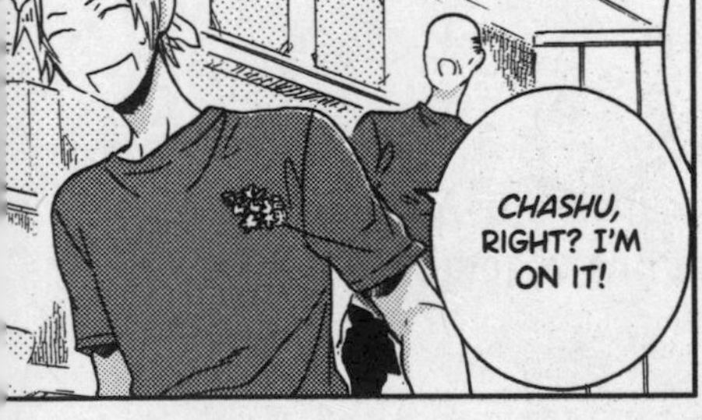
CHASHU, RIGHT? I'M ON IT!

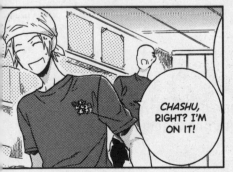

***Chashu*, page 65**
Chashu is stewed pork, often served with ramen. Its origins are in Chinese barbecue pork, or *char siu*.

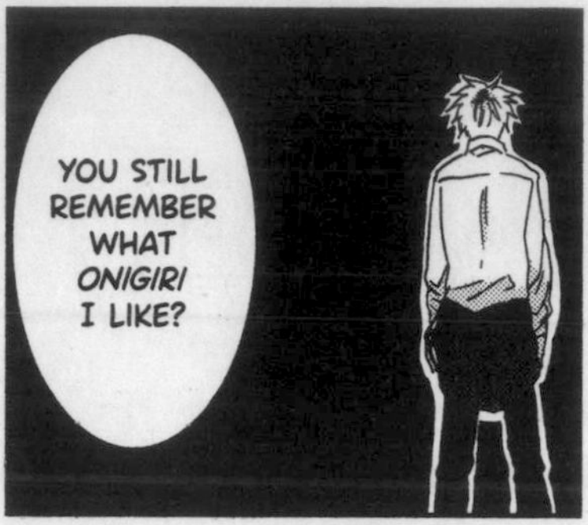
YOU STILL REMEMBER WHAT ONIGIRI I LIKE?

***Onigiri*, page 77**
Onigiri, also known as rice balls, are a Japanese food made from rice that is shaped into a triangular, spherical, or cylindrical shape and wrapped in seaweed. The rice can be filled with many different things, such as tuna fish, *ume* (pickled plum), or the different flavors Masahiro gets from the convenience store on page 4.

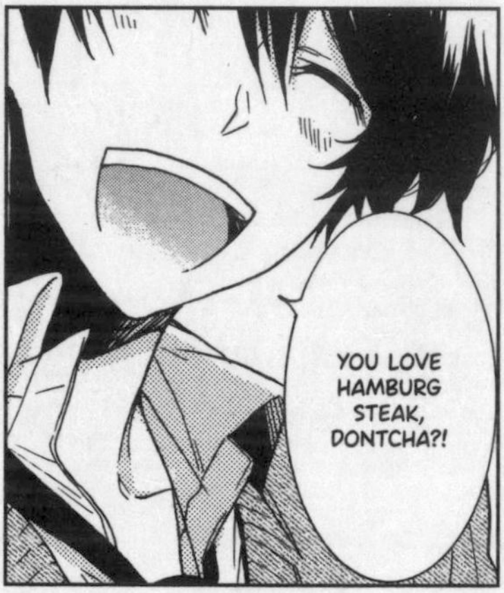
YOU LOVE HAMBURG STEAK, DONTCHA?!

Hamburg steak, page 79
Hamburg steak is a ground beef patty served with toppings such as gravy, cheese, or curry. It often comes with rice.

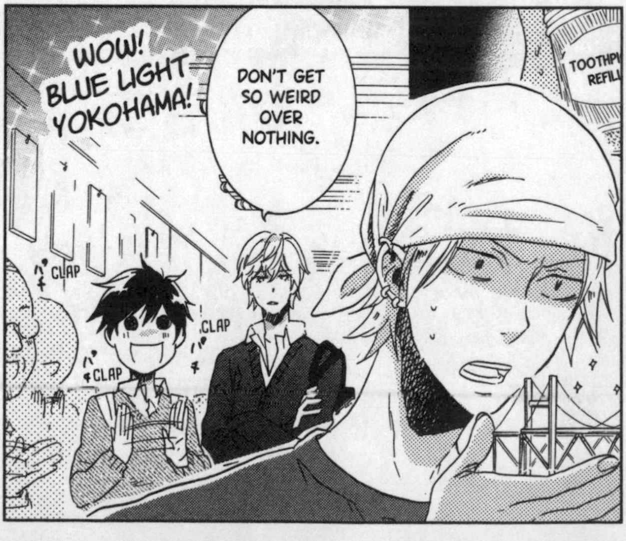
DON'T GET SO WEIRD OVER NOTHING.
WOW! BLUE LIGHT YOKOHAMA!
CLAP
CLAP
CLAP

Blue Light Yokohama, page 140
The bridge Masahiro made out of tooth-picks is the Yokohama Bay Bridge. Kensuke's referencing a famous love song about Yokohama by Ayumi Ishida, "Blue Light Yokohama."

Taking a bath, page 145
In Japan, taking a bath and cleansing oneself before sex has become a well-known trope. By inviting Masahiro to bathe, Kousuke is (jokingly?) making his intentions known.

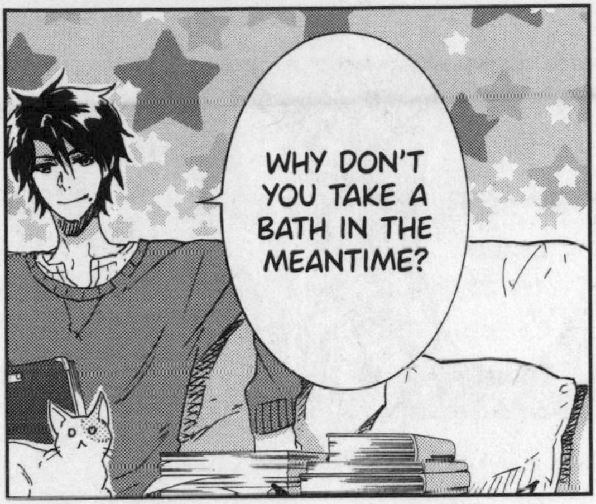
WHY DON'T YOU TAKE A BATH IN THE MEANTIME?

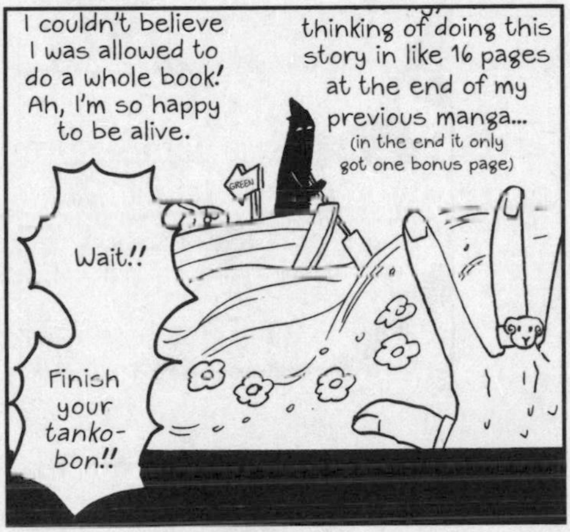
thinking of doing this story in like 16 pages at the end of my previous manga...
(in the end it only got one bonus page)
I couldn't believe I was allowed to do a whole book! Ah, I'm so happy to be alive.
Wait!!
Finish your tanko-bon!!

***Tankobon*, page 169**
A *tankobon* is a bound volume of collected manga chapters. What you're reading now!

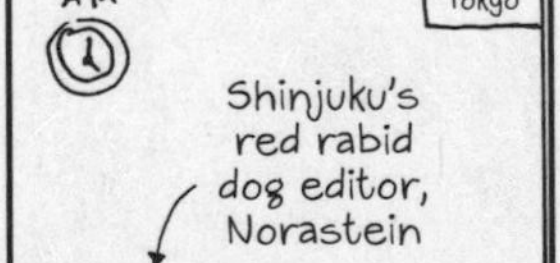
Tokyo
AM
Shinjuku's red rabid dog editor, Norastein

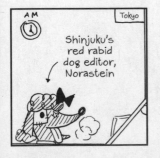

Norastein, page 171
Norastein is a combination of *nora,* the word for stray (as in "stray dog") and the "-stein" from Frankenstein.

Cast off figure, page 171

A "cast off" type of figure means that the figure comes with clothes or other items that are fully removable, allowing the figure to become partially or totally nude. So-co seems to be a parody of Super Sonico.

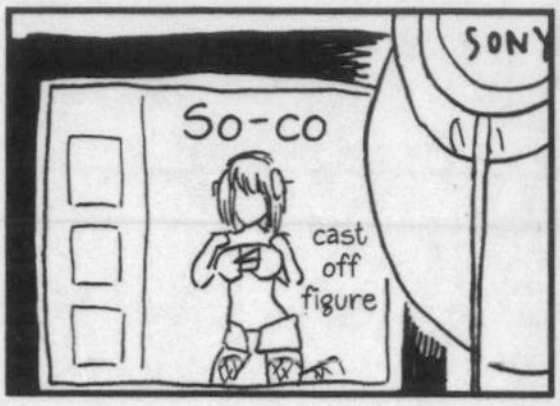
SONY
So-co
cast off figure

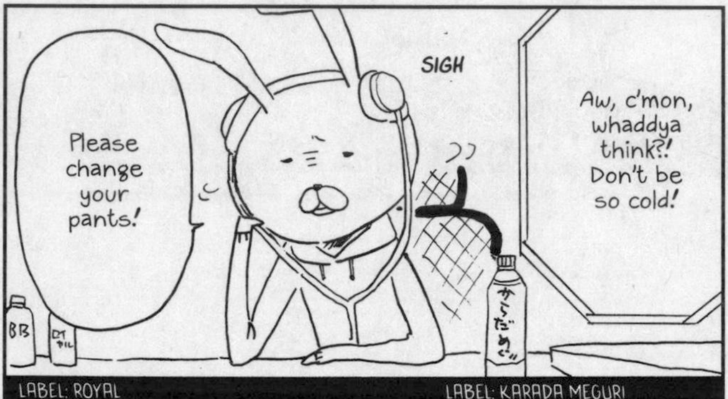
Aw, c'mon, whaddya think?! Don't be so cold!
SIGH
Please change your pants!
LABEL: ROYAL
LABEL: KARADA MEGURI

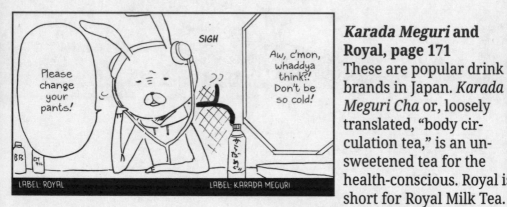

***Karada Meguri* and Royal, page 171**

These are popular drink brands in Japan. *Karada Meguri Cha* or, loosely translated, "body circulation tea," is an unsweetened tea for the health-conscious. Royal is short for Royal Milk Tea.

***a*an*, page 173**

*a*an* is a reference to the popular Japanese fashion and lifestyle magazine, *an·an*.

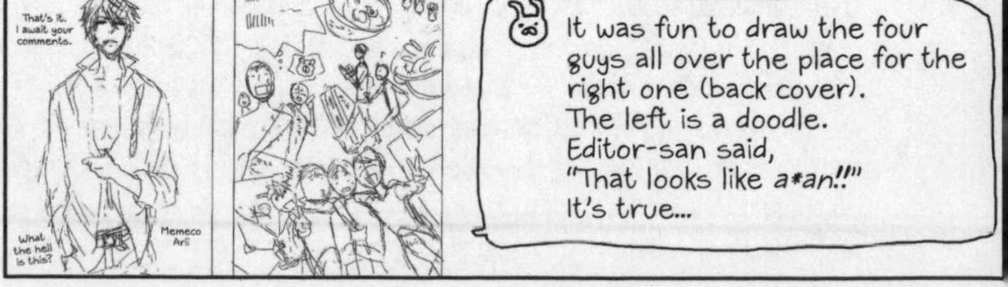
It was fun to draw the four guys all over the place for the right one (back cover).
The left is a doodle.
Editor-san said,
"That looks like *a*an!!*"
It's true...
That's it. I await your comments.
Memeco Arii
What the hell is this?

THE STORY STARTS **HERE!**

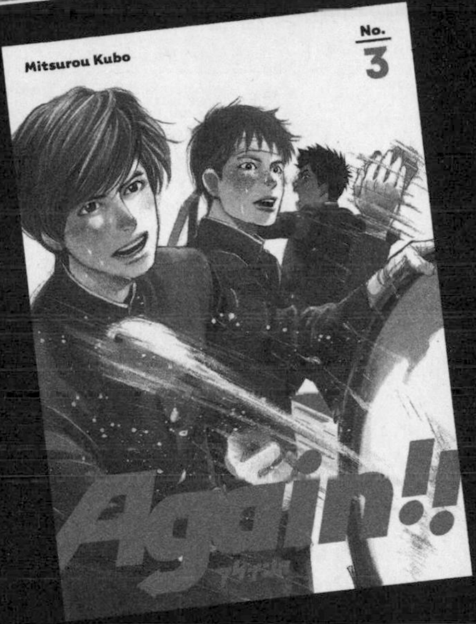
Mitsurou Kubo
No. 3
Again!!

Again!!

アゲイン!!

Kinichiro Imamura isn't a bad guy, really, but on the first day of high school his narrow eyes and bleached blonde hair made him look so shifty that his classmates assumed the worst. Three years later, without any friends or fond memories, he isn't exactly feeling bittersweet about graduation. But after an accidental fall down a flight of stairs, Kinichiro wakes up three years in the past... on the first day of high school! School's starting again—but it's gonna be different this time around!

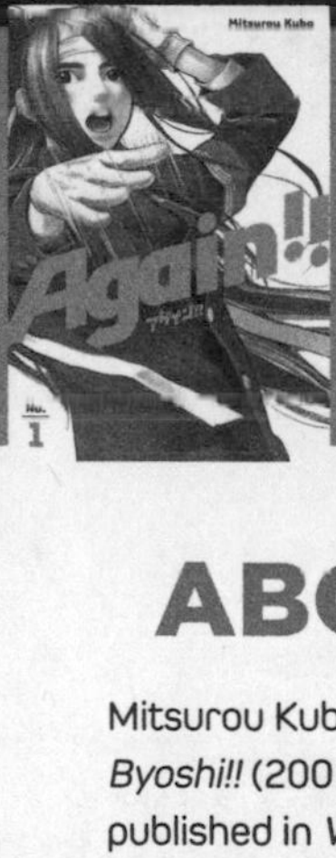
Mitsurou Kubo
Again!!
No. 1

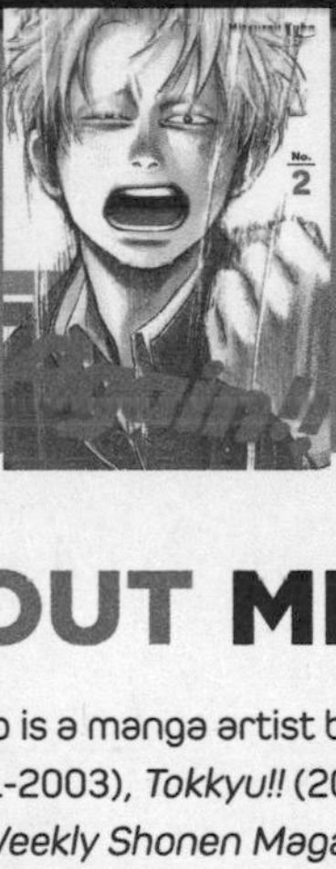
Mitsurou Kubo
No. 2

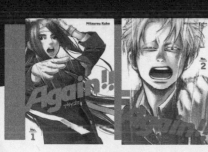

Vol. 1-3 now available in **PRINT** and **DIGITAL**!
Vol. 4 coming August 2018!

Find out **MORE** by visiting:
kodanshacomics.com/MitsurouKubo

ABOUT MITSUROU KUBO

Mitsurou Kubo is a manga artist born in Nagasaki prefecture. Her series *3.3.7 Byoshi!!* (2001-2003), *Tokkyu!!* (2004-2008), and *Again!!* (2011-2014) were published in *Weekly Shonen Magazine*, and *Moteki* (2008-2010) was published in the seinen comics magazine *Evening*. After the publication of *Again!!* concluded, she met Sayo Yamamoto, director of the global smash-hit anime ***Yuri!!! on ICE***. Working with Yamamoto, Kubo contributed the original concept, original character designs, and initial script for ***Yuri!!! on ICE***. *Again!!* is her first manga to be published in English.

KODANSHA COMICS

Princess Jellyfish

Akiko Higashimura

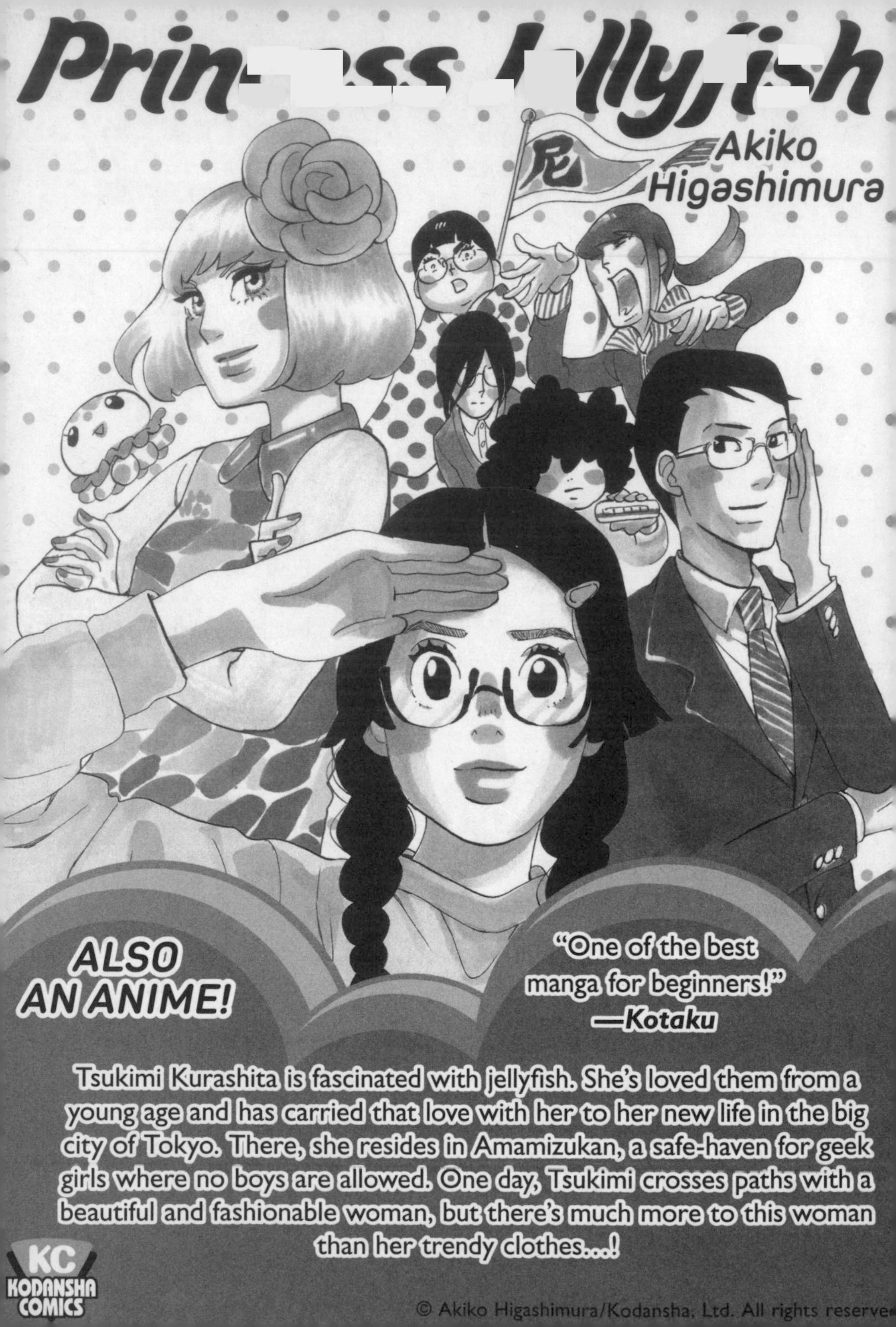

ALSO AN ANIME!

"One of the best manga for beginners!"
—*Kotaku*

Tsukimi Kurashita is fascinated with jellyfish. She's loved them from a young age and has carried that love with her to her new life in the big city of Tokyo. There, she resides in Amamizukan, a safe-haven for geek girls where no boys are allowed. One day, Tsukimi crosses paths with a beautiful and fashionable woman, but there's much more to this woman than her trendy clothes...!

KC KODANSHA COMICS

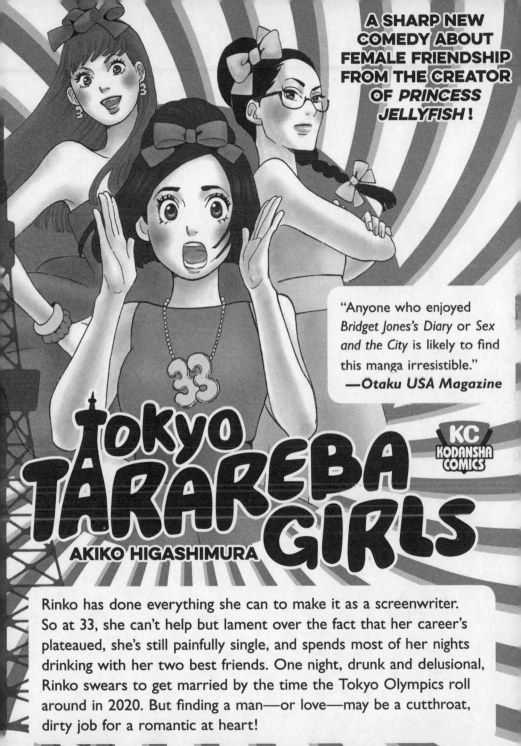

A SHARP NEW COMEDY ABOUT FEMALE FRIENDSHIP FROM THE CREATOR OF *PRINCESS JELLYFISH*!

"Anyone who enjoyed *Bridget Jones's Diary* or *Sex and the City* is likely to find this manga irresistible."
—**Otaku USA Magazine**

Tokyo TARAREBA GIRLS

AKIKO HIGASHIMURA

Rinko has done everything she can to make it as a screenwriter. So at 33, she can't help but lament over the fact that her career's plateaued, she's still painfully single, and spends most of her nights drinking with her two best friends. One night, drunk and delusional, Rinko swears to get married by the time the Tokyo Olympics roll around in 2020. But finding a man—or love—may be a cutthroat, dirty job for a romantic at heart!

KC
KODANSHA
COMICS

Japan's most powerful spirit medium delves into the ghost world's greatest mysteries!

Story by Kyo Shirodaira, famed author of mystery fiction and creator of *Spiral*, *Blast of Tempest*, and *The Record of a Fallen Vampire*.

Both touched by spirits called yôkai, Kotoko and Kurô have gained unique superhuman powers. But to gain her powers Kotoko has given up an eye and a leg, and Kurô's personal life is in shambles. So when Kotoko suggests they team up to deal with renegades from the spirit world, Kurô doesn't have many other choices, but Kotoko might just have a few ulterior motives...

IN/SPECTRE

STORY BY KYO SHIRODAIRA
ART BY CHASHIBA KATASE

KC
KODANSHA
COMICS

In love, there are
no save points.

NOW AN
ANIME!

ヲタクに恋は難しい

WOTAKOI:
LOVE IS HARD FOR OTAKU

by FUJITA

Narumi has had it rough: Every boyfriend she's had dumped her
once they found out she was an otaku, so she's gone to great
lengths to hide it. At her new job, she bumps into Hirotaka, her
childhood friend and fellow otaku. When Hirotaka almost gets
her secret outed at work, she comes up with a plan to keep him
quiet. But he comes up with a counter-proposal:
Why doesn't she just date him instead?

ANIME COMING OUT SUMMER 2018!

Mikami's middle age hasn't gone as he planned: He never found a girlfriend, he got stuck in a dead-end job, and he was abruptly stabbed to death in the street at 37. So when he wakes up in a new world straight out of a fantasy RPG, he's disappointed, but not exactly surprised to find that he's facing down a dragon, not as a knight or a wizard, but as a blind slime monster. But there are chances for even a slime to become a hero...

"A fun adventure that fantasy readers will relate to and enjoy." —AiPT!

THAT TIME I GOT REINCARNATED AS A SLIME

KC
KODANSHA
COMICS

"I'm pleasantly
surprised to find
modern shojo using
cross-dressing as a
dramatic device to deliver
social commentary...
Recommended."

-Otaku USA
Magazine

The prince in his dark days

By **Hico Yamanaka**

A drunkard for a father, a household of poverty... For 17-year-old Atsuko, misfortune is all she knows and believes in. Until one day, a chance encounter with Itaru-the wealthy heir of a huge corporation-changes everything. The two look identical, uncannily so. When Itaru curiously goes missing, Atsuko is roped into being his stand-in. There, in his shoes, Atsuko must parade like a prince in a palace. She encounters many new experiences, but at what cost...?

"An emotional and artistic tour de force! We see incredible triumph, and crushing defeat... each panel [is] a thrill!"
—Anitay

"A journey that's instantly compelling."
—Anime News Network

WELCOME TO THE BALLROOM

By Tomo Takeuchi

Feckless high school student Tatara Fujita wants to be good at something—anything. Unfortunately, he's about as average as a slouchy teen can be. The local bullies know this, and make it a habit to hit him up for cash, but all that changes when the debonair Kaname Sengoku sends them packing. Sengoku's not the neighborhood watch, though. He's a professional ballroom dancer. And once Tatara Fujita gets pulled into the world of ballroom, his life will never be the same.

KC KODANSHA COMICS

Based on the critically acclaimed classic horror manga

The first new *Parasyte* manga in over 20 years!

NEO
PARASYTE f

BY ASUMIKO NAKAMURA, EMA TOYAMA, MIKI RINNO, LALAKO KOJIMA, KAORI YUKI, BANKO KUZE, YUUKI OBATA, KASHIO, YUI KUROE, ASIA WATANABE, MIKIMAKI, HIKARU SURUGA, HAJIME SHINJO, RENJURO KINDAICHI, AND YURI NARUSHIMA

A collection of chilling new *Parasyte* stories from Japan's top shojo artists!

Parasites: shape-shifting aliens whose only purpose is to assimilate with and consume the human race... but do these monsters have a different side? A parasite becomes a prince to save his romance-obsessed female host from a dangerous stalker. Another hosts a cooking show, in which the real monsters are revealed. These and 13 more stories, from some of the greatest shojo manga artists alive today, together make up a chilling, funny, and entertaining tribute to one of manga's horror classics!